SHELTON STATE COMMUNITY
COLLEGE
JUNIOR COLLEGE DIVISION
LIBRARY

DISCARDED

✓ Y0-CCG-969

E
468.5
.B49

Beyond the Civil War synthesis

DATE DUE

DEC 2 8 1988			
JAN 1 7 1990			
MAY 1 4 1998			

SHELTON STATE COMMUNITY
COLLEGE
JUNIOR COLLEGE DIVISION
LIBRARY

Beyond
the Civil War
Synthesis

RECENT TITLES IN CONTRIBUTIONS IN AMERICAN HISTORY

Series Editor: Jon L. Wakelyn

BEYOND
THE CIVIL WAR
SYNTHESIS

Political Essays of the Civil War Era

Robert P. Swierenga
Editor

Contributions in American History No. 44

GREENWOOD PRESS

Westport, Connecticut • London, England

To Theodore S. and Annette Boomker

Library of Congress Cataloging in Publication Data
Main entry under title:

Beyond the Civil War synthesis.

(Contributions in American history ; no. 44)
"A collection of . . . articles in American political history that originally
appeared in Civil War history."
Includes bibliographical references and index.
CONTENTS: The historiography of the Civil War: Silbey, J. H. The Civil
War synthesis in American political history. Foner, E. The causes of the American
Civil War. Curry, R. O. The Civil War and Reconstruction, 1861-1877. Oates, S. B.
John Brown and his judges: a critique of the historical literature. [etc.]
1. United States—History—Civil War, 1861-1865—Historiography—Addresses,
essays, lectures. 2. Reconstruction—Historiography—Addresses, essays, lectures.
3. United States—Politics and government—Civil War, 1861-1865—Addresses, essays,
lectures. I. Swierenga, Robert P.
E468.5.B49   973.7   75-10046
ISBN 0-8371-7960-2

Copyright © 1975 by Robert P. Swierenga

All rights reserved. No portion of this book may be reproduced, by any process
or technique, without the express written consent of the author and publisher.

Library of Congress Catalog Card Number:75-10046
ISBN: 0-8371-7960-2

First published in 1975

Greenwood Press, a division of Williamhouse-Regency Inc.
51 Riverside Avenue, Westport, Connecticut 06880

Printed in the United States of America

CONTRIBUTORS

Michael Les Benedict is a professor of history at the Ohio State University. He is the author of *A Compromise of Principle: Congressional Republicans and Reconstruction, 1863-1869*, and *The Impeachment and Trial of Andrew Johnson*.

Richard E. Beringer is a professor of history at the University of North Dakota, Grand Forks. He is co-author of *The Anatomy of the Confederate Congress*.

Allan G. Bogue is Frederick Jackson Turner Professor of American History at the University of Wisconsin. He has published *Money at Interest* and *From Prairie to Corn Belt*, and is co-editor of *The West of the American People, Dimensions of Quantitative Research in History*, and *Emerging Theoretical Models in the Social Sciences*.

Richard O. Curry is professor of history at the University of Connecticut. He is the author of *A House Divided*, co-author of *The Shaping of American Civilization*, editor of *The Abolitionists: Reformers or Fanatics?* and co-editor of a number of books.

Phyllis Field is a visiting professor of history at the State University of New York, Stony Brook. She is co-author of an article in William Flanigan, Allan Bogue, and Joel Silbey (eds.), *Quantitative Studies of Popular Voting Behavior*.

Eric Foner is a professor of history at the City College of New York. He has published *Free Soil, Free Labor, Free Men* and edited *America's Black Past*.

Edward L. Gambill is a professor of history at the University of Minnesota, Saint Cloud.

Larry Gara is professor of history at Wilmington College (Ohio). He is the author of *Liberty Line* and the editor of *The Narrative of William Wells Brown*.

Richard Jensen is professor of history at the University of Illinois, Chicago Circle, and Director of the Family History Center at Newberry Library. He is the author of *The Winning of the Midwest* and co-author *Historian's Guide to Statistics*.

Glenn M. Linden is a professor of history at the Southern Methodist University. He is the author of several articles on Radical Republicanism.

David E. Meerse is a professor of history at the State University of New York at Fredonia. He has published several articles on the Northern Democrats in in the late 1850s.

August Meier is University Professor of history at Kent State University. He is the author of *Negro Thought in America*, co-author of *From Plantation to Ghetto* and *CORE: A Study in the Civil Rights Movement*; and co-editor of *Black Protest Thought in the Twentieth Century*, *The Making of Black America*, *Black Nationalism in America*, and *The Transformation of Activism.*

Stephen B. Oates is professor of history at the University of Massachusetts, Amherst. His publications include *Confederate Cavalry West of the River*, *Visions of Glory*, *To Purge This Land With Blood: A Biography of John Brown*, and he is editor of *Rip Ford's Texas* and *Portrait of America.*

Lawrence N. Powell is a doctoral student at Yale University and a research assistant with the Frederick Douglass Papers.

Joel H. Silbey is professor of history at Cornell University and author of *The Shrine of Party*, editor of *The Transformation of American Politics, 1840-1860* and *Political Ideology and Voting Behavior in the Age of Jackson*, and co-editor of *Voters, Parties and Elections.*

James B. Stewart is a professor of history at Macalester College and has written *Joshua R. Giddings and the Tactics of Radical Politics.*

Robert P. Swierenga is professor of history at Kent State University. He is the author of *Pioneers and Profits* and *Acres for Cents*, and editor of *Quantification in American History.*

Leonard Tabachnik is a professor of history at Queens College and has written a dissertation on the Native American party in Philadelphia.

Gerald W. Wolff is a professor of history at the University of South Dakota, Vermillion, and is co-author of *The Three Affiliated Tribes and the Comanche People, Indian Tribal Series, Phoenix, Arizona.*

Bertram Wyatt-Brown is professor of history at the Case Western Reserve University. He is the author of *Lewis Tappan and the Evangelical War Against Slavery* and editor of *The American People in the Antebellum South.*

CONTENTS

PREFACE

This book is a collection of twenty significant articles in American political history that originally appeared in *Civil War History,* the premier scholarly journal of the mid-nineteenth century. All of the contributions are contemporary—most were published within the last five years and the earliest was written barely a decade ago. The essays reflect the latest scholarship in political studies of the Civil War and Reconstruction years. They contain "revisionist" viewpoints that often are derived from new social scientific methods. Students and general readers will find the fresh viewpoints provocative, and specialists will appreciate the conflicting philosophical perspectives.

The collection is divided into five main parts. Within each major part, the arrangement is roughly chronological. Part I is historiographical and includes four "overview" articles, two of which were presented at the 1972 meeting of the Organization of American Historians. Part II contains five articles on political parties and popular voting behavior. This is followed in Part III by five articles on Congressional roll call voting. Part IV includes three essays that illuminate the ethnic, religious, and racial dimensions of the Middle Period. The final three essays, comprising Part V, offer differing interpretations of antislavery political ideologies. An index is appended to aid readers in using the book for reference purposes.

I am indebted to the contributors for permission to include their works; to John T. Hubbell, editor of *Civil War History,* for his assistance and advice; to the Kent State University Press, the publisher of Civil War History; and its director Paul H. Rohmann for attending to the technical details; to Jon L. Wakelyn, editor of the Contributions in American History series of Greenwood Press, who initially encouraged me to prepare this book; and to Mrs. Jeannette Lindsay, managing editor for original books of Greenwood Press, for guiding the book from initial copy to final text. Finally, I wish to thank my wife, Joan Boomker Swierenga, for typing assistance.

EDITOR'S INTRODUCTION

The American Civil War was such a cataclysmic event that in the aftermath contemporaries could not view it in perspective. The pre-war years were antediluvian and the Reconstruction era was post-diluvian. The traumatic wartime experiences provided a "sense of meaning" for the survivors, a focal point around which memories centered and people measured the significance of things.

This same fixation with the Civil War has subsequently plagued American historians, especially those of the antebellum period. This at least is the contention of Joel H. Silbey in the opening essay of this book. The war, Silbey asserts, has had a "pernicious influence on the study of American political developments that preceded it" because it tempts historians to read history backwards, to look first at the war and then to interpret all earlier events from hindsight. Specifically, since the Civil War demonstrated the fact of sectionalism in an ultimate sense, all major political developments from 1828 or even earlier are ipso facto viewed as steps in the "road to war." Such an ahistorical approach, Silbey maintains, seriously "distorts the reality" of antebellum political life and has led to a "false" picture, which he calls the "Civil War Synthesis."

The Civil War Synthesis is an interpretation of the Middle Period that stresses the deepening sectional rift between North and South (and East and West) over the issue of slavery. From this standpoint, historians such as Frederick Jackson Turner, Merrill Jensen, Avery Craven, and Roy Nichols studied national elections, Congressional alignments, and the ideological battles over the morality and legality of slavery. The "disruption of American democracy," they believed, was the result of a "persistent sectional pattern." This stress on sectionalism, which is essentially a conflict model of society based on regional determinism, has clearly predominated as the major theme of American historiography of the Civil War era.[1]

Silbey's seminal article of 1964 is the first major attack on the sectional synthesis. Writing from a behavioral or "social scientific" perspective—an approach that is shared by many, though not all, contributors to this book—Silbey challenged historians to break free from their "universal preoccupation with the sectional issue." Instead, he urged his colleagues to consider nonsectional variables such as ethnocultural and religious conflicts, partisanship, and racism. Single-factor explanations of human behavior, Silbey insisted, are not only naive but a distortion of reality. The only remedy to such tunnel vision is for historians to borrow more sophisticated behavioral models from modern political theorists and to employ statistical methods whenever possible to evaluate their data.

The faint beginnings of the social scientific[2] reorientation that Silbey advocated were apparent from the works quoted or mentioned in his article. Indeed, several of the colleagues that he cited, all fellow members of the "Iowa School" of New Political Historians,[3] subsequently published their works in *Civil War History.* These articles, and others of a similar nature that are included below, testify to the fundamental reorientation in American political studies in the 1960s. Consequently, readers will find interspersed within the narrative of this book a liberal sprinkling of tables of figures and cross tabulations, Guttman "scales," and social statistical measures. Even more significant than the quantitative apparatus is the fact that social theory is reflected in both the narrative and the data manipulation.

While the imprint of the New Political Historians is stamped clearly on many of the contributions of this volume, Eric Foner's historiographical essay, "The Causes of the American Civil War," published in 1974, vividly indicates that the behavioralists have not swept the field. From his essentially Marxian ideological perspective, Foner sarcastically chides the New Historians for writing off the Civil War as a non-event and for being ahistorical themselves by substituting "one-dimensional 'religious man'" for "economic man." Sectional social cleavages are at the root of the civil conflict, Foner insists. "The Civil War was, at base, a struggle for the future of the nation," he says. "Each side fought to preserve a society it believed to be threatened." The war pitted the static "world the slaveholders made" against the dynamic world of "free soil, free labor, free men."[4] These opposing "world-views," ideologies, or "Gestalts" were irreconcilable, Foner concludes. Thus does the ideologue defend the traditional Civil War Synthesis based on the notion of intransigent sectional patterns of thought and behavior.

Richard O. Curry's companion piece to Foner's essay, which covers the historical literature of the War and Reconstruction years from 1861 to 1877, also reflects the viewpoint of an intellectual historian. But Curry is an irenic ideologue; he seeks to blend the strengths of the qualitative and quantitative approaches. What emerges is a consensus view. Curry defends northern Copperheads (Democrats) for their loyal support of the war effort. He pictures President Lincoln as a shrewd politician who used conservative rhetoric to prepare the American public for drastic antislavery action. Curry dismisses the term "Radical Republican" as meaningless, and he insists that President Andrew Johnson's impeachment was a political necessity. In essence, Curry offers a consensus interpretation of Reconstruction history, one that posits the basic continuity of the 1860s and 1870s and the thoroughgoing rejection of radicalism by the political leaders.

The final contribution in Part I is Stephen B. Oates's critique of the historical literature on the enigmatic John Brown. This article again illustrates how events in the present influence the writing about events in the past. The impact of the politics of protest in the civil rights and antiwar movements of the 1960s is obvious. For the same philosophical reasons that Curry could deplore the "tragedy" of the First Reconstruction to "engineer a social and political revolution" in the South, so Oates from his radical perspective can portray John Brown as a deeply religious revolutionary who lashed out in righteous indignation at a hypocritical racist society that claimed to be Christian and free when in fact it was neither. Along the way, Oates is sharply critical of the inept attempts of Allan Nevins in *Ordeal of the Union* to place Brown on the psychiatrist's couch and to probe his mind and motives by psychoanalysis.

The five articles in Part II center around questions of party politics and mass voting behavior. The methodology varies from a simple case study approach to a sophisticated statistical analysis using partial and multiple regression coefficients. Despite the varied approach, these essays reflect common underlying themes. All are revisionist in the sense that they challenge conventional wisdom. All suggest the salience of state and local issues, rather than national ones, in determining popular voting behavior. Instead of reacting to such national issues as tariff and land policy or the extension of slavery into the territories, people in the local communities were moved by nativist ethnocultural issues such as naturalization and temperance laws, by personality factors, and by internecine party patronage squabbles.

In the first article in Part II, David E. Meerse, a long-time student of the Buchanan Democrats, analyzes the key 1858 off-year election in which the Democratic party lost twenty-six of its forty-nine House seats. The traditional thesis is that the Buchanan administration's support of the Lecompton Constitution spelled disaster for the northern Democrats at the party nominating conventions and then at the polls. Taking each of the four pillars of the accepted view, Meerse patiently dissects them one at a time, and shows each to be erroneous. In his conclusion, the author reiterates Silbey's criticism of the Civil War Synthesis:

Foreshadowing the sectional solidarity of the 1860s, historians have tended to depict a single response, repudiation, on the part of a homogeneous mass, the northern electorate, to a single issue, Kansas, with a single result, Democratic disaster. Yet a reexamination of the electoral criteria reveals that complexity, not solidarity, was the characteristic of northern politics.

Analyses of the 1860 election lend credence to the notion of the complex local mosaic of the American electorate. Large blocs of voters responded to very personal issues and remained virtually unmoved by the national debate in Washington over slavery and sectionalism. In a study of a Dutch immigrant settlement in central Iowa, for example, Robert P. Swierenga found that nativism was the key factor in determining voting patterns. The Dutch had personally felt the sting of nativism in the mid-1850s at the hand of local Know Nothings and Whig prohibitionists and restrictionists, and no amount of persuasion or blandishments by their "Dominie," a Lincoln Republican, could convince them to desert the Democracy in 1860. Republican promises of free homesteads, a transcontinental railroad, and no slavery extension fell on deaf ears; the Dutch clung tenaciously to their traditional Democratic allegiance. To those scholars who would understand immigrant voting behavior in the nineteenth century, the lesson is clear: be alert to local issues and study voter behavior rather than the rhetoric of the elite. They did not always deliver the vote.

This advice to immigrant historians would appear to apply with equal force to all Middle Period political historians, at least judging from Lawrence N. Powell's study of the 1866 Congressional elections. Powell investigated the seventeen districts where Republican incumbents lost renomination bids. Since the early twentieth century, historians had always assumed that voters rejected these men for reasons of national Reconstruction politics. Republican voters supposedly purged moderates in favor of radicals who could carry the fight against President Johnson. Powell found, however, after extensive research in local sources in each of the districts, that "reconstruction had very little bearing on the nominations. In the overwhelming majority of cases incumbents were replaced for entirely local reasons." Local cabals and popularity contests, one-term rules and rotation customs, were more important than whether the defeated South should be punished.

The "pervasive localism" that Powell uncovered in the 1866 election is reiterated in Phyllis Field's statistical study of black suffrage referenda in New York State in 1846, 1860, and 1869. Field focused on the "grass-roots response" rather than on party leaders and their rhetoric because she believed that "the conduct of the Republican party on the racial questions could be better understood if the base of the party pyramid received as much attention as its apex." At the base, Field found that the party structure was badly fissured. The old Yorker sections in the southeast, where slavery had once flourished and Dutch traditions persisted, were opposed to black suffrage, whereas western and northern Republican voters were overwhelmingly in favor of equal suffrage. These local divisions were masked by a superficial party unity and, until Field dug below the surface with her detailed correlation analyses of the actual voting patterns, historians remained unaware of them.

At the national level the Republican party was also sharply divided between radicals and conservatives. Michael Les Benedict's study of the issues and voting results of the fall state races in 1867 suggests that the Radical influence within the party had crested and the conservative forces were on the upsurge. The northern electorate had served notice that radicalism was no longer a "viable political creed," Benedict concluded. Thus, the state elections of 1867 signaled a "turning point" in Republican party history. In addition to the substantive conclusions of Benedict and the other contributors in Part II, there is a lesson to be learned in research design. All five of these studies suggest that more attention can profitably be given to state and local events in the Civil War era.

This is not to assert that the national scene is either unimportant or fully understood. Indeed, all five articles in Part III indicate that rich, untapped sources await the innovative researcher. Countless scholars, for example, have pored over the record of Congressional debates and roll calls in the hope of understanding the development of sectionalism, the conflict between conservatives and liberals, and the like. But until the development of quantitative techniques of roll call analysis and computer programs to assimilate the more than 500,000 individual roll call responses of Congress from 1836 to 1877, political historians were forced to focus attention on the formal speeches and private correspondence of the lawmakers, and to pick a few "key" votes, such as the Kansas-Nebraska Bill, for in-depth study. Now *all* the roll calls can be included in the analysis and the voting patterns of individuals and groups of legislators can be uncovered.

Even more important than the mathematical and mechanical tools is the intellectual reorientation among the New Political Historians. Instead of concentrating on sectional manifestations, scholars such as Allan G. Bogue now view Congress as a "political system" in which a variety of determinants of voting behavior are interacting—party, section or constituency, faction or bloc, and individual biography. The task of the scholar is to measure the relative strength over time of these reciprocating forces and to account for the shifting emphases in various historical contexts.

The Civil War era, broadly defined, included both the second and third party systems—the Whigs and Democrats and then the Republicans and Democrats. Given the strength of these rival national parties and the emotional attachment of millions of voters to one or the other party, one is not surprised to find that partisan considerations played a major role in legislative decision making. All five of the articles in Part III suggest that party is the most important determinant. Senators and congressmen consistently voted with their party more than with their geographical section or factional bloc. Even on such an emotional issue as the Kansas-Nebraska Act, Gerald W. Wolff's Guttman scalogram analysis[5] reveals that "both party and sectional influences" were strong. In the end, sectionalism triumphed on the Nebraska question, Wolff concluded, "but not without the partial triumph of party allegiance."

If the party spirit survived the Nebraska controversy, could it outlive the War itself? Both Bogue and Richard Beringer prove that partisanship did remain strong during the war, even in the Confederate Congress, and Glenn Linden discovered that in the final Reconstruction years, 1873 to 1877, party ties were the "most important characteristic" in voting behavior. Even the Radical Republicans were party men. Bogue's study of "bloc and party," the first systematic roll call study of the Thirty-seventh Congress, indicates that the Radicals substantially disagreed with Republican Moderates on only one out of four votes on the issues of slavery and confiscation. Some factionalism, of course, is to be expected in a virtual one-party legislature, yet Bogue concludes that "party objectives were by no means forgotten; Democrats hoped for a comeback and many Republicans had both the present and future in mind."

That this goal of party resurgence in the Reconstruction years was realized is hinted at in Edward Gambill's study of the Thirty-ninth Senate and is clearly demonstrated in Glenn Linden's analysis of the Forty-third and Forty-fourth Senates. Gambill's is the first scalogram research published in *Civil War History* and his purpose is simply to identify the Radicals and measure their group cohesiveness. He discovered that the Radicals only numbered ten out of thirty-eight Republican Senators and that they were a less cohesive group than the Moderates. Linden's study is more detailed and complex. He singled out more than one hundred Senate roll calls on political and economic measures and by "scaling" the votes he noted that "there was no longer a marked division" between Radicals and Moderates. During the last four years of Reconstruction, in short, the Senate at least had "returned to its normal voting habits."

Surprisingly, even in the Confederate Congress, where the beleaguered lawmakers had an inate antipathy to politics, Beringer detected an "unconscious 'spirit of party'." Proto-party attitudes were being "nurtured in the womb of crisis." Because the baby died in embryo, Beringer explained, is no reason for the doctor to conclude that "none was ever conceived." Indeed, conception was inevitable, the author concluded in somewhat of a mixed metaphor, given the "bountiful crop of divisive issues" that Confederate leaders faced during the war. The conclusion to the roll call scales in Part III, then, is that the Congress functioned within a strong two-party system that survived even the Civil War itself. This fact, if nothing else, is a testimony to the fundamental party spirit in American politics that served to reunify a divided people.

Americans have always paid a price for consensus politics, however, as the three articles in Part IV illustrate. The foreign-born experienced severe discrimination in political patronage during the antebellum decades. All Americans with strong religious convictions were frustrated when political decisions clashed with their view of the good society. And blacks had their hopes and aspirations for legal equality dashed in the Reconstruction era because politicians returned to "business as usual" as soon as the War crisis had passed. These negative assessments of the Civil War era undoubtedly reflect the turmoil of the 1960s. In that tumultuous decade, American society moved "beyond the melting pot" into one of a "new ethnicity" of "unmeltable ethnics." Religious and cultural movements surfaced everywhere and civil rights activists ushered in the Second Reconstruction.

The major social-demographic change in the antebellum years was the influx of five million immigrants. Did the political parties welcome these new citizens and open jobs to them or did nativist prejudices prevail? According to Leonard Tabachnik's actual headcount of foreign-born citizens in the federal Customhouse Service from 1821 to 1861, the answer is a resounding "No." Immigrants were significantly underrepresented in both Republican and Democratic administrations, with the non-Anglo-Saxon groups bearing the brunt of the discrimination.

The ethnoreligious patterns in patronage appointments were also reflected in party affiliation. Nowhere is this more evident than in the midwestern county directories of the 1870s that list party, religion, and occupation for all voters. Richard Jensen sampled and statistically analyzed these virgin local sources and discovered that religion was the key determinant in party affiliation. This finding ran counter to the American axiom that religion and politics "do not mix." But mix they did, and in a vital way. The more pietistic the voter's religious outlook, the more likely the person was a Republican (or Whig). Conversely, the more liturgical the voter's church or denomination, the more likely the person was a Democrat. Religion, Jensen concluded, "exacerbated" political tensions in the Middle Period.

Race also agitated the waters of the political pool during Reconstruction. As August Meier describes so pointedly, black leaders hoped that the moral impetus of the abolitionist campaign and Emancipation Proclamation would culminate after the war in full-fledged legal and political rights for the freedmen, and perhaps even land reforms. But the movement fizzled out and blacks were bitterly disappointed, although the more realistic leaders had fully expected failure. Meier concludes: "To put the matter baldly, most of the people in a position of political influence were not really interested in the Negroes' welfare." This attitude was "simply part and parcel of the whole pattern of northern indifference to the status of Negroes in American society." Having recently witnessed the abortive ending of the Second Reconstruction, who of us can disagree with the dismal assessment of this renowned scholar who himself has been a civil rights advocate since the 1940s.

A large part of the explanation for the postwar failure to ensure racial equality lies in the superficial commitment of the American people and their political leaders in the antebellum years. The three final articles, which comprise Part V, consider the ideology of the antislavery crusade from oppositional viewpoints. Larry Gara insists that the moral indignation against slavery of the Garrisonians contributed much less to the abolitionist movement than did the perceived threat that the expansionist-minded and militant "slave power" leaders would ultimately dominate the national government. Northerners were opposed to the political challenge of proslavery leaders rather than the immorality of slavery itself. The issue was pure self-interest, although happily in this case morality coincided with power politics.

James B. Stewart, a student of the tactics of radical politics in the antebellum years, takes issue with Gara's thesis. Stewart argues that moral suasion was the "realistic" approach. The Garrison forces, he believes, gained many converts to the banner of anti-slavery by their radical pressure group methods that deliberately polarized the American public. This strategy of noncompromise was "sophisticated" and "productive," Stewart claims. Bertram Wyatt-Brown adds yet a third variation, which admits to the effectiveness of Garrison's radical rhetoric in helping to "force stronger antislavery postures among antislavery man." But the effectiveness, Wyatt-Brown insists, derived not from the radical tactics of the rhetoricians but from the message itself. Garrison and his followers were in the mainstream of the nonviolent reform tradition in America and Great Britain. They "were actors in the last great era of Christian faith, and their appeal naturally focused on the deeply entrenched feelings of a conscience-minded northern community." Garrison, in short, reached the Christian conscience of middle class America in the same way that Martin Luther King, Jr., did in the 1960s, by the force of moral argument.

The question of which scholar makes the stronger case can best be left to the reader. If you view the Civil War era from a "conflict" perspective, Stewart's radical thesis will be most attractive. But if yours is a concensus viewpoint, Gara or Wyatt-Brown will be most appealing. Gara stresses the nonpartisan, amoral, institutional approach of the antislavery crusade and Wyatt-Brown emphasizes the appeal to the Christian moral tradition in America. The difference between these scholars appears great, but it centers on the question of the essential nature of American society, whether secular pragmatist or Christian idealist, and not on the radical "confrontation" tactics, per se, of the abolitionists. Whatever your conclusion, you the reader face the same task at the end of the book as at the beginning. You must judge whether or not those scholars who would move beyond the Civil War Synthesis have a clearer picture of the political history of the times than their colleagues who are satisfied with the sectional synthesis.

This review has summarized the latest concepts, conclusions, and methods used by political historians of the Civil War era. The impact of political events of the 1960s is noteworthy, as is the social scientific approach that has reached maturity among historians in the past decade. In contrast to earlier or traditional interpretations these recent studies stress the essential continuity between the pre- and postwar years. They indicate the importance of party as well as section in political decision making, especially in the Congress. At the grass roots, party allegiance rested on local ethnoreligious and cultural factors as much as, if not more than, on national issues such as free soil and free land that appealed more to native-born citizens than ethnics. In studies of immigrant voters, these articles suggest that the votes themselves should be examined and not only the rhetoric of ethnic leaders. Methodologically, the articles show the "pay-off" of the New History, which is based upon intensive research in nominal or statistical records such as roll calls, election poll books, county directories, and customs reports. Finally, in reflecting upon these articles in terms of Joel Silbey's 1964 critique of the Civil War Synthesis, it is clear that many scholars have moved beyond the simplistic sectional focus and discovered the complexity of what actually happened in American politics in the Civil War era. The influences of party, religion, race, and jobs were interacting with sectional forces and, except for a brief period during the early war years, these nonsectional influences prevailed.

NOTES

[1] A detailed critique of the Civil War Synthesis is in Joel H. Silbey, *The Shrine of Party: Congressional Voting Behavior, 1841-1852* (Pittsburgh, 1967), chap. 1 entitled "Sectional Complexity and Interplay."

[2] The term is explained in David S. Landes and Charles Tilly (eds.), *History as Social Science* (Englewood Cliffs, N.J., 1971). ·

[3] The best introduction is Allan G. Bogue, "United States: The 'New' Political History," *Journal of Contemporary History*, III (Jan., 1968), 5-27, reprinted in Robert P. Swierenga (ed.), *Quantification in American History: Theory and Research* (New York, 1970), pp. 36-52. This entire anthology contains examples of the New history. The latest overview is Swierenga, "Computers and American History: The Impact of the 'New' Generation," *Journal of American History*, LX (March, 1974), 1045-1070.

[4] A full-length exposition of Foner's view is in his book, *Free Soil, Free Labor, Free Men: The Ideology of the Republican Party Before the Civil War* (New York, 1970).

[5] In addition to the footnote references in the articles in this book, see for Guttman scaling Duncan MacRae, Jr., *Issues and Parties in Legislative Voting: Methods of Statistical Analysis* (New York, 1970).

PART I:

THE HISTORIOGRAPHY OF THE CIVIL WAR ERA

THE CIVIL WAR SYNTHESIS IN
AMERICAN POLITICAL HISTORY

Joel H. Silbey

THE CIVIL WAR has dominated our studies of the period between the Age of Jackson and 1861. Most historians of the era have devoted their principal attention to investigating and analyzing the reasons for differences between the North and the South, the resulting sectional conflict and the degeneration of this strife into a complete breakdown of our political system in war. Because of this focus, most scholars have accepted, without question, that differences between the North and the South were the major political influences at work among the American people in the years between the mid-1840's and the war.[1] Despite occasional warnings about the dangers of overemphasizing sectional influences, the sectional interpretation holds an honored and secure place in the historiography of the antebellum years.[2] We now possess a formidable number of works which, in one way or another, center attention on the politics of sectionalism and clearly demonstrate how much the Civil War dominates our study of American political history before 1861.[3]

Obviously nothing is wrong in such emphasis if sectionalism was

[1] The primary evocation of the sectional theme is found in Frederick Jackson Turner, *The Significance of Sections in American History* (New York, 1932). The persistence of the concept is illustrated in the titles and contents of the two books in the "History of the South" series on this period: Charles Sydnor, *The Development of Southern Sectionalism, 1819-1848* (Baton Rouge, 1948), and Avery O. Craven, *The Growth of Southern Nationalism, 1848-1861* (Austin, 1953).

[2] Both Charles Sellers and Thomas P. Govan have called attention to the presence of nonsectional ideas and influences in Southern politics in the 1840's and 1850's. See Charles Grier Sellers, Jr., "Who Were the Southern Whigs?", *American Historical Review*, LIX (1954), 335-337; Thomas P. Govan, "Americans Below the Potomac," in Charles Grier Sellers, Jr. (ed.,) *The Southerner as American* (Chapel Hill, 1960), pp. 19-39.

[3] We have, for example, books on the secession movements in the individual states of the South and which usually begin in the 1840's or 1850 at the latest. See, for instance, Henry T. Shanks, *The Secession Movement in Virginia, 1847-1861* (Richmond, 1934); J. Carlyle Sitterson, *The Secession Movement in North Carolina* (Chapel Hill, 1939); Dorothy Dodd, "The Secession Movement in Florida, 1850-1861," *Florida Historical Quarterly*, XII (1933), 3-24, 45-66. Others in this same tenor include Ulrich B. Phillips, *The Course of the South to Secession* (New York, 1939), and Craven, *Southern Nationalism.*

indeed the dominant political influence in the antebellum era. However, there is the danger in such emphasis of claiming too much, that in centering attention on the war and its causes we may ignore or play down other contemporary political influences and fail to weigh adequately the importance of nonsectional forces in antebellum politics. And, in fact, several recent studies of American political behavior have raised serious doubts about the importance of sectional differences as far as most Americans were concerned. These have even suggested that the sectional emphasis has created a false synthesis in our study of history which increases the importance of one factor, ignores the significance of other factors, and ultimately distorts the reality of American political life between 1844 and 1861.

I

Scholars long have used the presidential election of 1844 as one of their major starting points for the sectional analysis of American political history. In a general sense they have considered American expansion into Texas to be the most important issue of that campaign. The issue stemmed from the fact that Texas was a slave area and many articulate Northerners attacked the movement to annex Texas as a slave plot designed to enhance Southern influence within the Union. Allegedly because of these attacks, and the Southerners' defending themselves, many people in both North and South found themselves caught up in such sectional bitterness that the United States took a major step toward civil war.[4] Part of this bitterness can be seen, it is pointed out, in the popular vote in New York state where the Whig candidate for the presidency, Henry Clay, lost votes to the abolitionist Liberty party because he was a slaveholder.[5] The loss of these votes cost him New York and ultimately the election. As a result of Clay's defeat, historians have concluded that as early as 1844 the problem of slavery-extension was important enough to arouse people to act primarily in sectional terms and thus for this episode to be a milestone on the road to war.

Recently Professor Lee Benson published a study of New York state politics in the Jacksonian era.[6] Although Benson mainly concerned him-

[4] "But the antislavery crusade had already gained such momentum that no Northern man could take a public stand in favor of annexation . . . [of Texas]." Charles Wiltse, *John C. Calhoun, Sectionalist, 1840-1850* (Indianapolis, 1951), p. 156.

[5] Charles Wiltse, *The New Nation, 1800-1845* (New York, 1961), p. 187; George Rawlings Poage, *Henry Clay and the Whig Party* (Chapel Hill, 1936), p. 151. There is a less certain discussion of this problem in John Garraty, *Silas Wright* (New York, 1949), pp. 327-328.

[6] Lee Benson, *The Concept of Jacksonian Democracy: New York as a Test Case* (Princeton, 1961).

self with other problems, some of his findings directly challenge the conception that slavery and sectional matters were of major importance in New York in 1844. In his analysis Benson utilized a more systematic statistical compilation of data than have previous workers in the field of political history.[7] Observing that scholars traditionally have looked at what people said they did rather than at what they actually did, Benson compiled a great number of election returns for New York state in this period. His purpose was to see who actually voted for whom and to place the election in historical perspective by pinpointing changes in voting over time and thus identifying the basic trends of political behavior. Through such analysis Benson arrived at a major revision of the nature of New York state voting in 1844.

. Benson pointed out, first of all, that the abolitionist, anti-Texas Liberty party whose vote total should have increased if the New York population wanted to strike against a slave plot in Texas, actually lost votes over what it had received in the most immediate previous election, that of 1843.[8] Further analysis indicated that there was no widespread reaction to the Texas issue in New York state on the part of any large group of voters, although a high degree of anti-Texas feeling indeed existed among certain limited groups in the population. Such sentiment, however, did not affect voting margins in New York state.[9] Finally, Benson concluded that mass voting in New York in 1844 pivoted not on the sectional issue but rather on more traditional divisions between ethnic and religious groups whose voting was a reaction to matters closer to home. These proved of a more personal and psychological nature than that of Texas and its related issue of slavery-extension.[10] Sectional bitterness, contrary to previous historical conceptions, neither dominated nor seriously influenced the 1844 vote in New York. Although Benson confined his study to one state, his conclusions introduce doubts about the influence of sectionalism in other supposedly less pivotal states.

II

Another aspect of the sectional interpretation of American politics in the pre-Civil War era involves Congress. Political historians have considered that body to be both a forum wherein leaders personally expressed attitudes that intensified sectional bitterness, as well as an arena which reflected the general pattern of influences operative in the coun-

[7] Benson's methodology is discussed throughout the book and also in his article, "Research Problems in American Political Historiography," in Mirra Komarovsky (ed.), *Common Frontiers of the Social Sciences* (Glencoe, 1957), pp. 113-183.
[8] Benson, *Concept*, p. 260.   [9] *Ibid.*, p. 267.
[10] *Ibid.*, chap. xiv.

try at large.[11] Therefore, writers on the period have considered the behavior of congressmen to have been more and more dominated by sectionalism, particularly after David Wilmot introduced his antislavery extension proviso into the House of Representatives in 1846. Although there may have been other issues and influences present, it is accepted that these were almost completely overborne in the late 1840's and 1850's in favor of a widespread reaction to sectional differences.[12]

In a recently completed study, I have analyzed congressional voting in the allegedly crucial pivotal decade 1841-1852, the period which historians identify as embodying the transition from nationalism to sectionalism in congressonal behavior.[13] This examination indicates that a picture of the decade as one in which sectional influences steadily grew stronger, overwhelmed all other bases of divisions, and became a permanent feature of the voting behavior of a majority of congressmen, is grossly oversimplified and a distortion of reality. In brief, although sectional influences, issues, and voting did exist, particularly between 1846 and 1850, sectional matters were not the only problems confronting congressmen. In the period before the introduction of the Wilmot Proviso in 1846, national issues such as the tariff, financial policy, foreign affairs, and land policy divided congressmen along political, not sectional, lines.[14] Furthermore, in this earlier period issues which many have believed to have shown a high degree of sectional content, such as admittance of Texas and Oregon, reveal highly partisan national divisions and little sectional voting.[15]

[11] F. J. Turner, for example, suggested that on fundamental issues Congress demonstrated "a persistent sectional pattern." Turner, *Significance of Sections*, pp. 40, 198. And in his *The United States, 1830-1850; The Nation and its Sections* (New York, 1935), Turner consistently used congressional votes to demonstrate the growth of political sectionalism.

[12] Craven, *Growth of Southern Nationalism*, chap. i.

[13] Joel H. Silbey, "Congressional Voting Behavior and the Southern-Western Alliance, 1841-1852" (Ph.D. dissertation, State University of Iowa, 1963).

[14] Part of the evidence for these conclusions was presented as a paper, "The Response to Recovery: Congressional Voting Behavior, 1841-1845," before the Mississippi Valley Historical Association at Detroit in April, 1961.

[15] For example, when the House of Representatives voted on the group of issues involving expansion into Oregon and Texas, 82.3 per cent of the Democrats voted in favor of expansion while 74.5 per cent of the Whigs voted against such expansion. In the Senate the Whigs were 100 per cent united against expansion while 78.1 per cent of the Democrats supported a more expansionist policy than did the Whigs. Each party contained members, of course, from both sections of the Union. Furthermore, the dissenters from the party positions exhibited here were not sectional blocs, but, in general, scattered individuals reacting to local or personal considerations.

In connection with nationwide support for expansion, see also John Hope Franklin, "The Southern Expansionists of 1846," *Journal of Southern History*, XXV (1959), 323-338.

Even after the rise of the slavery-extension issue, other questions of a national character remained important. Slavery was but one of several issues before Congress and it was quite possible for congressmen to vote against one another as Northern and Southern sectionalists on an issue and then to join together, regardless of section, against other Northerners and Southerners on another matter. Certainly some men from both geographic areas were primarily influenced by sectional considerations at all times on all issues, but they were a minority of all congressmen in the period. The majority of congressmen were not so overwhelmingly influenced by their being Northerners or Southerners, but continued to think and act in national terms, and even resisted attempts by several sectionally minded congressmen to forge coalitions, regardless of party, against the other section.[16]

A careful study of congressional voting in these years also demonstrates that another assumption of historians about the nature of politics is oversimplified: the period around 1846 did *not* begin the steady forward movement of congressional politics toward sectionalism and war. Rather, it was quite possible in the period between 1846 and 1852 for congressmen to assail one another bitterly in sectional terms, physically attack one another, and even threaten secession, and still for the majority of them to return in the following session to a different approach—that of nonsectional political differences with a concomitant restoration of nonsectional coalitions. For example, it was possible in 1850, after several years of sectional fighting, for a national coalition of Senators and Representatives to join together and settle in compromise terms the differences between North and South over expansion. And they were able to do this despite the simultaneous existence of a great deal of sectional maneuvering by some congressmen in an attempt to prevent any such compromise. Furthermore, during this same session Congress also dealt with matters of railroad land grants in a way that eschewed sectional biases.[17] Obviously the

[16] John C. Calhoun tried for years to organize the Southern congressmen into a unified bloc to resist Northern pressures. However, his efforts were always opposed by some other Southerners, both Whigs and Democrats, who did not see any reason to organize or vote sectionally and who preferred to maintain their national partisan commitments. Examples of this feeling can be seen in the resolutions of the Democrats of the Sixth Congressional District of Georgia, in the Washington *Union,* June 17, 1847; the resolutions of the Alabama State Democratic Convention, February 1848, in *ibid.,* Feb. 25, 1848; Howell Cobb, *et al.,* "To Our Constituents," Feb. 26, 1849, in Robert Brooks (ed.), "Howell Cobb Papers," *Georgia Historical Quarterly,* V (1921), 51 ff.

Calhoun's organ, the *Charleston Mercury,* finally admitted that "the antipathies of Whig and Democrat are too strong in Washington, and their exercise forms too much the habit of men's lives there. . . ." for there to be sectional unity. See issue of Jan. 22, 1849.

[17] In the thirty-first Congress, 95.2 per cent of the Southerners in the House

usual picture of an inexorable growth of sectional partisanship after 1846 is quite overdone. And lest these examples appeared to be isolated phenomena, preliminary research both by Gerald Wolff and by myself demonstrates that as late as 1854 there was still no complete or overwhelming sectional voting even on such an issue as the Kansas-Nebraska Act.[18]

Such analyses of congressional behavior in an alleged transition period reinforce what Lee Benson's work on New York politics demonstrated: many varieties and many complexities existed with respect to political behavior in the antebellum period, so that even slavery failed to be a dominating influence among all people at all times—or even among most people at most times—during the 1840's and early 1850's. Again, our previous image of American politics in this period must be reconsidered in light of this fact and despite the emergence of a Civil War in 1861.

III

Perhaps no aspect of antebellum politics should demonstrate more fully the overpowering importance of sectional influences than the presidential election of 1860. In the preliminaries to that contest the Democratic party split on the rock of slavery, the Republican party emerged as a power in the Northern states with a good chance of winning the presidency, and loud voices in the Southern states called for secession because of Northern attacks on their institutions.[19] In dealing with these events, historians, as in their treatment of other aspects of antebellum politics, have devoted their primary attention to sectional bickering and maneuvering among party leaders, because they considered this activity to be the most important facet of the campaign and the key to explaining the election.[20] Alhough such a focus obviously has merit if one is thinking in terms of the armed conflict which broke out only five months after the election, once again, as in the earlier cases considered here, recent research has raised pertinent questions about the political realities of the situation. We may indeed ask what were the issues of the campaign as seen by the majority of voters.

Earlier studies of the 1860 election, in concerning themselves pri-

---

voted together on issues rising out of the slavery-extension debate and then they turned around and split fairly evenly, (45.6 per cent, 11.4 per cent, 43.0 per cent) into three positions on issues of internal improvements. In the succeeding sessions of Congress such sectional divisions remained the rule on the issues considered.

[18] Gerald Wolff, "A Scalogram Analysis of the Kansas-Nebraska Act" (unpublished manuscript lent by author).

[19] The background of this election is well covered in Roy F. Nichols, *The Disruption of American Democracy* (New York, 1947).

[20] See, for example, Emerson D. Fite, *The Presidential Campaign of 1860* (New York, 1911); James G. Randall and David Donald, *The Civil War and Reconstruction* (2nd ed.; Boston, 1961), pp. 129-132.

marily with the responses and activities of political leaders, have taken popular voting behavior for granted. This aspect has either been ignored or else characterized as reflecting the same influences and attitudes as that of the leadership. Therefore, the mass of men, it is alleged, voted in response to sectional influences in 1860. For instance, several scholars concerned with the Germans in the Middle West in this period have characterized the attitudes of that group as overwhelmingly antislavery. Thus the Republican party attracted the mass of the German vote because the liberal "Forty-Eighters" saw casting a Lincoln vote as a way to strike a blow against slavery in the United States.[21] Going beyond this, some historians have reached similar conclusions about other Middle Western immigrant groups.[22] As a result, according to most historians, although narrowly divided, the area went for Lincoln thanks in large part to its newest citizens, who were Northern sectionalists in their political behavior. Such conclusions obviously reinforce the apparent importance of geographic partisanship in 1860.

Testing this hypothesis, two recent scholars systematically studied and analyzed election returns in Iowa during 1860. Such examinations are important because they should reveal, if the sectional theory is correct, preoccupation among Iowa voters—especially immigrants—with the slavery question and the increasingly bitter differences between North and South. Only one of these studies, that of Professor George H. Daniels of Northwestern University, has appeared in print.[23] But Daniels' findings shatter earlier interpretations which pin-pointed sectional concerns as the central theme of the 1860 election.

Briefly stated, Daniels isolated the predominantly German townships in Iowa and, following Lee Benson's methodological lead, analyzed their vote. He found that, far from being solidly Republican voters, or moved primarily by the slavery question, the Germans of Iowa voted overwhelmingly in favor of the Democratic party. And Daniels discovered that the primary issue motivating the Germans in 1860 was an ethnic one. They were conscious of the anti-alien Know-Nothing movement which had been so strong in the United States during the 1850's and they identified the Republican party as the heir and last refuge of Know-Nothingism.[24] If the Germans of Iowa were attracted

21 See, for example, Lawrence S. Thompson and Frank X. Braun, "The Forty-Eighters in Politics," in Adolf E. Zucker, *The Forty-Eighters* (New York, 1950), p. 120; Ray Allen Billington, *Westward Expansion* (2nd ed.; New York, 1960), p. 611; William E. Dodd, "The Fight For the Northwest, 1860," *American Historical Review*, XVI (1911), 774-788.

22 Donnal V. Smith, "The Influence of the Foreign Born of the Northwest in the Election of 1860," *Mississippi Valley Historical Review*, XIX (1932), 193.

23 George H. Daniels, "Immigrant Vote in the 1860 Election: The Case of Iowa," *Mid-America*, XLIV (1962), 146-162.

24 *Ibid.*, 155-157.

to the Republicans by the latter's antislavery attitudes, such attraction
was more than overcome by the Republicans' aura of antiforeignism.[25]
Furthermore, the Republicans were also identified in the minds of the
Iowa Germans as the party of prohibitionism, a social view strongly
opposed by most Germans.[26] Thus, as Daniels concludes, ". . . The rank
and file Germans who did the bulk of the voting considered their own
liberty to be of paramount importance. Apparently ignoring the advice
of their leaders, they cast their ballots for the party which consistently
promised them liberty from prohibition and native-American legislation."[27] As a result, the Germans of Iowa voted Democratic, not Republican, in 1860.

Lest this appear to be an isolated case, the research of Robert Swierenga on Dutch voting behavior in Iowa in 1860 confirms Daniels' findings. Swierenga demonstrated that the Dutch also voted Democratic
despite their vaunted antislavery attitudes; again, revulsion from certain
Republican ideals overpowered any attraction towards that party on
the slavery issue.[28]

Such research into the election of 1860, as in the earlier cases of the
election of 1844 and congressional voting behavior in the 1840's and
early 1850's, suggests how far the sectional and slavery preconceptions
of American historians have distorted reality. Many nonsectional
issues were apparently more immediately important to the groups
involved than any imminent concern with Northern-Southern differences. Once again, the Civil War synthesis appears to be historically
inaccurate and in need of serious revision.

IV

Several other provocative studies recently have appeared which, while
dealing with nonpolitical subjects, support the conclusion that sectional
problems, the slavery issue, and increasing bitterness between North
and South were not always uppermost concerns to most Americans in
the fifteen years before the outbreak of the war. Building upon the
work of Leon Litwack, which emphasizes the general Northern antagonism toward the Negro before 1860, and that of Larry Gara demonstrating the fallacy of the idea that a well-organized and widespread
underground railroad existed in the North,[29] Professor C. Vann Wood-

[25] Other issues such as a Massachusetts voting law, which would have made it
more difficult for aliens to exercise the franchise, reinforced this feeling during
the election of 1860. See *ibid.*, 156-157.
[26] *Ibid.*, 156.   [27] *Ibid.*, 157.
[28] Robert P. Swierenga, "The Ethnic Leader and Immigrant Voting" (unpublished manuscript lent by author).
[29] Leon Litwack, *North of Slavery: The Negro in the Free States, 1790-1860*
(Chicago, 1961); Larry Gara, *Liberty Line: The Legend of the Underground
Railroad* (Lexington, 1961).

ward has cautioned students against an easy acceptance of a "North-Star" image—a picture of a universally militant Northern population determined to ease the burden of the slave in America.[30] Rather, as Woodward points out, a great many Northerners remained indifferent to the plight of the slave and hostile to the would-be antislavery reformer in their midst.[31]

In this same tenor, Milton Powell of Michigan State University has challenged long-held assumptions that the Northern Methodist church was a bulwark of antislavery sentiment after splitting with its Southern branch in 1844. As Powell makes clear, Northern Methodists were concerned about many other problems in which slavery played no part, as well as being beset by conditions which served to tone down any antislavery attitudes they may have held. More importantly, this led many of them to ignore slavery as an issue because of its latent tendency to divide the organization to which they belonged.[32] Thus, even in areas outside of the political realm, the actual conditions of antebellum society challenge the validity of the sectional concept in its most general and far-reaching form.

V

This review of recent research indicates that much of our previous work on the prewar period should be re-examined free from the bias caused by looking first at the fact of the Civil War and then turning back to view the events of the previous decade in relation only to that fact. Although it is true that the studies discussed here are few in number and by no means include the entire realm of American politics in the antebellum era, their diversity in time and their revisionist conclusions do strongly suggest the fallacy of many previous assumptions. No longer should any historian blithely accept the traditional concept of a universal preoccupation with the sectional issue.

But a larger matter is also pointed up by this recent research and the destruction of this particular myth about political sectionalism. For a question immediately arises as to how historians generally could have accepted so readily and for so long such oversimplifications and inaccuracies. Fortunately for future research, answers to this question have been implicitly given by the scholars under review, and involve methodological problems concerning evidence and a certain naïveté about the political process.

Historians generally have utilized as evidence the writings and commentaries of contemporary observers of, and participants in, the

---

[30] C. Vann Woodward, "The Antislavery Myth," *American Scholar*, XXXI (1962), 312-328.

[31] *Ibid.*, 316-318.

[32] Milton B. Powell, "The Abolitionist Controversy in the Methodist Episcopal Church, 1840-1864" (Ph.D. dissertation, State University of Iowa, 1963).

events being examined. But, as both Benson and Daniels emphasize, this can endanger our understanding of reality. For instance, not enough attention has been paid to who actually said what, or of the motives of a given reporter or the position he was in to know and understand what was going on around him. Most particularly, scholars have not always been properly skeptical about whether the observer's comments truly reflected actuality. As Daniels pointed out in his article on German voting behavior, "contemporary opinion, including that of newspapers, is a poor guide."[33]

If such is true, and the evidence presented by these studies indicates that it is, a question is raised as to how a historian is to discover contemporary opinion if newspapers are not always reliable as sources. The work of Benson, Daniels, and myself suggests an answer: the wider use of statistics. When we talk of public opinion (that is, how the mass of men acted or thought) we are talking in terms of aggregate numbers, of majorities. One way of determining what the public thought is by measuring majority opinion in certain circumstances—elections, for example, or the voting of congressmen—and then analyzing the content and breakdown of the figures derived. If, for example, 80 per cent of the Germans in Iowa voted Democratic in 1860, this tells us more about German public opinion in 1860 than does a sprightly quote from one of the Germans in the other 20 per cent who voted Republican "to uphold freedom." Historians are making much more use of statistics than formerly and are utilizing more sophisticated techniques of quantitative analysis. And such usage seems to prelude, judging by the works discussed here, a fuller and more accurate understanding of our past.

There are also other ways of approaching the problems posed by the 1850's. Not enough attention has been paid, it seems to me, to the fact that there are many different levels of political behavior—mass voting, legislative activity, leadership manipulation, for example—and that what is influential and important on one level of politics may not be on another. Certainly the Germans and Dutch of Iowa in 1860 were not paying much attention to the desires of their leaders. They were responding to influences deemed more important than those influences shaping the responses of their leaders. As Swierenga pointed out in his analysis of Dutch voting:

While Scholte [a leader of the Dutch community] fulminated against Democrats as slave mongers, as opponents of the Pacific Railroad and Homestead Bills, and as destroyers of the Constitution, the Dutch citizens blithely ignored him and the national issues he propounded and voted their personal prejudices against Republican nativists and prohibitionists.[34]

[33] Daniels, "Immigrant Vote," 158.
[34] Swierenga, "Ethnic Leader," p. 24.

Obviously, when historians generalize about the nature of political behavior they must also be sure which group and level of political activity they mean, and so identify it, and not confuse different levels or assume positive correlations between the actions of people on one level with those on another level. Such precision will contribute greatly to accuracy and overcome tendencies toward distortion.

Finally, based on the work under discussion here, it is clear that historians must become more aware of the complexities of human behavior. All people, even of the same stratum of society or living in the same geographic area, do not respond with the same intensity to the same social or political stimuli. Not everyone perceives his best interests in the same way, or considers the same things to be the most important problems confronting him. Depending upon time and circumstances, one man may respond primarily to economic influences; another one, at the same time and place, to religious influences; and so on. Sometimes most people in a given community will respond to the same influences equally, but we must be careful to observe *when* this is true and not generalize from it that this is *always* true. Single-factor explanations for human behavior do not seem to work, and we must remain aware of that fact.

With improved methodological tools and concepts historians may begin to engage in more systematic and complete analyses of popular voting, legislative voting, and the motivations and actions of political leaders. They will be able to weigh the relative influence of sectional problems against other items of interest and concern on all levels of political behavior. Until this is done, however, we do know on the basis of what already has been suggested that we cannot really accept glib explanations about the antebellum period. The Civil War has had a pernicious influence on the study of American political development that preceded it—pernicious because it has distorted the reality of political behavior in the era and has caused an overemphasis on sectionalism. It has led us to look not for what was occurring in American politics in those years, but rather for what was occurring in American politics that tended toward sectional breakdown and civil war—a quite different matter.

THE CAUSES OF THE AMERICAN CIVIL WAR: Recent Interpretations and New Directions

Eric Foner

In 1960, as Americans prepared to observe the centennial of the Civil War, one of the foremost historians of that conflict published a brief article entitled, "American Historians and the Causes of the Civil War."[1] Most readers probably expected another survey of the changing course of civil war interpretation. Instead the author announced that as a subject of serious historical analysis, Civil War causation was "dead."

Looking back over the decade and a half since David Donald wrote, it would appear that he somewhat exaggerated the death of this field of inquiry. In the 1950's, historians were concerned with investigating periods of consensus in America's past. But in the 1960's, as the issues of race and war came to the forefront of national life, earlier times of civil strife in American history attracted renewed attention.

The 1960's, for example, witnessed a renascence of the study of slavery. It is now no longer possible to view the peculiar institution as some kind of accident or aberration, existing outside the mainstream of national development. Rather, slavery was absolutely central to the American experience, intimately bound up with the settlement of the western hemisphere, the American Revolution and industrial expansion. It was what defined the Old South and drew southern society along a path of development which set it increasingly apart from the rest of the nation.[2]

* This paper was read before the 1972 meeting of the Organization of American Historians, at one of a series of "Overview" sessions, reviewing the last fifteen years of historical writing on various periods of American history. The author is extremely grateful to the following scholars for their helpful criticisms of earlier drafts of this paper: Richard O. Curry, Herbert Gutman, David Rothman, James P. Shenton, and James B. Stewart.

[1] David Donald, "American Historians and the Causes of the Civil War." *South Atlantic Quarterly*, LIX (Summer, 1960), 351-55.

[2] To cite only a few of the host of works related to this point, David Brion Davis, *The Problem of Slavery in Western Culture* (1966), and Edmund S. Morgan, "Slavery and Freedom: The American Paradox," *Journal of American History*, LIX, (June, 1972), 5-29 stress the centrality of slavery to the American experience. Douglass North, *The Economic Growth of the United States, 1790 to 1860* (1961), shows how the profits of the cotton trade paid for the economic development of antebellum America. Staughton Lynd, *Class Conflict, Slavery, and the United States Constitution* (1967), Donald L. Robinson, *Slavery and the Structure of American Politics* (1971), Richard H. Brown, "The Missouri Crisis, Slavery and the Politics of Jacksonianism," *South Atlantic Quarterly*, LXV (Winter, 1966), 55-72, William W. Freehling, *Prelude to Civil War* (1966), and Eric Foner, *Free Soil, Free Labor,*

At the same time, a striking reversal of interpretations of the abolitionists took place.[3] In fact, there was a paradoxical double reversal.
On the one hand the abolitionists, previously castigated as fanatics and
agitators, suddenly emerged as the conscience of a sinning nation—
much as the Garrisons and Welds had portrayed themselves a century
earlier. At the same time, a number of writers argued that not only
were the friends of the slave not immune from racism, but, far from
being truly "radical," they seemed to accept the middle-class values of
northern society.[4]

The flood of studies of slavery, abolitionism, and the race issue does
not seem, however, to have brought historians much closer to a generally accepted interpretation of the coming of the Civil War than they
were fifteen years ago. As the late David Potter pointed out, the irony
is that disagreements of interpretation persist in the face of a greatly increased body of historical knowledge.[5] This is partially because the
Civil War raised so many still unresolved issues. Perhaps, however,
there is another reason. Historians' methodologies and value judgments
have changed considerably over the past fifteen years, but the questions
historians have asked of their data have remained relatively static.
Like the debate over slavery before the appearance of Stanley Elkins'
study in 1959, discussion of the causes of the Civil War continues to be
locked into an antiquated interpretive framework. Historians of the
Civil War era seem to be in greater need of new models of interpretation and new questions than of an additional accumulation of data.

There have, however, been a number of works in the past fifteen
years which have attempted to develop entirely new ways of looking
at ante-bellum America and the origins of the Civil War. One of the
most striking developments of these years has been the emergence of
the "new political historians," who have attempted to recast our understanding of ante-bellum political alignments. They have de-emphasized
"national" issues like slavery and the tariff, and substituted ethno-cul-

---

Free Men: The Ideology of the Republican Party Before the Civil War (1970)
place slavery at the center of politics at various points in ante-bellum history. Eugene D. Genovese, *The Political Economy of Slavery* (1965), makes clear the centrality of slavery to the society of the Old South.

[3] Rather than citing the scores of works on abolitionism, let me simply refer to
an admirable historiographical survey: Merton L. Dillon, "The Abolitionists: A
Decade of Historiography, 1959-1969," *Journal of Southern History*, XXXV, (Nov.,
1969), 500-22.

[4] On the racism of anti-slavery advocates, see, for example, William H. Pease
and Jane H. Pease, "Anti-Slavery Ambivalence: Immediatism, Expediency, Race,"
American Quarterly, XVII (Winter, 1965), 682-95; Eric Foner, "Racial Attitudes
of the New York Free Soilers," *New York History*, XLVI (Oct., 1965), 311-29; Eugene H. Berwanger, *The Frontier Against Slavery* (1967); and James H. Rawley,
Race and Politics (1969). For the limitations of abolitionist radicalism, see William
Appleman Williams, *The Contours of American History* (London ed., 1961), p.
254; Aileen Kraditor, *Means and Ends in American Abolitionism* (New York, 1969),
pp. 244-53); George F. Fredrickson, *The Black Image in the White Mind* (1971),
pp. 36-37.

[5] David Potter, *The South and the Sectional Conflict* (1968), p. 146.

tural conflicts between Protestants and Catholics, or between pietistic and ritualistic religious groups, as the major determinants of voting behavior. These works have broadened our understanding of ante-bellum political culture, and demonstrated the inevitable failure of any "monistic interpretation" of political conflict. And they should force historians to abandon whatever economic determinism still persists in the writing of political history. Perhaps most important, they have demonstrated the virtues of viewing voters not as isolated individuals, but as men and women embedded in a complex network of social and cultural relationships.[6]

The "new political history" involves both a new methodology—the statistical analysis of quantitative data—and a distinctive model of historical explanation. The broadening of the methodological tools available to historians can only be applauded, although some writers may at times be guilty of mistaking correlations for causes, and inducing the behavior of individuals from aggregate data. It sometimes seems that the very sophistication of the new methodology has unfortunate effects on these writers' approach to historical data. Not only is undue weight often assigned to historical variables such as ethnicity for which quantifiable data happens to be available, but the definition of basic concepts is reduced to the most easily quantifiable elements. Thus, class is measured by data on occupation and assessed property holdings, culture is reduced to a mixture of ethnicity and religion, and religion is measured purely by Church affiliation.[7]

It is in the realm of explanation, and as a contribution to our under-

[6] The major works of "new political history" dealing with ante-bellum politics are Lee Benson, *The Concept of Jacksonian Democracy: New York as a Test Case* (1961); Ronald P. Formisano, *The Birth of Mass Political Parties: Michigan 1827-1861* (1971); Paul Kleppner, *The Cross of Culture* (1970); the essays collected in Frederick C. Luebke (ed.), *Ethnic Voters and the Election of Lincoln* (1971); and Michael F. Holt, *Forging a Majority: The Formation of the Republican Party in Pittsburgh, 1848-1860* (1969). The phrase "monistic interpretation" is quoted from Holt, p. 125. I should note that obviously not all these writers agree on every interpretation. Holt, for example, tends to give anti-slavery attitudes more credence as a determinant of voting behavior than do the other writers.

[7] Some of these methodological criticisms are raised in Allen G. Bogue, "United States: The 'New Political History,'" *Journal of Contemporary History*, III (Jan., 1968), 22-24; James E. Wright, "The Ethnocultural Model of Voting," *American Behavioral Scientist*, XVI (May-June, 1973), 653-74; and James R. Green, "Behavioralism and Class Analysis: A Review Essay on Methodology and Ideology," *Labor History*, XIII (Winter, 1972), 89-106. Among other methodological problems is the tendency of some writers to infer the behavior of voters in heterogeneous areas from the actions of those who lived in homogenous ethnic communities, and difficulties created by the use of census data on the number of church seats of each religion in a specified area, as a measure of the breakdown of religious affiliations of that area. There are also simple problems of interpreting data. Formisano, for example, presents a table of the voting of evangelical townships in Michigan in 1860. In eastern Michigan, six of eleven such townships gave Lincoln over 60 per cent of the vote, but Lincoln carried the state with 57 per cent of Michigan's ballots. The table shows that in five of eleven evangelical townships, Lincoln received less than his state-wide percentage. The figures hardly justify the conclusion that evangelical townships voted "strongly Republican" in 1860. Formisano, *Birth of Mass Political Parties*, pp. 312-13.

standing of the coming of the Civil War, that the "new political history" is most open to criticism. First, while rightly rejecting the economic determinism of progressive historians, the new political historians
seem to be in danger of substituting a religious or cultural determinism of their own. Indeed, the interpretive framework of the new school
is strikingly similar to that of the progressives. Both pose a sharp distinction between "real" and "unreal" issues, both put thousands of persons in the quasi-conspiratorial position of concealing their real intentions, and both take an extremely limited view of individual motivation.
For the "economic man" of the progressives, the new political history
has substituted an equally one-dimensional "religious man."

Most important, this new mode of explanation is fundamentally
ahistorical; its key variables exist independently of historical context.
Religion and ethnicity are generally treated as "uni-dimensional concepts, without reference to time, place, rate of acculturation, or individual personality." The point is that all historical variables are interrelated, and change as society develops. To take one key variable—
religious belief in this case, or an over-simplified version of class for the
progressives—and abstract it from its social context and the processes
of historical change, is to distort and fracture historical reality.[8]

The arguments of the "new political historians" have profound implications for the question of Civil War causation. Their basic outlook
was announced in 1964, in Joel Silbey's influential article, "The Civil
War Synthesis," which chided historians for writing the history of the
1850's solely from the vantage point of the slavery issue, ignoring questions, like nativism, which seemed to have little to do with the coming
of war. Subsequent writers have agreed with Silbey that a split existed
between northern political elites and the mass of voters. The former
were, for a variety of reasons, increasingly anti-southern, the latter
were "basically unmoved" by the issues of slavery and sectional conflict and were more concerned with so-called "cultural" questions like
immigration and temperance.[9]

While often criticizing traditional historians for using such "elite
sources" as newspapers, speeches and letters, this new interpretation
of ante-bellum politics has its own elitist bias. It assumes that "large portions of the electorate do not have meaningful beliefs,"[10] that only elites

[8] Some of these criticisms are noted in the Wright and Green articles cited
above, and in David P. Thelen, review of Kleppner, *Civil War History*, XVII
(Mar., 1971), 84-86, and Thelen, review of Formisano, *Civil War History*, XVIII
(Dec., 1972), 355-57. The quotation is from Wright, "The Ethnocultural Model of
Voting," 664. Wright and Green question whether these studies are adequately controlled for class and status variables. All three critics question whether class can be
adequately measured by looking at units like "farmers" or "workers," or by measuring the wealth of rural and urban precincts without considering the internal
class structure of these units.

[9] Joel H. Silbey, "The Civil War Synthesis in American Political History," *Civil
War History*, X (June, 1964), 130-40; Luebke, *Ethnic Voters*, p. xi.

[10] This incredible statement is quoted by Formisano from Philip E. Converse,
"The Nature of Belief Systems in Mass Publics," in David E. Apter, *Ideology and*

are truly issue-oriented. This kind of reasoning, however, can never illuminate the relationship between political leaders and voters in a democratic political culture. Nor can it explain under what circumstances local issues will dominate politics and when national issues will come to the fore, or tell us why Republicans in the late 1850's were constantly trying to play down the issues of temperance and nativism which had supposedly created their party in the first place.[11] The view of the Republican party as the political expression of pietistic Protestantism can hardly encompass a figure like Lincoln, who was southern-born and whose religious beliefs were akin to the deism of that infidel Thomas Paine, whom Lincoln greatly admired.[12] According to the aggregate data, Lincoln should have been a pro-slavery Democrat. At best, he was a historical accident, an ecological fallacy.

But what of the Civil War? Supposedly, when the scientist Laplace described the Newtonian system to Napoleon, the emperor asked, "But where is God in your system?" To which Laplace replied, "I have no need for that hypothesis." Similarly, the "system" of the new political history has no need for the Civil War. Unfortunately, the Civil War did take place. But the new interpretation leaves a yawning gap between political processes and the outbreak of war. Recently, Lee Benson has tried to bridge this gap by arguing that a "small group" of southern conspirators, taking advantage of the "irresponsible character" of the political system, caused the war.[13] To pursue our Enlightenment analogy and paraphrase Voltaire, if Benson's explanation did not exist, we would have to invent it. If only elites cared about the slavery question, we are logically driven back to a neo-revisionist conspiracy theory of the coming of the war. One does not have to assume that great events always have great causes to believe that conspiracy theories are rarely satisfactory as historical explanations.

A second school of historical writing places the coming of the Civil War within the process political scientists have termed "modernization." This is as yet an imprecisely defined concept, but it involves such basic changes in the structure of a society as rapid economic development, urbanization, industrialization, the creation of an integrated national economic and political structure, and generally, the spread of market-oriented capitalist economic relations and of mental attitudes viewing continuous social change as natural and desirable.[14] Within this context, the Civil War becomes the process by which the "modern" or "modernizing" North integrated the "pre-modern" South into a national political and economic system. As Raimondo Luraghi explains, "So, in

---

Discontent (1964), p. 245. Formisano, *Birth of Mass Political Parties*, pp. 11-12. Cf. Leubke, *Ethnic Voters*, p. xiv.

[11] On this last point, see Foner, *Free Soil, Free Labor, Free Men*, ch. 7.

[12] Richard N. Current, *The Lincoln Nobody Knows* (1958), pp. 58-59.

[13] Lee Benson, *Toward the Scientific Study of History* (1972), pp. 316-26.

[14] See, in general, A. S. Eisenstadt, *Modernization: Protest and Change* (1966), and C. E. Black, *The Dynamics of Modernization* (1966).

the nineteenth century, as the industrial revolution was expanding on a worldwide scale, the days of wrath were coming for a series of agrarian, pre-capitalistic, 'backward' societies throughout the world, from the Italian and American South down to India."[15] Aside from Luraghi's work, the modernization framework has not yet been systematically applied to the coming of the Civil War, although in many respects it is compatible with the work of Eugene Genovese on the South and with my own discussion of the Republican party in the 1850's.[16]

As Robert Kelley demonstrates, the ethno-cultural and modernization interpretations are not necessarily incompatible. In his book, *The Transatlantic Persuasion*, the Republicans in America and the Tories in England become the nationalists, homogenizers and cosmopolitans. Intolerant of any social diversity within their societies, they attempted to impose their values on dissident groups—temperance legislation on the Irish immigrants, anti-slavery on the South—while the party of the regional and ethnic minorities (Democrats in America, Liberals in Britain), called for cultural pluralism and local autonomy.[17]

The problem with this analysis is that it views the sectional conflict primarily as a struggle between local and national institutions. It is significant that in Kelley's stimulating book, the institution of slavery is conspicuous by its absence. But slavery was what made the South distinct—it was central to the moral, economic and political antagonisms between the sections.

Nonetheless, this framework has much to offer toward an understanding of the politics of the 1850's. Lincoln's House Divided speech, as J. R. Pole has written, can be viewed as the outlook of a man "who had grasped the essentials of the process of nationalisation that was overtaking the main institutions of American life." Conversely, Stephen A. Douglas's objection to what he termed Lincoln's belief that "there must be uniformity in the local laws and domestic institutions of each and all states of the Union," and his plea for recognition of "diversity and dissimilarity" within the nation, can be read as the cry of all the out-groups

[15] Raimondo Luraghi, "The Civil War and the Modernization of American Society: Social Structure and Industrial Revolution in the Old South Before and During the War," *Civil War History*, XVIII (Sept., 1972), 242.

[16] Also relevant is Barrington Morroe, Jr., *Social Origins of Dictatorship and Democracy* (1966), ch. 3. I should note that describing the South as "pre-modern" does not necessarily contradict the findings of Stanley Engerman and Robert Fogel that slavery was a highly profitable investment. Engerman and Fogel, *Time on the Cross: The Economics of American Negro Slavery* (1974). In a forthcoming essay, George Fredrickson applies the concept of modernization to the Civil War itself, and the question of why the North was victorious, but he explicitly denies its applicability to the question of the causes of the Civil War. Fredrickson, "Blue Over Gray: Sources of Success and Failure in the Civil War," in Fredrickson (ed.), *A Nation Divided: Essays on the Civil War and Reconstruction* (forthcoming).

[17] Robert Kelley, *The Transatlantic Persuasion: The Liberal Democratic Mind in the Age of Gladstone* (1969).

and backward areas confronted by the process of modernization in the nineteenth century.[18]

Having said this, I hasten to add that there are certain problems in applying this model to the causes of the Civil War. First, there is the imprecision of the term "modernization." At times, it seems to be used more or less interchangeably with "industrialization," and, in effect, becomes a restatement of the Beardian view of the Civil War as a conflict between industrial and agrarian economies. In this form, the model exaggerates the extent to which northern society itself was as yet fully modernized in the ante-bellum years. Historians, indeed, have not yet produced the studies which will enable us to state with assurance what the class structure of the North was, or how far industrialization had advanced by 1860. Before we can assess the effects of modernization, in other words, we need to know exactly what kind of society was undergoing that process. Ante-bellum northern society may well have been "modern" in some respects. Certainly capitalist economic relations and democratic political procedures prevailed, and according to Richard Brown, the "modern personality" had been dominant since colonial days. But the economy was almost certainly pre-industrial, and the ideals of the yeoman farmer and independent artisan, their belief in the natural right of each individual to the fruits of his labor (which became in the hands of Lincoln so damning an indictment of slavery), still permeated society.[19]

Nevertheless, the modernization model does have two great virtues. First, it enables us to see that what happened in nineteenth century America was not a unique or local occurrence, but a process which had deep affinities with events in many other areas of the world. Secondly, it demands that political historians place their work in the largest context of the development of American society, for, as Albert Soboul writes, "all studies of political history entail a study of social history."[20] To me, moreover, it suggests a framework for beginning to answer the crucial question raised by David Brion Davis in *The Problem of Slavery in Western Culture*. Why does slavery, which for centuries had been considered a normal part of the social order, suddenly come to be

[18] J. R. Pole, *Abraham Lincoln and the American Commitment* (1966), p. 32; Paul Angle (ed.), *Created Equal? The Complete Lincoln-Douglas Debates of 1858* (1958), p. 18. Cf. Bertram Wyatt-Brown, "Stanley Elkins' Slavery: The Antislavery Interpretation Reexamined," *American Quarterly*, XXV (May, 1973), 167.

[19] Richard D. Brown, "Modernization and the Modern Personality in Early America, 1600-1865: A Sketch of a Synthesis," *Journal of Interdisciplinary History*, II (Winter, 1972), 201-28. E. A. Wrigeley comments on the impecision of the modernization concept, and how it often seems to be used simply as a synonym for industrialization, in "The Process of Modernization and the Industrial Revolution in England," *Journal of Interdisciplinary History*, III (Autumn, 1972), 228, 228n. The general question of the persistence of pre-industrial work habits and ideals in nineteenth century America is raised in Herbert G. Gutman, "Work, Culture and Society in Industrializing America, 1815-1919," *American Historical Review*, LXXVIII (June, 1973), 531-88.

[20] Albert Soboul, *The San-Culottes*, trans. Remy Inglis Hall (1972) p. xv.

viewed by large numbers of men and women as a totally unacceptable form of labor and social organization? Why, that is, does an anti-slavery movement emerge?

To answer this question, we must place the Civil War in the context of the general abolition of unfree labor systems in the nineteenth century, from slavery in the western hemisphere, to serfdom in Russia and robot in the Austrian Empire. Within this context, we need to relate the emergence of the modern anti-slavery movement to two related processes—changes in attitudes toward labor and the condition of laboring classes,[21] and the enormous economic and social transformations of the nineteenth century. Of course, American anti-slavery thought did not emerge full-blown in the 1830's. As C. Vann Woodward has pointed out, patterns of derogatory sectional imagery stretch back into the colonial era. Many New England Federalists employed anti-southern and anti-slavery rhetoric highly suggestive of the Republican assaults of the 1850's. They not only condemned the three-fifths clause of the Constitution and southern domination of the national government, but spoke of the superiority of free labor, the economic stagnation of the South, and the differences in "manners, habits, customs, principles and ways of thinking" between the sections.[22]

The elements of an anti-slavery ideology, therefore, had long been present in America, but a coherent critique of slavery had not. Why could the Federalists not develop one? For one thing, until 1800 they had powerful allies in the South, and after then, the dream of a reunited and triumphant Federalist party never entirely disappeared. Moreover, as several recent writers have emphasized, the Federalist world view centered on a society of order, harmony and organic unity, one composed of stable and distinctly separated ranks and orders.[23] It was not until this older organic conception of society broke down that a complete anti-slavery ideology could emerge.

We know of course that in the 1820's and 1830's this older vision was thoroughly disrupted, and replaced by one of a society of competing individuals, a vision more in keeping with the requirements of an expanding, market-oriented capitalist society. Why this ideological transformation occurred is not yet, in my opinion, entirely clear. The transportation revolution was a major determinant, but we know too little about the nature of economic change in the ante-bellum era to be able to

[21] This point is suggested in J. H. Plumb, "Slavery, Race, and the Poor," *New York Review of Books*, Mar. 13, 1969, 4. After writing this paper, David Brion Davis's new volume, *The Problem of Slavery in the Age of Revolution* (forthcoming), came to my attention. Davis relates the growth of anti-slavery in England to changes in attitudes toward labor in a way similar to my argument in the paragraphs below.

[22] C. Vann Woodward, *American Counterpoint* (1971), p. 6; Linda Kerber, *Federalists in Dissent* (1970), pp. 24-44; James M. Banner, *To the Hartford Convention* (1970), pp. 99-108; Richard J. Buel, *Securing the Revolution* (1972), p. 235.

[23] Banner, *To the Hartford Convention*, pp. 108-09; Kerber, *Federalists in Dissent*, pp. 50, 59-63.

place this ideological development in its proper social setting. We do know that the ideological transformation had profound effects on the nature of anti-slavery thought. As Rowland Berthoff observes, "if classes supposedly did not exist, they could not be accepted as constituent institutions of American society; rank or degree was no longer an admissible principle for organizing or even thinking about the social order." That abolitionist thought was utterly individualistic and atomistic has by now become an axiom of historical writing. Historians as diverse in their ideological preconceptions as Stanley Elkins and William Appleman Williams severely chide the abolitionists for viewing slavery not as a functioning institution, embedded in a distinct society, but as a personal sin of the individual master against the individual slave.[24] But it may be that it was only when the ideas of an organic society, and the permanent subordination of any class of men, had been overthrown, that anti-slavery thought could develop in a consistent form. Only a movement which viewed society as a collection of individuals, which viewed freedom as the property of every man, which believed every individual had the right to seek advancement as a unit in competitive society, could condemn slavery as utterly and completely as, in their own ways, abolitionists and Republicans did.[25]

Anti-slavery thus fed on the anti-monopoly, anti-corporate, egalitarian ethos of Jacksonian America. At the same time, as a vision of labor, anti-slavery was curiously ambiguous. Anti-slavery men exalted "free labor," meaning labor working because of incentive instead of coercion, labor with education, skill, the desire for advancement, and also the freedom to move from job to job according to the changing demands of the marketplace.[26] On the other hand, many anti-slavery men

[24] Rowland Berthoff, *An Unsettled People* (1971), p. 182; Stanley Elkins, *Slavery* (1959), ch. 4; Williams, *Contours*, p. 158. Cf. Fredrickson, *Black Image in the White Mind*, pp. 19-33.

[25] The highly competitive, individualistic nature of ante-bellum society also helps to explain the apparent paradox that both racism and anti-slavery thought became more pervasive in the North at the same time. As Stanley Elkins points out, "in a stratified society with strong aristocratic attitudes, there is no need to define the Negro as hopelessly inferior, because the greater portion of society is inferior in varying degrees." In America, by contrast, where freedom implied the ability to compete for advancement, the idea of freeing the slaves inevitably raised the question of social equality. Elkins, in John A. Garraty, *Interpreting American History* (1970), I, 188-89. Cf. Fredrickson, *Black Image in the White Mind*, p. 95, and David Brion Davis, "The Emergence of Immediatism in British and American Antislavery Thought," *Mississippi Valley Historical Review* (Sept., 1962), 209-30, one of the many works which relates the new anti-slavery outlook of the 1830's to a faith, engendered by evangelical religion, in the perfectability of individual men and to a decline in deference to institutions which blocked the path to reform.

[26] On notions of "free labor," see Foner, *Free Soil, Free Labor, Free Man*, ch. 1; David Montgomery, *Beyond Equality* (1965) ch. 1. Cf. the remark by sociologist Wilbert E. Moore; "If one were to attempt a one-word summary of the institutional requirements of economic development, that word would be *mobility*. Property rights, consumer goods, and laborers must be freed from traditional bonds and restraints, from aristocratic traditions, quasi-feudal arrangements, paternalistic and other multi-bonded relations." Moore, "The Social Framework of Economic De-

were also opponents of union activity, and were closely involved in
other reforms—such as the creation of prisons and asylums, temperance,
and poor relief (with the ever-present distinction between the deserving and undeserving poor) which to a certain extent can be interpreted
as attempts to transform the life style and work habits of labor in an
industrializing society.

One could argue that the anti-slavery movement, by glorifying northern society and by isolating slavery as an unacceptable form of labor
exploitation, while refusing to condemn the exploitative aspects of
"free" labor relations, served to justify the emerging capitalist order of
the North. In fact, it is possible that the growing ideological conflict
between the sections had the effect of undermining a tradition of radical criticism within northern society.[27] Men like Horace Greeley,
highly critical of certain aspects of their society in the 1840's, became
more and more uncritical when faced with the need to defend the North
against southern assaults. The choices for America came to be defined
as free society versus slave society—the idea of alternatives within free
society was increasingly lost sight of.[28]

To develop this point further, many anti-slavery men believed in an
ideal of human character which emphasized an internalized self-discipline. They condemned slavery as a lack of control over one's own destiny and the fruits of one's labor, but defined freedom as more than a
simple lack of restraint. The truly free man, in the eyes of ante bellum
reformers, was one who imposed restraints upon himself. This was
also the ideal, as David Rothman shows, of the reformers who con-
structed the prisons and asylums of this era—to transform the human
personality so that the poor, insane and criminal would internalize a
sense of discipline, order and restraint.[29]

---

velopment," in Ralph Brabanti and Joseph J. Spengler (eds.), *Tradition, Values
and Socio-Economic Development* (1961), p. 71.

[27] Of course certain northern intellectuals, alienated from the more materialistic
aspects of their own culture, turned to the South for the qualities lacking in northern society—"the vestiges of an old-world aristocracy, a promise of stability, and
an assurance that gentility . . . could be preserved under republican institutions."
William R. Taylor, *Cavalier and Yankee* (1961), p. xviii and *passim*. I would argue
however, that by the 1840's and 1850's most northerners saw much more to criticize than to admire in southern life.

[28] This argument would suggest that the process, described by George Fredrickson, in which ante-bellum radicals abandoned their position as independent critics
of American institutions and uncritically identified themselves with their society—
which he attributes to the Civil War experience—may have already begun during
the 1850's. Fredrickson, *The Inner Civil War* (1965). John Thomas makes an argument similar to Fredrickson's in "Romantic Reform in America, 1815-1865," *American Quarterly*, XVII (Winter, 1965), 656-81. However, Richard O. Curry has criticized both these works, arguing that anti-institutional radical thought persisted
after the Civil War. Curry. "The Abolitionists and Reconstruction: A Critical Appraisal," *Journal of Southern History*, XXXIV (Nov., 1968), 527-45.

[29] David Rothman, *The Discovery of the Asylum* (1971), pp. 107, 129, 214. Two
works which deal with the transformation of personality and life styles required by
industrial society are Herbert G. Gutman, "Work, Culture, and Society in Indus-

There are parallels between this aim, and Lincoln's condemnation in his famous lyceum speech of 1838, of "the increasing disregard for law which pervades the country," of vigilanteeism, mob violence and those who hoped for the "total annihilation of government." For Lincoln, law, order and union, commonly accepted and internalized, allowed civilization and progress to exist in America, especially given the highly competitive nature of the society. Or, to quote Theodore Weld, "restraints are the web of civilized society, warp and woof." Of course, on one level, slavery, as some pro-slavery writers argued, solved the problem of disciplining the labor force, but the ideal of the reformers was a society of free (self-governing) individuals. Slavery may have been like an asylum or a school in some respects, but it lacked one essential element of those institutions—release, or graduation. Moreover, it allowed full rein to the very passions which so many northerners desired to see repressed—it encouraged greed, self-indulgence, and all sorts of illicit personal and sexual activities on the part of the masters. When Lincoln in 1861 declared, "plainly, the central idea of secession, is the essence of anarchy," he could have chosen no more damning description.[30]

Thus the anti-slavery movement exalted the character traits demanded by a "modernizing" society while it condemned an institution which impeded that "modernization." Interpreted in this way, the modernization thesis can assimilate some of the insights of the new political history. For example, the ethnoculturalists never deal directly with the relationship between ethno-cultural identity and class relations in the setting of a modernizing society. We know how closely related certain ethnic and class patterns were—how, in urban areas, Irish immigrants were overwhelmingly lower-class unskilled laborers, and how, to quote Ronald Formisano, "prosperity and evangelical political character often went together." It is also well known that class and ethnic prejudices were inextricably linked in nativist attacks on Irish immigrants.[31]

If we do expand our notion of culture beyond a relatively narrow

---

trializing America, 1815-1919," and E. P. Thompson, "Time, Work Discipline and Industrial Capitalism," *Past and Present*, XXXVIII (1967), 58-97.

[30] Roy F. Basler, *et al.* (eds.), *The Collected Works of Abraham Lincoln* (1953-55), I, 108-15; IV, 268. Weld is quoted in Ronald G. Waters, "The Erotic South: Civilization and Sexuality in American Abolitionism," *American Quarterly*, XXV (May, 1973), 187. Weld's statement suggests that abolitionists' "anti-institutionalism" may be interpreted as a belief that in the absence of powerful social institutions, "restraints" usually imposed by those institutions would have to be internalized by each individual. Also relevant to the above discussion is George Dennison's argument that the forcible suppression of internal disorder in the North in the 1830's and 1840's set a moral and legal precedent for the northern refusal to allow peaceable secession in 1861. Dennison, " 'The Idea of a Party System:' A Critique," *Rocky Mountain Social Science Journal*, IX (Apr., 1972), 38-39n.

[31] Foner, *Free Soil, Free Labor, Free Men*, pp. 231-32; Gutman, "Work, Culture and Society," 583; Douglas V. Shaw, "The Making of an Immigrant Community: Ethnic and Cultural Conflict in Jersey City, New Jersey, 1850-1877," (Ph.D. dissertation, University of Rochester, 1972), pp 27-40, 75, 119; Formisano, *Birth of Mass Political Parties*, pp. 146-47.

definition of ethnicity and religious belief, we may find that "pietists" were much more hospitable to the Protestant work ethic and the economic demands of a modernizing society than were "ritualists" and Catholic immigrants.[32] Is it possible that the resistance of the Irish to "Americanization," rather than simply a desire to maintain cultural identity, was the attempt of a pre-industrial people to resist the hegemony of a modernizing culture, with all that that implied for character structure, work patterns and life styles? May we view the Democratic party as the representative of the great pre-modern cultures within American society—the white South and the Irish immigrants—and perhaps then better understand why the nativist image of the Irish and the anti-slavery critique of the southern slaveholder stressed the same "undesirable" traits of lack of economic enterprise and self-discipline, and the attack on the Slave Power and Catholic Church denounced corporate monoliths which restricted individual freedom? Was the northern Democratic machine at the local level attuned to the communal, traditionalist behavior of the peasant immigrants, while the intense individualism of the Republicans had little to offer them?

Before we attempt to locate the crusade against slavery within the social history of ante-bellum America, there is a more basic historical question to answer. We still do not understand the social composition of that movement. We do have information about the abolitionist leadership, but also disagreement as to whether abolitionists were a declining elite, using reform as an effort to regain a waning status,[33] or a rising group, challenging older elites, North and South, for social dominance. This latter would seem to be the implication of Leonard Richards's recent study of anti-abolitionist mobs, which concludes that in Utica and Cincinnati, the mobs were composed of members of the pre-industrial upper class of commercial and professional men, while abolitionist membership drew much more heavily on artisans, manufacturers, and tradesmen.[34] Generally, however, to quote David Davis, "little is known of the rank and file members, to say nothing of the passive supporters, of a single reform movement."[35] Historians of reform over the past fifteen years have been much more successful in explicating ideologies than in giving us a clear picture of the movements' social roots.

Without such studies, we have been guilty of accepting an oversimplified version of reform, e.g., the temperance movement was an effort

[32] This is suggested in James R. Green, "Behavioralism and Class Analysis," 98.

[33] This is suggested in David Donald, *Lincoln Reconsidered* (1956), pp. 19-36, and Clifford S. Griffen, *Their Brothers' Keepers: Moral Stewardship in the United States 1800-1865* (1960).

[34] Richards, *Gentlemen of Property and Standing* (1970), ch. 5.

[35] David Brion Davis (ed.), *Ante-Bellum Reform* (1967), p. 10. A recent study which attempts to probe this question is Joseph E. Mooney, "Antislavery in Worcester County, Massachusetts: A Case Study," (Ph.D. dissertation, Clark University, 1971). It is marred by the use of categories like "the common man" as units of social analysis, but its study of signers of an anti-slavery document of 1840 finds a large majority of farmers and artisans. (278-79).

of middle-class Yankees to exert their cultural dominance over immigrant Catholics and the unruly poor. That for many supporters the movement did have this character cannot be doubted, but we need only to read Brian Harrison's study of the English temperance movement to see that our studies have been noticeably one-dimensional. Harrison showed that temperance was a cross-class movement which had deep roots in the working class, appealing to aspirations for self-help and social betterment. It was not simply an attempt "to impose middle-class manners on the working class."[36] The same, I suspect, can be said for temperance in this country, and for other reforms, such as the movement for expanded public education, which have been interpreted through the eyes of their middle-class proponents, without considering the very different aims of workingmen who also supported the reform. But at present, we know far too little of the extent to which workers, skilled or unskilled, were sympathetic to one phase or another of the anti-slavery movement, or whether anti-slavery workingmen viewed slavery differently than did its middle-class foes. Thus, while Garrison drew a sharp distinction between slavery and the northern system of free labor, how many workingmen were impressed by the *similarities* between the chattel slavery of the South and the "wage slavery" of the North?

Many labor spokesmen were initially hostile to the abolitionists precisely because they believed the Garrisons and Welds were diverting attention from the pressing social problems of the industrializing North. But in the late 1840's and 1850's many workingmen were attracted to free-soilism and the Republican party by the issues of land reform and opposition to the expansion of slavery.[37] To what extent did workingmen oppose the extension of slavery to preserve the safety-valve which, they believed, guaranteed the independence of the northern laborer, and prevented him from being subjected to the degrading discipline of the factory or from being permanently trapped in the status of wage-earner? In other words, anti-slavery could have served as an ideological vehicle for both the proponents of modernization and for those whose objective was to preserve the pre-modern status of the independent artisan.

In a similar vein, many questions remain about the social history of ante-bellum South. Several recent studies emphasize the "obsession" of the secessionist leadership with internal unity, their fear that slavery was weak and declining in the border area and that the loyalty of the

---

[36] Brian Harrison, *Drink and the Victorians: The Temperance Question in England, 1815-1872* (1971). The quotation is from page 24.

[37] This is suggested in Williams, *Contours*, p. 280, and in Bernard Mandel, *Labor: Free and Slave* (1955). Michael Holt shows that in the mid-1850's, Know-Nothing lodge membership came disproportionately from manual workers and skilled artisans. Many of these workers presumably went into the Republican party. Holt, "The Politics of Impatience: The Origins of Know-Nothingism," *Journal of American History*, LX (Sept., 1973), 329-31.

non-slaveholding whites was questionable. The secession of the South
on the election of Lincoln, these works argue, was motivated not by
paranoia or hysterical fear, but by a realistic assessment that the unity
of their society could not survive the open debate on the future of
slavery which Republicans seemed determined to stimulate within the
South.[38]

Before we can assess this interpretation, we must take a new look at
the social and economic structure of the Old South. The non-slaveholding whites are probably the least studied of all our social classes. Of
course, such an investigation may indeed reveal that the hegemony of
the planter class was complete.[39] Or we may find that the loyalty of the
non-slaveholders, while real, was unstable; that, especially in the back-
woods areas outside direct planter control, there had developed a culture which was in many ways hostile to planter rule, while at the same
time, cut off from both the market economy and from effective political
power.

Fear of internal disunity can explain the belief of Edmund Ruffin
that a Republican government could accomplish "the ruin of the South"
without a direct assault upon slavery.[40] Ruffin was convinced that in the
event of civil war, a Southern victory would ensue, a belief he predi-
cated on the continued loyalty of the slaves. But if we are to look at the
question of internal disunity and its relation to secession, the slaves
themselves cannot be ignored. Southerners knew that to exist as a regional institution within a larger free society, slavery required a community consensus, voluntary or enforced. Division among the whites
had always been disastrous for discipline of the slaves. This was why
the South had suppressed its own anti-slavery movement and continually demanded the silencing of nortnern abolitionists. Once a Republican administration was inaugurated, who knew what ideas would cir-
culate in the slave quarters? Before we can answer these questions,

[38] William Barney, *The Road to Secession* (1972); William W. Freehling, "The
Editorial Revolution, Virginia, and the Coming of the Civil War: A Review Essay,"
Civil War History, XVI (Mar., 1970), 64-72; Michael P. Johnson, "Secession and
Conservatism in the Lower South: The Social and Ideological Bases of Secession in
Georgia, 1860-1861" (Ph.D. dissertation, Stanford University, 1973).

[39] Carl Degler concludes that southern dissenters were remarkable largely for
their weakness. Degler, *The Other South* (1974). Cf. Otto Olsen, "Historians and
the Extent of Slave Ownership in the Southern United States," *Civil War History*,
XVIII (June, 1973), 101-16. On the other hand, William Barney suggests that there
were severe divisions within the slaveholding class itself. The upper echelons of that
class, he argues, became an increasingly closed elite in the 1850's, and younger and
lesser planters found the route to upward mobility blocked by the rising price of
slaves and concentration of wealth. Secession and slave expansionism, for them,
was a route to renewed social mobility. Barney, *The Road to Secession*, p. 135.

[40] [Edmund Ruffin], *Anticipations of the Future* (1860), pp. viii-ix. Published in
the fall of 1860, Ruffin's book in a sense is the first contribution to civil war historiography. It details the administrations of Presidents Abraham Lincoln and William Seward, and the course of a war in 1867 in which the South wins a glorious
military victory, New York City is destroyed by a mob, and Washington becomes
the capital of a new southern republic.

we need to know more about how the slaves themselves were affected by, and perceived, the vast changes which took place in the South in the fifty years preceding secession—the ending of the slave trade, the rise of the cotton kingdom, and the expansion of slavery southward and westward.

In this connection, one of the most intriguing findings of Robert Fogel and Stanley Engerman's new study of the economics of slavery is the extent to which the lower level of the slave system was in the hands of blacks—how slaves were becoming a larger and larger proportion of the drivers and managers on plantations. This is precisely the class which, in the British West Indies, during the agitation of the years 1816-1833, was most strongly influenced by humanitarian anti-slavery ideas and which developed a campaign of non-violent resistance which undermined West Indian slavery in the years immediately preceding emancipation. Of course, the situation in the United States was vastly different from that in the islands, but the experience there, and similar events in the 1880's in Brazil, should remind us again of the dangers of subversive ideas among the slave population, and the reality of southern fears that the very existence of a hostile central government was a threat to the stability of their peculiar institution.[41]

Having previously called on political historians to pay more attention to social history, I would like to conclude by reversing this equation. Of course, our knowledge of the social history of ante-bellum America is still in some ways in its infancy. One of the striking features of the writing of the past fifteen years is the curious disjunction between a growing body of knowledge about nineteenth century American society, and the reluctance or inability of social historians to relate this information either to the politics of the period or the question of Civil War causation.[42] As one of our most creative social historians, Rowland Berthoff, reminds us, "any basic interpretation of American history will have to account for . . . the coming of the Civil War." And no such interpretation can be complete which does not encompass the course of American political development. "Politics bears critical importance to

[41] Engerman and Fogel, *Time on the Cross*, pp. 39-40. My analysis of the situation in the British West Indies is derived from a dissertation in progress at Columbia University by George Tyson. Robert Brent Toplin shows how Brazilian slaveholders actually experienced in the 1880's what southerners may have feared in 1861—the emergence of abolitionism near plantations, slaves running away in large numbers, and the gradual disintegration of control over the black population. Toplin, "The Spectre of Crisis: Slaveholder Reactions to Abolitionism in the United States and Brazil," *Civil War History*, XVIII (June, 1973), 129-38.

[42] It is perhaps appropriate to add that this disjunction exists for other periods of American history as well. Writings on the origins of the American Revolution seem to be as devoid of a clear linkage between social and political history as does Civil War historiography. For a speculative attempt to remedy this situation, see Kenneth A. Lockridge, "Social Change and the Meaning of the American Revolution," *Journal of Social History*, VI (Summer, 1973), 403-39. Cf. Jack P. Greene, "The Social Origins of the American Revolution: An Evaluation and an Interpretation," *Political Science Quarterly*, LXXXVIII (March, 1973), 1-22.

the history of society, for politics affects the social structure, the economy, and the life of a people."[43]

In other words, the social cleavages that existed in ante-bellum America were bound to be reflected in politics. This was an era when the mass political party galvanized voter participation to an unprecedented degree, and in which politics formed an essential component of American mass culture. Politics became the stage on which the sectional conflict was played out, and it was not an accident that the break-up of the nation succeeded by less than one year the break-up of the last major national party, or that it was a presidential election, not any "overt act" which precipitated the final crisis.[44]

Lawrence Stone has identified as an essential prerequisite to any revolution the "polarization into two coherent groups or alliances of what are naturally and normally a series of fractional and shifting tensions and conflicts within a society."[45] For most of the ante-bellum period, the political system served to prevent such a polarization. The existence of national political parties necessitated both the creation of linkages and alliances between elites in various parts of the country, and the conscious suppression of disruptive sectional issues. We can, in fact, view the political history of the coming of the Civil War as an accelerating struggle between the demands of party and those of sectional ideology, in which the latter slowly gained the upper hand. But the triumph was late and never complete. As late as 1860 major political leaders like Stephen A. Douglas hoped to curtail sectional controversy by restoring the political system to its traditional basis, with slavery carefully excluded from partisan debate.

Changes in the political system itself, changes related in ways still obscure to changes in the structure of American society, doomed the old basis of sectional political balance. If the anti-slavery crusade could not have emerged without the transformation of northern society, it could not have entered politics until the instruments of mass democracy had developed. It was no accident that the same decade witnessed the rise of the anti-slavery movement and the height of "Jacksonian democracy." The same institutions which created mass participation in politics also made possible the emergence of the sectional agitator—the radical, North and South, who consciously strove to influence public opinion through speeches, newspapers, lectures and postal campaigns. This was now an efficacious way both to affect political de-

[43] Berthoff, *An Unsettled People*, p. 510; Michael Kammen, "Politics, Science and Society in Colonial America," *Journal of Social History*, III (Fall, 1969), 63.

[44] The paragraphs which follow are based on my essay, "Politics, Ideology, and the Origins of the American Civil War," which will appear in George M. Fredrickson (ed.), *A Nation Divided: Essays on the Civil War and Reconstruction* (forthcoming).

[45] Lawrence Stone, *The Causes of the English Revolution 1529-1642* (1972), p. 10.

cision-making and, if Richards is right, to challenge the social and political dominance of older entrenched elites.

Just as the abolitionist assault emerged in the 1830's, so too, spurred by it, did the coherent southern defense of slavery. The process of ideological response and counter-response, once set in motion, proved extremely difficult to curtail. In the next two decades, these sectional ideologies became more and more sophisticated. As each came to focus on its lowest common denominator, with the widest possible base of support in its society, the political system proved incapable of preventing first the intrusion, then the triumph of sectional ideology as the organizing principle of political combat.

The Civil War was, at base, a struggle for the future of the nation. Within the context of modernization, one can agree with Luraghi that it became part of the process of "building a modern, centralized nation-state based on a national market, totally and unopposedly controlled by an industrial capitalistic class."[46] But is not there a danger here of transposing consequences and causes? It might be more accurate to say that each side fought to preserve a society it believed was threatened. Southerners fought to preserve the world the slaveholders made. As for the North, Lincoln expressed the hopes of his section, when he defined the union cause as a struggle to preserve a system in which every man, whatever his station at birth, could achieve social advancement and economic independence. Lincoln's Union was one of self-made men. The society he was attempting to preserve was, in this respect, also pre-modern—the world of the small shop, the independent farm and the village artisan. Republicans certainly condemned slavery as an obstacle to national economic development and as a "relic of barbarism" out of touch with the modern spirit of the nineteenth century. They exalted the virtues of economic growth, but only within the context of a familar social order. If modernization means the growth of large-scale industry, large cities and the leviathan state, northerners were no more fighting to create it than were southerners.

Yet modern, total war, against the intentions of those who fought, was a powerful modernizing force.[47] In the South, the war experience not only destroyed slavery, but created the opportunity for the two subordinate pre-modern classes, the poor whites and the slaves, to organize and express their resentment of planter control. In the North, the war gave a tremendous impetus to the rationalization of capitalist enterprise, the centralization of national institutions, and, in certain in-

---

[46] Luraghi, "Civil War and Modernization," 249. To be fair, Luraghi elsewhere observes that the Civil War "had not so much the task of making free a complete capitalistic structure yet existing, but mainly that of creating the conditions for such a structure to grow." (241).

[47] For the South, see Emory Thomas, *The Confederacy as a Revolutionary Experience* (1971); for the North, Allan Nevins, *The War for the Union: The Organized War 1863-64* (1971), and *The War for the Union: From Organized War to Victory, 1864-65* (1971).

dustries, mechanization and factory production. The foundations of the industrial capitalist state of the late nineteenth century, so similar in individualist rhetoric yet so different in social reality from Lincoln's America, were a large extent laid during the Civil War. Here, indeed, is the tragic irony of that conflict. Each side fought to defend a distinct vision of the good society, but each vision was destroyed by the very struggle to preserve it.

THE CIVIL WAR AND
RECONSTRUCTION, 1861-1877:
A Critical Overview of Recent Trends
and Interpretations

Richard O. Curry

PROFESSOR FONER, IN HIS PAPER, has concentrated primarily on the politics of the 1850s, the secession crisis, and that historical perennial, the causes of the Civil War.[1]

The major themes I have chosen to deal with are: an evaluation of Civil War party struggles in the North; an assessment of Lincoln's role as war leader; the aims, objectives and ideological commitments of Congressional Republicans; the impeachment of Andrew Johnson; the role of the Supreme Court in the Reconstruction and post-Reconstruction periods; an analysis of Congressional Reconstruction in the South—with particular emphasis upon the role of blacks; the identity, location and motives of "Scalawags" and a brief evaluation of the recent exchange between Professors Woodward and Peskin as to the reality and significance of the Compromise of 1877. In addition, we need to consider the implications of recent studies which have extended the scope of Reconstruction historiography to embrace both border and northern states. Recent methodological innovations, especially in the behavioral and quantitative realms also demand attention, as well as important new research currently in the planning or writing stages.

First, let me say that the politics of the Civil War and Reconstruction era ought to be considered as a unit. In recent years Harold Hyman, Herman Belz, Hans Trefousse, Peyton McCrary and others, have emphasized that the analysis of Reconstruction historiography properly begins with 1861, with greater emphasis upon the wartime origins of

---

[1] An abbreviated version of this paper was read in the Civil War and Reconstruction Overview Session at the meetings of the Organization of American Historians in Denver, April 19, 1974. No one, of course, is aware of everything going on in any field; but during the planning stages for this paper a number of scholars were considerate enough to share with me their own thoughts about the period, and in several instances provided extended written commentaries on their current projects. Especially helpful were: Thomas B. Alexander, Steven Channing, Joanna Cowden, Robert Cruden, Leonard Curry, Carl Degler, Charles Dew, Robert Dykstra, Eric Foner, William Harris, W. D. Jones, Frank Klement, Stanley Kutler, Peyton McCrary, James Mohr, John Niven, Walter Nugent, William Parrish, J. R. Pole, Thomas Pressly, James Roark, Loren Schweninger, Joel Silbey, Russell Weigley, Robin Winks and Bertram Wyatt-Brown.

postwar conflicts and processes.[2] This theme is most thoroughly developed in Belz's study, which deals primarily with events on the Congressional and Presidential levels. Moreover, McCrary's dissertation on the failure of Reconstruction in Louisiana is perhaps the most thoroughly documented study of wartime Reconstruction efforts in any Southern state. I would extend the argument further by maintaining that the issue of Reconstruction constitutes the central theme in explaining the Civil War party struggles in the loyal states. As Frank L. Klement has phrased it, there was, in a sense, "a war within the war."[3] Stated another way, the war produced a massive political and ideological confrontation in the loyal states as to the type of Union that would or ought to emerge from the ashes of war. In short, was the war simply a struggle to preserve the old federal Union of 1860 with slavery intact and the rights of the states unimpaired? Or was the war to be successfully transformed by Republicans into a crusade to preserve the Union, and to eradicate forever the cancer of slavery.

Until late 1864, after Lincoln's convincing victory over McClellan, the answer was not entirely clear. Throughout most of the war, a majority of northern Democrats, who supported a war for Union, bitterly opposed its transformation into a crusade to subjugate the South and destroy slavery. As Leonard P. Curry has convincingly demonstrated, the vast majority of Democratic members of Congress voted men and measures to suppress the rebellion despite their opposition to emancipation.[4]

Other revisionists maintain that Republican charges of widespread subversion among northern "Copperheads" (or Democrats) to subvert the Union war effort and recognize the independence of the Confederacy simply does not conform to reality.[5] Totally reactionary in their racial attitudes and strongly traditionalist in their constitutional doctrines and economic views they most assuredly were, but traitorous and subversive they most assuredly were not, unless, of course, one equates opposition to

[2] Hyman (ed.), *The Radical Republicans and Reconstruction, 1861-1870* (1967); Belz, *Reconstructing the Union: Theory and Practice During the Civil War* (1970); Trefousse, *The Radical Republicans: Lincoln's Vanguard for Racial Justice* (1969); and McCrary, "Moderation in a Revolutionary World: Lincoln and the Failure of Reconstruction in Louisiana" (Ph.D. dissertation, Princeton University, 1972).

[3] Klement, *The Copperheads in the Middle West* (1960), p. 1.

[4] L. Curry, "Congressional Democrats, 1861-1863," *Civil War History*, XII (1966), 213-29.

[5] Richard O. Curry's "The Union As It Was: A Critique of Recent Interpretations of the 'Copperheads'" *Civil War History*, XIII (1967), 25-39 contains a useful discussion of "Copperhead" historiography. Revisionist studies not analyzed in Curry's article include: V. Jacque Voegeli, *Free But Not Equal: The Midwest and the Negro During the Civil War* (1967); Klement, *The Limits of Dissent: Clement L. Vollandigham and the Civil War* (1970); Joel H. Silbey, "A Respectable Minority: The Democratic Party, 1860-1868" (unpublished manuscript), 1968; Ronald Formisano and William G. Shade, "The Concept of Agrarian Radicalism," *Mid-America*, LII (1970), 3-30; and Van M. Davis, "Individualism on Trial: The Ideology of the Northern Democracy During the Civil War" (Ph.D. dissertation, University of Virginia, 1972).

the emancipation policies of the Lincoln Administration with treason. Some Republican campaign orators, generals, government officials and newspapers did precisely this—and with great effect in some parts of the country. On the other hand, Democrats were equally accusatory of Republicans whom they condemned as "wild-eyed" Jacobins who, in their lust for power, would transform the federal republic into a monstrous authoritarian state under the control of Father Abraham, his henchmen and their "big business" allies. Not the least of their fears concerned the possibility that hordes of "ignorant and depraved Negroes," would, after emancipation, flock northward and in combination with their "Black Republican" allies dominate Northern society and destroy the purity of Anglo-Saxon civilization—in *sexual* as well as political, economic and cultural terms.[6] In sum, revisionist scholarship convinces me that the vast majority of Northern Democrats supported a war for Union, if not emancipation, and that dismissing them as traitors or quasi-secessionists tends to obscure the depths of racism and conservatism in American society, the continued existence of which still poisons our efforts to create a just and humane society.

To press this point further, my conviction is that a remarkable degree of continuity exists as regards Democratic policies and political philosophy from the 1790's until the late 1920's. However, Jacksonian Democrats are ordinarily placed in the American liberal tradition; and high marks are usually awarded to Woodrow Wilson's "New Freedom" doctrines. Yet, the position of the Jacksonians on slavery and race were equally as reactionary as that of the northern Democracy during the Civil War; and all three groups (Jacksonians, "Copperheads" or Conservative Union Democrats and Wilsonian Democrats) adhered to strict constructionist views of the Constitution—espousing the doctrines of *laissez-faire* individualism and the conception of the negative liberal state. The failure to recognize marked similarities in the ideological commitments of Democrats throughout the nineteenth and the first three decades of the twentieth century not only does violence to our understanding of Civil War and Reconstruction party struggles but of the political process itself—inhibiting meaningful analyses of conflict, change and continuity.[7]

I am not suggesting that no Northern Democrats opposed the war, anymore than I would argue that all Southerners supported the Con-

---

[6] On Northern fears of miscegenation see Forrest G. Wood, *Black Scare: The Racist Response to Emancipation and Reconstruction* (1968); and George M. Fredrickson, *The Black Image in the White Mind: The Debate on Afro-American Character and Destiny, 1817-1914* (1971).

[7] Richard O. Curry, "Copperheadism and Ideological Continuity: Anatomy of a Stereotype," *Journal of Negro History*, LVII (1972), 29-36. The fact that numerous individuals deserted Democratic ranks and joined the Republican party during the 1850's detracts but little from the accuracy of this point which focuses upon the decades of the 1820's and 1830's. Besides, the machinations of the "slave power" and not the institution of slavery itself was the only common denominator which unified disparate elements in the Republican coalition.

federacy. What I object to is the failure of historians to make precise distinctions when using such terms as Copperhead, War Democrat, conservative Democrat or peace-at-any-price Democrat. Despite the revisionist assault on the bastions of traditionalist scholarship in recent years, many scholars with solid academic credentials still tend to tar all, or nearly all, northern Democrats with the "Copperhead" brush.[8] The literature is riddled with semantic and conceptual confusion. Such disagreements can be resolved only by intensive study at the state and local levels—utilizing quantitative analysis, among other tools—in an effort to determine the composition of the Democratic party and the relative strength of various factions.[9]

A recent dissertation by Joanna Dunlap Cowden on Connecticut politics, 1863-1868, demonstrates that a sizable minority of Connecticut Democrats, led by Thomas Hart Seymour, opposed the war from its inception and called for a negotiated peace settlement throughout the conflict. After Seymour's defeat in his bid for the governorship in 1863, the influence of the "peace faction" in the Connecticut Democracy declined precipitously. Yet, in spite of Seymour's anti-war views and his outspoken demands for a negotiated peace, it is by no means clear that he favored Confederate independence. In fact, it seems more likely that Seymour was convinced that the Union could not be restored in any way other than by negotiation. Such a position was unrealistic and unenlightened, as well as politically, morally and intellectually bankrupt—considering the determination of the Confederacy to win its independence and maintain the institution of slavery at all hazards. But Seymour and the peace men in Connecticut did not engage in overt acts of treason, sabotage and obstructionism; and more important, they did not succeed in dominating the Democratic party. But to repeat, we des-

---

[8] For example, see William G. Carleton, "Civil War Dissidence in the North: The Perspective of a Century," *South Atlantic Quarterly*, LXV (1966), 390-402; Eugene C. Murdock, *Patriotism Limited, 1862-1865: The Civil War Draft and the Bounty System* (1967); William Dusinberre, *Civil War Issues in Philadelphia, 1856-1865* (1965); Harold M. Hyman, "The Election of 1864," in Arthur M. Schlesinger, Jr. (ed.), *History of American Presidential Elections* (4 vols., 1971), II, 1155-1244; and Stephen Z. Starr, *Colonel Grenfel's Wars: The Life of a Soldier of Fortune* (1971).

[9] Recent surveys and synthetic works reflect the "interpretive schizophrenia" that characterizes "Copperhead" historiography. David M. Potter, *Division and the Stresses of Reunion* (1973); James A. Rawley, *The Politics of Union* (1974); and David Lindsey, *Americans In Conflict: The Civil War and Reconstruction* (1974) occupy revisionist ground. Somewhat ambiguous in dealing with the issue of alleged disloyalty are: Robert Cruden, *The War That Never Ended: The American Civil War* (1973); W. R. Brock, *Conflict and Transformation: The United States, 1844-1877* (1973); and Thomas H. O'Connor, *The Disunited States: The Era of the Civil War and Reconstruction* (1972). Robert H. Jones, *Disrupted Decades: The Civil War and Reconstruction Years* (1972) does not occupy a clearcut position but leans toward the views expressed by revisionists. Emory M. Thomas' *The American War and Peace, 1860-1877* (1973) is also unclear on the issue but tends toward the traditional view of the "Copperhead" as subversive. Donald M. Jacobs and Raymond H. Johnson, *America's Testing Time, 1848-1877* (1973) take no position whatever.

perately need studies of almost every loyal border and northern state to determine the extent to which the work of revisionists themselves stands in need of revising. Until that day arrives, I am not prepared to modify my own views all that much—despite the findings of Cowden in Connecticut which may or may not apply elsewhere.

Thus far, I have approached Civil War politics primarily from the point of view of the intellectual historian—being concerned with such phenomena as ideology, perception and values—although I did "count numbers" in my own dissertation which enabled me to correct a number of misconceptions as regards the disruption of Virginia and the creation of the state of West Virginia.[10] From the point of view of a trained "Cliometrician" (another term for quantifier), my methods were unsophisticated at best, and frankly it did not occur to me that I was engaging in a rudimentary form of quantification. Rather, I was using common sense; and I fully agree with Pardon E. Tillinghast, author of *The Specious Past* (1972), an intriguing book on the nature of history and historical writing, that common sense remains one of the historian's most effective weapons. No doubt one could create quite a stir if one tried to determine the degree to which each of us possesses this rare quality.

Having defended the bastions of "traditional scholarship" (after all, modern intellectual history is at least 35 years old), it cannot be too strongly emphasized that the behavioral and quantitative approaches are beginning to have a significant impact on recent American scholarship.[11] Not all of these scholars have written about the Civil War and Reconstruction era, but recent studies of Congressional voting behavior that utilize various techniques involved in roll call analysis represent an

[10] Richard O. Curry, *A House Divided: A Study of Statehood Politics and the Copperhead Movement in West Virginia* (1964).

[11] Thomas Alexander, *Sectional Stress and Party Strength: A Computer Analysis of Roll-Call Voting Patterns in the United States House of Representatives, 1836-1850* (1967); Alexander and Richard Beringer, *The Anatomy of the Confederate Congress: A Study of the Influences of Member Characteristics on Legislative Voting Behavior, 1861-1865* (1972); Lee Benson, *Toward the Scientific Study of History* (1972); Allan Bogue, "Bloc and Party in the United States Senate, 1861-1863," *Civil War History*, XIII (1967), 221-41; Bogue "The Radical Voting Dimension in the U.S. Senate During the Civil War," *Journal of Interdisciplinary History* III (1973), 449-74; Bogue, "Some Dimensions of Power in the Thirty-Seventh Congress," in W. O. Aydellotte, A. Bogue and R. Fogel (eds.), *The Dimensions of Quantitative Research in History* (1972), 285-318; Ronald Formisano, *The Birth of Mass Parties: Michigan, 1827-1861* (1971); Edward Gambill, "Who Were the Senate Radicals?", *Civil War History*, XI (1965) 237-44; Richard Jensen, "The Religious and Occupational Roots of Party Identification: Illinois and Indiana in the 1870s," *ibid.*, XVI (1970), 325-44; Jensen, *The Winning of the Midwest: Social and Political Conflict, 1888-1896* (1971); Paul Kleppner, *The Cross of Culture: A Social Analysis of Midwestern Politics, 1850-1900* (1970); Glenn Linden, "Radicals and Economic Policies: The House of Representatives, 1861-1873," *Civil War History*, XIII (1967), 51-65; Linden, "Radical Political and Economic Policies: The Senate, 1873-1877," *ibid.*, XIV (1968), 240-49; Frederick C. Luebke (ed.), *Ethnic Voters and the Election of Lincoln* (1971); and John L. McCarthy, "Reconstruction Legislation and Voting Alignments in the House of Representatives, 1863-1869" (Ph.D. dissertation, Yale University, 1970).

exciting new dimension in political history; and the analysis of political party structure in social terms—especially the emphasis upon religious and ethnic factors at the state and local levels, holds great promise for the understanding of cultural and hence, political processes. Clearly, more extensive studies along these lines can help to resolve "some" of the contradictions and ambiguities of Civil War and Reconstruction politics. In addition, historians such as John Blassingame, W. McKee Evans, Joel Williamson, Peter Kolchin and Otto H. Olsen have produced pioneer studies of inestimable value in the realm of social and political history of black Americans during the Reconstruction era.[12]

In light of these studies, it scarcely needs stating that the quantifier and the intellectual historian have much of value to learn from each other. By no means, however, is it clear that historians of various persuasions are in process of forming mutual admiration societies. As Thomas J. Pressly has observed, ". . . it would be human, [but] it would still be tragic if the (perhaps unwitting) intellectual intolerance and arrogance which has characterized some opponents of the use of quantitative evidence in historical study should also come to characterize the proponents of such use."[13]

Having dealt with the Civil War Democracy, and having "resolved" all of the methodological disputes that divide the historical community, I now want to focus attention upon Lincoln and the Republicans —especially upon Lincoln's role as war leader, and the strategy and tactics utilized by Lincoln and his party on the related questions of slavery and emancipation. Lincolnian historiography remains a colorful and controversial topic, as evidenced by recent books and articles by Herman Belz, David Donald, John Hope Franklin, Harold Hyman, Ludwell H. Johnson, J. R. Pole, Benjamin Quarles, James A. Rawley, Hans Trefousse, V. Jacque Voegeli, and T. Harry Williams.[14] Stephen Oates, one of the biographers of John Brown, is now writing a new biography of the sixteenth President.

Most Civil War scholars generally agree that Lincoln's (and the Republican party's) war policies consisted of a blend of political expediency, idealism, radicalism and conservatism. However, no agreement exists as to which element(s) predominated or ought to receive pri-

[12] Analysis of these works appears below.

[13] Pressly, review of David Donald, The Politics of Reconstruction, 1863-1867 (1965), Civil War History, XII (1966), 267-70.

[14] Belz, Reconstructing the Union; Current, The Lincoln Nobody Knows (1958); Donald, "Devils Facing Zionwards," in Grady McWhiney, (ed.), Grant, Lee, Lincoln and the Radicals (1964), 72-91; Franklin, The Emancipation Proclamation (1963); Hyman, "Lincoln and Equal Rights for Negroes," Civil War History, XII (1966), 258-66; Johnson, "Lincoln and Equal Rights: A Reply," ibid., XIII (1967), 66-73; Johnson. "Lincoln and Equal Rights," Journal of Southern History, XXXII (1966), 83-87; Pole, Abraham Lincoln and the American Commitment (1966); Quarles, Lincoln and the Negro (1962); Rawley, Turning Points of the Civil War (1967); Trefousse, The Radical Republicans; Voegeli, Free But Not Equal; and Williams "Lincoln and the Radicals: An Essay in Civil War History and Historiography," in McWhiney, Lincoln and the Radicals, 92-117.

mary emphasis. For example, Current portrays Lincoln as a cautious and somewhat reluctant emancipator who "veered to an actively anti-slavery line for reasons of wartime expediency"—that the President was at odds with the Radical wing of his party, that he favored combining emancipation with colonization, and that in issuing the Emancipation Proclamation, his motives were ambiguous at best. Yet, Current deals with the contradictions in Lincoln's character by concluding that by war's end, the President had demonstrated an amazing capacity for personal growth, moving inexorably towards total abolition as a war aim. "Lincoln," Current concludes, "as a symbol of man's ability to outgrow his prejudices, still serves the cause of human freedom."[15] Hyman's position is not identical to Current's but their conclusions are similar. Johnson, in an exchange with Hyman on "Lincoln and Equal Rights" disputes the idea that Lincoln was "moving by his own volition" toward equalitarianism, and that it has yet to be demonstrated beyond reasonable doubt that Lincoln ever acted for reasons other than political expediency.[16]

To complicate matters further, Trefousse and Belz argue that Lincoln had no serious differences with the Radicals (including the question of Reconstruction)—that in fact Radical agitation gradually enabled the President to occupy higher ground. Beyond this, Donald suggests that the Radical-Conservative dichotomy in Republican ranks ought to be discarded as the majority of Republicans agreed that slavery ought to be destroyed, and that the Radicals did not become a cohesive faction until war's end. Williams agrees that all Republicans were anti-slavery but contends that the Radicals "are still identifiable as a faction" both in terms of attitude and temperament. Williams describes what he terms "the essence of the paradox" in Republican division as follows:

Lincoln and the Radicals *were* in agreement on the ultimate goal, the extinction of slavery. On the great end there was no fundamental difference between them. But they *were* divided on the methods and the timing, on how fast and in what manner they should move toward the goal. Both were committed to bringing about a wrenching social change. One would do it with the experimental caution of the pragmatist, the other with the headlong rush of the doctrinaire. And this matter of method on this particular issue was a fundamental difference. If a question of semantics arises concerning the use of fundamental, it can at least be said that the difference was deeper and darker than the fissures normally separating American political groups. It should not be exaggerated. But it cannot be exorcised.[17]

There is something to be said for each of these viewpoints. Two important elements in Lincoln's thinking that may clarify some of the contradictions or apparent contradictions are those of *timing* and *calculated risk*. In sum, what good is lofty idealism or radicalism if it is not tempered by political realism? When Lincoln repudiated Fre-

[15] Current, *Lincoln Nobody Knows*, p. 236.
[16] Johnson, "Lincoln and Equal Rights: A Reply," 73.
[17] Williams, "Lincoln and the Radicals," 113-14.

mont in 1861, he could hardly have done otherwise whatever his private beliefs. Shaken by the adverse reaction in the border states to Fremont's ill-timed and unauthorized emancipation decree, Lincoln rescinded it. "I think to lose Kentucky," Lincoln wrote to Orville H. Browning, "is nearly the same as to lose the whole game, Kentucky gone we cannot hold Missouri nor as I think Maryland. These all against us, and the job on our hands is too large for us. We would as well consent to a separation at once. . . ."[18] Equally important, the President not only had to consider the reactions of loyal border slaveholding states, but the distinct possibility of a resurgent northern Democratic party in 1862, 1863 and 1864. If Lincoln proceeded with caution, and with scrupulous regard to constitutional principles in attacking the institution of slavery; and if he couched his language in terms of military necessity, what does this indicate?

Richard Hofstadter may have been right by concluding that the Emancipation Proclamation contained "all the moral grandeur of a bill of lading."[19] But it occurs to me that he misses the point. That Lincoln did act decisively in January 1863 after the critical fall elections of 1862 allowed the Republicans to retain control of the national government. If the proclamation freed no slaves immediately, it *did* commit the nation to abolition if the Union army won the war. If it did not win, all the moral grandeur in the world would not have amounted to a tinker's dam. Lincoln's famous reply to Horace Greeley's "Prayer of Twenty Millions" has been too often used as evidence of Lincoln's conservatism. He would save the Union, Lincoln said, with or without slavery. Saving the Union, the President continued, was his primary objective; and he would do so "the shortest [possible] way under the Constitution." If he attacked slavery, the President concluded, he would do so, only on grounds of military necessity, and this despite his own "*personal* wish that all men could be free."[20]

Far from establishing Lincoln's fundamental conservatism, this statement demonstrates beyond question his shrewdness as a politician. After all, Lincoln had already announced to his Cabinet in July, 1862 his intention of issuing an emancipation proclamation; and he accepted Seward's suggestion that he wait until the Union won a decisive victory before issuing it. In the interim, Greeley's "Prayer" allowed him to educate the public. By playing down his radicalism, by using conservative rhetoric, he was in fact trying to prepare the public for drastic action. Even when Lincoln issued the preliminary proclamation in September, 1862, he not only stressed the idea of military necessity, but offered the Confederates the opportunity to lay down their arms and

[18] Lincoln to Orville H. Browning, Sept. 22, 1861, in Roy Basler (ed.), *The Collected Works of Abraham Lincoln* (1953), IV, 532.

[19] Hofstadter, *The American Political Tradition and the Men Who Made It* (1949), p. 132.

[20] "To Horace Greeley," Aug. 22, 1962, in Basler (ed.), *Collected Works of Lincoln*, V, 388-89.

return to the Union with slavery intact. It occurs to me that when Lincoln couched the preliminary proclamation in these terms, one need not conclude that the President was an arch-consverative.

First of all, is it conceivable that the President seriously believed that the Confederates would accept his offer? And second, considering the potential strength of the Democratic party in general, and the immediacy of the fall elections of 1862 in particular, what sagacious political leader would boldly proclaim a holy war when such a stance could readily lead to disaster? In short, to whom was Lincoln speaking? Certainly not the Confederates. In my opinion, his rhetoric was calculated to prevent extreme polarization in the Union camp. On the one hand, he could subdue, if not pacify, the Radicals by announcing his intention to take some action; and, on the other, he could, perhaps, partially allay the fears of some Democrats and some conservative Republicans who would not support an administration which based its war policies upon radical antislavery principles. But to repeat: once the Republican party passed its first acid test, the elections of 1862, Lincoln, despite the fears of Radicals, not only issued the Emancipation Proclamation, but authorized the enrollment of black soldiers into the Union army.[21] And this issue, of course, had not only provoked dissent in Democratic ranks, but in Republican as well. It is possible to continue in this vein indefinitely—citing still other examples of Lincolnian and Republican strategy and tactics in which the radical implications of Republican war aims were covered by a smokescreen of conservative rhetoric.

'Lincoln may or may not have been committed to colonization in principle; but as Professor Voegeli has convincingly demonstrated, Lincoln never again *publicly* implemented or mentioned colonization schemes after the smashing Republican political victories in 1863 and the triumph of Union arms at Gettysburg and Vicksburg—"mute evidence," Voegeli concludes, that Lincoln "felt it was no longer politically essential" to use a conservative mask to hide a radical face.[22]

Lack of conclusive evidence may make it impossible to measure, be-

---

[21] For the many and diverse roles played by Negroes during the Civil War see especially: Herbert Aptheker, *The Negro in the Civil War* (1938); Dudley Cornish, *The Sable Arm* (1956); W. E. B. DuBois, "The Negro and the Civil War," *Science and Society*, XXV (1961), 347-52; Robert F. Durden, *The Gray and the Black: The Confederate Debate on Emancipation* (1972); Louis S. Gerteis, *From Contraband to Freedom: Federal Policy Toward Southern Blacks, 1861-1865* (1973); James McPherson (ed.), *The Negro's Civil War* (1965); Benjamin Quarles, *The Negro in the Civil War* (1953); George W. Smith and Charles Judah, *Life in the North During the Civil War* (1966); Charles L. Wagandt, "The Army Versus Maryland Slavery, 1862-1864," *Civil War History*, X (1964), 141-48; Bell I. Wiley, *Southern Negroes, 1861-1865* (1938); and Wiley, Billy Yank and the Black Folk," *Journal of Negro History*, XXXVI (1952), 35-52.

[22] Voegeli, *Free But Not Equal: The Midwest and The Negro During the Civil War* (1967), p. 112. On colonization plans see Walter A. Payne, "Lincoln's Carribbean Colonization Plan," *Pacific Historian*, VII (1963), 65-72; and Paul J. Scheips, "Lincoln and the Chiriqui Colonization Project," *Journal of Negro History*, XXXVII (1952), 418-53.

yond any shadow of doubt, Lincoln's precise aims, motives and objectives. Lincoln's death in April 1865 reduces us to the game of IF history as regards the actions he would have taken toward the South and the freedmen had he lived. Yet, one thing is clear, at least in my mind, that unless historians give greater weight to the elements of *timing* and *calculated risk* in Lincolnian, and indeed, Republican party strategy, we will never understand the essential Lincoln.

Turning now to Reconstruction historiography, the first major area of controversy concerns Andrew Johnson's clash with Congress, his subsequent impeachment and the aims, objectives, successes and failures of Congressional—not Radical—Reconstruction in the South. Several historians have argued that the term "Radical" Republican has meaning only in terms of a common commitment to the destruction of slavery—that in fact they agreed on little else—certainly not on economic issues; and clearly, there was no agreement on the roles that freedmen would be allowed to play after emancipation.[23] In short, how many Republicans agreed with Thaddeus Stevens that Rebel property should be confiscated, deeded to freedmen, and thousands of "Nabobs" sent into exile so that a truly radical transformation of Southern society might occur?

Herman Belz, in a penetrating review essay of recent books, attacks what he terms "The New Orthodoxy in Reconstruction Historiography" which places the failure of confiscation and land distribution to freedmen at the core of the failure of Reconstruction. "The number of Republicans," Belz writes, who favored confiscation "is acknowledged to be small, but their existence is taken as proof than an alternative existed, that there was a decisive moment out of which an entirely different and more satisfactory solution to the problem of Reconstruction could have come." "I like the idea of redistributing property as much as the next person," Belz concludes, "But I think that to make it the key to interpretations of Reconstruction is unhistorical."[24] With that judgment, the present writer could not agree more.

When considering Andrew Johnson should he be viewed as Eric McKitrick's "outsider," as Kenneth Stampp's "last Jacksonian" whose ideological rigidity rendered him incapable of compromise, or as the Coxes' shrewd politician whose appeal to states' rights and Negrophobia conceivably could have sustained his position? Or should one agree with John Niven's more recent view that "Johnson, far from being a cool, cal-

---

[23] Stanley Coben, "Northeastern Business and Radical Reconstruction: A Reexamination," *Mississippi Valley Historical Review*," XLVI (1959), 67-90; Walter Nugent, *The Money Question During Reconstruction* (1969); Robert Sharkey, *Money, Class and Party* (1959); Irwin Unger, *The Greenback Era: A Social and Political History of American Finance, 1865-1879* (1964); and Peter Kolchin, "The Business Press and Reconstruction, 1865-1868," *Journal of Southern History*, XXXIII (1967), 183-96.

[24] Robert Cruden, *The Negro in Reconstruction* (1969); Thomas H. O'Conner, *The Disunited States*; and Allen W. Trelease, *Reconstruction: The Great Experiment* (1971), in Belz, "The New Orthodoxy in Reconstruction Historiography," *Reviews in American History*, I (1973), 106-13.

culating, shrewd politician, as pictured by the Coxes and others, was a bumbling, fumbling, politically inept individual, who spent most of the war years remote from eastern and middle-western political power centers; who was ignorant of the various Union Republican factions and who relied too much on the advice of a polarized cabinet"—especially William H. Seward.[25] Whatever view one chooses to adopt (though I tend to agree with the "ideological rigidity" and "bumbling politician" schools of thought), one thing is perfectly clear: the Coxes demonstrate beyond reasonable doubt that if Johnson had been willing to compromise with moderate and conservative Republicans in 1866 by agreeing to the principle of federal protection of civil rights for freedmen, short of suffrage, he might have averted the collision with Congress.[26] Michael Perman may or may not be correct in concluding that Draconian measures could or would have produced a drastic societal reformation in the South.[27] But once again the point is irrelevant precisely because it is unhistorical. One can hardly characterize Congressional Reconstruction as being radical or even having contained the potential for radicalism. The Military Reconstruction Acts, and the Fourteenth and Fifteenth Amendments were rather slender reeds upon which to engineer a social and political revolution. Numerous recent works or commentaries clearly reveal the limitations and handicaps—in ideological, political, economic and constitutional terms—that constituted the tragedy of post-Civil War America.[28]

[25] McKitrick, *Andrew Johnson and Reconstruction* (1960); Stampp, *The Era of Reconstruction, 1865-1877* (1965); Lawanda and John H. Cox, *Politics, Principle and Prejudice, 1865-1866* (1963); and Niven to R. O. Curry, October 11, 1973.

[26] Eric Foner disagrees with this point of view—maintaining that "your argument may impose a kind of static attitude on a very dynamic situation. Sure, there didn't have to be a break in February 1866—but could a break really have been averted at some point, as long as Republicans held the very un-radical aims of seeing 'loyal' men in control of the South, and really protecting the freedman? And what would have been Johnson's role? In a modus vivendi he would have had to give up his ambitions, since Republicans were not going to accept him for 1868. So I think the speculation that the whole fight might been avoided is questionable." Foner to R. O. Curry, March 13, 1974.

[27] Perman, *Reunion Without Compromise: The South and Reconstruction, 1865-1868* (1973). See also Lawanda Cox's review essay of Perman's book, "Reconstruction Foredoomed?: The Policy of Southern Consent," *Reviews in American History,* I (1973), 541-47.

[28] See W. R. Brock, *An American Crisis: Congress and Reconstruction, 1865-1867* (1963); John H. and LaWanda Cox, *Politics, Principle and Prejudice, 1865-66* (1963); John Hope Franklin, *Reconstruction After the War* (1961); Hyman, "Reconstruction and Political-Constitutional Institutions: The Popular Expression," in Harold Hyman (ed.), *New Frontiers of the American Reconstruction* (1966), 1-39; Hyman, *A More Perfect Union: The Impact of the Civil War and Reconstruction on the Constitution* (1973); Alfred H. Kelly, "Comment on Harold M. Hyman's Paper," in Hyman (ed.), *New Frontiers,* 40-58; Stanley I. Kutler, *Judicial Power and Reconstruction Politics* (1968); William McFeely, *Yankee Stepfather, General O. O. Howard and the Freedmen* (1968); James McPherson, *The Struggle for Equality: Abolitionists and the Negro in the Civil War and Reconstruction* (1964); David Montgomery, *Beyond Equality: Labor and the Radical Republicans, 1862-1872* (1967); Rembert Patrick, *The Reconstruction of the Nation* (1967); Willie Lee Rose, *Rehearsal for Reconstruction: The Port Royal Experiment* (1964); Patrick A. Rid-

In part, the failure of Congressional Reconstruction may be attributed to conflicts of race. The fear of white recalcitrance was a real, not an imaginary threat to Republican policymakers. But equally important, the Republican majority demonstrated a remarkable commitment to what Alfred Kelly has termed "the Republicans' self-imposed constitutional dilemmas"—not the least of which was their reluctance to enhance power on any level of the federal system, especially the national.[29] In short, the Fifteenth Amendment did not enfranchise anybody. It merely forbade state discrimination on grounds of "race, color, or previous condition of servitude." Such discrimination would be extremely difficult to prove in a court of law on these grounds and these grounds alone if state authorities chose to violate the spirit, or even the letter of the law. Intrastate voluntarism did not—indeed, could not work, once the so-called "Redeemers" seized control of Southern state governments by fair means and foul, and once the Supreme Court surrendered the principle of equality before the law for blacks in the Slaughter House cases, in *United States v. Reese* (1876), and the famous, or rather infamous, civil rights cases in 1883 which declared unconstitutional the much vaunted Civil Rights Act of 1875.[30] But even if this act had withstood the assault of the Court, would it really have changed anything? Bertram Wyatt-Brown argues:

if the bill could claim any significance, it lay in its demonstration of the bankruptcy of Republican Reconstruction principles. Rather than being a true memorial to Charles Sumner and his cause, it was a travesty of racial justice, because neither the white public nor its representatives expected or wanted the Act's enforcement.[31]

Beyond this, Richard Curry has demonstrated, to his own satisfaction, that even the abolitionists, the most advanced social thinkers of their time, were not precursors of twentieth century social planners. "One may . . . suggest," Curry writes,

without challenging the idea that most abolitionists were dedicated equalitarians, that their conception, in practice if not in theory, was that of equality before the law—nothing more. And even this modest institutionalization of equalitarian prin-

---

dleberger, "The Radicals' Abandonment of the Negro During Reconstruction," *Journal of Negro History*, XLV (1960), 88-102; Riddleberger, *George Washington Julian, Radical Republican: A Study in Nineteenth Century Politics and Reform* (1966); Kenneth M. Stampp, *Era of Reconstruction*; and C. Vann Woodward, "Seeds of Failure in Radical Race Policy," in Hyman (ed.), *New Frontiers*, 125-47.

[29] Kelly, "Comment on Harold Hyman's Paper" *ibid.*, 53.

[30] Astute analyses of these cases are found in Kutler, *Judicial Power* and William Gillette, "Anatomy of a Failure: Federal Enforcement of the Right to Vote in the Border States During Reconstruction," in Richard O. Curry (ed.), *Radicalism, Racism and Party Realignment: The Border States During Reconstruction* (1969), 265-304.

[31] Wyatt-Brown "The Civil Rights Act of 1875," *The Western Political Quarterly*, XVIII (1965), 775. See also James M. McPherson, "Abolitionists and the Civil Rights Act of 1875," *Journal of American History*. LII (1965), 493-510; and William P. Vaughn, "Separate But Unequal: The Civil Rights Act of 1875 and the Defeat of the School Integration Clause," *Southwest Social Science Quarterly* XLVIII (1967), 146-54.

ciples . . . necessitated a modification of ideological commitments by many Garrisonians who found it difficult to embrace political activism after years of dedication to the idea that moral reform and social change were not matters 'of laws to be passed . . . but of *error* to be rooted out and *repentance* . . . exacted.'[32]

Having painted such a bleak picture in analyzing the failure of Congressional Reconstruction, should we then reject the Coxes' position that the Republicans acted not from political expediency, but despite political risk? I think not. The point at issue is not the *ends* which Republicans sought—equality of all men before the law—but the fact that those ends were limited and the *means* employed to achieve even these were inadequate. Thus, within the self-imposed limits under which the Republicans operated, they were able to act—and often decisively.[33]

For example, Michael Les Benedict in his recent study, *The Impeachment and Trial of Andrew Johnson* (1973), convincingly demonstrates that the President was impeached for two major reasons: (1) Johnson,

[32] Curry, "The Abolitionists and Reconstruction: A Critical Appraisal," *The Journal of Southern History*, XXXIV (1968), 527-45. For opposing points of view, see especially: George M. Fredrickson, *The Inner Civil War: Northern Intellectuals and the Crisis of the Union* (1965); John G. Sproat, "Blueprint for Radical Reconstruction," *Journal of Southern History*, XXIII (1957), 25-44; Rose, " 'Iconoclasm Has Had Its Day': Abolitionists and Freedmen in South Carolina," in Martin Duberman (ed.), *The Antislavery Vanguard: New Essays on the Abolitionists* (1965), 178-205; John L. Thomas, "Antislavery and Utopia," *ibid.*, 240-69; and Thomas, "Romantic Reform in America, 1815-1865," *American Quarterly*, XVII (1965), 656-81.

[33] The question of Republican motivation has long been a major issue in Reconstruction historiography. The most recent and influential interpretations are those of William Gillette and John H. and LaWanda Cox. See the Coxes, "Negro Suffrage and Republican Politics: The Problem of Motivation in Reconstruction Historiography," *Journal of Southern History*, XXXIII (1967), 303-30; Gillette, *The Right To Vote: Politics and the Passage of the Fifteenth Amendment* (1965, 1969). The 1969 edition of Gillette's book contains a new epilogue (pp. 166-90), "The Black Voter And The White Historian: Another Look At Negro Suffrage, Republican Politics, And Reconstruction Historiography." The Coxes, in the article cited above, take Gillette to task for maintaining that political expediency was the primary force behind the Fifteenth Amendment—that the "primary object of the Amendment was to get the Negro vote in the North." The Coxes forcefully argue that the Republican leadership committed the nation "to equal suffrage for the Negro not because of . . . expediency but *despite* political risk." In his 1969 epilogue, which in fact is a reply, Gillette chides the Coxes for oversimplifying the issues by creating an artificial "dichotomy between idealism and expediency." The point at issue, therefore, is: to what extent did Republicans recognize the dangers involved as opposed to the practical advantages to be derived from enfranchisement. If I read the Coxes and Gillette correctly, their positions are not irreconcilable—reflecting differences in emphasis rather than fundamentals. Conceding that "idealism" played a role, Gillette writes, "The Amendment was a step in the right direction—no less and no more. It represented neither an unalloyed victory nor an unforgivable sellout; it represented only 'practical wisdom.' " "As I see it," LaWanda Cox wrote recently, "The surprising thing is not that the Republicans didn't do more, but that they did as much as was the case" (LaWanda Cox to R. O. Curry, May 11, 1974). It occurs to me that Gillette's argument that the Coxes are guilty of hindsight in constructing their argument can be used against his own contention that Negro suffrage did, in fact, make a difference in numerous elections during the 1870s, 1880s, and 1890s. In short, could anyone predict in 1869 what the outcome of ratification would be, regardless of *perceived* advantages by contemporaries?

by his actions was violating the principle of the separation of powers in government; and (2) the President's obstructionism in failing to carry out the spirit, and in some instances, the letter of the Military Reconstruction Acts—once they had been passed over his veto, threatened the success of the Congressional program.[34] In sum, it could not have been as clear to contemporaries as it now appears to historians, that their program was doomed from the beginning. Far from being a mindless or vindictive act, Johnson's impeachment was a political necessity as viewed by the Republican majority. As Stanley Kutler observes,

now that Benedict has somewhat redressed the balance on Andrew Johnson's impeachment and trial [it cannot be too strongly emphasized that historians] have been terribly guilty of counter-factual thinking on this subject. For example, note how they have accepted *prima facie* [Lyman] Trumbull's contention that the President had to be acquitted or all future presidents would have been in jeopardy for disagreeing with Congress. Preposterous.[35]

Speaking of Kutler, his book *Judicial Power and Reconstruction Politics* (1968) is a brilliant revisionist study which not only demolishes old characterizations of the role of the Supreme Court during the Reconstruction era and the attitudes of Republicans toward the Court, but demonstrates convincingly that the origins of the modern judicial system lie in this period. Especially compelling is Kutler's analysis of the Jurisdiction and Removal Act of 1875 which was partially responsible for broadening the Court's jurisdiction in the late nineteenth and twentieth centuries. Unfortunately, limitations of space prohibits the extended analysis here that Kutler's work so richly deserves.[36] The same holds true for Hyman's *A More Perfect Union: The Impact of the Civil War and Reconstruction on the Constitution* (1973). While some historians "may be a bit disconcerted to find it pervaded throughout with a fervent liberal nationalism," most will undoubtedly agree with William Wiecek's judgment that *A More Perfect Union* is not only a provocative work of synthesis, but a book which "strikes out in new directions, searching for both the scattered wellsprings of policymaking and for the way contemporaries themselves saw their current history unfolding."[37]

[34] Raoul Berger occupies a more traditional position on Johnson's impeachment and trial in *Impeachment: The Constitutional Problems* (1973). See Stanley Kutler's review essay of the Benedict and Berger books in *Reviews in American History*. I (1973) 480-87. See also James E. Sefton, "The Impeachment of Andrew Johnson: A Century of Writing," *Civil War History*, XIV (1968), 120-47.

[35] Kutler to R. O. Curry, Sept. 16, 1973.

[36] Kutler argues persuasively that the Republican majority, being committed to the principle of separation of powers, was not hostile to the Supreme Court as an institution, and that the court was not inclined to interfere with the Congressional Reconstruction program despite fears in some circles that it was. For an opposing view as regards the attitudes of Congressional Republicans toward the Supreme Court, see Charles Fairman, *Reconstruction and Reunion, 1864-88* (1971), pp. 258-514.

[37] Wiecek, "The Reconstruction of the Constitution," *Reviews in American History*, I (1973), 548-53.

Turning to Reconstruction in the South, one is delighted to reiterate that at long last the old Dunningite stereotype of "vindictive Carpetbaggers, ignorant Negroes, and unprincipled Scalawags" has been consigned to the scrapheap of historical blindness and perversity—a fate it so richly deserves. The work of early revisionists including W. E. DuBois, A. A. Taylor, Francis B. Simkins, Howard K. Beale, David Donald, T. Harry Williams, Vernon L. Wharton and John Hope Franklin undermined the assumptions on which traditional views were based.[38] But only in the last decade has the *coup de grace* been delivered by the massive outpouring of revisionist works. In the limited space available here, I would like to address myself briefly to two principal themes: (1) the structure of the Republican party in the South and the reasons for its failure aside from the lack of national support; and (2) the effects of emancipation upon the lifestyle of blacks in social, cultural, and economic terms.

In recent years studies by scholars such as John Blassingame, W. McKee Evans, Robert Cruden, Peter Kolchin, Joe Richardson, Willie Lee Rose, and Joel Williamson have extended pioneering efforts to look at Reconstruction in the South from the black man's point of view.[39] In his study of the social history of Alabama blacks, Kolchin directly attacks the Sambo stereotype; but clearly the others do so by implication. All make important contributions in treating such topics as the relative strength of the black family, the crucial roles played by the Negro church, educational opportunities, and intellectual life and social patterns in general. Certainly, Williamson's book is by far the most comprehensive in dealing with a single state, but the strength of Blassingame's study, the first major monograph on the Southern Negro during Reconstruction in an urban setting, stems, in part, from the greater availability of evidence from black rather than white sources. Moreover, he uses demographic and quantitative methods with great effect. In the period that he covers, 1860-1880, Blassingame paints a rather

38 DuBois, *Black Reconstruction* (1935); Taylor, *The Negro in South Carolina During Reconstruction* (1924); *The Negro in the Reconstruction of Virginia* (1926); and *The Negro in Tennessee, 1865-1880* (1941); Simkins, "New Viewpoints of Southern Reconstruction," *Journal of Southern History,* VI (1939), 49-61; Beale, "On Rewriting Reconstruction History," *American Historical Review,* XLV (1940), 807-27; Donald, "The Scalawag in Mississippi Reconstruction," *Journal of Southern History,* X (1944), 447-60; Williams, An Analysis of Some Reconstruction Attitudes," *ibid.* (1946), 469-86; Wharton, *The Negro in Mississippi* (1947); and Franklin, "Whither Reconstruction Historiography," *Journal of Negro Education,* XVII (1948), 446-61.

39 Blassingame, *Black New Orleans, 1860-1880* (1973); Evans, *Ballots and Fence Rails: Reconstruction on the Lower Cape Fear* (1967); Cruden, *The Negro in Reconstruction* (1969); Kolchin, *First Freedom: The Response of Alabama's Blacks to Emancipation and Reconstruction* (1972); Richardson, *The Negro in the Reconstruction of Florida, 1865-77* (1965). Rose, *Rehearsal for Reconstruction;* and Williamson, *After Slavery: The Negro in South Carolina During Reconstruction, 1865-1877* (1965). See also John Hope Franklin, "Reconstruction and the Negro," in Hyman, *New Frontiers,* 59-76 and August Meier, "Comment on John Hope Franklin's Paper," *ibid.,* 77-86. Closely related is Evans' *To Die Game: The Story of the Lowry Band, Indian Guerillas of Reconstruction* (1971).

progressive, if not totally optimistic picture, in pointing to the ability
of blacks to make substantial economic progress. Similar views are expressed both by Kolchin and Williamson. However, Joseph Logsdon,
in a perceptive review essay of the Kolchin and Blassingame books, suggests that "their picture of improvement in the lives of black people
during Reconstruction" fails to consider "the enormous setbacks that
followed, in what DuBois termed the move 'Back Toward Slavery.'"
"When further work is done on social developments from 1880-1900,"
Logsdon continues, "perhaps utilizing similar census data which will
become available to historians in 1975, that reaction can be ascertained."
"For New Orleans," Logsdon speculates, "the reversal may well be of
catastrophic proportions." In short, as exciting as recent contributions
to the history of blacks during Reconstruction are, the exploration of
the field has just begun.[40]

As regards political developments in the South, it is now generally
agreed that despite some corruption in Republican regimes in the South,
these governments, while they survived, enacted basic social, economic
and political reforms. In fact, the corruption of Republican Reconstruction governments is minor relative to corruption in the North and to
"Redeemer" governments in the South. Blacks participated in all of the
governments but black officeholding was never commensurate at any
level with the size of the black electorate. All this is well-known, but
we still need intensive studies of black voting behavior and political
consciousness for nearly all Southern states, evidence for which is not
all that easy to come by.

Another intriguing and complex problem in the political realm involves the identity, location and motives of Southern white Republicans—or if we must use the more traditional term—who were the Scalawags? Professor Donald opened the debate on this subject in 1944,
arguing that former Whigs in Mississippi, many of whom had opposed
secession, and could not abide the prospect of Democratic dominance,
joined ranks with Carpetbaggers and blacks to form the Republican
party. Former Whigs, led by Governor James L. Alcorn, dominated the
Republican party, 1869-1873. Donald estimates that by 1873 approximately 25-30 per cent of white voters in Mississippi had joined the Republicans. Why? "By recognizing the legal equality of the Negroes,"
Donald writes, "Alcorn hoped to gain their political support for his own
policies" which favored the planter class. But this coalition was doomed
to failure. By 1873, blacks, who cared nothing about Whig economic
policies, demanded a greater share voice in government and policies
calculated to serve their own interests. As a result, blacks threw their
support to and elected Adelbert Ames, a principled Carpetbagger—if
we must also use that term—to the governorship. Shortly thereafter,
the Republican coalition disintegrated. "The basic trouble was," Don-

[40] Logsdon, "Black Reconstruction Revisited," *Reviews in American History*, I
(1973), 553-58.

ald concludes, that the Southern planter, "though he might advocate legal equality and civil rights [for blacks] as a matter of expedience . . . could not accede to the Negro's demand for social equality." In short, the race question—then as now—dominated the Southern white's consciousness.[41] In recent years, Donald has extended his Unionist former Whig thesis to include most of the South, the chief exceptions being Alabama and North Carolina, where the Scalawags primarily were hillcountry farmers who had opposed the planter class before, during and after secession.[42]

The most comprehensive challenge to Donald's point of view has come from Allen Trelease, who has done a county-by-county quantitative analysis of Republican voting patterns for every Southern state, focusing attention upon the Presidential election of 1872. In striking contrast to Donald, Trelease argues that in only three states—Tennessee, North Carolina, and to a lesser extent Virginia "was there much ground for identifying postwar Republicans with pre-war Whigs, and even there the correspondence was by no means complete." Moreover, Whig areas that did go Republican

were the habitat of the Appalachian highlander. The planter-businessman aristocracy to which Professor Donald and others have referred seems in general to have found the postwar Democratic or Conservative camp more congenial. Doubtless the minority of this group who did join the Radicals carried more weight in terms of leadership and prestige than their numbers would indicate, but they were hardly more typical of the white Republicans as a whole than of their own class.[43]

According to Trelease, the evidence suggests rather that most white Republican voters were small farmers, who lived in counties containing few Negroes, who were predominately Democratic before the war, who were poorer by far than the Southern average, and had little in common with former slaveholders who "had frequently dominated affairs in their respective states." These small farmers, therefore, were free "to join (or not to join) the antiplanter, Radical, Union party with less reference to the albatross of Negro equality or to other major issues of Reconstruction policy." In most areas of the South "there were enough freedmen to constitute at least the illusion of a threat to white supremacy; thus few Republicans joined the Republican party to begin with and many of those who did dropped out early. Personal conviction united with social pressure—often expressed physically—to keep a large majority in the party of conservatism and white supremacy." If this

[41] Donald, "The Scalawag in Mississippi Reconstruction," *Journal of Southern History*, X (1944), 447-60, esp. pp. 450 and 452.

[42] Donald and James G. Randall, *The Civil War and Reconstruction* (revised edition, 1961), 627-28. By implication, at least, the work of Thomas B. Alexander lends support to Donald's position. See Alexander, "Persistent Whiggery in Alabama and the Lower South, 1860-1867," *Alabama Review* XII (1959), 35-52 and "Persistent Whiggery in the Confederate South, 1860-1877," *Journal of Southern History*, XXXVII (1961).

[43] Trelease, "Who Were the Scalawags?" *Journal of Southern History*, XXVIV (1963), 445-68. Quote taken from p. 462.

preoccupation with race was indeed the "central theme of Southern history," it not only confirms "the highlanders' isolation from the mainstream of Southern life," but demonstrates that W. E. B. DuBois's "vision of democracy across racial lines" was—alas—too utopian.[44]

Shortly after Trelease's work appeared, Donald challenged the validity of his findings—arguing that Trelease's work contained serious methodological shortcomings. Trelease, Donald observes, omitted from consideration in his analysis all counties in which the Republican voting percentage did not exceed

the percentage of Negro population by at least twenty. . . . To put it another way, Professor Trelease's method excludes, by definition, virtually all counties with a heavy Negro population as sources of possible scalawag strength. . . . As Professor Trelease admits, his index eliminates 'about two thirds of the black belt counties' and 'a majority of all counties which were more than 40 per cent Negro in composition.' What is left is the hill and mountain counties of the South. . . . Of course there were few Whig-planter-businessmen in the impoverished counties, and Mr. Trelease's method does not permit him to identify this element in the black belt counties and the growing cities, where research has repeatedly revealed strong and persistent Southern Whiggery.

Donald admits, however, that the existence of methodological flaws in Trelease's analysis "does not . . . prove that Whig planters and businessmen became Republican in large numbers. To establish, or to refute, that argument will require much more thought and much more research."[45] Donald penned these words in 1964. In the interim, the debate has by no means been resolved, but several historians—including Otto H. Olsen, Lillian Pereyra, Elizabeth Nathans, John V. Mering, Warren Ellem and William M. Cash have made important contributions which underscore the difficulties involved in making accurate generalizations about the nature and sources of Scalawag strength.[46]

Olsen's work on North Carolina supports Donald's view that the "Tar Heel" state was a major exception to the Unionist former Whig thesis. Curiously enough, North Carolina is one of three states in which Trelease concedes that the former Whig thesis has a degree of validity. On the other hand, Elizabeth Nathans' recent study of Reconstruction in Georgia maintains that whereas former Whigs from black belt counties played an important role in the Republican party, former Democratic voters from the hill country of North Georgia and the wire grass

[44] Ibid., 467-68.

[45] Donald, Communication to the Editor of the Journal of Southern History, XXX (1964), 254-56. For Trelease's vigorous reply to Donald, see ibid., 256-57.

[46] Olson, "Reconsidering the Scalawags," Civil War History, XII (1966), 304-25; Pereyra, James Lusk Alcorn: Persistent Whig (1966); Nathans, Losing the Peace: Georgia Republicans and Reconstruction, 1865-1871 (1968); Mering, "Persistent Whiggery in the Confederate South: A Reconsideration," South Atlantic Quarterly, LXIX (1970), 124-43; Ellem, "Who Were the Mississippi Scalawags?" Journal of Southern History, XXXVIII (1972), 217-40; Cash, "Alabama Republicans During Reconstruction: Personal Characteristics, Motivations, and Political Activity of Party Activists, 1867-1880" (unpublished Ph.D. dissertation, University of Alabama, 1973).

country in the southern part of the state also voted the Republican ticket in large numbers.

To complicate matters even further, Donald modified his own position considerably in 1967 in a review of Lillian Pereyra's biography of
Governor Alcorn of Mississippi. Pereyra, Donald wrote,

> might well have been advised to minimize Whiggery as Alcorn's cardinal principle
> and to stress instead his consistent advocacy of the interests of the Mississippi Delta
> area, as opposed to those of the hill country. Indeed it seems likely that persistent
> patterns of intra-state sectionalism . . . were more important in shaping Southern
> politics during the Reconstruction period than ideology, class, or even race.[47]

Three years later, John Mering elaborated upon this theme by arguing,
as Warren Ellem observes, "that Whigs—either as a group or individuals—did not act consistently enough to permit historians to examine
meaningfully their reaction to the issues of Reconstruction in terms of
Whiggery, considered either as a class ideology or a political entity."[48]

At this point, the reader might well be forgiven for washing his hands
in despair—at least temporarily—considering the wide disparity in historians' findings. However, a recent article by Ellem on the Mississippi
Scalawags rejects Trelease's analysis as well as Mering's position and
Donald's modification of his earlier views. Although Ellem argues that
Mississippi Scalawags numbered approximately 9,000 rather than
20,000-25,000, he vigorously reasserts the validity of the Unionist former Whig thesis—leaving the major premises of Donald's original argument intact.[49] Equally important, William Cash extends the Unionist
former Whig thesis to include Alabama. According to Thomas B. Alexander, Cash's study identifies 2,700 Republican activists and concludes
that

> they were not chiefly from the hill country but predominantly from the Black Belt,
> Tennessee Valley, and larger cities of Alabama. Of the 258 men for whom he could
> identify antebellum party affiliations . . . 21% were too young to have voted in
> 1860, 60 per cent had been Whigs or Constitutional Unionists, 16 per cent had been
> Democrats and 4 per cent Northern Republicans.[50]

In conclusion, it is clear that the Unionist former Whig thesis, far
from being passe, remains the most influential frame of reference thus
far developed by historians to characterize the Scalawags. As Ellem
demonstrates (and to some extent Trelease), this thesis does not necessarily preclude the importance of intrastate sectional cleavages in explaining divisions among Southern whites. Even so, a consensus does
not exist, and we still need studies of nearly every Southern state before

[47] *American Historical Review*, LXXII (1967), 707-08.

[48] Ellen, "Mississippi Scalawags," 217.

[49] *Ibid.*, 240.

[50] Being unable to utilize Cash's thesis personally, I am indebted to Professor
Alexander for providing the above analysis. Equally important, Alexander was extremely helpful in providing bibliographical data for other materials that I had
overlooked (Alexander to R. O. Curry, April 27, 1974).

historians can make accurate generalizations (replete with the proper qualifying factors and distinctions) for the South as a whole.

There is little point in repeating here the familiar story of the fall of various Republican regimes in the South—the lack of national support, the influence of the race issue in destroying shaky and ultimately unviable Republican coalitions, and the use of terrorism, fraud and subterfuge by Southern "redeemers" to destroy the opposition.[51] Republican Reconstruction in Lousiana, South Carolina and Florida lasted until 1877 in large measure because of the size of the black electorate. But even these regimes could not hold out forever without some degree of national support which, of course, was not forthcoming. C. Vann Woodward's *Reunion and Reaction: The Compromise of 1877 and The End of Reconstruction* (1951) is the standard account of this subject and has enjoyed wide acceptance. Recently, Allan Peskin, in an article entitled, "Was There A Compromise of 1877?" launched the first major assault upon Woodward's influential thesis.[52]

Space does not permit an extended analysis of the arguments pro and con. However, it is clear that in all probability that we will never know all the details involved nor will we know the relative importance of various concessions made. Beyond this, the motives of some individuals who either delivered or reneged on promises or alleged promises are not entirely clear. On balance, however, I think Professor Woodward has provided the far more persuasive argument. "The subject under discussion," Woodward reminds his critic, was not the disputed election of 1876, "but the compromise of 1877 and its consequences." The compromise was not concluded until after the Electoral Commission, the creation of which was originally considered a Democratic victory, had already voted for Hayes.

"Tilden's defeat then," Woodward writes, "was not a consequence of the compromise." But the "elimination of Tilden from 'consideration' . . . did not assure the constitutional election and peaceful inauguration of Hayes." After the Electoral Commission's decision, as Peskin admits, "the choice was no longer between two candidates but between Hayes and chaos."[53] Peskin suggests that the failure of many key features of the compromise to materialize stemmed from what Ellis Paxon Oberholtzer termed Republican "honeyfuggling." Woodward is far more persuasive in suggesting that if anyone "honeyfuggled" anyone it was the Southerners, not the Republicans, who succeeded.[54]

However, I do have one criticism of Professor Woodward's analysis.

[51] On violence and terrorism, including the failure of Republican regimes to use effectively black militia to protect themselves, see especially: Otis A. Singletary, *Negro Militia and Reconstruction* (1957); James E. Sefton, *The United States Army During Reconstruction, 1865-1877* (1967); and Allen W. Trelease, *White Terror: The Ku Klux Klan Conspiracy During Southern Reconstruction* (1971).

[52] *Journal of American History*, LX (1973), 63-75.

[53] Woodward, "Yes, There Was a Compromise of 1877," *ibid.*, 222, 220.

[54] Peskin, "Was There A Compromise," 72; Woodward, "Yes," 222-23.

As regards the return to "home rule," Woodward argues that "in this respect [at least] the Compromise of 1877 outlasted all the other compromises [ever made in the United States] and enjoyed a life span exceeding that of all of them combined."[55] It occurs to me that long before 1877 Republican Reconstruction in the South was a moribund experiment, and that Woodward may have overemphasized both the importance of the compromise and its long-range significance. In sum, the compromise of 1877 paved the way for the orderly inauguration of "Rutherfraud" B. Hayes (as some contemporaries called him); but Congressional Reconstruction was doomed from the beginning, and even the limited objectives envisioned by northern Republicans could not be long sustained in South Carolina, Louisiana or Florida—the only states then remaining under Republican rule, compromise or no compromise.

Other extremely important new dimensions in Reconstruction historiography must receive at least passing mention here. A jointly authored book edited by Richard O. Curry, *Radicalism, Racism and Party Realignment* brings the history of the "dark and bloody" border states into the mainstream of Reconstruction historiography for the first time.[56] Equally important, numerous studies of society and politics in Northern states during the Reconstruction era are currently being undertaken; thus far four books and several articles have reached print.[57] In ad-

[55] *Ibid.*, 217-18. I was unable to secure a copy of Keith Ian Polakoff's *The Politics of Inertia: The Election of 1876 and the End of Reconstruction* (1973) before this paper was completed. According to William P. Vaughn, whose review of Polakoff's book appeared in *Civil War History*, XX (1974), 87-88, *The Politics of Inertia* is not a refutation of Woodward's landmark study, "but it is a revision of that part of Woodward's thesis which emphasized 'the secret deal by which southern Democrats of (Old Whig) antecedents assented to the seating of . . . Hayes in return for various political and economic concessions. . . .'" Woodward, Polakoff states, concentrated too heavily on the maneuvers and negotiations of a few politicians, lobbyists and journalists, "ignoring the internal strife of the Republicans and the defeatist attitude of Democratic standard bearer Samual J. Tilden. . . . Polakoff insists that it was the almost total inability of both the Republican and Democratic leaders to control their own organizations, 'even in a crisis demanding centralized direction, which assured a peaceful, though clumsy solution to the disputed election.'" Having effectively countered Peskin's arguments, Professor Woodward's reactions to Polakoff's book are anticipated with interest.

[56] See also Thomas B. Alexander, *Political Reconstruction in Tennessee* (1950 and 1968); William E. Parrish, *Missouri Under Radical Rule* (1965); Norma L. Peterson, *Freedom and the Franchise: The Political Career of B. Gratz Brown* (1965); Margaret L. Calcott, *The Negro in Maryland Politics, 1870-1912* (1969); Ross A. Webb, *Benjamin Helm Bristow: Border State Politician* (1969); and Jean H. Baker, *The Politics of Continuity: Maryland Politics from 1858 to 1870* (1973).

[57] Erwin H. Bradley, *The Triumph of Militant Republicanism: A Study of Pennsylvania and Presidential Politics, 1860-1872* (1964); Frank B. Evans, *Pennsylvania Politics, 1872-1877: A Study in Political Leadership* (1966); Felice Bonadio, *North of Reconstruction: Ohio Politics, 1865-1870* (1970); James C. Mohr, *The Radical Republicans and Reform in New York* (1973); Philip D. Swenson, "The Midwest and the Abandonment of Radical Reconstruction, 1864-1877 (Ph.D. dissertation, University of Washington, 1971); David Montgomery, "Radical Republicanism in Pennsylvania, 1866-1873," *Pennsylvania Magazine of History and Biography*, LXXXV (1961), 439-57; Ira V. Brown, "Pennsylvania and the Rights of the Negro, 1865-1887," *Pennsylvania History*, XXVIII (1961), 45-57; Leslie H. Fishel, "Wis-

dition, James C. Mohr is now editing a collection of original essays on
Reconstruction in the North for the Johns Hopkins Press. Beyond this,
I was extremely impressed by the number of papers presented at the
1973 meetings of the Southern Historical Association in Atlanta on variations of this significant new theme.[58]

Other important topics on which significant writings have appeared
recently concern Anglo-American and Franco-American relations during the war years. For example, Lynn Case and Warren Spencer have
produced the first authoritative account of France's role in the American Civil War.[59] Moreover, Melvyn Dubofsky's essay review of Mary
Ellis's *Support for Secession: Lancashire and the American Civil War*
(1973) shows that the debate over the attitude of English workingmen
toward slavery and the war itself is far from over.[60] The same holds true
for the impact of the American Civil War on the passage of the British
Reform Bill of 1867. Especially useful on this topic are the writings of
Joseph Hernon, Jr., Gertrude Himmelfarb, W. D. Jones, and H. C. Allen.[61] Equally important is Harold Hyman's edited volume, *Heard
Round the World: The Impact Abroad of the Civil War* (1969) which
deals with England, France, Russia, Canada and Latin America.[62]

Another major topic that deserves extended treatment is the long-
range significance of the American Civil War in social, constitutional,
economic and political terms. Especially important is the work of
Thomas C. Cochran and his critics on the economic consequences of the

---

consin and Negro Suffrage," *Wisconsin Magazine of History*, XLVI (1963), 180-96;
Fishel, "Repercussions of Reconstruction: The Northern Negro, 1870-1883," *Civil
War History*, XIV (1968), 325-45; and Edgar A. Toppin, "Negro Emancipation In
Historic Retrospect: Ohio, The Negro Suffrage Issue in Postbellum Ohio Politics,"
Journal of Human Relations, XI (1963), 232-46.

[58] Richard Mendales, "Republican Defectors to the Democracy During Reconstruction"; James Quill, "Northern Public Opinion and Reconstruction, April-De-
cember 1865"; Phyllis Field, "New York Voters and the Issue of Black Suffrage,
1846-1869"; and Kermit Hall, "Judicial Politics and Regional Reward: Congress
and the Federal Courts, 1861-1869." I wish to thank these scholars for providing
me with copies of their papers.

[59] Case and Spencer, *The United States and France: Civil War Diplomacy*
(1970). See also Daniel B. Carroll, *Henri Mercier and the American Civil War*
(1971); and Stuart L. Bernarth, *Squall Across the Atlantic: American Civil War
Prize Cases and Diplomacy* (1970). In addition the entire issue of *Civil War History*, XV (December 1969) is devoted to new perspectives on Anglo-American diplomacy.

[60] Dubofsky, "Myth and History," in *Reviews in American History*, I (1973), 396-
99. See also Joseph Hernon, Jr., "British Sympathies in the American Civil War:
A Reconsideration," *Journal of Southern History*, XXXIII (1967), 356-67.

[61] Hernon, *Celts, Catholics and Copperheads: Ireland Views the American Civil
War* (1968); Himmelfarb, *Victorian Minds* (1968); W. D. Jones, "The British Conservatives and the American Civil War," *American Historical Review*, LVIII
(1953), 527-43 and H. C. Allen, "Civil War, Reconstruction and Great Britain,"
in Harold Hyman (ed.), *Heard Round the World: The Impact Abroad of the
Civil War* (1969), 3-96.

[62] See also Belle B. Sideman and Lillian Friedman, eds., *Europe Looks at the
Civil War* (1960) and Robin Winks, *Canada and the United States: The Civil War
Years* (1960).

war,[63] Kutler's and Hyman's work on constitutional development and the various volumes (either completed or in preparation) in The Impact of the Civil War Series sponsored by the Civil War Centennial Commission.[64]

Important new research—either recently completed or now in progress—must be treated briefly here. Along these lines, I think Thomas J. Pressly's forthcoming study of comparative slave societies at the time of emancipation promises to be an extremely enlightening work, as does the projected study by Steven Channing on the collapse of slavery in the South during the war itself and James Roark's forthcoming book on Southern planters during the Civil War and Reconstruction era.[65] Equally important, as Professors Lee Benson and Robin Winks have suggested, the comparative study of civil wars ought to place the American experience in clearer perspective. "I hope that one day," Winks writes, "we might see a symposium volume on civil wars in which the American example is just one essay, with Cyprus, and Aden, and Malaysia, and Mexico, and Spain, and a dozen others, examined within a sophisticated, perhaps Deutschian frame." Professor Raimondo Luraghi's recent article comparing Italian unification to the American Civil War is highly suggestive.[66]

In conclusion, let me say that if there can be no salvation without sin, neither can there be justification for graduate study in history without ignorance. As Peyton McCrary wrote recently:

On the whole I would say the field is in a healthy state. It continues to attract some of the best scholarly minds, and its close relationship to the literature on slavery and black history should be a further source of strength (since that is also one of the exciting areas of American scholarship). If the behavioral revolution in political history and the so-called new social history continue to find appreciative reception

[63] See Cochran, "Did the Civil War Retard Industrialization?" *Mississippi Valley Historical Review,* XLVIII (1961), 197-210; Stephen Salsbury, "The Effect of the Civil War on American Industrial Development," in Ralph Andreano (ed.), *The Economic Impact of the American Civil War* (1962), 161-68; Harry N. Scheiber, "Economic Change in the Civil War Era: An Analysis of Recent Studies," *Civil War History,* XI (1965), 396-411; David T. Gilchrist and David Lewis (eds.), *Economic Change in the Civil War Era* (1965); Stanley L. Engerman, "The Economic Impact of the Civil War," *Explorations in Enterpreneurial History,* 2nd series, III (1965), 176-99; and Richard F. Wacht, "A Note on the Cochran Thesis and the Small Arms Industry in the Civil War," *ibid.,* IV (1966), 57-62.

[64] Thus far Mary Elizabeth Massey's *Bonnet Brigades* (1966) and Paul Gates' *Agriculture and the Civil War* (1965) have appeared. See also Robert H. Bremner, "The Impact of the Civil War on Philanthropy and Social Welfare," *Civil War History,* XII (1966), 293-303.

[65] Pressly to R. O. Curry, Sept. 14, 1972 and Apr. 12, 1974; Channing to Curry, Oct. 9, 1973 and Roark to Curry, Nov. 13, 1973. See also Channing's "Slavery and Confederate Survival: The Debate on Arming and Freeing the Slave," *Reviews in American History,* I (1973), 400-05.

[66] Benson, *Toward the Scientific Study of History* (1972), esp. pp. 310-40; and Winks to R. O. Curry, Dec. 27, 1973. Luraghi, "The Civil War and the Modernization of American Society: Social Structure and Industrial Revolution in the Old South Before and During the War," *Civil War History,* XVIII (1972), 230-50.

by Civil War and Reconstruction historians, then I think we may add a major new dimension to our understanding of the period.[67]

Subject to the reservations expressed by Professor Foner on these approaches, most of which I share, I wholeheartedly agree with McCrary's analysis. Let me close by saying that a critical overview of the Civil War and Reconstruction era in a brief paper was an intriguing, exasperating, exciting and impossible thing to ask anyone to do. Nevertheless, it needed to be done. I only wish that some themes that were only alluded to, mentioned in passing, or omitted altogether could have been elaborated upon. Compression has its advantages—in fact, several— which, I hope, will compensate for some of its inherent, unavoidable liabilities.

[67] McCrary to R. O. Curry, Oct. 4, 1973.

JOHN BROWN AND HIS JUDGES:
A Critique of the Historical Literature

Stephen B. Oates

AMERICANS HAVE ALWAYS FOUND IT DIFFICULT to write objectively about controversial figures in their past, and this has been especially true of John Brown. Since he died on the gallows for attempting to incite a slave insurrection in the South, those who have dealt with him—biographers, poets, novelists, essayists, and, alas, professional historians—have with rare exception been either passionately for or against the man. Either Brown was *right* or he was *wrong*. Either he was an authentic and immortal hero who sacrificed his life so that America's "poor, despised Africans" might be free, or he was a "mean, terrible, vicious man," a demented horsethief, a murderer, a psychopath. For over one hundred years, American writers—popular and scholarly alike—have engaged in such heated controversy over whether Brown was right or wrong, sane or crazy, hero or fanatic, that scarcely anyone has taken the time to try to understand him.[1]

The legend of Brown as hero was molded by a succession of worshipful biographies that appeared between 1860 and 1910. Those written by James Redpath, Franklin B. Sanborn, and Richard J. Hinton[2]—all

---

* This article is dedicated to the memory of Boyd B. Stutler, Civil War scholar and John Brown expert, whose help to me was invaluable and indispensable.

[1] There have been exceptions, of course. Mary Land's "John Brown's Ohio Environment," *Ohio State Archaeological and Historical Quarterly*, LVII (Jan. 1948), 24-47, showed how Brown was influenced by the antislavery controversies that raged in Ohio's Western Reserve and concluded that Brown was not an insane fanatic but an extreme product of that intensely antislavery region. C. Vann Woodward's "John Brown's Private War," in *The Burden of Southern History* (Baton Rouge, 1960), pp. 41-68, provided a trenchant analysis of the impact of the Harpers Ferry attack on the South, but was marred by the author's acceptance of controversial documents regarding Brown's alleged "insanity" at their face value. David M. Potter's "John Brown and the Paradox of Leadership among American Negroes," in *The South and the Sectional Conflict* (Baton Rouge, 1968), pp. 201-218, included a fair appraisal of Brown's relationship with Negro leaders like Frederick Douglass, although the essay ignored the influence of Brown's religious beliefs on the Harpers Ferry attack. Other thoughtful essays are [Floyd C. Shoemaker], "John Brown's Missouri Raid: A Tale of the Kansas-Missouri Border Retold with Some New Facts," *Missouri Historical Review*, XXVI (Oct., 1931), 78-83; and Boyd B. Stutler's "Abraham Lincoln and John Brown—A Parallel," *Civil War History*, VIII (Sept., 1962), 290-299.

[2] Redpath, *The Public Life of Capt. John Brown* (Boston, 1860); Sanborn, *Life and Letters of John Brown* (Boston, 1885); and Hinton, *John Brown and His Men, with Some Account of the Roads They Traveled to Reach Harpers Ferry* (New York, 1894).

57

of whom had been friends and associates of Brown—portrayed him as a deeply principled "Puritan soldier," "an idealist with a human intent," "a simple, brave, heroic person, incapable of anything selfish or base."[3] The legend-builders did not always agree on facts. Redpath, the propagandist of the Brown legend, asserted that the Old Hero did not commit the Pottawatomie murders, that he was somewhere else when they occurred. Sanborn, followed by Hinton, gave evidence that Brown had instigated the massacre, but argued that he was justified in doing so, inasmuch as the victims were crude, violent, proslavery "poor whites" who would likely have massacred Brown and his free-state neighbors had he not killed them first.[4] But facts aside, all three biographers, disregarding unfavorable aspects of Brown's character and career, presented him as a great man in the manner of Samson, Hercules, and Oliver Cromwell—a steadfast warrior who saved Kansas for liberty in 1856 and then gave his life in Virginia so that the slaves might be free. He was "a saint," Hinton asserted; "Our bravest martyr," said Redpath.[5] Brown was as heroic as Lincoln and as noble as Socrates, declared Sanborn, one of the Secret Six who furnished Brown with guns and money for the Virginia invasion. "What he did in Kansas for a single State, he did in Virginia for the whole nation,—nay, for the whole world."[6]

Other early biographies—those by Richard D. Webb, Hermann von Holst, Joseph Edgar Chamberlin, William E. Connelley, and W. E. Burghardt Du Bois—none of whom had been associated with Brown, but all of whom idolized what he stood for—also depicted the Old Hero in legendary terms.[7] Connelley, rebutting those writers and politicians who had attacked the Brown legend in post Civil War Kansas, argued that the Pottawatomie massacre was "the most important work of John Brown in Kansas" and that he was *still* a martyr, no matter what his detractors said.[8] The Du Bois volume, while exhibiting a cheerful disregard for factual accuracy, was a scathing indictment of slavery and an impassioned defense of Brown as a revolutionary symbol, as a man who

[3] Sanborn, *Life and Letters of John Brown*, pp. 626-628, and *Recollections of Seventy Years* (Boston, 1909), I, 82; Hinton, *John Brown and His Men*, p. 438.

[4] Redpath, *Public Life of Capt. John Brown*, pp. 115-119; Sanborn, *Life and Letters of John Brown*, pp. 247-282; Hinton, *John Brown and His Men*, pp. 61-97.

[5] Hinton, *John Brown and His Men*, p. 415; Redpath, *Public Life of Capt. John Brown*, p. 406.

[6] Sanborn, *Recollections of Seventy Years*, I, 252, and *Life and Letters of John Brown*, pp. 631-632.

[7] Webb, *The Life and Letters of Captain John Brown . . . with Some Notice of His Confederates* (London, 1861); von Holst, *John Brown* (Boston, 1889); Chamberlin, *John Brown* (Boston, 1899); Connelley, *John Brown*, (Topeka, 1900); and Du Bois, *John Brown* (Philadelphia, 1909).

[8] Connelley, *John Brown*, p. 153. For a discussion of the political feud that raged in post Civil War Kansas between Charles Robinson and the followers of James Henry Lane and the martyred Brown—a feud which prompted Connelley to write his biography—see James C. Malin, *John Brown and the Legend of Fifty-Six* (Philadelphia, 1942), pp. 359-439.

was "eternally right" in his decision to destroy an institution that was "eternally wrong."[9]

The early biographies, then, were either defenses or eulogies of Brown as the abolitionist martyr. None of them attempted to examine the whole range of Brown's personality, to account for his mistakes and faults (his egotism, his cruelty, his intolerance, his self-righteousness) as well as his courage and his uncompromising abolitionism.

The first serious effort to give a rounded portrait of Brown was Oswald Garrison Villard's now classic biography, published initially in 1910 and reissued in a second edition, without textual revision, in 1943.[10] Based on prodigious research in manuscript and printed sources and on numerous interviews with Brown's surviving relatives and friends, Villard's book was a compendium of not always well-digested facts, letters, and recollections. Yet, such a compendium is useful indeed, not only for the research scholar, but for anyone who might want to know about some of the more controversial aspects of Brown's life. Although Villard was a pacifist and a deeply committed humanitarian who sympathized with Brown, he was not afraid to quote from those who recalled how severe Brown had been with his children and his employees and how stubborn and incompetent he had been as a businessman. Still, Villard tended to apologize for the harsher sides of Brown's personality, and the interpretation of Brown that emerged from his encyclopedic work was a tempered version of the traditional view. True, Villard conceded, Brown had made mistakes in his life. True, he had instigated that "bloody crime" on Pottawatomie Creek in Kansas, a crime which his "wealth of self-sacrifice, and the nobility of his aims," could not justify.[11] But, the Pottawatomie massacre aside, Brown was still a hero doing battle with injustice, a man who possessed "straightforward unselfishness" and a willingness "to suffer for others"—traits dramatically exhibited when he made his sacrifice "for the altar of liberty" at Harpers Ferry and on the gallows at Charlestown.[12] Thus, Villard believed that the "story of John Brown will ever confront the spirit of despotism, when men are struggling to throw off the shackles of social or political or physical slavery. His own country, while admitting his mistakes without undue palliation or excuse, will forever acknowledge the divine that was in him by the side of what was human or faulty, and blind and wrong. It will cherish the memory of the prisoner of Charlestown in 1859 as at once a sacred, a solemn and an inspiring American heritage."[13]

While Villard deserves credit for the extensiveness of his research and

---

[9] Du Bois, *John Brown*, pp. 339-356.

[10] Villard, *John Brown, 1800-1859: A Biography Fifty Years After* (1st ed., Boston, 1910; revised ed., New York, 1943). My references are to the 1943 edition.

[11] *Ibid.*, p. 188.

[12] *Ibid.*, pp. 78, 425.

[13] *Ibid.*, p. 589.

for his sincere effort to be fair and honest in recounting Brown's life, his biography left several vital questions unanswered. For one thing, Villard only paid lip service to Brown's "Puritan" religion; he made no attempt to show how Brown's religious beliefs, based in large measure on the mystical New Light Calvinism of Jonathan Edwards, not only shaped his vision of himself in the world and his nonconformist brand of abolitionism, but also influenced his Harpers Ferry plans. Theologically, Brown was an orthodox nineteenth-century Calvinist who believed in foreordination, the doctrine of election, innate depravity, and in man's total dependence on a just and sovereign God. He believed, too, that once God saved "poor dependent, sinning, & self condemned mortals" like himself, then God remained a constant, all-powerful, directive force in his life.[14] Brown's notion that he was "an instrument of God" to free the slaves—a notion that lay behind his invasion of Virginia—was an outgrowth of his intense Calvinist faith. As one of Brown's recruits, George B. Gill, phrased it, Brown was certain that whatever flaws his plan of operations contained, and whatever mistakes he made, "God would be his guard and shield, rendering the most illogical movements into a grand success."[15] Surely Brown's conviction that God would take care of everything to suit His own purpose (as well as Brown's ineptitude as a strategist) accounts for many of the blunders and much of the lack of planning in the Harpers Ferry attack.

If Villard did not adequately deal with Brown's religion, he also failed to show how Brown was influenced by his environment. For example, what effect did the abolitionist movement in Ohio—and in the North at large—have in shaping Brown's own antislavery views? How much did his work on the Underground Railroad, and his association with such Negro leaders as Frederick Douglass and Henry Highland Garnet, contribute to his growing conviction that slavery could only be destroyed by violence? And when exactly did Brown's decision to fight slavery in the South become the "greatest or principal object" of his life?

Villard did address himself to the latter question, but his answer is open to dispute. He asserted that Brown was committed to the destruction of slavery from about 1846 on—in other words, all other considerations were of secondary importance—and that by 1855 he had more or less perfected a plan that called for full-scale guerrilla warfare against

[14] On this point, one could cite Brown's letters almost at random; but see especially Brown to his father, June 12, 1830, John Brown Papers, Ohio Historical Society; Brown to John Jr., Sept. 25, 1843, John Brown Letters, Illinois State Historical Library; Brown to John Jr., Aug. 26, 1853, and Brown's Notes for a Sermon (probably written in the 1830s), Boyd B. Stutler Collection, Charleston, W. Va. See also James Foreman to James Redpath, Dec. 28, 1859, Richard Hinton Papers, Kansas State Historical Society; George B. Delamater, address about John Brown given at Meadville, Pa., sometime after Brown's death, MS, Stutler Collection; statements of John Brown Jr. and Ruth Brown Thompson in Sanborn, *Life and Letters of John Brown*, pp. 91-95.

[15] Gill, Reminiscences, MS, Hinton Papers, Kansas State Historical Society.

slavery in the South. He might have put that plan into operation around 1856 had not trouble broken out in Kansas, compelling him to fight slavery there before he undertook the grand scheme. In support of his thesis, Villard relied chiefly on recollections of Brown's children and acquaintances, given long after the Civil War, and on memorandum entries in the second volume of Brown's private notebooks. Among other things, these entries contained references to Mina's guerrilla operations in Spain during the Napoleonic Wars and included a list of American cities and towns, most of them in the South, where Federal forts or arsenals were located. Villard claimed that these notes were "probably recorded early in 1855" and consequently supported the contention of some members of the Brown family that Brown planned an invasion of the South, to commence at Harpers Ferry, before he went to Kansas.[16]

In point of fact, the entries in question were made not in 1855, but in the summer of 1857—*after* Brown's experiences in the Kansas civil war.[17] The evidence seems fairly convincing that Brown did not conceive the Harpers Ferry or Virginia scheme, which involved a slave insurrection in the South, until the fall of 1856 or spring of 1857, as a result of his own private war against the "Slave Power" which began with the Pottawatomie massacre.

Not that Brown lacked ideas about opposing the South with force before that time. On the contrary, long before he went to Kansas—in 1847 or 1848—he composed an essay called "Sambos Mistakes" in which he chided Negroes for passively submitting to white oppression. He also befriended Negro militants like Henry Highland Garnet, who in 1843 had given a speech that urged the slaves to revolt. One story goes that Brown put up the money to have the speech published.[18] However that may be, Brown did exhort Negroes to kill any southerner or Federal officer who tried to enforce the Fugitive Slave Law and enlisted forty-four Negroes from Springfield, Massachusetts, into a mutual-defense organization called the "Branch of the United States League of Gileadites." The League was based on the Book of Judges, Chapter 7, which told how God had called on Gideon to deliver Israel from the Midianites and sent him, with an army of three hundred, to defeat the host in a violent, running battle.[19] Also, Brown appears to have developed by 1847 a secret project called the Subterranean Pass Way, which probably derived from his experiences with the Ohio Underground Railroad.[20]

---

[16] Villard, *John Brown*, p. 53.

[17] The Notebooks are located in the Boston Public Library. The entries in question are undated, but obviously were made in the summer of 1857 as the notes that precede and follow them were recorded at that time.

[18] Henry Highland Garnet, *A Memorial Discourse* (Philadelphia, 1865), pp. 44-52.

[19] Brown, "Words of Advice; Branch of the United States League of Gileadites," in Louis Ruchames (ed.), *A John Brown Reader* (London and New York, 1959), pp. 76-78.

[20] On Brown and the Underground Railroad, see Louis Filler (ed.), "An Interview with Charles S. S. Griffing," *Ohio Archaeological and Historical Quarterly*, LVIII

The project called for an armed guerrilla contingent, with Brown as commander, to run slaves out of the South through the Allegheny Mountains (long an escape route for fugitives). In Brown's mind, these operations would reduce the value of slave property, thereby rendering the institution so "insecure" that southerners would have to abolish it themselves. Frederick Douglass, who claimed that Brown revealed this plan to him in 1847 (and there seems no reason to dispute him), said that Brown did not intend to incite an insurrection at this time. But he was quite prepared to fight slaveowners in the mountains, because he did not believe they could "be induced to give up their slaves, until they felt a big stick about their heads." The Subterranean Pass Way scheme was a sort of hobby of Brown's (if one may call it that) from 1847 until he left for Kansas in 1855. While the scheme never got beyond the planning stage, it clearly became the basis of his Harpers Ferry project.[21]

Still, it is not accurate to assert that Brown was single-mindedly devoted to the destruction of slavery in those years between 1847 and 1855. He *was* a deeply committed abolitionist, to be sure. But he was just as deeply involved in a number of business ventures, as he tried without success to pay his debts, restore his fortunes, and provide for his large and tragedy stricken family.[22]

Villard's assertion that Brown went to Kansas in 1855 to fight for freedom, without giving a thought to settlement there, is inaccurate.[23] The evidence indicates that Brown initially planned to follow his sons to the Territory to engage in surveying and investigate business prospects there. By relocating in Kansas and later bringing out his family from their farm in upstate New York, he could do his part to settle the Territory with antislavery pioneers who would vote to make it free. But when John Jr. wrote that business opportunities were not promising in Kansas, when he described how a great war between freedom and slavery was about to break out there, beseeching his father to gather a number of guns for free-state forces, Brown altered his original intentions for going to Kansas. He solicited a number of weapons in New

(Apr., 1949), 213-218; James Harris Fairchild, *The Underground Railroad* (Cleveland, 1895), pp. 103-106.

[21] Douglass, *Life and Times* (Hartford, Conn., 1882), pp. 338-342. Douglass, an honest and intelligent man, had no vested interest in perpetuating myths about Brown in order to defend himself. On the contrary, since he refused to accompany Brown and came under some criticism for his "cowardice," he could easily have avoided any detailed discussion of his connections with Brown's plans. For this reason, I see no cause to doubt him when he claimed that Brown told him about his Subterranean Pass Way scheme in 1847. Boyd B. Stutler, who spent more than fifty years doing research on Brown and who owned one of the most valuable Brown collections in the United States, agreed with me, contending that Brown definitely had it in his mind to interfere directly with slavery in the South in 1846 or 1847. During the genesis of the Harpers Ferry raid after the Kansas civil war, Brown and some of his Negro allies made repeated references to his old Subterranean Pass Way scheme.

[22] For an elaboration of this point, see my book, *To Purge This Land with Blood: A Biography of John Brown* (New York, 1970), pp. 51-93.

[23] Villard, *John Brown*, pp. 76-78, 84-85, 93.

York, Massachusetts, and Ohio, and set out for the Territory to fight the armies of the "Slave Power," should war break out there as John Jr. had predicted.[24]

Villard's assessment of Brown's role in the Kansas troubles of 1855 and 1856 contained some errors and overstatements, but Villard was not so "blind" in his "hero-worship" of Brown as James C. Malin charged.[25] In all fairness to Villard, he dismissed as myth the contention that Brown saved Kansas for freedom. He pointed out that "no one man decided the fate of Kansas" and that much of Brown's lone-hand activities in the summer of 1856 actually impeded the free-state cause.[26]

Villard stated that once peace had been restored to Kansas, Brown turned back to his Virginia plan, which he had set aside in 1855, and traveled east to solicit guns and money for that operation as well as for any additional fighting he might have to undertake in the Territory. While Villard provided a mass of information about Brown's movements from 1857 to 1859, as he gathered supporters and recruits for his Virginia scheme, Brown the complex and messianic revolutionary figure never came alive in Villard's pages. The man was lost in a vortex of facts and block quotations. Nor did Villard offer any real insights into the personalities and motivations of the six abolitionist reformers who backed Brown—Franklin B. Sanborn, Thomas Wentworth Higginson, Gerrit Smith, Theodore Parker, George Luther Stearns, and Samuel Gridley Howe. The closest Villard came to explaining Brown's motives (beyond an implacable opposition to slavery) was the following declaration: "Something compelled him to attack slavery by force of arms, and to that impulse he yielded."[27] Given little more than that, one sets the book aside knowing a great deal of factual information, but with only scant understanding of Brown himself, of what it was that convinced him and his secret backers that only violent revolution could solve the slavery problem in their time.

Because Villard portrayed Brown as the immortal if imperfect hero (one capable of making mistakes), he was criticized both by Brown's defenders and his detractors.[28] The most scathing denunciation came from the pen of Hill Peebles Wilson, a Kansas politician who claimed that he had been an admirer of Brown until he learned "the facts," that

[24] John Jr. to Brown, May 20, 24, and 26, 1855, Ferdinand Julius Dreer Collection, Historical Society of Pennsylvania; John Brown, "A Brief History of John Brown Otherwise (old Brown, & his family: *as connected with Kansas*: by one who knows," MS, *ibid.*; John Jr. to Brown, June 22, 1855, John Brown Papers, Kansas State Historical Society; John Jr. to Brown, June 29, 1855, copy in Franklin B. Sanborn Folder, Houghton Library, Harvard University.

[25] Malin, *John Brown and the Legend of Fifty-Six*, p. 482.

[26] Villard, *John Brown*, pp. 265-266.

[27] *Ibid.*, p. 586.

[28] For example, Sanborn declared that Villard's biography "is useful for some facts which do not appear elsewhere, but is vitiated by a false estimate of Brown's character, which leads him to make foolish guesses instead of giving the facts as they were." Sanborn to Charles E. Rice, Apr. 29, 1912, Stutler Collection.

the Old Hero was not a hero at all, but a crook. After Villard published his "jargon of facts and fancies," his "fulsome panegyrics" and "extravagantly illogical attributes" about Brown, Wilson decided to tell the public "the truth." The result was his *John Brown, Soldier of Fortune: A Critique*, which was privately printed in Lawrence, Kansas, in 1913. Drawing those facts from Villard that would suit his thesis, Wilson categorized Brown as a swindler even before he went to Kansas, citing as evidence his "fraudulent and criminal" business ventures, especially in Ohio (an accusation that itself was a gross distortion of the record). Wilson asserted that Brown migrated to Kansas in hopes that some criminal opportunity would turn up, that he murdered those five men on Pottawatomie Creek to steal their horses and prevent them from testifying against him in the proslavery court, that he looted and plundered under the pretext of fighting for the free-state cause, and that ultimately he sought to pursue his nefarious activities on a larger scale by invading the South. If Brown had a tradition, said Wilson, it was not as a great hero, but as "a soldier of fortune, an adventurer. He will take his place in history as such; and will rank among adventurers as Napoleon ranks among marshals; as Captain Kidd among pirates; and as Jonathan Wild among thieves."[29]

Wilson's book is so biased and so rife with unsupported conjectures that nobody should take it seriously as history. Indeed, it is not history at all but high-decibel polemicism—the anti-Brown counterpart of the work of James Redpath. As it turned out, Mrs. Sara T. Robinson, whose late husband and one-time governor of Kansas had challenged the Brown legend as presented in the hero-worshipping biographies, had commissioned Wilson to write a book that would "reverse" Villard's favorable portrait of Brown "in Kansas and afterwards." She offered Wilson $5,000 to do the job, but died without paying up. He had to sue her heirs to get his money. Those sympathetic with Brown, of course, castigated Wilson. "The would-be historian who sells himself for such a purpose trebly prostitutes his powers," wrote Villard; "he is untrue to himself, to his state, and to our mistress, History."[30] Later, James C. Malin, who also wrote to destroy the Brown legend, claimed that Wilson had arrived at his views before Mrs. Robinson approached him.[31] If so, that still does not alter what the book is: an anti-Brown tract that will always be enjoyed, as C. B. Galbreath put it, "by the critically inclined who place a low estimate upon humanitarian endeavor and reluctantly accord unselfish motives to others."[32]

In the South, a counter-legend had grown up about John Brown, but

[29] Wilson, *John Brown, Soldier of Fortune: A Critique* (Lawrence, Kans., 1913), pp. 24, 99, 116, 217, 343, 383, 387, 395, 401, 404, 407.

[30] Kansas State Historical Society, *Publications* (Topeka, 1875-1928), XIII, 423-429; Ruchames, *A John Brown Reader*, p. 364.

[31] Malin, *John Brown and the Legend of Fifty-Six*, pp. 486-487.

[32] Galbreath, "John Brown," *Ohio Archaeological and Historical Quarterly*, XXX (July, 1921), 194.

no full-scale biography that argued the southern view existed until Robert Penn Warren, a native of Kentucky, published *John Brown, the Making of a Martyr*, in 1929. Eschewing original research in manuscript sources, Warren borrowed his facts from Sanborn and Villard in order to construct a case against Brown and his abolitionist supporters and followers. Flippant, condescending, and contemptuous of Brown throughout his volume, Warren described him as an inept and warped Yankee businessman who became a violent abolitionist fanatic. The central trait of Brown's personality, Warren suggested, was his genius at rationalizing his faults and failures, a genius glaringly evident when he posed as a saint during his trial and execution. "It was all so thin," Warren observed, "that it should not have deceived a child, but it deceived a generation." In Warren's opinion, Brown was a criminal whose only virtue was his courage (the same opinion which Edmund Ruffin, the Virginia secessionist, had expressed after Brown's execution).[33] Warren's interpretation was so partisan that even Avery Craven, who was himself sympathetic toward the southern point of view, found it "an indictment, not an unbiased biography."[34]

Thus far no professional historian had produced a book-length treatment of Brown, one based on exhaustive research and imbued with an objective and critical spirit. In 1942, James C. Malin, professor of history at the University of Kansas, published a volume that claimed to perform this laudable task, a volume that purported to make "a scientific study" of Brown by applying "to the problem in full measure the critical technique of modern historiography."[35] In reality, despite its wealth of detail and its demolition of many myths, Malin's *John Brown and the Legend of Fifty-Six* was not a scientific study but a partisan work of the anti-Brown school. Malin based the 794-page volume almost exclusively on holdings in the Kansas State Historical Society, ignoring (or using in only a limited manner) indispensable Brown materials in the private collection of Boyd B. Stutler and in a number of other libraries, repositories, and historical societies in the United States.[36] But the

---

[33] Warren, *John Brown, the Making of a Martyr* (New York, 1929), p. 414; Edmund Ruffin's Diary, Dec. 2, 1859, Stutler Collection.

[34] *Books* (Jan. 12, 1930), 17.

[35] Malin, *John Brown and the Legend of Fifty-Six*, p. 1.

[36] In his bibliographical note, Malin claimed that, in addition to materials in the Kansas State Historical Society, he used the Byron Reed Collection in the Omaha, Nebraska, Public Library and Franklin Sanborn's letters in the Atlanta University Library. Apparently he did not see fit to utilize invaluable Brown manuscripts and related materials in the Boston Public Library, Houghton Library of Harvard University, Yale University Library, the Library of Congress, the Historical Society of Pennsylvania, the Illinois State Historical Library, the Ohio Historical Society, the Henry E. Huntington Library, and the collections of Clarence S. Gee and Boyd B. Stutler. Malin did say in his preface that Stutler gave him "many courtesies in pursuit of elusive material," but Stutler wrote me on Nov. 6, 1968, that he "rendered no help to [Malin] directly. The citations are for material furnished one of his graduate students for use in her dissertation, *John Brown in American Literature*, which she fashioned to fit the Malin conception."

least scientific feature of Malin's study was its biased portrait of Brown himself. Commencing with an examination of Brown's pre-Kansas career, Malin argued that Brown was a restless and dishonest speculator. He insisted that "two or more" of Brown's many business ventures involved "crime" (Malin did not specify which ones) and that Brown's "flagrant dishonesty" in both his business and family relations made him unreliable as a character witness. Accepting only four "authentic episodes" in which Brown was connected with "the negro question," Malin concluded that Brown's views and activities did not "differ materially from those of any number of the active anti-slavery or abolitionist people of the time."[37]

Let me examine these points one at a time. First, while Malin rightly rejected the myth that all Brown had ever been interested in was overthrowing slavery by the sword, his contention that Brown was merely another abolitionist hardly did him justice. A Calvinist and a thoroughgoing nonconformist, he had refused to join any antislavery organization and argued with his abolitionist acquaintances about their religious convictions, especially those who believed in free will and the perfectibility of man. Moreover, from 1847 to 1855 Brown became increasingly belligerent, rejecting the doctrines of both the political abolitionists and the nonresistant Garrisonians and advocating a policy of violent opposition to the aggressions of the "Slave Power." Furthermore, what about Brown's friendship with Frederick Douglass and Henry Highland Garnet? And what about the Subterranean Pass Way scheme? Malin not only refused even to bring up the latter project for analysis (either to accept or reject it), but also dismissed Brown's involvement with Douglass as not "particularly important"[38]—although the Negro leader viewed Brown as one of the most forceful and extraordinary white abolitionists he had met. After visiting Brown in late 1847 and hearing the details of the Subterranean Pass Way scheme, Douglass wrote the *North Star* that he had had "a private interview" with Brown, who, "though a white gentleman, is in sympathy, a black man, and as deeply interested in our cause, as though his own soul had been pierced with the iron of slavery." Brown, for his part, could scarcely restrain his joy at finding black men like Douglass—men who "possessed the energy of head and heart to demand freedom for their whole people." The result would be—must be—"the downfall of slavery."[39] Douglass visited Brown again in 1848. And in the months that followed, his own antislavery utterances "became more and more tinged by the color of this man's strong impressions." At an abolitionist convention at Salem, Ohio,

---

[37] Malin, *John Brown and the Legend of Fifty-Six*, pp. 3-7.

[38] Malin to Philip S. Foner, Feb. 6, 1947, in Foner, *Frederick Douglass* (New York, 1964), p. 405.

[39] *North Star* (Rochester, N.Y.), Feb. 11, Nov. 17 and 24, and Dec. 8, 1848; Foner, *Douglass*, pp. 137-138; and Douglass, *Life and Times*, pp. 277-282.

Douglass repeated what Brown had told him and said he feared that only bloodshed could annihilate slavery now.[40]

Secondly, Malin's contention that Brown's business activities before he went to Kansas involved "crime" and "flagrant dishonesty" was unfairly slanted. True, Brown had a talent for overstatement and exaggeration, especially when he was excited. But he could also be scrupulously and commendably honest. It is a fact that in 1838 he took money a New England wool company had entrusted to him and used it to pay his private debts. Yet the company did not press charges, and Brown vowed —and seriously attempted—to pay the money back, until forced into bankruptcy in 1842. Moreover, when Brown opened his wool agency in Springfield in 1846, he pledged part of his commission toward paying this and other debts. While most of his business deals did end in disaster and while he was plagued with endless litigation for not meeting his obligations and settling his debts, few if any of the businessmen who took him to court accused him of crime or "flagrant dishonesty." Rather, they accused him of being negligent, careless, and inept.[41]

Malin's account of Brown in Kansas is equally one-sided—an elaboration on the theme of the restless and dishonest speculator. If Brown was an unscrupulous operator with only an ordinary interest in slavery, it followed that he could never have been genuinely concerned with the free-state cause in the Territory. Thus Malin insisted that Brown set out for Kansas, in a wagon loaded down with guns and swords, only to find a business deal! This assertion not only ignored Brown's fighting temperament, but dismissed John Jr.'s letters of June 22 and 29, 1855, which reported that business opportunities were not at all promising in Kansas. Although Malin actually quoted John Jr. to that effect, he proceeded to ignore the very quotation in asserting that Brown migrated to the Territory for purposes of business and settlement. In the letter of June 29 (which Malin either dismissed or never read), John Jr. also declared in his most impassioned prose that a great war was about to erupt between free-state and proslavery partisans in Kansas and again pleaded with his father to bring guns with him. Malin to the contrary, it would seem that Brown himself most accurately described his ultimate reason for going to the Territory. "Four of my sons had gone there to settle, and they induced me to go," he told a retinue of interrogators after Harpers Ferry. "I did not go there to settle, but because of the difficulties."[42]

In Malin's opinion, Brown became involved in the difficulties in Kansas after he arrived there, not because he hated slavery and its Missouri and Kansas defenders, or because he thought their efforts to force slav-

---

[40] Douglass, *Life and Times*, p. 282; Foner, *Douglass*, pp. 138-141.

[41] Villard, *John Brown*, pp. 29-41.

[42] Malin, *John Brown and the Legend of Fifty-Six*, pp. 14-16; John Jr. to Brown, June 29, 1855, Sanborn Folder, Houghton Library, Harvard University; Brown's "Interview" after the Harpers Ferry raid, in New York *Herald*, Oct. 21, 1859.

ery on Kansas were unjust and a sin against God, but because the struggle brought out his basic criminal nature and afforded him an opportunity to steal horses (which was Wilson's thesis). Rejecting a considerable body of evidence to the contrary, Malin argued that all the threats of murder and annihilation issued by proslavery forces had no impact on Brown, that enemy atrocities did not disturb him either, and that he instigated the Pottawatomie massacre largely for political reasons. According to Malin, Brown selected his victims on the one hand because they had been associated with Cato's proslavery court when it sat in session at Pottawatomie Creek, and on the other hand because they were going to testify against Brown at the Lykins County session of the court, to open on May 26, 1856, on a charge of treasonably resisting the proslavery territorial government. Yet Malin conceded that one problem existed in his interpretation: Brown had spared the life of James Harris, who had also been a juror on Cato's court. "If the assassination was directed at those who participated in the court, why was he permitted to go free?"[43]

Malin did not answer his own question. Nor did he address himself to other problems which his thesis contained. For one thing, since neither Brown nor any of his sons had been indicted at the Pottawatomie session of Cato's court, why should Brown have been preoccupied with the personnel of the court? Why, indeed, did Brown allow Harris, as well as other members of the proslavery court who resided on the creek, to live? It is most likely that he did so because they had not actively aided Missouri intruders or threatened their free-state neighbors, as the victims evidently had done.[44] Furthermore, Malin gave no evidence that Brown knew he was going to be indicted for treason by the court when it opened in Lykins County (I could find no such evidence either). And even if Brown had known, would he have cared? Although the Cato court had indicted several free-state men for crimes and misdemeanors,

[43] Malin, *John Brown and the Legend of Fifty-Six*, pp. 537-592, 754-755. The proslavery Westport (Missouri) *Border Times*, in its issue of May 27, 1856, argued that the only reason for the murders was to prevent the victims from testifying against free-state troublemakers at the Lykins County session of the court. Malin accepted and elaborated on this story as one of the reasons why Brown committed the massacre.

[44] Brown and his self-styled "Northern Army" asked both Harris and another man at Harris' cabin whether they had ever assisted proslavery intruders, participated in "the last troubles at Lawrence," or ever harmed or intended harm to the free-state party. They obviously answered no on all counts because Brown spared them both. Surely Brown used the same criteria in determining the fate of his actual victims. (Harris' affidavit, June 6, 1856, "Howard Report," *U.S. House Committee Reports* [3 vols., 34 Cong., 1 sess., 1855-1856], Vol. II, no. 200, p. 1179.) Numerous free-state settlers asserted shortly after the massacre that the victims, all of them connected with the proslavery court and the proslavery party, had thrown out threats and insults to their free-state neighbors. There is no contemporary evidence, however, that the victims had actually done violence to their free-state opponents, as Villard asserted. See, for example, James Hanway's Memorandum Book, entry about June 1, 1856, Hanway Papers, Kansas State Historical Society; and Samuel Adair to "Dear Bro. & Sis. Hand & Other Friends," late May or early June, 1856, Oswald Garrison Villard Collection, Columbia University Library.

no attempt had been made to arrest them. And if it was feared that arrests might be made this time, why did not John Jr. and some of the others who had resisted the laws (and who were subsequently indicted by the court on treason charges) accompany Brown on the massacre? Because of these unanswered questions, the political assassination theory would hardly seem a plausible explanation of the massacre. While the exact motives which prompted Brown to kill those men may never be known, I am inclined to accept the retaliatory blow thesis—that Brown instigated the massacre both to avenge proslavery atrocities (the murder of six free-state men, the sacking of Lawrence) and to create "a restraining fear." He wished to show "by actual work" that he was one free-state partisan who was not afraid to fight back. The retaliatory blow thesis seems to fit the logic of events and Brown's own behavior during the sack of Lawrence better than the other explanations given for the Pottawatomie killings.[45]

Perhaps bothered by his own interpretation, Malin wrote elsewhere in his volume that Brown may also have had some devious psychological purpose for perpetrating the murders. Since John Jr. (who was commander of the Pottawatomie column which marched to the defense of Lawrence) had overruled Brown "on all points relative to the expedition," the massacre may have been in part "the explosive self-assertion of a frustrated old man . . . a means by which he might enjoy untrammelled authority and restore his confidence in himself."[46]

Malin accepted Wilson's thesis that, in the civil war of 1856, Brown used the free-state cause as a cloak to steal the horses and property of "innocent settlers." In truth, Brown did steal horses from proslavery people (proslavery partisans also stole horses from free-state people). Yet plundering and horsestealing (as well as distortion and lies, secrecy and terrorization) were perfectly justifiable in Brown's mind, because he believed that he was waging a holy war against obstinately wicked men. His letters contained telling references to God, "who has not given us over to the will of our enemies but has moreover delivered them into our hands" and who "will we humbly trust still keep & deliver us."[47] Anyway, "a state of war existed," as one of Brown's recruits asserted, "and it was quite proper to dispoil the enemy." Yet there is no evidence

[45] Among the other explanations are: (1) that free-state leaders conceived the massacre and Brown merely executed it; (2) that Brown had reason to kill his victims because they had actually done violence to free-state settlers; (3) that he learned they were part of a conspiracy to exterminate their free-state neighbors and that Brown killed them to prevent them from doing so. For lack of convincing corroborative evidence, I have rejected these explanations. For an account which incorporates the retaliatory-blow thesis, see my book, *To Purge This Land with Blood*, pp. 112-137.

[46] Malin, *John Brown and the Legend of Fifty-Six*, p. 563.

[47] Brown to his wife and children, June 24 and 26, and July 4 and 5, 1856, John Brown Letters, Illinois State Historical Society; Brown to Jason, Aug. 11, 1856, John Brown Letters, Kansas Collection, University of Kansas; Brown to his wife and children, Sept. 7, 1856, Brown Papers, Kansas State Historical Society.

that he kept the money made from the sale of stolen horses for his own personal gain. On the contrary, he used the money and stolen supplies "for the continuation of the struggle."[48]

As for Brown's importance in the Kansas civil war, Malin argued that an analysis of contemporary sources—especially proslavery newspapers —suggested that Brown did little in either "making or marring Kansas history." He was never a major factor; his exploits were eruptions of disorder that had no relationship with either radical or conservative free-state strategy. Thus, destroying Brown as no other writer had ever done, Malin described him as "no more outstanding as a villain than as a hero."[49] Malin is, of course, entitled to his opinion. But it would be fairer to say that Brown was simply not an organization man; a nonconformist all his adult life, he refused to take orders from conservative, "broken-down" politicians like Charles Robinson who, in Brown's judgment, were afraid to fight. The old man elected to wage his own private war—in his own way—against the proslavery enemy. And he *did* fight —at Black Jack, at Sugar Creek, and at Osawatomie. Consequently, he *was* in Kansas history and cannot be dismissed (as Malin himself had to concede). Moreover, Brown's experiences in Bleeding Kansas convinced him that he should expand his war against the South, that God, who remained an *"all wise & all powerful"* directive force in Brown's life, wished him to do so.[50] When fighting in Kansas seemed at an end in 1857, he conceived his Virginia plan to attack slavery directly. And in this respect the significance of Brown in Kansas takes on an added dimension of importance which has been too little emphasized.

Was Brown crazy? Malin suggested that he was, using as evidence a letter written in 1859 by C. G. Allen, a Christian minister, who recalled that he had heard several persons say that they thought Old Brown was "insane" after the battle of Osawatomie. Malin pronounced this "a damaging piece of evidence," although in his analysis of the Pottawatomie massacre and the growth of the Brown legend, he repeatedly attacked pro-Brown writers for using hearsay evidence.[51]

As for Brown's career after the Kansas civil war, Malin agreed that Brown turned to his Harpers Ferry plan less to free the slaves than to loot and plunder on a grand scale in the South itself. While Brown

48 Luke F. Parsons to J. H. Beach, Apr. 21, 1913, John Brown Papers, Kansas State Historical Society; August Bondi, "With John Brown in Kansas," Kansas State Historical Society, *Publications*, VIII, 284. See also John Brown's Covenant and By-Laws of his company of "Kansas Regulators," Notebook, II, MS, Boston Public Library.

49 Malin, *John Brown and the Legend of Fifty-Six*, pp. 245, 487.

50 Again, one could cite Brown's letters of 1857, 1858, and 1859 almost at random. But see especially Brown to John Jr., Apr. 15, 1857, and Brown to Henry Stearns, July 15, 1857, Stutler Collection; Brown to his wife and children, Feb. 20, 1858, and Brown to Sanborn, Feb. 24, 1858, John Brown Jr. Papers, Ohio Historical Society; and Brown to Higginson, May 14, 1858, Higginson Papers, Boston Public Library.

51 Malin, *John Brown and the Legend of Fifty-Six*, p. 298.

failed in this enterprise, he nevertheless "possessed a capacity for self-justification for his failures which amounted almost to genius [Warren's thesis], and on his final rôle he staked his claims to immortality and worked himself to a state of religious immolation."[52] As far as I can discover, this was the only time Malin discussed Brown and religion in his entire study, although a belief in an implacable and sovereign God is evident in most of the letters Brown wrote from about 1830 until he was hanged in 1859.

Thus far I have concentrated on Malin's conception of Brown and have said little about the merits of his work. Malin reappraised Brown's role in both the Wakarusa War and in the last defense of Lawrence in September, 1856, pointing out that Villard overstated Brown's importance in those events. Malin also gave a valuable account of the organization of the proslavery court system and of the activities of the Hoogland Commission in the summer of 1856. In addition, he demonstrated that the struggle between proslavery and free-state men was not always over slavery, but sometimes involved conflicting land claims. Malin provided a helpful analysis of free-state and proslavery newspapers and included an assessment of the growth of John Brown historiography from Redpath to Robert Penn Warren, showing how some of the principals in the Brown controversy—among them, James Hanway, Charles Robinson, and Franklin Sanborn—changed positions regarding the Pottawatomie massacre. Yet *John Brown and the Legend of Fifty-Six* was essentially a biased and one-sided study of Brown the man. And this was especially unfortunate in view of the large number of historians who accepted Malin's interpretation as a "scientific" one.[53]

If Malin's conception of Brown found wide acceptance among historians, so did the case study of Brown which Allan Nevins included in Volume II of *The Emergence of Lincoln*.[54] Indeed, the views of Malin and Nevins in large part became the conventional wisdom about Brown in the historical profession. Although Nevins's study contained brilliant insights into the Harpers Ferry attack and revealed more of the contradictions and complexities of Brown's personality than any of the other works discussed thus far, the account was marred by a highly questionable approach. For Nevins insisted on psychoanalyzing Brown largely on the basis of partisan testimony given nearly a century before. In diagnosing Brown's "mental disease," his "psychogenic malady," Nevins maintained that Brown, partly from his inheritance and partly from a lifetime of sickness and hardship, was suffering from "reasoning insan-

---

[52] *Ibid.*, p. 286.

[53] Wrote David M. Potter: "James C. Malin . . . has applied the rigorous pruning hook of historical method to the luxuriant growth of unsupported assertion about John Brown in Kansas. The residue of fact which remains presents such startling contrasts to the legend that Malin's study has value, apart from the Kansas question, as a case study in historical method." Potter, *South and the Sectional Conflict*, p. 140.

[54] Nevins, *Emergence of Lincoln* (New York and London, 1950), II, 5-27, 70-112.

ity" or "ambitious paranoia," a mental disease characterized by "systematized delusions."[55] It is not without significance that of all the extremists (southern racists and fire-eaters included) described in *The Emergence of Lincoln*, Brown was the only one Nevins psychoanalyzed. To be sure, his diagnosis only reinforced what Brown's detractors had said all along—the man was crazy. And because he was crazy, it was not necessary to understand him in the context of the problems and paradoxes of American society which helped bring him to Harpers Ferry. Once again, this "stone in the historians' shoe," as Truman Nelson phrased it, could be conveniently dismissed as a madman.[56]

I do not suggest, of course, that the historian has nothing to learn from psychology and what it has discovered about human behavior. As Paul Murray Kendall said, "Psychology and psychoanalysis have thrust fingers of light into the cave of the human mind, have deepened our sense of the complexities, the arcane tides, of personality, have enabled us to penetrate some of the dark corners of motive and desire, to detect patterns of action, and sense the symbolic value of word and gesture."[57] It is one thing to learn from what psychology has taught us about human beings. It is quite another for the historian to assume the role of the psychiatrist, as Nevins did with Brown, and to persist in diagnosing the "mental disease" of some long-dead historical figure whose hidden anxieties and inner conflicts cannot be probed in psychiatric sessions. One may doubt whether many responsible psychiatrists today would want to analyze the troubles of their patients strictly on the basis of their letters and what others (friends and enemies alike) have written about them. Furthermore, once the historian poses as psychiatrist, he intrudes upon his craft all the controversies and disagreements of what is still an imprecise and incipient science. The historian who does that is likely to confuse the very issues he seeks to clarify and understand.

If one can question the validity of Nevins's clinical approach, one can also criticize much of the evidence used to support it. He not only re-

---

[55] *Ibid.*, 9, 11. Everybody makes mistakes, of course, but there seems to be an unusually large number of them in Nevins's account of Brown. Among them: Brown's business associates did not "rue" their partnerships with him. Brown's mother did not die insane. The League of Gileadites was formed in 1851, not 1850. Brown did not lose his reputation for probity during his business disasters of 1837-1841 (Heman Oviatt, Seth Thompson, and Simon Perkins all formed partnerships with him afterwards). Brown did not relocate in North Elba, N.Y., and then see his sons off to Kansas. He saw them off before he moved east. Brown was not so much a "cranky skeptic" about Christ and the New Testament as he was a Calvinist who rooted his theology in the Old. One may not "question the sanity of a nearly penniless man with a large family who devotes a month" to writing a letter of exhortation to John Jr. regarding his religious views. Brown wrote some of the letter, then waited a month before he came back to finish it. Equally wrong is the assertion that Brown, in the letters he wrote in 1859, "makes but one reference to Christ, and none to Christian mercy." In fact, Brown made at least seven major references to Jesus in his prison letters, and exhorted his children both to hate slavery and to strive to do good and help the poor.

[56] Nelson, "John Brown Revisited," *The Nation* (Aug. 31, 1957), 88.

[57] Kendall, *The Art of Biography* (New York, 1965), p. 121.

ferred to Brown's "deluded," "irrational" behavior during the genesis and execution of his raid and ensuing trial, but also placed heavy reliance on nineteen affidavits that were given by Brown's friends and relatives shortly after he was sentenced to hang. These documents claimed that "insanity" ran in the maternal side of the family and that Brown himself suffered from mental disorders. Using these documents as his evidence, Nevins asserted that Brown inherited part of his mental aberrations from his mother, Ruth Mills Brown, who, "like his maternal grandmother, died insane."[58] Not only does this statement ignore the whole question as to whether or not mental aberrations can be inherited, it is also inaccurate. There is no evidence that Brown's mother was ever "insane." None of the affidavits claimed that she had been "insane" or peculiar in any way.[59] Thus, if one insists on arguing that Brown labored from "hereditary insanity," one must rest one's case on the assumption that his disorders came from his grandmother. And there is no evidence at all as to what her problem was. True, the affidavits claimed that she was "insane," but that is of little help to us: the word "insanity" is a vague, emotion-changed, and clinically meaningless term. Even in a historical context (as C. Vann Woodward has reminded us), the term is misleading, ambiguous, and relative—it has meant different things to different peoples in the past, and what seems "insane" in one period may seem perfectly "sane" at other times.[60] Even in nineteenth-century parlance, "insanity" was a catch-all term used to describe a wide range of odd or unacceptable behavior. Therefore, when the affiants speak of the "insanity" of Brown's grandmother, we do not know what sort of disorder they were describing. Maybe she was simply senile.

The affiants also claimed that a number of Brown's uncles, aunts, and cousins on his mother's side were "insane," that his only sister and his brother Salmon were "insane" or "said to be insane," that his first wife Dianthe and two of their sons (John Jr. and Frederick) had exhibited symptoms, and that Brown, too, was mentally disturbed, although opinions differed as to the nature and source of his affliction. Historians must beware of using these claims as clinical evidence. As Louis Ruchames has pointed out, the affidavits contained a great deal of information based not on direct knowledge of the cases they described, but on hearsay (as Sylvester Thompson admitted).[61] In the case of Brown's immediate family, there is no evidence that Salmon Brown, who was

[58] Nevins, *Emergence of Lincoln*, II, 5, 9, 11, 91.

[59] The affidavits are located in the John Brown Papers, Library of Congress. I examined these documents as painstakingly as I could, but found no references in them to any "insanity" on the part of Brown's mother.

[60] C. Vann Woodward, "John Brown's Private War," in *Burden of Southern History*, p. 46. Woodward warns us to be careful in approaching the insanity question, because it can blind us to the meaning of Harpers Ferry and confuse the whole issue. Then he procedes to confuse the issue by accepting those controversial affidavits at their face value.

[61] Ruchames, *A John Brown Reader*, pp. 30n-31n.

the editor of the New Orleans *Bee*, was "insane." As for Brown's sons (John Jr. and Frederick), if one accepts the assumption that mental disorders can be hereditary, then one must face the argument that both sons inherited their difficulties from Dianthe, not Brown.[62] Actually a much more plausible explanation is that John Jr.'s depression and melancholia resulted from his experiences in Kansas: the haggling with his father as to what they should do during the Lawrence crisis, the tension and lack of sleep, the humiliation he had suffered when his political friends turned against him after the Pottawatomie massacre, and the cruel treatment he received at the hands of U.S. troops following his capture. And what of Frederick? If we may believe Samuel Adair, Brown's preacher brother-in-law, Frederick was suffering from what doctors at that time diagnosed as "an accumulation of blood on the brain" that caused "blinding headaches" and left him temporarily incoherent and "flighty."[63] He could have had a brain tumor. Or perhaps his trouble was epilepsy.

Finally—and this is a crucial point—the affidavits were intended first and foremost to save Brown's life, by convincing Governor Henry A. Wise and the state of Virginia that Brown was "insane," that he was not responsible for his acts, and that he should be placed in an asylum. The documents were not objective clinical evidence gathered by doctors who wanted to establish as clearly as possible what Brown's mental "disorders" were. When the affiants asserted that Brown was "insane," they were giving their opinions for a partisan objective. Although many of them doubtlessly believed that their opinions were true, they were still opinions. Except for Dr. Jonathan Metcalf of Hudson, Ohio, none of the affiants was educated in medical matters, and none of them was a psychologist.

All this is not to go to the other extreme and argue that Brown was a "normal," "sane," "well-adjusted" individual. These terms are meaningless, too. That Brown was a revolutionary who believed himself called by God to a special destiny, that he had an excitable temperament and could get carried away with one idea, that he was inept, extremely egotistical, hard on his sons, afflicted with chronic attacks of the ague, worn down from a lifetime of hardship, and enraged enough at his "slave-cursed" country to contemplate destroying it, that he could have five men he regarded as his enemies assassinated in cold blood (after proslavery forces had killed six free-state men in cold blood), and that he wanted to become either an American Spartacus at the head of a slave army or a martyred soldier who was the first to die in a sectional war over slavery—all this is true. Yet Brown could also be kind and

---

[62] When the subject of Dianthe's emotional troubles came up during the trial, Brown did not deny that she had had problems. Relatives and friends, who were not connected with the affidavits and the move to save Brown from the gallows, recalled that she had suffered. But of course we do not know specifically what her affliction was.

[63] Adair, "Life of Frederick Brown," MS, Kansas Collection, University of Kansas.

gentle—extremely gentle. He could rock a baby lamb in his arms. He could stay up several nights caring for a sick child, or his ailing father, or his afflicted first wife. He could hold children on both knees and sing them the sad, melancholy refrains of Isaac Watts's old hymn, "Blow ye the trumpet, blow."[64] He could stand at the graves of four of his children who had died of dysentery, weeping and praising God in an ecstasy of despair.[65] He could teach his children to fear God and keep the Commandments—and exhibit the most excruciating anxiety when they began questioning the value of religion.[66] He could treat Negroes as fellow human beings, allowing them to eat at his table with his family and addressing his black workers as "Mr."—a significant trait in view of the anti-Negro prejudice that prevailed among a majority of northerners and almost all southerners in his time.[67] He could offer to take a Negro child into his home and educate him. He could dream for years of establishing a Negro school, and he could move his family to North Elba, New York, to help a Negro community there.[68] He could deplore racial discrimination in Ohio, especially in the churches.[69] And he could feel an almost paralyzing bitterness toward slavery itself and all the people in the United States who sought to preserve and protect it.[70] Thus, to label Brown as an "insane" man—even a reasoning "insane" man—is to disregard or minimize the more favorable traits of his personality, especially his sympathy for the suffering of the black man in the United States. And it is to ignore the piercing insight he had into what his raid

[64] Ruth Brown Thompson's statement in Sanborn, *Life and Letters of John Brown*, pp. 33-40, 93-95; Salmon Brown, "My Father, John Brown," *Outlook*, CIII (Jan. 25, 1913), 212-214; Annie Brown Adams's statement in Villard, *John Brown*, p. 387; Brown to John Jr., June 26, 1854, John Brown Jr. Papers, Ohio Historical Society.

[65] Brown to John Jr., Sept. 25, 1843, John Brown Letters, Illinois State Historical Library.

[66] Brown to Ruth and Henry Thompson, Jan. 23, 1852, John Brown Letters, Chicago Historical Society; Brown to John Jr., Aug. 6, 1852, in Villard, *John Brown*, p. 70; Brown to Ruth and Henry Thompson, Aug. 10, 1852, John Brown Papers, Huntington Library; Brown to John Jr., Aug. 26, 1853, Stutler Collection.

[67] Samuel Shapiro, *Richard Henry Dana, Jr., 1815-1882* (East Lansing, Mich., 1961), p. 34; Dana, "How We Met John Brown," *Atlantic Monthly*, XXVIII (July, 1871), 6-7; Brown to his father, Jan. 10, 1849, John Brown Papers, Kansas State Historical Society.

[68] Brown to his brother Frederick, Nov. 21, 1834, in Sanborn, *Life and Letters of John Brown*, pp. 40-41; Brown to John Jr., Apr. 24, 1848, John Brown Jr. Papers, Ohio Historical Society; Brown to his father, Jan. 10, 1849, John Brown Papers, Kansas State Historical Society; Ruth's statement in Sanborn, *Life and Letters of John Brown*, p. 101.

[69] Cincinnati *Philanthropist*, Jan. 20, 1837; Milton Lusk's statement in Sanborn, *Life and Letters of John Brown*, p. 53; Land, "John Brown's Ohio Environment," 30-32; statements of John Jr. and Ruth Brown Thompson in Sanborn, *Life and Letters of John Brown*, pp. 37, 52-53; Brown to Ruth and Henry Thompson, June 30, 1853, and Jan. 25, 1854, in *ibid.*, pp. 109-111, 155.

[70] See, for example, Brown's letter of Jan. 9, 1854, in *Frederick Douglass' Paper* (Rochester, N.Y.), Jan. 27, 1854; the Preamble to Brown's Provisional Constitution, ratified at the Chatham Convention in May, 1858, in Ruchames, *A John Brown Reader*, p. 111; and W. A. Phillips, "Three Interviews with Old John Brown," *Atlantic Monthly*, XLIV (Dec., 1879), 738-744.

—whether it succeeded or whether it failed—might do to sectional tensions that already existed. Nor can John Brown be removed from the context of the violent, irrational, and paradoxical times in which he lived. A man of "powerful religious convictions" who believed to his bones that slavery was a sin against God, he was profoundly distressed that a nation which claimed to be both Christian and Free should condone, protect, and perpetuate that "sum of villanies."[71] It was not only his angry, messianic mind, but the racist, slave society in which he lived—one that professed "under God" to provide liberty and justice for all—that helped bring John Brown to Harpers Ferry.

[71] *Ibid.* One could cite any number of Brown's letters on this point, especially those written during and after the Kansas civil war. In addition, many of the affiants who testified to Brown's "insanity" conceded that he was a man "of powerful religious convictions."

PART II:

POLITICS AT
THE GRASS ROOTS:
Elections and Voters

THE NORTHERN DEMOCRATIC PARTY AND THE CONGRESSIONAL ELECTIONS OF 1858

David E. Meerse

WHATEVER THEIR DISAGREEMENTS ON OTHER POINTS, historians of the antebellum decade have displayed a remarkable unanimity in their analyses of the northern congressional elections of 1858. In his Pulitzer-prize winning *Disruption of American Democracy*, Roy F. Nichols calls it "truly the most significant congressional election in the history of the Democratic party" and, pointing to the net loss of eighteen of their forty-nine congressional seats, terms the result a "Democratic debacle." Don E. Fehrenbacher asserts that the elections were "a Democratic disaster in the free states and especially in Pennsylvania," which latter state he declares underwent "a political revolution." Allan Nevins, in his monumental *The Emergence of Lincoln*, proclaims the elections a "slaughter heavy enough to choke Scamander" for the Democrats.[1]

Although these historians disagree to some extent about the role of peripheral issues like the homestead and the tariff in producing this result, they are in basic agreement concerning what Nevins calls the "central impulse" of the election: northern condemnation of the pro-slave Lecompton constitution for Kansas and the English bill. This latter measure resubmitted the Lecompton constitution to the people of Kansas with a proviso that should they reject admission under that constitution they could not again seek statehood until they had population sufficient to entitle them to one representative in the lower house of Congress. Support for the primacy of Administration Kansas policy as a causal factor in the election outcome is based upon the following considerations: (1) the re-election of Democratic congressional opponents of the English bill, such as "the President's arch enemy" John B. Haskin of New York, who, according to Nevins, "won a smashing victory." (2) Repudiation of that part of the English bill which Nevins calls the "population test." Repudiation took a variety of forms, but generally consisted of a Democratic candidate's pledge to vote for the admission of Kansas under a new constitution regardless of the number of inhabi-

---

[1] Roy F. Nichols, *The Disruption of American Democracy* (New York, 1967), p. 223. Don E. Fehrenbacher, comment on "Why the Republican Party Came to Power" in George H. Knowles (ed.), *The Crisis of the Union, 1860-1861* (Baton Rouge, 1965), p. 28. Allan Nevins, *The Emergence of Lincoln* (New York, 1950), I, 402. For other examples, see Philip Klein, *President James Buchanan: A Biography* (University Park, 1962), pp. 328-331, and Damon Wells, *Stephen Douglas: The Last Years 1857-1861* (Austin, 1971), pp. 132-133, 137.

tants. Nevins holds it "significant that nearly all Northern Congressmen who supported the [English] bill . . . had run pell-mell for cover
as soon as they faced the voters," and asserts that "almost every . . .
Democratic candidate in Indiana, Ohio, Pennsylvania and New York"
repudiated the test. (3) The failure of Administration supporters to
gain renomination. Nevins points to the "two . . . Lecompton Representatives" from Pennsylvania who failed of renomination, while Nichols
singles out Ohio's William Lawrence to epitomize those who "avoided
defeat only by not running." (4) Finally, sizeable accretions to Republican ranks of voters determined to rebuke Democratic policies at the
polls. Fehrenbacher points to massive voter shifts in Pennsylvania while
Nichols declares that the Democracy there was "engulfed." Nevins
speaks of "a passionate revolt of the voters" against J. Glancy Jones of
Pennsylvania and a "Republican upsurge" in Ohio. He finds that the
Republicans "swept Maine and Vermont," and that that party had a
"decisive plurality" in New York. "Not only did Buchanan's policies fail
to command a majority of the [Northern] electorate," concludes Douglas' biographer George F. Milton, "but the Democratic rank and file had
no heart in their defense." Any attempt to re-examine the impact of
the congressional elections of 1858 on the Northern Democratic party
must deal with these four criteria.[2]

A re-evaluation of voter performance in the election could well begin with a division of the northern constituencies into "metropolitan"
and "rural," on the assumption that both the political structures and
the interests of the two types of constituencies create different voter responses.[3] Also, such re-evaluation must take into consideration the factor of voter apathy. Today it is generally accepted that voting declines
in the off-year congressional elections following a presidential contest.
In discussing the elections of 1858, however, historians have tended to
assume that the opposite occurred: a significant increase in Republican votes, accompanied by large declines in the Democratic poll.
Neither assumption is universally valid for the election of 1858, as Table
I shows.

<hr />

[2] Nevins, *Emergence*, I, 400-403. Nichols, *Disruption*, pp. 223-225. Fehrenbacher, *Crisis*, pp. 28-29. George Fort Milton, *The Eve of Conflict: Stephen A.
Douglas and the Needless War* (Boston, 1934), p. 352.

[3] The term "metropolitan" designates those congressional districts of New York
City, Brooklyn, Philadelphia, Pittsburgh, and Cincinnati, wherein the district
boundaries comprise only a part of a county. The term "rural" applies to those
congressional districts wherein the basic division of the district is the county. This
produces some anomalies: Chicago, Cleveland, and Buffalo are "rural" although
not greatly different in size from Cincinnati, which is "metropolitan." But the political organizations of the "metropolitan" areas took positions which affected and
were affected by the conditions of more than a single congressional district, while
the organizations of the "rural" districts affected only a single congressman. It is
my opinion also that the organizations in the metropolitan areas were approaching
those conditions usually described as a "machine" while those of such "rural" districts as Chicago, Buffalo, and Cleveland were not. My thinking on these divisions
owes much to Roy F. Nichols' discussion of "metropolitanism" in his *Disruption
of American Democracy*, pp. 37-39.

TABLE I[4]

Mean drop-off in votes for congressional candidates, rural constituencies,
1856 to 1858.

State	Republican Drop-off (%)	Democratic Drop-off (%)
Maine	12.09	− 1.69
Vermont	13.88	− 8.42
Massachusetts	25.65	12.54
New York	− 6.96	−25.43
Pennsylvania	1.00	27.66
New Jersey	−22.82	12.16
Michigan	8.47	− 3.68
Ohio	− 1.42	− .75
Indiana	− 1.86	14.53
Illinois	− 5.41	−15.35
Wisconsin	2.94	− 4.15
Iowa	−23.39	−38.74
Mean Northern Drop-off	2.17	−31.33

These figures serve to show that while apathy may have been a factor affecting party fortunes in some northern states, most markedly among the Pennsylvania Democracy, it seems to have been more prevalent in Republican than in Democratic ranks. These figures also show that only New Jersey and Indiana voters acted as historians have assumed the entire North performed, and certainly not to the extreme degree which historians have implied. Most importantly, as the table indicates, the Democracy in 1858 improved its position from 1856, in terms of votes cast, in the non-metropolitan areas of eight of the twelve

[4] The county voting returns are published in The [New York] Tribune Almanac and Political Register for 1857 (New York, nd), pp. 44-64, and for 1859 (New York, nd), pp. 44-63. The concept of "drop off" as a measure of voter participation is developed in Walter Dean Burnham, "The Changing Shape of the American Political Universe," American Political Science Review, LIX (Mar., 1965), 7-28, reprinted in Robert P. Swierenga (ed.), Quantification in American History (New York, 1970), pp. 196-197. The drop-off is the reciprocal "of the percentage of the presidential-year total vote [in this case, the vote cast for congressional candidates in 1856] which is cast in the immediately-following off-year election [in this case, the congressional elections of 1858.]" As Burnham notes, a negative drop-off indicates that the total vote in the off-year election exceeds that cast in the immediately preceding presidential year. Comparing the presidential years 1848-1872 with the off-year periods 1850-1874, Burnham calculates a mean national drop-off of 7% which indicates that both parties performed quite well in 1858, with the Democratic performance markedly better than the Republican. This is reinforced by Burnham's findings for Ohio for the period 1857-1879 of a drop-off of 9.7%, and for New York for the period 1834-1858 of 3.3% (although he specifically excludes from this computation the elections from 1854 to 1858 because of the presence of the Native American party.) It should be pointed out that certain statistical difficulties arise from comparing a single election with the mean of a series of elections, from comparing a sectional mean with a national mean, as well as in separating the party performances and then comparing them with a series based on the combined performance of both parties. Nevertheless, the comparison is here made to show the relation of the election under study with a norm, without attempting to state categorically the degree of differentiation from the norm.

TABLE II[5]

Party Performance by Counties, Rural Constituencies, 1856-1858

| | Counties | | Gross Repub. Change | Gross Dem. Change | Mean Repub. Change | Mean Dem. Change | Majority Party in County | | | |
	No.	%					Republican 1856	1858	Democratic 1856	1858
Both Parties Increased, 1856-1858.	191	32.4	+58,792	+45,182	+45.67%	+55.06%	114[a]	123	76	68
Both Parties Decreased, 1856-1858.	185	31.4	−50,703	−46,230	−14.34%	−13.91%	105	110	80	75
Repub. Increase, Dem. Decrease, 1856-1858.	90	15.2	+27,441	−31,593	+26.70%	−15.19%	24	63	66	27
Repub. Decrease, Dem. Increase, 1856-1858.	123	21.0	−43,116	+39,880	−16.08%	+29.54%	97[b]	80	25	43
Total	589		− 7,586	+ 7,239			340	376	247	213

[a] Printed returns show identical Repub. & Dem. votes, Guthrie county, Iowa, 1856

[b] Printed returns show identical Repub. & Dem. votes, Sandusky county, Ohio, 1856

[5] *Tribune Almanac, 1857*, pp. 44-64 and *Tribune Almanac, 1859*, pp. 44-63. Excluded are the following counties which were created between 1856 and 1858: Union, New Jersey; Newaygo, Alpena, Bay, Cheboygan, Chippewa, Emmet, Iosco, Mackinac, Manistee, Manitou, Marquette, and Ontonagon, Michigan; Chippewa, Douglas, Dunn, LaPointe, Pierce, Polk, Door, Kewaunee, and Oconto, Wisconsin; Calhoun, Carroll, Cherokee, Clay, Dickinson, Hamilton, Hancock, Humbolt, Ida, Plymouth, Winnebago, and Worth, Iowa. In analyzing the votes, the following procedures were utilized: (1) in districts where an incumbent Democrat with Republican backing ran as the only candidate against a Democrat, the votes for the incumbent Democrat were counted as Republican. (2) In districts where both a

TABLE III[6]

Party Performance by Congressional Districts, Maine and Massachusetts, 1856-1858

	District No.	District %	Gross Repub. Change	Gross Dem. Change	Mean Repub. Change	Mean Dem. Change	Majority Party in District Republican 1856	1858	Democratic 1856	1858
Both Parties Increased, 1856-1858.	1	5.88	+ 808	+ 378	+11.84%	+ 8.34%	1	1	0	0
Both Parties Decreased, 1856-1858.	12	70.58	−12,366	− 6,628	−27.91%	−12.76%	12	12	0	0
Repub. Increase, Dem. Decrease, 1856-1858.	0	0	......	......	......	......	..	..	..	..
Repub. Decrease, Dem. Increase, 1856-1858.	4	23.54	− 3,501	+ 1,457	− 7.89%	+ 4.26%	4	4	0	0
Total	17		−15,059	− 4,793			17	17	0	0

Lecompton and an anti-Lecompton Democrat (to use contemporary, if somewhat misleading, appelations) appeared against a Republican candidate, the votes of the two Democrats were combined to get the Democratic totals. This latter procedure was deviated from only in the case of the third congressional district in Indiana, where the votes for the anti-Lecompton Democrat were not given by counties; hence, only the votes for the Lecompton Democrat were used. Combining the two wings of the Democracy seems most questionable in Illinois, where the antagonism was almost greater between the two wings than between Democrat and Republican. However, excluding the Lecompton or anti-Douglas Democratic votes would have changed the county patterns in only six counties. Excluding the anti-Douglas votes in Illinois (all of which were Democratic) would, of course, have reduced the overall Democratic vote totals.

[6] Published voting returns by counties are not available for Maine and Massachu-

states voting in 1858, while the Republicans improved their position in only six states.

The reversal of traditional assumptions of northern voter behavior is borne out by an examination of the parties' performances at the county level. The county was the basic political unit in the mid-nineteenth century; more importantly, it was the key unit in the partisan political structure.[7] If the traditional analyses of the 1858 elections were correct, it would be anticipated that Republican votes would increase while Democratic votes would decline, most noticeably in those congressional districts represented by "Lecompton Representatives." However, as Tables II and III show, this did not occur.

In terms of the vote cast in 1856, these tables show that where both parties increased their votes, Democratic increases were greater than their opponents (except in Maine and Massachusetts). Similarly, where both parties' votes declined, Democratic losses were slightly less than Republican. And, in those counties where the two parties diverged, Democratic gains outpaced Republican gains, while Democratic losses were smaller than those of their opponents. In sum, outside of the metropolitan areas of New York City, Brooklyn, Philadelphia, Pittsburgh, and Cincinnati, the Republican congressional candidates of 1858 (of whom seven were former Democrats) lost 22,645 votes from those garnered by their party compatriots in 1856, while the Democratic candidates, supposedly burdened by an unpopular President and an unpopular Kansas policy, were able to increase their total non-metropolitan congressional vote over that cast in 1856 by 2,446. Not only does it seem that "the Democratic rank and file" had "heart" to support Democratic candidates, but also that Democrats had more "heart" than did their opponents.

This analysis of the election returns calls into question the other three criteria used to evaluate the elections of 1858. In re-examining these criteria it should be kept in mind that not two but three groups emerged among the fifty-three Northern Democrats during the Congressional struggles over slavery in Kansas. Eleven Democrats consistently voted against both the original Lecompton constitution and the English bill. Twenty-six Democrats just as consistently voted for both measures. A third group of sixteen shifted their position, largely from opposition to the Lecompton constitution to support for Administration policy.[8] Exam-

---

setts, necessitating the analysis of the two states by congressional districts. The use of the mean as a measure of central tendency, as well as its limitations, is described in V. O. Key, Jr., *A Primer of Statistics for Political Scientists* (Crowell paperback edition, New York, 1966), pp. 9-15.

[7] On the importance of the county as a partisan political unit, and the key political role played by the county committees, see my "James Buchanan, the Patronage, and the Northern Democratic Party, 1857-1858" (Ph. D. dissertation, University of Illinois, 1969), 21-28.

[8] The grouping is based upon the votes on Lecompton and the English bill found in *Journal of the House of Representatives of the United States: Being the First Session of the Thirty-Fifth Congress: Begun and Held at the City of Washington, December 7, 1857* (Washington, 1857), 279-283, 342-349, 477-482, 490-491, 572-

ining each of these criteria with respect to each of the three groups of Northern Democratic Congressmen suggests the need to examine additional factors influencing the election outcome.

(1) THE TEST OF RENOMINATION. Of the twenty-six consistent friends of the Administration, only three did not seek renomination. One, John Kelly, sought successfully the post of sheriff of New York City. Another, John Ahl of Pennsylvania, resided in a district which followed what was conventionally known as the "yearling" policy, i.e., regardless of circumstances a man was entitled to only one congressional term. Only William F. Russell of New York refused a contest.[9] Of the remaining twenty-three, two, James Gregg of Indiana and Paul Leidy of Pennsylvania, were denied renomination, but over federal appointments that alienated their Democratic backers.[10] Thus, of the

---

581, 604-605, 617-620, 675-683, 692-694, 718-721, as analyzed in my "Buchanan, Patronage, and the Northern Democracy," 307-359. The Congressmen and their positions are as follows:

CONSISTENT FRIENDS OF THE ADMINISTRATION

Samuel Arnold, Conn.
John A. Searing, N.Y.
William D. Bishop, Conn.
George Taylor, N.Y.
Daniel E. Sickles, N.Y.
William B. Maclay, N.Y.
Elijah Ward, N.Y.
Erastus Corning, N.Y.
John Huyler, N.J.
Thomas B. Florence, Penn.
Henry M. Phillips, Penn.
Paul Leidy, Penn.
Allison White, Penn.

James L. Gillis, Penn.
James M. Gregg, Ind.
John Kelly, N.Y.
John Cochrane, N.Y.
William F. Russell, N.Y.
Israel T. Hatch, N.Y.
Jacob R. Wortendyke, N.J.
James Landy, Penn.
J. Glancy Jones, Penn.
William H. Dimmick, Penn.
John A. Ahl, Penn.
James Hughes, Ind.
Charles R. Scott, Calif.

CONSISTENT OPPONENTS OF THE ADMINISTRATION

John B. Haskin, N.Y.
Henry Chapman, Penn.
John G. Davis, Ind.
Thomas L. Harris, Ill.
Robert Smith, Ill.
James C. McKibben, Calif.

John Hickman, Penn.
William Montgomery, Penn.
Isaac N. Morris, Ill.
Aaron Shaw, Ill.
Samuel S. Marshall, Ill.

CONGRESSMEN WHO CHANGED THEIR POSITION

Horace F. Clark, N.Y.
Owen Jones, Penn.
Wilson Reilly, Penn.
Willaim S. Groesbeck, Ohio
Lawrence Hall, Ohio
Samuel S. Cox, Ohio
William Lawrence, Ohio
William H. English, Ind.

Garnett B. Adrain, N.J.
William L. Dewart, Penn.
George Pendleton, Ohio
Joseph R. Cockerill, Ohio
Joseph B. Miller, Ohio
Joseph Burns, Ohio
William E. Niblack, Ind.
James B. Foley, Ind.

[9] On Kelly, see New York *Times*, Oct. 12, 1858. On Ahl, see J. F. Shunk to Jeremiah S. Black, Harrisburg, Sept. 26, 1858, Jeremiah S. Black manuscripts, Library of Congress (microfilm edition). Kelly had carried his district in 1856 with 72.02% of the vote; Ahl with 53.65%; Russell, in a three-way race, had only 38.88% of the total district vote.

[10] On Gregg, who fell afoul of Senator Jesse D. Bright while trying to exercise an independent course on federal appointments, see James Talbot to (A. Hayton?), Indianapolis, Mar. 17, 1858, Letters of Application for Federal Land Office Regis-

twenty-six Administration friends only one "refused" a contest, while two were denied renomination for reasons not connected with Kansas matters. Twenty-one of the twenty-six (80.7 per cent) sought and obtained party endorsement for their past actions. In the group of sixteen who shifted position, three did not seek renomination, two of whom (Joseph R. Cockerill and William Lawrence of Ohio) fell victim of the "yearling" policy.[11] Again, only one (James B. Foley of Indiana) refused to submit his record to the voters. Of the remaining thirteen, two failed of renomination. However, it was their anti-Lecomptonism, not their support of Administration policy, which cost Horace E. Clark of New York and Garnett B. Adrain of New Jersey renomination *as Democrats*. The other eleven (70 per cent) were successful in gaining their party's endorsement of their past actions. Thus, Democratic voters seemed inclined to reward rather than punish these two groups of Administration friends; Democratic Congressmen seemed eager to avail themselves of their constituents' inclinations.

If the test of renomination is deemed a good one, however, it should apply equally to all. What of those eleven Democratic Congressmen who were consistent opponents of the Administration? Four (36.3 per cent) including three of Douglas' loyal Illinois followers, did not seek renomination. The men nominated in place of the three Illinois Congressman

ters and Receivers, Indiana—Indianapolis, Papers of James Talbot, Records of the Interior Department, Record Group 48, National Archives [future citations to this group of papers will be: LOR&R, (location of office), Papers of (name of applicant), RG 48, NA.] Ashbel P. Willard and six others to James Buchanan, Indianapolis, Feb. 7, 1857, LOR&R, Ind.—Indianapolis, Papers of Elijah G. B. Waldo, RG 48, NA. S. E. Perkins, J. M. Talbott, Ashbel P. Willard and six others to Buchanan, Jan. 8, 1858, LOR&R, Ind.—Indianapolis, Papers of Myron North, RG 48, NA. John L. Robinson to Jacob Thompson, Indianapolis, Mar. 7, 1858, LOR&R, Ind.—Indianapolis, Papers of George McOuat, RG 48, NA. James M. Gregg to Jacob Thompson, Washington, Mar. 18, 1857, LOR&R, Ind.—Indianapolis, Papers of Charles C. Campbell, RG 48, NA. "Brief of Recommendations, Indianapolis, Apr. 19, 1858," RG 48, NA. Aquilla Jones and six others to John G. Davis, Indianapolis, May 11, 1858; W. W. Wick to Davis, Indianapolis, May 11, 1858; Austin H. Brown to Davis, Indianapolis, May 13, 1858; Ad. Seidensticker to Davis, Indianapolis, May 27, 1858; George W. Sample to Davis, Cleveland, Nov. 9, 1858, John G. Davis manuscripts, Indiana Historical Library, Indianapolis (microfilm edition). Washington *Union*, Aug. 27, 1858. On Leidy see B. K. Rhodes to William Bigler, Danville, Jan. 7, 1858, William Bigler manuscripts, Historical Society of Pennsylvania. Temporary commission of Laton S. Fuller (Scranton), June 5, 1857; temporary commission of Eleazer B. Collins (Wilkes-Barre), July 23, 1858, *Temporary Commissions of Deputy Postmasters*, records of the Department of State, Record Group 59, National Archives. *Journal of the Executive Proceedings of the Senate of the United States....* (106 vols to date, Washington, 1828–), X, (Charles Gorman, Pittstown), 420, 432.

11 Lewis W. Sifford to Samuel S. Cox, Chillicothe, Aug. 6, 1858, Samuel S. Cox manuscripts, Rutherford B. Hayes Memorial Library (microfilm edition). Matthew Johnson to James Buchanan, Cleveland, July 31, 1858, James Buchanan manuscripts, Historical Society of Pennsylvania. Washington *Union*, Aug. 10, 1858. Cleveland *Plain Dealer*, Aug. 14, 21, 26, 28, 30, Sept. 8, 21, 1858. Cockerill and Lawrence both faced two opponents in 1856. Cockerill won with 48.71% of the total district vote, while Lawrence's plurality was 47.83%. In 1858 Cockerill's Democratic successor won with 51.58% of the vote in a two-way race; Lawrence's successor lost, although increasing the Democratic proportion of the vote in a two-way race to 49.68% of the district total.

did not denounce their predecessors' course, but they certainly did not have to run on their own congressional records, as did the thirty-two friends of the Administration who successfully sought renomination. And the candidate nominated in place of the Pennsylvania anti-Lecomptonite Henry Chapman refused to endorse his predecessor's course. Four other Administration opponents sought renomination as Democrats, but were defeated in Democratic congressional conventions. Only three Administration opponents (27.3 per cent) were returned as regular Democratic candidates to the Thirty-sixth Congress, as compared with four candidates (25.0 per cent) from districts represented by those who shifted their positions, and six (23.1 per cent) consistent friends of the Administration.[12] Moreover, if the fact of renomination is significant, what is to be said of the eight (of eleven) incumbent Massachusetts Republicans, the thirteen (of twenty-one) incumbent New York Republicans, or the six (of ten) incumbent Pennsylvania Republicans, all opponents of both Lecompton and the English bill, who failed of renomination in 1858?[13] In terms of the turnover of personnel, it was the Republican party, not the Democracy, that was "revolutionized" in the party nominating conventions of 1858.

(2) RE-ELECTION OF DEMOCRATIC OPPONENTS OF THE ENGLISH BILL. Again, results seem to justify the value of this criterion. Four consistent opponents of the Administration, in addition to the three regularly elected, were denied renomination as Democrats and thereupon ran as independent candidates. Three were returned to the Thirty-sixth Congress.[14] However, one of the three was John B. Haskin of New York, who, running with the support of the Republicans, actually defeated the regular Democratic candidate by a "smashing" thirteen votes. Equally important, the regularly-nominated Democrat

---

[12] The four who did not seek renomination were Aaron Shaw, Robert Smith, and Samuel S. Marshall of Illinois, and Henry Chapman of Pennsylvania. On Chapman and his successor see Harrisburg *Herald*, Aug. 7, 1858, and the Philadelphia *Press*, Sept. 28, Nov. 10, 1858. The campaign has been analyzed from the viewpoint of Marshall's successor in James P. Jones, *"Black Jack": John A. Logan and Southern Illinois in the Civil War* (Tallahasee, 1967). The four who sought renomination but were denied it *as Democrats* were John B. Haskin of New York, John Hickman of Pennsylvania, John G. Davis of Indiana, and James C. McKibben of California.

[13] *Congressional Directory for the First Session of the Thirty-Fifth Congress of the United States of America* (Washington, 1858), pp. 3-6. *Congressional Directory for the First Session of the Thirty-Sixth Congress of the United States of America* (Washington, 1860), pp. 3-7. 33 1/3% of the incumbent Democratic congressmen were not renominated *as Democrats*, while 47.6% of Republican congressional incumbents failed of renomination.

[14] Haskin, Hickman, and Davis were returned. McKibben was renominated in 1858 by his wing of the California Democracy. But the 1858 legislature had changed the date for electing Congressmen, and the opposition wing of the Democracy refused to nominate candidates, contending that congressional elections could not take place until 1859. In 1859 both wings of the Democracy nominated candidates. McKibben, who had beaten a Republican candidate in 1858, was defeated by another Democrat in 1859. Winfield J. Davis, *A History of Political Conventions in California, 1849-1892* (Sacramento, 1892), pp. 86-95. *Tribune Almanac, 1859*, p. 63. *Tribune Almanac 1860* (New York, nd), p. 58.

polled 429 more votes in 1858 than Haskin himself had in 1856, and a comparison of Haskin's 1858 votes with those of the candidates on the state tickets indicates that he drew off only about 6.6 per cent (543 votes) of the Democratic strength. Yet even this Democratic defection was insufficient to bring victory to a Republican-backed candidate in that district; Haskin's victory was due more to the fusion of the Republicans and Native Americans than to Democratic defections. Similarly, John G. Davis of Indiana and John Hickman of Pennsylvania drew off 15.6 and 18.3 per cent of the Democratic votes in their districts.[15] These figures suggest that the anti-Lecompton sentiment among Northern Democratic voters has been somewhat overestimated both as a factor determining anti-Administration Democrats to seek re-election and as a factor in their re-election.

Moreover, historians have assumed that the Administration sought to defeat all Democratic congressmen who had opposed its Kansas policy. The Administration did endeavor to defeat nine of its consistent opponents, but not two Pennsylvanians who had received regular party nominations.[16] Thus it is questionable that all congressional opponents of the English bill won re-election because of their opposition to the English bill or against Administration wishes.

(3) REPUDIATION OF THE "POPULATION TEST" OF THE ENGLISH BILL. Repudiation is seen by historians as critical in the case of those few Democrats elected in 1858; its significance is shown by Nevins' declaration that "almost every . . . Democratic candidate" was a repudiator. That many Democrats did repudiate the "population test" is undeniable, but that "almost every" candidate did is questionable, as is, more importantly, that a direct relationship exists between repudiation and the outcome of the election. In Pennsylvania, for example, evidence in the form of speeches, party resolutions, etc., indicates that three incumbent Democratic Congressmen and four other Democratic candidates repudiated the English bill. Yet only one incumbent and one candidate were elected; the former because of the presence of an avowed anti-Lecompton Democrat in the triangular race, the latter because he was running with Republican support. Moreover, the other five repudiators ran from 6 per cent to 25 per cent behind their party compatriots of 1856, hardly the voter response traditionally attrib-

[15] *Tribune Almanac, 1857*, pp. 47-48, 58. *Tribune Almanac, 1859*, pp. 45-46, 52-59. Nevins, *Emergence*, I, 402. New York *Times*, Oct. 13, 1858. Haskin won in 1856, in a three-way race, with only 39.50% of the total district vote. The Democratic candidate in 1858, also in a three-way race, polled 48.23% of the total vote.
[16] The two were Stokes L. Roberts, who succeeded Henry Chapman, and William Montgomery. On Roberts, see Harrisburg *Herald*, Aug. 8, 1858, and Philadelphia *Press*, Sept. 28, Nov. 10, 1858. On Montgomery, see George W. Miller to Jeremiah S. Black, Washington, Apr. 30, 1858; John L. Dawson to Black, Brownsville, May 12, 31, June 7, 1858; William Montgomery to Black, Washington, June 25, 1858; Black to Montgomery, Washington, July 6, 1858 (copy), Black MSS. Cleveland *Plain Dealer*, June 18, 1858. *Illinois State Journal*, June 21, 1858. Harrisburg *Herald*, June 28, 1858.

uted to those candidates with the "courage" to resist the "proscriptive means of the Administration" to enforce its unpopular policies upon reluctant candidates. Or, taking New York as a "test case," seventeen regular Democratic candidates did not repudiate the test, while six did. Of the seventeen, three were elected while fourteen (including one incumbent Congressmen) were defeated. Of the six repudiators, only one regularly-nominated Democrat was re-elected, while five (including one incumbent Congressman) were not. Of the seventeen non-repudiators, eight lost votes from those cast in 1856, but nine increased the party's vote from the previous race. Of the six repudiators, three lost votes from those cast in 1856, while three increased their party's vote.[17] Thus it seems questionable that the position which candidates took on the "population test" was universally the critical factor in their success or failure at the polls in 1858.

Having questioned the traditional analyses of the 1858 elections, how then can the net loss of eighteen Democratic Congressmen be explained? Consideration will first be given to the fourteen Democratic Congressmen (26.4 per cent of Northern Democrats) elected in 1856 from the metropolitan areas of New York City, Brooklyn, Philadelphia, and Cincinnati. The performance of the parties in these metropolitan areas is indicated in Table IV.

As the figures indicate, seven of the fourteen Democrats elected in 1856 won their seats by pluralities rather than majorities. With the exception of Philadelphia, where the shift had occurred earlier, by the election of 1858 the American party had disintegrated as a force in metropolitan politics. It has been traditionally assumed that the Americans gave up their separate political existence to fuse with the Republicans. It is true that some American party members, particularly the party

17 Nevins, *Emergence*, I, 402. Nevins' statement is based upon Stephen A. Douglas' speech in his Oct. 7, 1858, debate with Lincoln at Galesburg, as found in Paul M. Angle (ed.), *Created Equal? The Complete Lincoln-Douglas Debates of 1858* (Chicago, 1958), p. 288. Douglas spoke before all Northern Democrats had been nominated and before many had begun to campaign extensively; Nevins applies the statement to the entire campaign. Historical analysis of the Pennsylvania election seems based on the editorial claims of John W. Forney's Philadelphia *Press*, which claimed stridently before the election *editorially* that all Democratic candidates had repudiated the population test, but modified this position, again editorially, after the election. Most importantly, it gave surprisingly few details about the repudiations. An examination of the *Press* revealed details for the seven candidates here discussed, including Congressmen Florence, Owen Jones, and Wilson Reilly, and the Democratic candidate in Buchanan's own Lancaster district, a fact of which the *Press* made much. *Press*, Aug. 6, Sept. 11, 13, 15, 16, 17, 22, 24, 25, 26, 27, Oct. 7, 10, 11, 14, 1858. On the New York contest, see New York *Times*, Oct. 8, 19, 20, 29, 1858. Albany *Atlas & Argus*, Sept. 27, Oct. 1, 6, 8, 14, 18, 20, 1858. In New York, the three non-repudiators who were elected were Daniel E. Sickles, Thomas Barr (in place of John Kelly), and William Maclay. The defeated non-repudiator was Erastus Corning. Of the repudiators, only John Cochrane was reelected; the incumbent repudiator who was defeated was Israel T. Hatch. *Tribune Almanac, 1859*, p. 46. Washington *Union*, Oct. 13, 14, 1858. New York and Pennsylvania are given special attention because in the two states Democrats lost twenty (58.82%) of the seats lost in 1858 (including two seats whose Democratic incumbents were re-elected with Republican help in 1858).

TABLE IV[18]

Party Performance in Metropolitan Areas, 1856 to 1858

	Candidate elected in 1856	Republican				Democratic				American				Candidate elected in 1858
		1856 vote	% of total	1858 vote	% of total	1856 vote	% of total	1858 vote	% of total	1856 vote	% of total	1858 vote	% of total	
Brooklyn														
dist. 1	D	5449	26.84	8122	52.53	8960	44.41	7339	47.47	5892	29.02	.....	.....	R
dist. 2	D	5869	29.44	6475	36.77	8591	43.09	4578	26.00	5476	27.47	974	5.53	R
								5581	31.70					
New York														
dist. 3	D*	2126	19.78	3015	33.26	5716	53.19	3177	35.04	2905	27.03	.....	.....	D*
								2874	31.70					
dist. 4	D	1487	12.96	2290	22.99	8319	72.02	2671	26.82	1735	15.02	340	3.41	D
								3949	39.65					
								710	7.13					
dist. 5	D	3274	23.21	4982	42.82	5863	41.56	5780	49.75	3798	26.93	855	7.36	D*
						1169	8.30							
dist. 6	D	3991	26.29	5520	42.94	7531	49.61	7336	57.06	3658	24.10	.....	.....	D*
dist. 7	D	4100	25.71	8306	55.76	6531	40.96	6591	44.24	854	5.36	.....	.....	R
										4461	27.98			
dist. 8	D	3760	25.25	9035	58.77	7482	50.24	6338	41.23	3651	24.51	.....	.....	ALD*
Philadelphia														
dist. 1	D	7275	43.12	6492	40.94	9495	56.28	2442	15.40	.....	.....	.....	.....	D*
								6823	43.03					
dist. 2	O	6411	51.58	5653	58.38	6018	48.42	4030	41.62	.....	.....	.....	.....	O*
dist. 3	D	6753	45.98	6977	54.46	7933	54.02	5834	45.54	.....	.....	.....	.....	O
dist. 4	D	2457	13.43	9749	59.25	9279	50.72	6451	39.21	6560	35.85	253	1.54	O
dist. 5	D	7961	45.14	9701	57.37	9674	54.86	7209	42.63	.....	.....	.....	.....	O
Cincinnati														
dist. 1	D	4256	32.66	6785	48.76	6133	47.06	7131	51.24	2642	20.27	.....	.....	D*
dist. 2	D	4343	32.63	8054	52.58	5738	43.11	7263	47.42	3229	24.26	.....	.....	R

* Re-election of 1856 incumbent in 1858.

leadership, did make the transition to Republican ranks. Both the absolute increase in Democratic votes and the increase in the Democratic proportion of the total vote, however, (with Philadelphia again the exception) suggest that the American-Republican fusion was far from a mass migration of the former into the ranks of the latter.[19] Therefore, factors internal to the Democratic party must be examined to help explain the loss of eight metropolitan seats.

The six New York City seats were involved in the struggle between ex-mayor Fernando Wood and Tammany Hall, which latter organization had nominated the 1856 congressional candidates. Both Wood and Tammany had endorsed the admission of Kansas under the Lecompton constitution and the English bill. Embarrassed by the President's refusal to support wholeheartedly his ally, federal Customs Collector Augustus Schell, and by the President's refusal to offer him the Governorship of Nebraska Territory, Wood ran his own Congressional candidates in two districts and refused to support the Tammany candidates in one other. This division of the party cost the Democrats two seats.[20] In Brooklyn a similar division between the "Bradley" and "Vanderbilt" organizations existed. The Bradley organization endorsed both incumbent Congressmen, whereupon the Vanderbilt followers mirrored Wood's tactics, causing the defeat of both incumbents.[21] In Philadel-

---

[18] The metropolitan voting returns are published in *Tribune Almanac, 1857,* pp. 47-49, 56, and *Tribune Almanac, 1859,* pp. 46, 52-53, 57. The exclusion of the two Pittsburgh congressional districts is based upon the fact that in 1858 candidates ran upon issues connected with local taxes; "anti-tax" rather than "anti-Lecompton" candidates appear. The complicated story of Pittsburgh politics is admirably treated by Michael Fitzgibbons Holt, *Forging A Majority* (New Haven, 1968).

[19] The movement of Native Americans into Democratic ranks had been presaged in the elections of 1856 when, in four upstate New York districts, the two parties fused behind a single congressional candidate to oppose the Republican nominees: *Tribune Almanac, 1857,* p. 47.

[20] The Wood-Tammany feud is discussed briefly in Nichols, *Disruption,* p. 213. On the Wood and Tammany endorsements of Lecompton and the English bill, see New York *Herald,* Dec. 5, 9, 16, 17, 18, 23, 24, 1857, and Feb. 10, 26, 27, Mar. 3, 4, 5, 8, 1858. On Wood, Schell, and Nebraska, see Howell Cobb to James Buchanan, Washington, Aug. 4, 6, 1858; Daniel E. Sickles to Buchanan, Aug. 5, Sept. 8, 1858; Fernando Wood to Buchanan, New York, Sept. 8, 10, 1858; Isaac V. Fowler to Buchanan, New York, Sept. 8, 1858; John Cochrane and John Kelly to Buchanan, New York, Sept. 15, 1858; James Buchanan to Fernando Wood, Washington, Sept. 9, 1858, Buchanan MSS. Augustus Schell to Daniel E. Sickles, New York, Sept. 18, 1858, in Albany *Atlas & Argus,* Sept. 21, 1858. On the Wood and Tammany nominations, see Washington *Union,* Oct. 17, 1858; New York *Herald,* Oct. 3, 13-20, Nov. 1, 1858; New York *Times,* Oct. 12, 1858. Wood supported Hiram Walbridge against Daniel E. Sickles, and Thomas J. Barr in John Kelly's district against the Tammany candidate James Farmer. In Horace Clark's district Wood gave no support to Tammany's Anson Herrick, and one of his loyal henchmen, corporation counsel Richard Busteed, campaigned for Clark. Wood did support Tammany candidates John Cochrane, Elijah Ward (nominally), and William Maclay. The seats of Ward and Clark were lost to the Democrats; Tammany suffered additional loss in the election of Barr.

[21] William H. Ludlow to Stephen A. Douglas, Sayville, Nov. 6, 1858, Stephen A. Douglas MSS., University of Chicago. Washington *Union,* July 23, Aug. 5, Oct. 29, 1858. New York *Herald,* Oct. 5, 6, 8, 11, 13, 15, 19, 20, 1858. New York *Times,* Oct. 12, 19, 1858. New York *Dispatch,* quoted in New York *Times,* Oct. 6, 1858.

phia, the President had "imported" a Lancastrian, Joseph B. Baker, to be customs collector, which antagonized federal District Attorney and aspirant-Presidential spokesman James C. Van Dyke. Failure to obtain a vacant federal judgeship, a failure which he ascribed to Baker's interference, further alienated Van Dyke. The Baker-Van Dyke feud contributed largely to the loss of three seats to the opposition.[22] In Cincinnati, Congressmen Pendleton and Groesbeck had followed an almost identical course. They wavered on Lecompton but finally supported the English bill, repudiated the population test, and faced a united opposition in 1858 as opposed to separate Republican and American candidates in 1856. They differed only in supporting a candidate for surveyor of the port of Cincinnati, with Groesbeck being successful. But the appointee proved very unpopular, and those angered by the Surveyor's

---

The two congressmen who were defeated were John Searing and George Taylor. Searing's case is significant for showing the relative weights to be ascribed to anti-Lecompton sentiment and to struggle for party dominance. Searing defeated William H. Ludlow, an avowed Douglas supporter, in the regular Democratic convention, whereupon Ludlow vowed to defeat the incumbent by staying away from the polls. In Suffolk county, Ludlow's home, Searing's vote declined from his 1856 total by 337 votes (15.7%). But in that portion of his district which encompassed a portion of Brooklyn, Searing aligned himself with the Bradley organization, whereupon the Vanderbilt Democracy refused to support him. In the Brooklyn portion of his district Searing's vote declined by 1751 (66.5%) from his poll of 1856. *Tribune Almanac, 1857*, p. 47; *Tribune Almanac, 1859*, p. 46.

[22] On Baker, Van Dyke, and the judgeship, see James C. Van Dyke to James Buchanan, Philadelphia, Mar. 14, 1857, Buchanan MSS (Van Dyke supported Hendrick B. Wright for the office given to Baker.) John W. Forney to Buchanan, Philadelphia, Mar. 5, 1857; Thomas B. Florence to Buchanan, Washington, Mar. 4, 1857; Henry M. Phillips and James Landy to Buchanan, np, nd; J. Edgar Thompson to Buchanan, Philadelphia, Mar. 5, 1857; Joseph Baker to J. Buchanan Henry, Harrisburg, Mar. 10, 1857, with enclosures; William B. Reed to Baker, Philadelphia, Mar. 11, 1857, Collector of Customs applications, Penn.—Philadelphia, Papers of Joseph B. Baker, records of the Treasury Department, Record Group 56, National Archives. James C. Van Dyke to Buchanan, Philadelphia, Jan. 31, Mar. 20, 1858 (two letters); Van Dyke to Buchanan, Philadelphia, Apr. 6, 1858, enclosing Buchanan to Van Dyke, Washington, Apr. 7, 1858; Van Dyke to Buchanan, Philadelphia, Apr. 7, 1858; Joseph B. Baker to Buchanan, Philadelphia, Mar. 8, Apr. 12, 1858; Richard Vaux to Buchanan, Philadelphia, Feb. 6, 1858; William A. Porter to Lewis Cassidy, Philadelphia, Apr. 12, 1858, enclosed in Cassidy to Buchanan, np. Apr. 14, 1858; Buchanan to Van Dyke, Washington, Apr. 17, 1858, Buchanan MSS. Lewis C. Cassidy to Jeremiah S. Black, Philadelphia, Mar. 13, 1858; Henry W. Phillips to Black, np, Apr. 11, 1858; W. F. Boone to Black, Philadelphia, Apr. 8, 1858, Black MSS. On Baker and Van Dyke's actions in the congressional nominating conventions, see Joseph B. Baker to Buchanan, Philadelphia, Aug. 16 and nd (c. August 16), 1858; Henry M. Phillips to Buchanan, Philadelphia, Aug. 5, 1858; James C. Van Dyke to Buchanan, Philadelphia, Sept. 13, 1858, Buchanan MSS. Henry M. Phillips to Jeremiah S. Black, Philadelphia, June 20, 1858; Jeremiah McKibben to Black, Philadelphia, Sept. 11, 1858, Black MSS. Jesse Johnson to William Bigler, Philadelphia, Aug. 19, 1858, Bigler MSS. New York *Herald*, June 18, 1858. Washington *Union*, Aug. 25, 1858. Harrisburg *Herald*, Aug. 27, 1858. In only one district, Thomas Florence's, was John Forney able to secure an anti-Lecompton candidate to run against a regular Democrat in Philadelphia. The anti-Lecomptonite was George W. Nebinger, an unsuccessful applicant for a post in the Navy Yard. Nebinger polled 2442 votes, and caused Florence's vote to decline by 28.1% from 1856 (the votes of Florence's Republican-Opposition opponent declined by 10.8%). For a different interpretation of Philadelphia Democratic politics, see William Dusinberre, *Civil War Issues in Philadelphia, 1856-1865* (Philadelphia, 1965).

actions vented their rage upon his Congressional patron at the ballot box. Groesbeck lost, Pendleton won.[23] Thus, a significant factor in the loss of eight of the fourteen metropolitan seats was internecine warfare which antedated Buchanan's Kansas policies, and not the English bill, which served as a convenient excuse for, rather than a cause of, the divisions.

What of the twenty-eight "rural" seats held by consistent or quondam friends of the Administration during the Kansas difficulties, of which the Democrats lost eighteen?[24] Five of those districts were "marginal" Democratic districts, where the Democrats won in 1856 because both the Republicans and Americans ran separate candidates. In 1858 the two opposition parties united to defeat the Democratic candidate. The fact that Democratic votes increased between 1856 and 1858 in four of the five districts indicates no major dissatisfaction with the position these men occupied on Kansas affairs.[25] Of the remaining thirteen districts, the regular Democratic nominees were replaced by so-called "anti-Lecompton" Democrats in three, Erastus Corning's in New York, J. Glancy Jones' in Pennsylvania, and John Huyler's in New Jersey. The anti-Lecomptonism in Corning's district grew directly from the fact that Corning had control of two major post office appointments in his dis-

[23] For Groesbeck's and Pendleton's course on Lecompton and the English bill, see the citations in fn. 8, above. Pendleton actually voted for the Administration position more often than did Groesbeck. Cleveland *Plain Dealer*, Sept. 8, 21, 1858. Cincinnati *Daily Enquirer*, Sept. 22, 1858. *Tribune Almanac, 1857*, p. 56. *Tribune Almanac, 1859*, p. 57. George H. Pendleton to James Buchanan, Washington, June 2, 1858, Surveyors' of Customs Applications, Ohio—Cincinnati, Papers of Francis Linck, records of the Treasury Department, Record Group 56, National Archives [hereafter cited as: SCA, (location of office), Papers of (name of applicant), RG 56, NA.] E. A. Ferguson and Alexander Long to Buchanan, Cincinnati, Jan. 4, 1858; W. S. Groesbeck to Buchanan, Washington, June 4, 1858, SCA, Ohio—Cincinnati, Papers of T. Jefferson Sherlock, RG 56, NA. *Senate Executive Journal*, X, 442, 450. Louis R. Harlan (ed.), "The Autobiography of Alexander Long, 1858," *Bulletin* of the Historical and Philosophical Society of Ohio, XIX (Apr., 1961), 124-125.

[24] Of the twenty-eight seats, those of Samuel Arnold and William D. Bishop in Connecticut were not filled until Apr., 1859, leaving twenty-six seats contested in 1858. The seat of Garnett B. Adrain was lost to the New Jersey Democracy by Adrain's re-election as an anti-Lecompton Democrat with Republican backing. Of the remaining twenty-five, the Democrats won in seven districts: William H. Dimmick of Pennsylvania, Charles L. Scott of California, Samuel S. Cox of Ohio, and William E. Niblack and William H. English of Indiana were re-elected, while William Howard was elected in place of Joseph Cockerill in Ohio, and William S. Holman in place of James Foley in Indiana. The remaining eighteen seats are those under consideration.

[25] The marginal districts were those of Israel Hatch and William Russell in New York, Jacob Wortendyke in New Jersey, Joseph Miller and William Lawrence in Ohio. Democratic votes increased in all except Lawrence's district. Hatch, Russell, and Wortendyke were all consistent supporters of the President in Kansas affairs; only Russell refused a contest. Miller was renominated, but Lawrence fell to the "yearling" policy. In New York, fusion of Democratic opponents was achieved only at the congressional level and there only partially; fusion efforts at the state level failed, indicating that other issues were viewed as more prominent than opposition to Administration Kansas policy. *Tribune Almanac, 1857*, pp. 47, 50, 56-57. *Tribune Almanac, 1859*, pp. 45-46, 54, 57-58.

trict, at Albany and at West Troy (Watervliet). At Albany, Corning acceded to the wishes of party chieftain Peter Cagger and President Buchanan and replaced a popular incumbent with Calvert Comstock, editor of the Albany *Atlas & Argus*. Corning's choice outraged Michael McMahon, an Albany Irish Democratic leader. McMahon had sought the office for himself, as a symbol of the importance of the Irish Democracy, with the support of William A. Young, Recorder of the city of Albany. Similarly, at West Troy, Corning supported Cagger's candidate. Cagger's opponents carried their dissatisfaction into the Democratic state convention at Syracuse. Defeated there, they returned home and openly bolted. At a meeting in which Young served as president and McMahon nominated John H. Reynolds to oppose Corning, two resolutions on Kansas affairs were adopted, while four denounced Cagger, Corning, and spoilsmongering. The Democratic gubernatorial nominee, Amasa J. Parker, running on a platform praising Buchanan for settling the Kansas problem, carried Albany county over his two opponents; Corning polled 763 votes less and lost to Reynolds by 1200 votes.[26] In Jones' district, the disposal of the Reading postoffice and the U.S. Navy coal agency, as well as Jones' interference in state Democratic patronage, produced two Democratic conventions and the election of anti-Lecompton Democrat John Schwartz by nineteen votes.[27]

In two other Pennsylvania "rural" districts (John A. Ahl's and Henry Chapman's) Presidential postoffice appointments had been made. Had Democratic losses in the counties of appointment been held to the level of declines in the other counties of the district, the Democratic candidates would have been elected. In the Ohio district represented by Lawrence Hall, the Democratic decline in the one county where there was a Presidentially-appointed office was almost exactly equal to the margin by which Hall lost the district. Buchanan's staunchest Ohio supporter was Joseph Burns, who had won election by a 51-vote margin in 1856 and lost it in 1858 by only 230 votes, hardly a massive repudiation of Burns' pro-Administration position. In the single county in Burns'

[26] "Abstract of M. McMahon's recommendations for the Post office at Albany, N.Y."; John V. L. Pruyn to Erastus Corning, Albany, Apr. 5, 1858; M. McMahon to Corning, Albany, May 15, 1858; James Brady to Corning, West Troy, May 25, 1858; William P. Malburn to Edwin Croswell, Albany, June 7, 1858; William Cassidy to Corning, Albany, June 5, 1858; Calvert Comstock to Corning, Albany, June 10, 1858, Erastus Corning MSS., Albany Institute of History and Art. Albany *Atlas & Argus*, Sept. 16, 17, Nov. 4, 1858. Albany *Evening Journal*, Sept. 14, 1858. New York *Times*, Oct. 12, 1858. Washington *Union*, Oct. 15, 1858. *Tribune Almanac, 1859*, pp. 46-47. Corning ran 396 votes behind Parker in "the heavily Irish first, second, seventh, and eighth wards" of Albany: William E. Rowley, "The Irish Aristocracy of Albany, 1798-1878," *New York History*, LII (July, 1971), 289.

[27] George W. Woodward to Jeremiah S. Black, Pittsburgh, Oct. 31, 1857; George M. Lauman to Black, Reading, Nov. 4, 27, 1857, Black MSS. Harrisburg *Herald*, Aug. 5, 1858. Washington *Union*, Aug. 5, Sept. 4, 1858. Chicago *Times*, Oct. 16, 1858. The first anti-Jones convention in Berks was silent on the English bill; the second repudiated the population test in its platform, but Schwartz ignored the issue in his acceptance speech and seems to have concentrated the most of his attack on Jones' failure to support a protective tariff: Philadelphia *Press*, Aug. 6, Sept. 13, 1858.

district containing a Presidential office, Burns lost 140 votes. In the Pennsylvania district represented by Paul Leidy the concentration of Presidential appointments and the unpopularity of Leidy's selections cost Leidy renomination and his successor the election; the Democratic candidate for state supreme court judge carried the district while Leidy's successor lost it. Finally, there was the case of W. L. Dewart, representative of Schuylkill and Northumberland counties, and one of the sixteen who opposed Lecompton but supported the English bill. Schuylkill's large German element vied with the Irish for the appointment of postmaster at Pottsville. The office went first to Irish spokesman Michael Cochrane, whose name went to the Senate of the United States for confirmation. But before that body could approve, the nomination was withdrawn and given to a German, Henry L. Acker. Cochrane thereupon led his followers out of party ranks to nominate an "anti-Lecompton" ticket that pitted Joseph Cake against Dewart, while Cochrane took on Acker's leading backer for the latter's state senate seat. The result was the loss of both elective offices to the Democrats, although the combined votes of Dewart and Cake exceeded those of the successful Republican.[28]

Dewart's case typifies the election of 1858 and highlights a major weakness of historical explanations of antebellum political behavior in those elections. Foreshadowing the sectional solidarity of the 1860's, historians have tended to depict a single response, repudiation, on the part of a homogenous mass, the northern electorate, to a single issue, Kansas, with a single result, Democratic disaster. Yet a re-examination of the electoral criteria reveals that complexity, not solidarity, was the characteristic of northern politics. In only two of the twelve states did the two parties' performances approximate the historians' "norm" for the section. Elsewhere, the Democrats improved their voter appeal from 1856 in more states than did their opponents. Moreover, it was the Democratic friends of the Administration who faced the voters in 1858, while the Republican opponents of the Administration were giving way to new Republican faces with which to greet the electorate. The Democrats did suffer losses, both in popular votes and in congressional seats; for the party's future, an equally significant loss was in control of those counties where the Democratic vote declined while Republican votes were increasing, for this loss deprived the Democracy of control of local offices that were vital to ensuing campaigns. However, Democratic losses were a state, not a sectional phenomena. The Democracy suffered its greatest voter loss in Pennsylvania; but the Key-

[28] Lewis Cassidy to Jeremiah S. Black, Philadelphia, Mar. 16, 1857, Jan. 11, 1858; C. M. Straub to Black, Pottsville, June 8, 1858, Black MSS. *Senate Executive Journal*, X, 435, 452, 455. Harrisburg *Herald*, Mar. 4, Aug. 10, 1858, Mar. 1, 1859. *Tribune Almanac, 1857*, pp. 48-49, 56-57. *Tribune Almanac, 1859*, pp. 52-53, 57-58. The basic argument is that the position a candidate took on issues like Kansas would have a fairly uniform effect across his entire district, and that if vote patterns differ widely among the counties of the district, one must look to issues other than Kansas for the explanation.

stone state was atypical of the North, and the opposition did not
achieve large gains of popular votes there at the expense of the Democracy. And Pennsylvania popular-vote losses were offset by Democratic
gains elsewhere. Even the fusion of the Republicans and Native Americans, which probably accounted for one-fifth of the seats the Democrats
lost in 1858, was not a total disaster for the Democracy. The disappearance of the Native Americans as a separate political entity, a phenomenon deserving of much greater study, left the Democracy with prospects of garnering some of these voters, as the metropolitan voting
record revealed. Concentrating on those congressional districts where
incumbent Democrats were defeated in 1858, it is evident that in eight
of the fourteen metropolitan districts, and in twelve of the twenty-eight
rural districts, factors other than the Kansas issue contributed to Democratic losses.[29] Setting aside the Native American factor, the loss of
fifteen of the twenty-six seats lost by incumbent Democrats in 1858 was
the result of struggles for dominance within the institutional party
structure, for ethnic and personal pre-eminence, and for control of appointments. Democratic congressional losses in 1858 were as much
the result of power, prestige, and patronage as of unpopular Presidential policies about Kansas.

What was the significance of these congressional elections of 1858 for
the Northern Democracy? Implicit in the historical accounts of the period 1858 to 1860 is the assumption that the debacle of 1858 brought to
a finish the contest between Stephen A. Douglas and James Buchanan
for control of the remains of the Northern Democracy, with Douglas
clearly emerging the victor. Thereafter attention shifts to the South,
where Douglas' Freeport doctrine and John Brown's raid destroy the
few remaining bonds of party and national unity. It only remains for the
Charleston convention to bring into the open the irreparable breach between the Douglas-dominated Northern Democracy and the Southern
wing of the party controlled by the fire-eaters.[30]

Far from being a "debacle," the elections of 1858 revealed that the
party in the North had remarkable vitality. The decline in Republican
votes, the narrowness of Republican victories,[31] and the location of

[29] Nevins, *Emergence*, I, 402, cites the Albany *Atlas & Argus*, Nov. 3, 1858, to
the effect that "a Kansas swell" had overswept all other considerations in the race.
This was the reaction of the editors on the day following the election before all
returns were in. A more reasoned reaction, stressing other factors, came on the following day: see the editorial entitled "The Election in this Congressional District,"
Nov. 4, 1858. Nevins also ignores the analysis of the New York *Times* following
the Oct. elections that "the issue in Pennsylvania, Ohio, and Indiana has not been
the old question of Freesoil in Kansas. . . .": Oct. 15, 1858.

[30] Following his chapter on the Lincoln-Douglas debates, Nevins devotes four
pages to the 1858 elections outside of Illinois in a chapter titled, significantly, "Steps
toward Secession." Nichols' chapter on the elections of 1858, entitled "Repudiation
at the Polls," is contained in that portion of his book with the general heading
"Demoralization and Defeat."

[31] Aside from Haskin's and Schwartz' narrow victories, Republicans won by margins of less than 100 votes in four districts, by less than 200 in another, by less
than 300 in three others, and by less than 400 in two others. In 1860, Democrats

Democratic losses as well as the reasons therefore, combine to indicate that contemporaries saw neither the congressional elections of 1858 as a great struggle over Kansas nor the results as an epic defeat for a repudiated party, its past national policies, or its President. From the election figures and results both Stephen A. Douglas and James Buchanan could draw strength for a struggle for party supremacy, a struggle for which the elections themselves had provided no decisive answer.[32]

---

captured seven of these ten seats, as well as those of Schwartz and Haskin. *Tribune Almanac, 1859*, pp. 44-63; *Tribune Almanac, 1861*, (New York, nd), pp. 39-63.

[32] For examples of the claims that the election sustained both the party and the President, see Albany *Atlas & Argus*, Oct. 16, Nov. 4, 1858. Indianapolis *Sentinel*, Oct. 22, 1858, quoted in Washington *Union*, Oct. 26, 1858. Buffalo *Courier*, Nov. 6, 1858, quoted in Washington *Union*, Nov. 10, 1858. Washington *Union*, Nov. 18, 1858. See also Nichols, *Disruption*, p. 225, n. 30. This is not to belittle Stephen A. Douglas' achievements in 1858. He had clearly emerged as the most prominent individual in the ranks of the Northern Democracy. But it does not follow that he controlled the institutional apparatus of the party in that section.

A shorter version of this paper was presented at the fifth Duquesne History Forum. The author wishes to thank the following for support for portions of the research: The Civil War Round Table, Chicago, Illinois; Joint Awards Committee/ University Awards Council, Research Foundation of the State University of New York; Fredonia Foundation; the American Council of Learned Societies; and Gary B. Ross, Topeka, Kansas.

THE ETHNIC VOTER AND
THE FIRST LINCOLN ELECTION

Robert P. Swierenga

SCHOLARS, PARTICULARLY THOSE interested in the impact of ethnic groups on key national elections, have long been intrigued by Abraham Lincoln's victory in 1860. Ever since Professor William E. Dodd's classic article it has been axiomatic in the works of historians that the foreign-born of the Old Northwest, voting in solid blocs according to the dictates of their leaders, cast the decisive ballots. Lincoln could not have won the presidency, Dodd suggested, "but for the loyal support of the Germans and other foreign citizens led by Carl Schurz, Gustav Koerner, and the editors of the *Staatszeitung* of Chicago."[1]

A decade later, taking his cue from Dodd, Donnal V. Smith scrutinized the immigrant vote in 1860 and confidently declared that "without the vote of the foreign-born, Lincoln could not have carried the Northwest, and without the Northwest . . . he would have been defeated." Smith's statistics also confirmed the premise that the social solidarity characteristic of ethnic groups invariably translated itself into political solidarity, and that because of the language barrier the immigrants needed leaders to formulate the political issues for them. "The leaders who were so trusted," Smith maintained, "were in a splendid position to control the political strength of the foreign-born." And in the election of 1860, he continued, even to the "casual observer" the ethnic leaders in the Middle West were solidly Republican.[2] Therefore, except for isolated, insignificant minorities, the foreign-born of the Old Northwest voted Republican.

Most midwestern ethnic leaders, it is true, were predominately in the Republican camp in 1860. Foreign language newspapers generally

[1] "The Fight for the Northwest, 1860," *American Historical Review*, XVI (1910), 786. The idea was quickly accepted. See, for example, Arthur C. Cole, *The Era of the Civil War* (Springfield, 1919), pp. 341-342.

[2] "The Influence of the Foreign-Born of the Northwest in the Election of 1860," *Mississippi Valley Historical Review*, XIX (1932), 204, 193, 202. See also F. I. Herriott, "Iowa and the First Nomination of Lincoln," *Annals of Iowa*, 3rd Ser., VIII (1907), 196.

carried the Lincoln-Hamlin banner on their mastheads; prominent immigrants campaigned actively for Old Abe and played key roles at the Chicago convention.[3] It is also widely conceded that the anti-slavery movement, the free homestead idea, and the Pacific railroad issue were key factors attracting ethnic leaders to the Republicans.[4]

The really crucial question, however, concerns not the foreign-born leaders but the masses that they supposedly represented. Did the naturalized immigrants vote as their spokesmen desired? Except for Dr. Joseph Schafer's deathbed protest in 1941 that the Wisconsin Germans did not fit the pattern,[5] the Dodd-Smith thesis has stood unchallenged.[6] But a recent analysis of the 1860 election statistics for Iowa suggests that the foreign-born, and particularly the Germans, may not have supported Lincoln as strongly as historians have long assumed to be the case.[7]

A possibly critical factor thus far ignored in studies of the ethnic impact on the first Lincoln election is the time-gap between the date of immigrant settlement and the year 1860. That ethnic leaders initially influenced the ballots of their countrymen is highly probable. Yet it seems reasonable to assume that a leader's power would steadily wane as the rank-and-file newcomers attained a measure of economic security and cultural acclimatization. If true, the student of ethnic voting must be careful when relying on what spokesmen said as an indication of how the foreign-born voted, particularly if ten or fifteen years had elapsed since the trans-Atlantic migration. The collective experience of the Netherlanders who migrated to central Iowa in the mid-nineteenth century, in illustrating this danger, is a case study

[3] Besides Schurz of Wisconsin and Koerner of Illinois, prominent foreign-born campaigners included Frederick Hassaurek of Ohio, Theodore Hielscher of Indiana, and Henry P. Scholte and Nicholas Rusch of Iowa. See M. Halstead, *Caucuses of 1860: A History of the National Political Conventions* (Columbus, 1860), pp. 123, 127; Reinhard H. Luthin, *The First Lincoln Campaign* (Cambridge, 1944), pp. 185-187; Charles W. Emery, "The Iowa Germans in the Election of 1860," *Annals of Iowa*, 3rd Ser., XXII (1940), 421-433.

[4] Luthin, *First Lincoln Campaign*, p. 187; Paul W. Gates, *Fifty Million Acres: Conflicts Over Kansas Land Policy, 1854-1890* (Ithaca, 1954), pp. 104-105.

[5] "Who Elected Lincoln?" *American Historical Review*, XLVII (1941), 51-63. Schafer's revisionist view was quickly rebutted in a brief nonstatistical article: Jay Monaghan, "Did Abraham Lincoln Receive the Illinois German Vote?" *Journal of the State Historical Society of Illinois*, XXXV (1942), 133-139. Support of Schafer's viewpoint came from Hildegard B. Johnson, "The Election of 1860 and the Germans in Minnesota," *Minnesota History*, XXVIII (1947), 20-36; but this article has been virtually ignored.

[6] For textbook examples see Carl N. Degler, *Out of Our Past: The Forces that Shaped Modern America* (New York, 1959), p. 287; Ray Allen Billington, *Westward Expansion: A History of the American Frontier* (2nd ed.; New York, 1960), p. 611.

[7] George H. Daniels, "Immigrant Vote in the 1860 Election: The Case of Iowa," *Mid-America*, XLIV (1962), 146-162.

of the complex influences actually molding immigrant political patterns in the years immediately preceding the Civil War.

In 1847 the Hollanders—some eight hundred strong—established their colony, with the new town of Pella at its center, in Lake Prairie Township, Marion County. To insure complete control of the area, the colony's leaders had earlier bought up the claims and improvements of almost all pioneer squatters in the township. Along with the purchase of vacant government land the Netherlanders were thus able to engross some eighteen thousand choice acres between the Des Moines and Skunk rivers. Through the antebellum years the settlement grew rapidly under a continuing Dutch immigration, augmented by a growing minority of native Americans. In the decade of the fifties potential voters in the township increased by 340 European-born and 152 native-born men. With a maximum voting majority of 85 per cent in 1850 and 72 per cent in 1860, therefore, the Dutch clearly dominated local politics.[8]

The Reverend Mr. Henry Peter Scholte (pronounced Skol′-tuh), founder of the Pella colony, was one of the ethnic leaders cited by Donnal Smith as typical of those who led the foreign-born into Lincoln's camp.[9] The basis of Scholte's political influence, dating from the Old Country, was his position as president of the "Netherlandish Association for Emigration to the United States," formed at Utrecht in 1846 and consisting mainly of members of his religious congregation. Having seceded from the state-supported Dutch Reformed Church because of its alleged lack of spirituality, Scholte and his flock suffered a mild persecution from government officials. This, coupled with economic distress, prompted the Dutch minister to lead his followers to America.

Until his death in 1868, the "Dominie," as his followers affectionately addressed him, played an important part in the intellectual, economic, and political life of Pella, Marion County, and the state of Iowa. His versatility was truly remarkable. He served as minister, as editor of the English-language Pella *Gazette*, as lawyer, real estate developer, justice of the peace, school inspector, and mayor *ex officio*. Scholte was also an energetic capitalist. Besides owning almost one-third of the land in and around the town of Pella, his investments in local industry were substantial. He owned a brick kiln, steam flour mill, and limestone quarry, founded the Pella National Bank, and was

[8] Voting population figures were compiled from manuscript censuses on microfilm at the State Historical Society of Iowa, Iowa City. Lake Prairie Twp. was the only township in Iowa in this period (1850-1860) in which the Dutch were a clear majority over native American voters.

[9] "Influence of the Foreign-Born," 193, 196.

a benefactor and trustee of the local college. Athough he failed in his bid for nomination as state senator in 1852, he served as delegate-at-large and vice-president of the 1860 Republican national convention at Chicago. In 1864 President Lincoln appointed him United States minister to Austria, although the Senate refused to confirm the nomination because he was not a native American.[10]

The early political views of the Pella leader were decidedly Whig. Idolizing Henry Clay while still in the Netherlands, Scholte espoused the Whig cause upon his arrival in Iowa. Like Clay, he possessed a typical Whig attitude toward slavery and the important economic questions of the day. While no admirer of the Peculiar Institution he condemned abolitionism more than slavery since it embodied the greater threat to the survival of the Union.[11] The American economy, he divined from his study of recent history, "always flourished" under Whig administrations and slumped during Democratic misrule. Moreover, the Whigs were "more respectable and more intellectual," while the Democrats were "poorer and slower-witted citizens." The only explanation for the Democrats' ascendancy in Iowa since the state's birth in 1846, he convinced himself, was the constant influx of "poor folks from other states and from abroad. . . . All the poverty-stricken Irish and Germans that arrive are immediately incorporated by the Democrats who inform them that the Whigs are the wealthy aristocrats and blood-suckers of the common man."[12]

Political observers assumed that the Pella Dutch would follow the usual pattern and line up with the other immigrants behind the Democratic standard.[13] But they failed to contend with the Dutch leader and his Whig sympathies. The presidential election of 1852, the first

[10] Biographical data in Scholte Collection, Central College Archives, Pella, Iowa. A full-length biography—Lubbertus Oostendorp, *H. P. Scholte: Leader of the Secession of 1834 and Founder of Pella* (Franeker, Netherlands, 1964)—is mainly concerned with Scholte's theological ideas and his religious career. But see also Jacob Van Der Zee, *The Hollanders of Iowa* (Iowa City, 1912); Henry S. Lucas, *The Netherlanders in America: Dutch Immigration to the United States and Canada, 1789-1950* (Ann Arbor, 1955); Lenora Scholte, "A Stranger in a Strange Land: Romance in Pella History," *Iowa Journal of History and Politics*, XXXVII (1939), 115-203.

[11] Unpublished autobiographical sketch, Scholte Collection. The best expression of Scholte's views on slavery is in his pamphlet, *American Slavery in Reference to the Present Agitation of the United States* (Pella, 1856), p. 5. George M. Stephenson, *A History of American Immigration, 1820-1924* (Boston, 1926), errs in maintaining that Scholte affiliated with the Democrats "shortly after his arrival in this country" (p. 130).

[12] A. E. Dudok Bousquet to John Bousquet, Jan. 1, 1851, in "Letters of Abraham Everardus Dudok Bousquet to His Brother, John, 1849-1853," trans. Elizabeth Kempkes, Scholte Collection. For a similar expression of sentiment see Komer Van Stigt, *Geschiedenis van Pella, Iowa, en Omgeving* (Pella, 1897), II, 81.

[13] "Marion County will shortly become an important part of the Democracy of the State, for, besides being thoroughly democratic ever since her organiza-

in which the newcomers were eligible to vote,[14] clearly demonstrated the Dominie's power over his immigrant band. Contrary to all expectations, over 80 per cent of the new voters cast Whig ballots, as the table of election statistics indicates.[15] The thumping Whig majority

ELECTION STATISTICS, LAKE PRAIRIE TOWNSHIP, 1851-1860[*]

Elections	Whig/Republican		Democratic		Know-Nothing	
	No.	%	No.	%	No.	%
1851 State	9	18.0	41	82.0		
1852 National	89	60.1	59	39.9		
1854 State	52	34.9	97	65.1		
	(For)		(Against)			
1855 Prohibition	31	11.1	250	88.9		
1856 State	98	24.7	299	75.3		
1856 National	136	27.7	345	70.3	10	2.0
1857 County (spring)	55	20.4	214	79.6		
1857 County (fall)	58	17.1	282	82.9		
1857 State	56	16.3	287	83.7		
1858 County	102†	27.8	265	72.2		
1859 State	146	28.6	364	71.4		
1860 National	199	33.9	388	66.1		

[*]Compiled from Marion Co. newspapers and published county histories.
†Includes 66 (18 per cent) Independent votes.

can largely be explained in terms of Scholte's influence. The language barrier isolated the Hollanders from their neighbors and rendered unintelligible the newspaper editorials of the day. Therefore, they were completely dependent on the few bilingual leaders like Scholte.[16]

Dutch ethnic antagonism toward native Americans in the immediate

---

tion, she is about to receive an acquisition of a thousand Hollanders." Davenport *Gazette*, Oct. 17, 1847.

[14] Iowa law prescribed a five-year naturalization period, except with respect to voting in township elections. Iowa *Revised Code*, 1851, pp. 562-563.

[15] In the August, 1851, election, when only native American settlers in Lake Prairie Twp. participated, the Democrats captured forty-one out of fifty ballots (or 82 per cent), demonstrating a solid Democratic predilection for this group. In the presidential contest of 1852, with ninety-eight additional votes cast, the Democrats gained eighteen and the Whigs eighty. There is no evidence that the native Americans switched parties; and since the Dutch monopolized the land of the township (refusing as a matter of policy to sell to incoming Americans) it is safe to assume that almost all the new voters of 1852 were Hollanders.

[16] Historians of the Pella colony were later unable to comprehend the magnitude of Scholte's early power. Failing to consult the township vote, they assumed that the native Americans led their Dutch neighbors into the Democratic fold immediately upon their arrival. See Van Stigt, *Geschiedenis van Pella*, II, 81-82; Cyrenus Cole, "Pella—A Bit of Holland in America," *Annals of Iowa*, 3rd Ser., III (1898), 257-258; Van Der Zee, *Hollanders of Iowa*, p. 231; Lucas, *Netherlanders in America*, p. 542.

locale apparently aided Scholte's effort to indoctrinate his followers
with Whig dogmas. Such cultural conflict was by no means unique
to Marion County. New York state, originally settled by the Dutch,
had long witnessed bitter antagonism between "Yankees" and "Yorkers," as Professors Dixon Ryan Fox and Lee Benson have shown.
Fox traced nineteenth century Yankee-Dutch antagonisms back to the
seventeenth century and Benson demonstrated that in the Jacksonian
period the Dutch "ranged themselves politically against the Yankees
and Negroes—and voted accordingly."[17] The Pella settlers soon fell
into this pattern. A bitter county seat contest, for example, evoked
native American-Dutch ill-will.[18] Even such seemingly minor concerns
as different conceptions of proper farming techniques and animal hus-
bandry, and proper dress and domestic habits of women, proved ir-
ritating.[19]

Between the national elections of 1852 and 1856 the political patterns in the state, as well as in Lake Prairie Township, changed radically. In the so-called revolution of 1854 the Iowa Whigs finally over-
turned the Democratic ascendency in the state. Among the Dutch,
however, the trend was in the opposite direction as Scholte and more
than 80 per cent of the Lake Prairie voters now switched to the Democratic party.[20]

Why did most of the Iowa Hollanders defect to the Democrats?
Scholte's newspaper editorials perhaps provide the answer. The final
plank in the 1854 platform of the Iowa Whigs pledged the party to
enact a state liquor prohibition law. Scholte and his people bitterly
opposed prohibition, which they viewed as an unwarranted intrusion into their traditional way of life.[21] Comparable to the liquor issue in generating anger and anxiety was the nativist movement then
gaining ground in the United States—a crusade against Roman Catholicism in particular but all recent immigrants in general. By 1856

[17] Fox, *Yankees and Yorkers* (New York, 1940), *passim;* Benson, *The Concept
of Jacksonian Democracy: New York as a Test Case* (Princeton, 1961), p. 301.

[18] A. E. Dudok Bousquet to John Bousquet, July 14, 1852, "Letters," Scholte
Collection.

[19] One Dutchman reported to friends in the Netherlands that American farmers had no regard for their animals and that their women "are terribly lazy."
Moreover, he said, American consumption of whiskey was "scandalous." Quoted
in Sjoerd Aukes Sipma, *Belangrijke Berigten uit Pella* (Dockum, Netherlands,
1849), pp. 14-15.

[20] There were 343 more votes cast in 1856 than in 1852. Of this increase, 286
(or 83.6 per cent) were new Democratic votes and fifty-seven (16.4 per cent)
were new Republican votes.

[21] Scholte, in one of his early promotional broadsides, asserted that Pella needed
a brewery. He added, however, that "I would not encourage a distillery, since
I think that an increase in strong beverages would be harmful for the colony."
Tweede Stem uit Pella (Bosch, Netherlands, 1848), p. 32.

almost one in every ten voters in Marion County supported ex-President Millard Fillmore, candidate of the American (or "Know-Nothing") party, which had pledged itself to limit the political rights of naturalized citizens.[22] The Iowa Democrats, on the other hand, promised in their platform to resist "every attempt to abridge the privilege of becoming citizens," a plank that obviously appealed to the Dutch.[23]

Following their 1854 election victory, the new Whig majority in the Iowa legislature immediately pushed through a proposed constitutional amendment "for the suppresion of intemperance," and in early 1855 submitted it to the electorate for approval.[24] The Dominie campaigned heatedly against the measure. From February through April, 1855, every issue of the Pella *Gazette* devoted itself almost exclusively to this subject. On February 15, Editor Scholte printed the bill in its entirety and promised to "disect the corpse" in subsequent editorials. He emphasized that "no man in the State of Iowa" was more strongly opposed to intemperance and the "debasing practice of drunkedness" than he. The "Whig law," however, was "an abomination" which would "subvert . . . the principles of common justice. . . . We [must not] try to effect by law," he reasoned, "what can only be effected by the Gospel."[25]

A counterattack by the prohibition forces was immediate. Levi Leland, popular agent of the Iowa Temperance Society, lectured in Pella on two successive evenings. Besides issuing other inflammatory statements, he charged Scholte with advocating "intemperance and drunkedness" and remarked that judging from the faces he had seen about town the Dutch used too much alcohol.[26] Native Americans throughout central Iowa joined the anti-liquor clamor, specifically attacking Scholte.[27] The Dutch leader, possibly anticipating real

[22] Fillmore collected 225 out of 2,616 votes cast, or 8.6 per cent. *Census of Iowa*, 1869, p. 261.

[23] Herbert S. Fairall (ed.), *The Iowa City Republican Manual of Iowa Politics* (Iowa City, 1881), p. 36.

[24] Dan E. Clark, "History of Liquor Legislation in Iowa, 1846-1861," *Iowa Journal of History and Politics*, VI (1908), 55-87.

[25] Pella *Gazette*, Mar. 1, 1855. The only extant file of this newspaper is in the Scholte Collection.

[26] *Ibid.*, Mar. 8, 1855.

[27] The Eddyville *Free Press*, Mar. 8, 1855, published a bitter three-column editorial, and a Knoxville resident, Charles Burnham, sent Scholte a lengthy letter-to-the-editor which leveled a variety of charges. See Pella *Gazette*, Mar. 8, 1855. Native Americans, of course, harbored similar opinions of their Dutch neighbors. Recalled one pioneer Marion Co. resident: "The writer will never forget the Hollanders coming into Pella—strange people, at least strange at that time, in their appearance, their strange ways, their forms of dress and language." Pella *Chronicle*, July 18, 1912.

trouble, advised his "Christian soldiers" to "Put your trust in God and keep your powder dry."[28]

On March 10, a group of native Americans at Pella, led by Francis A. Barker, warden of the state penitentiary, met and drew up resolutions charging Scholte with "retarding the progress of the temperance cause." Unless the Dutchman capitulated on the issue, they threatened to urge readers to cancel their subscriptions to the *Gazette*. Scholte disdainfully replied that to him "Pecuniary profit is a secondary thing."[29]

Politicians from Knoxville, the local county seat, staged the next rally in Pella. William M. Stone, a future Republican governor of Iowa, was the main speaker. He not only charged the Dominie with injuring the anti-liquor movement, but he ridiculed "Father Scholte's" foreign birth and asserted that the Dutch leader was scheming to open a "saloon or doggery" in Pella for the sale of imported liquors. Stone's attack on Scholte was the beginning of a bitter personal vendetta. The feud took the form of a newspaper war, since Stone edited and published the Knoxville *Journal*. More important, Stone's blatant prejudice against foreign-born citizens demonstrated to the Dutch in a most personal way that the emerging Republican party was no place for them, thoroughly permeated as it was with nativism.

The next issue of the *Gazette* contained a four-column letter charging that Scholte merely wanted a law that was harsh on the drinker but lenient on the seller—the former being mostly native Americans and the latter German and Dutch. In reply Scholte labelled this charge "Know-Nothingism" and declared that "It would perhaps be difficult to find ten beer shops kept by Dutchmen; they are commonly Germans. In the cause of temperance," he continued, "it is perfectly wrong to set the Hollanders or Dutchmen on the side of favoring drunken-[n]ess, it is just the contrary." He ended by demanding that native Americans never lay upon the Netherlanders "what they will never bear."[30]

Scholte's bitterness was now open. He considered all antagonists to be Know-Nothing types and grew overly sensitive to references to his European birth. In one sarcastic editorial he wrote that

Some men have sneeringly alluded to the foreign birthplace of one of the editors of our Paper. Men tainted with, or immersed in Know-Nothingism have in their native presumption supposed that they had only to open their native babbling instrument, and bellow out their native wind-pipe,

---

28 Pella *Gazette*, Mar. 8, 1855.   29 *Ibid.*, Mar. 29, 1855.
30 *Ibid.*, May 17, 1855. The letter was written by S. N. Lindley of Monroe, Jasper Co.

and the foreign-born citizen would tremble upon his feet, his hearer would shudder for fear of the native ignoramouses. . . . They are mistaken.[31]

Election day proved Scholte a correct judge of the local temper. Lake Prairie Township rejected the prohibition law by an overwhelming 89 per cent, although state-wide the voters approved the law by a small majority. Nearby Knoxville Township, consisting mainly of native Americans, also rejected prohibition—but by only 51.5 to 48.5 per cent. Significantly, on the liquor issue as on the county seat question, Pella and Knoxville were sharply divided.

An important county election that occurred shortly afterwards further increased the Democratic sympathies of the Dutch and prompted Scholte openly to endorse a Democratic slate. The contest pitted the Democratic machine which controlled the courthouse at Knoxville against a slate of ex-Whigs who styled themselves "Independents" but who were in fact incipient Republicans.

A secret midnight political caucus of the Independents at Pella on a July evening in 1855 became a crucial event. Several Dutch Democrats learned of the meeting and immediately declared it to be a Know-Nothing conclave. They strengthened their charge by swearing an affidavit before a Pella justice of the peace. "In our Government," Scholte observed,

it is unfair, unmanly, and unchristian to so work in the dark, and to shun an open contest with political opponents. . . . Is it a wonder that the people begin to have strange thoughts about men, who . . . resort to such secret policy? No! It is no wonder, true and genuine Democrats must detest such an organization.

The Dutch leader demanded that the Independent candidates pledge under oath that the charge of the affidavit was not true. The aspirants promptly refused, claiming Scholte was merely

the tool of certain party managers, who exult in their power of wielding at their pleasure the votes of our Holland fellow-citizens. . . . We most emphatically deny the right of any man, or set of men in the town of Pella or elsewhere to establish a censorship over the minds of our people.

At the same time, the men denied that they were members of the Know-Nothing party. In reply Scholte argued that the candidates, if innocent, should have taken the oath because "the voters have a right to know. . . . To ask citizens of foreign birth to vote for men who are bound to exclude such citizens from office is more than an insult, it is to ask them to commit political suicide."[32]

The Dominie's editorial remarks soon bore fruit. The Dutch re-

31 *Ibid.*, Mar. 29, 1855.   32 *Ibid.*, Aug. 2, 1855.

mained convinced that the Pella "midnight meeting" provided a clear indication of the linkage of Know-Nothingism and Republicanism. Anyone who claimed otherwise, said Scholte, committed an "open, bare-faced falsehood." From now on, he concluded, the Pella Dutch had a clear-cut choice between the nativist and Democratic parties and the decision would "not be difficult" to make.[33] On election day the colonists flocked to the polls and delivered "a heavy majority" against the Republican ticket.[34]

Following the two emotion-charged elections of 1855, the Dutch and their leader clearly and consistently espoused the Democratic cause. In the local election of April, 1856, the Democrats carried the county by two hundred votes, the largest majority ever. A few days before the election a Knoxville citizen had predicted that Pella did not have enough wooden shoes to gain the victory. Afterward Scholte reported prophetically: "The men with wooden shoes . . . kicked the Know-Nothing Republicans badly now, and they will do it [again] next August."[35]

As the citizens prepared for the important state election of August 4, 1856, just three months prior to the presidential contest, Scholte worked hard to gain another Democratic victory. He delivered a series of lectures in Pella in the final week of the campaign in both the English and Dutch languages. So forceful were these speeches that an anonymous nativist charged him with driving the citizens of Lake Prairie to the polls "like cattle to the slaughter."[36] Despite the complaint, the great bulk of the Dutch inhabitants applauded Scholte's zeal. On election day, Lake Prairie went Democratic by 75.3 per cent, enough to put the entire county in the Democratic column.

To swell this majority for the Democratic presidential nominee, Scholte inserted three political columns in the weekly *Gazette* in the Dutch language for the duration of the national campaign. Since Republican politicians considered victory in Lake Prairie a prerequisite for gaining Marion County, they countered by importing their most prestigious personality, Governor James W. Grimes. The governor's rhetoric proved of little help. After the Pella rally Scholte observed that Grimes had gained very few converts and that "the demonstration was a total failure." This prediction proved correct. In one of the largest turnouts in the decade Lake Prairie gave Democrat James Buchanan 70.3 per cent of their ballots. Republican John C. Frémont attracted 27.7 per cent and Millard Fillmore of the nativist American party 2 per cent. The increased total vote reflected Scholte's heated editorials in the Dutch language, and his efforts to have all

33 *Ibid.*, Nov. 29, 1855.   34 *Ibid.*, Aug. 9, 1855.
35 *Ibid.*, Apr. 17, 1856.   36 *Ibid.*, Aug. 21, 1856.

eligible aliens naturalized so as to cast ballots. In response to his urging some fifty Hollanders had appeared at the August session of the district court.[37]

Politically, the years 1857-1858 saw little change in Lake Prairie. Citizens balloted five times, with the Democrats consistently garnering 70 to 80 per cent of the vote. These impressive majorities placed Marion County well within the Democratic fold, whereas neighboring counties returned strong Republican votes in all these elections.[38] Scholte, however, was beginning to have second thoughts about the Democracy. He blamed President Buchanan for the sectional violence in Kansas and expressed dissatisfaction with the increasingly pro-slavery complexion of the party.[39]

Disillusionment with the Buchanan administration in no way aided local Republicans, however, for in the spring of 1858 the Republican-controlled legislature proposed an election law which discriminated against naturalized citizens whose ballots were challenged at the polls.[40] Scholte declared the bill an "outrageous affront" which clearly illuminated the nativist bias of the new party. "We did not dream," he wrote,

that the stupidity and recklessness of our Iowa Nativists would go so far. . . . Native puppyism was never better illustrated. . . . It is a narrow mind indeed that cannot devise a law to preserve the purity of elections without exposing naturalized citizens to repeated insults. The proposed outrage will sink deep into the minds of Hollanders, and they will take care to resent it. . . . The Hollanders were nursed and craddled under the enjoyment of Republican liberties for centuries and . . . will not, without a remonstrance submit to the ignomy of begging for a vote . . . at the pleasure of any Know-Nothing demagogue that may choose to challenge them! . . . But we know also that the day of reckoning is coming. . . . Whenever there is an opportunity . . . the despised wooden shoe nation will be at hand to kick would-be despots and exclusivists into the abyss of political oblivion.[41]

The statistics of the 1858 election, in which Lake Prairie voters gave almost three-fourths of their ballots to the Democrats, prove that Scholte's desire to "kick would-be Republican despots" was shared by most Pella Dutchmen. This was the fourth straight year that the community returned solid Democratic majorities, but their convictions would soon be put to a severe test.

[37] *Ibid.*, Aug. 21, Sept. 4, 1856.
[38] Knoxville *Journal*, Oct. 27, 1857, Feb. 2, 1858.
[39] Pella *Gazette*, Dec. 3, 24, 1857, Jan. 7, 14, Feb. 11, Mar. 11, 1858.
[40] Naturalized citizens would have to swear under oath they were indeed naturalized, then prove it by presenting their papers, and then swear to the veracity of the papers. Iowa *House Journal*, 7th G.A. (1858), p. 233.
[41] Pella *Gazette*, Feb. 18, 1858.

In 1859 the over-confident Democratic party of Marion County was rocked by two jarring blows which all observers predicted would change the political complexion of the county. In April a longtime Democrat, Sebra U. Hammond, editor of the *Democratic Standard* of Knoxville, bolted his party with an editorial blast in which he labeled the local Democratic leadership a "selfish and unprincipled clique."[42] The second jolt came with the defection of the man who was believed to control the crucial Dutch votes of Lake Prairie Township—Henry Scholte. The Dominie had planned his move carefully to obtain maximum newspaper coverage and squeeze out the last ounce of propaganda value. On June 18, the county Democratic convention named the Pella leader as one of its thirteen delegates to the state convention at Des Moines on June 23.[43] To the astonishment of all, however, on June 22 Scholte appeared at the Republican convention (also meeting in the capital city) at the head of the Marion County delegation. Eager to publicize this coup, the state's Republicans honored Scholte with the convention vice-presidency.

Almost every prominent newspaper in Iowa commented on this "Incident at the Convention." The Republican press reported that Scholte had fallen in with a number of Republican delegates on the steamer en route for Des Moines. These partisans supposedly had convinced him of the error of his way. On the morning of the convention, the story went, the Marion County Republicans elected him as a delegate since he had "privately declared himself a Republican, and wanted to have done with modern Democracy forever."[44] The Democratic journals lamely asserted that Scholte had "wandered into the Republican Convention by mistake."[45] Scholte himself ambiguously explained that "the foolish and unreasonable action of the democrats of nominating me as a delegate to their State Convention, against my will and without my knowledge, has accelerated my decision to take an active part in the Republican Convention, where I did belong in reality."[46]

That the Dominie belonged in the Republican fold is obvious from his editorials. Whig even before coming to America, he had adhered to that dying party until convinced that abolitionists and Know-Nothings had captured it. Thereafter, along with many former Whigs, he supported the Buchanan administration "for the purpose of saving

[42] Knoxville *Democratic Standard*, Apr. 5, 14, 1859.

[43] *Ibid.*, Apr. 14, 1859; Pella *Gazette*, July 22, 1859.

[44] Muscatine *Weekly Journal*, July 1, 1859; Des Moines *Iowa Citizen*, June 29, July 13, 1859; Keokuk *Des Moines Valley Whig*, July 4, 1859; Dubuque *Daily Times*, June 30, 1859.

[45] Dubuque *Express and Herald*, cited in Burlington *Hawk-Eye*, July 30, 1859.

[46] Pella *Gazette*, July 22, 1859.

the Union."[47] But the President's support of the fraudulent proslavery Kansas constitution and the eruption of violence in the Sunflower State disillusioned him. Scholte, in short, had joined the Democrats only as a last resort and soon grew disenchanted.

The most important question is not why Scholte changed his party allegiance, however, but whether the Pella Dutch would follow his lead. Opinions of contemporaries varied widely, depending on political viewpoint. Typical of Republican editors was a flat statement that "the accession of Mr. Scholte and those he represents will give us Marion County, with a gain of two Representatives and one Senator."[48] The Knoxville *Journal* editor assured his readers that Scholte's defection was "likely to work a complete revolution in the political character of Marion County. The feeling and conviction that led Scholte to abandon the black democracy, has also induced most of his countrymen to take the same step."[49] Democratic newspapers, on the other hand, predicted that "Mr. Scholte will take with him into the Republican party exactly four men, himself one of the number. And a number of Hollanders, whose dislike to Scholte has placed them with the Republicans, will now come over to the Democracy."[50] The Oskaloosa editor labeled Scholte "another Benedict Arnold," whose "unprincipled course" would result in a larger majority for the Democracy of Lake Prairie "than they ever yet had."[51] A Netherlander from Muscatine, professing some acquaintance with the Pella colony, also judged that Dutchmen "possess a mind of their own," and could not be "turned by the voice of a traitor. . . . Hollanders are not such a set of fools as to change their political principles at the bidding of a man in whom they have no confidence."[52]

Republican politicians, particularly ex-Governor Grimes and the gubernatorial nominee, Samuel J. Kirkwood, were unwilling to accept this verdict. On July 29, Grimes encouraged Kirkwood to discount rumors that the Republicans were losing strength in Iowa, as just the reverse was true. "I just saw an intelligent man from Marion County," Grimes wrote. "He says the Hollanders are nearly all going with Scholte and that we shall carry the county by as large a maj[ority] as the democrats have usually done it, viz. 200."[53]

[47] Scholte, *American Slavery*, p. 78.

[48] Burlington *Hawk-Eye*, June 28, 1859. See also Iowa City *Republican*, July 6, 1859.

[49] Cited in Des Moines *Citizen*, July 6, 1859.

[50] Des Moines *State Journal*, reprinted in Davenport *Daily Iowa State Democrat*, July 3, 1859.

[51] Oskaloosa *Times*, July 28, 1859.

[52] Davenport *Democrat*, July 6, 1859.

[53] "Correspondence of James W. Grimes," *Annals of Iowa*, 3rd Ser., XXII (1941), 556.

Because of the wide publicity given to Scholte's defection, winning the Dutch vote became a matter of prestige for both parties. A Knoxville editor spoke for many when he noted the election was "one of unusual importance because all eyes are turned on Marion."[54] Maintaining the support of the Hollanders was a must for the Democrats. Should the Dutch defect, other Iowa immigrant groups, particularly the Germans, might be influenced to follow suit.

The politicians worked diligently as the gubernatorial election of 1859 approached. Scholte sponsored several Republican caucuses in Lake Prairie, thereby affecting the first permanent Republican organization in the township.[55] As in previous contests, the key issues seemed to be ones affecting the Dutch as an ethnic group. Instead of squatter sovereignty, free land, and a transcontinental railroad, local attention centered on the nativist Massachusetts naturalization law and the protection of naturalized Americans abroad.[56] The Massachusetts Act, an expression of eastern Republicanism which other states were being urged to emulate, banned foreign-born citizens from the polls of that state for a minimum of two years after gaining citizenship. Iowa Democrats, citing this issue, argued that for the Dutch to vote Republican was tantamount to "putting the rope around their own necks."[57] Republicans, however, countered by stressing the refusal of Buchanan's Secretary of State, Lewis Cass, to protect naturalized citizens from induction into foreign military service while temporarily visiting their old homelands.[58]

The balloting took place on October 10, 1859. Despite Scholte's strongest urgings, Lake Prairie citizens again cast Democratic votes in undiminished numbers. Over 71 per cent of the total went to the Democrats whereas in 1856, with Scholte campaigning ardently for the Democracy, the party had captured but 70.3 per cent. The turnout in both contests varied little—491 in 1856 to 510 in 1859. Instead of wholesale desertions to the Republicans, therefore, the Democrats actually showed a slight net gain. The Knoxville *Standard* editor was obviously correct when he concluded that "H. P. Scholte does not control the Hollanders."[59]

Scholte's loss of power highlights a significant fact—that the initial

---

54 Knoxville *Standard*, Aug. 12, 1859.

55 Pella *Gazette*, Aug. 17, Sept. 14, Oct. 5, 1859.

56 *Ibid.*, Sept. 14, 21, 28, 1859.

57 *Ibid.*, Aug. 17, Sept. 14, Oct. 5, 1859; Knoxville *Standard*, June 14, 1859.

58 Pella *Gazette*, July 22, 1859; Oskaloosa *Times*, July 28, Aug. 4, 1859.

59 Knoxville *Standard*, Oct. 22, 1859. Scholars, entirely ignoring the township vote, have assumed that Scholte's defection had a tremendous influence on his countrymen. See Stephenson, *History of American Immigration*, p. 130; Frank I. Herriott, "Republican Presidential Preliminaries in Iowa, 1859-1860," *Annals of Iowa*, 3rd Ser., IX (1910), 253.

power of the ethnic leader to control the ballots of the immigrant could be short-lived. It is difficult, however, to pin-point when the Dominie's political influence began to decline. A few disgruntled colonists had criticized him and dissentions already had erupted within his church in the early years, and by 1855 a group of "young Turks" had pushed through the municipal incorporation of Pella and taken office against Scholte's wishes.[60] Undoubtedly he had made enemies. Yet this probably had little impact on the outcome of the 1859 election. The voting pattern had been set and, regardless of attitudes toward Scholte, the people continued to think in terms of prohibition and nativism, as the Dominie subsequently complained.[61] No doubt the bitterness of these issues, both associated with Republicanism, still smarted within the rank-and-file. The sophisticated Scholte, his political contacts transcending the local scene, apparently proved to his own satisfaction that the Republican party had purged itself of nativism and that prohibition had become a relatively minor issue. But the mind of the average Dutchman, still largely isolated by the language barrier, could not easily be changed. "I don't bother much about politics," remarked a Dutch carpenter. "I put a Democratic ticket in the box and leave the rest to God."[62]

Seemingly not discouraged, Scholte labored for the Republicans throughout 1860. Returning full of enthusiasm from the national convention in Chicago he penned splendid tributes to Lincoln and castigated Democratic leaders.[63] He also publicized the Republican platform planks on the supposedly key issues—no extension of slavery into free territory, a homestead bill, a transcontinental railroad.[64]

The homestead principle, in particular, should have appealed to the Dutch of Marion County. By 1860 most of the vacant land within twenty miles of Pella had been taken up and the community considered itself overcrowded.[65] Colonists were discussing the feasibility of a mass migration to northwest Iowa where government land was still available. The idea of free—or at least cheap—land should have

[60] Sipma, *Belangrijke Berigten*, pp. 27-30; Pella *Gazette*, Aug. 9, 16, 23, 1855; Oostendorp, *H. P. Scholte*, pp. 168-173; "The Garden Square Controversy, April 1865," Scholte Collection.

[61] ". . . The Democratic leaders," wrote Scholte, "are continually trying to influence foreign-born citizens . . . [to think] that the Republican party is under the control of the party generally known as the Know-Nothing or Native Americans." This was "slander," he concluded. Pella *Gazette*, Jan. 25, 1860.

[62] Quoted in John Scholte Nollen, *Grinnell College* (Iowa City, 1953), p. 249.

[63] The Pella *Gazette* succumbed to financial difficulties in February, 1860, and thereafter Scholte published his views in the Burlington *Hawk-Eye* and the Sheboygan (Wisc.) *Nieuwsbode*, a Dutch-language paper read by many Pella Hollanders.

[64] Burlington *Hawk-Eye*, Nov. 3, 1860.

[65] Lucas, *Netherlanders in America*, p. 333.

been decisive. Yet the Hollanders rejected both the Republican platform and the party's rough-hewn candidate.[66] In November, 1860,
Lake Prairie Township awarded Lincoln only 33.9 per cent of its
ballots.[67]

Scholte's post-election editorials gave no indication that the Pella
colony had repudiated his political leadership; other politicians and
editors continued to treat him as an important ethnic leader. Only the
township statistics now contradict the assumption by historians that
the Dominie continued to deliver the Dutch vote.[68] Scholars might
well be cautious of other immigrant spokesmen who professed political leadership of their people.

But there is a larger lesson to be learned from the case of the Pella
Dutch. In recent years some students of the ethno-cultural approach
to voting—in stressing nativism and prohibition as hidden issues—have
implied that immigrants "rationally" defended their Old Country ways
of life at the ballot box. The case of the Pella colony, however, suggests
that after the first few years sheer political inertia governed—as Scholte
himself discovered. Influenced by personal attacks on himself and his
followers (attacks that he translated to the rank-and-file), the Dominie created such a stanch tradition of Democratic voting that he was
unable to alter it. Hence, while Scholte in 1860 fulminated against
Democrats as slave-mongers, as opponents of the Pacific railroad and
homestead bills, and as destroyers of the Constitution, the Dutch
citizens blithely ignored him and the national issues he propounded
and voted against nativism and prohibition—the issues of 1854-1856.

One suspects that if Scholte had initially championed slavery aboli-

[66] There is other evidence in addition to this negative Dutch vote that Buchanan land policy and the homestead issue may have been overemphasized by
historians such as Paul W. Gates ("The Homestead Law in Iowa," *Agricultural
History*, XXXVIII [1964], 73). Many northwest Iowa newspapers welcomed Buchanan's land sales of 1858-1860 and ignored his homestead bill vetoes, while
Stephen A. Douglas ran far ahead of his ticket in the same area.

[67] Although this was a net Republican gain of 5.3 per cent over the gubernatorial contest of 1859, the Republican increase was likely due to the influx of
native Americans attracted to Pella by Central Iowa University, which opened its
doors in 1857. A comparison of the 1850 and 1860 population censuses in Lake
Prairie Twp. shows that nearly two-thirds of the non-Dutch newcomers of the
fifties were from the New England, Middle Atlantic, and Upper Ohio Valley
states. Daniels, "Immigrant Vote," table II, demonstrates that most migrants
to Iowa from these areas voted Republican in 1860.

[68] See Stephenson, *History of American Immigration*, p. 131; Van Stigt, *Geschiedenis van Pella*, III, 44; Van Der Zee, *Hollanders of Iowa*, pp. 229, 408 n.
Lucas alone concluded the reverse. "In Pella," he wrote, "the majority still stub-
bornly adhered to the Democratic position and were suspicious of the abolitionist
elements in the new party." *Netherlanders in America*, p. 562. The "official abstract" of the Marion Co. vote was printed in the Knoxville *Republican*, Nov. 20,
1860. The only issue of the newspaper for that year known to be extant, it now
reposes in the State Historical Society of Iowa.

tion and had refrained from emphasizing the Know-Nothing and anti-liquor movements, he might have created a Whig-Republican tradition. Indeed, in failing to gravitate to Lincoln's support in 1860 the Pella Hollanders apparently ran counter to what occurred in Dutch settlements in Michigan, Illinois, and Wisconsin.[69] Lake Prairie Township, in fact, has been in the Democratic column in *every* national election since 1860 except for the Eisenhower and Kennedy contests.[70] For those who would understand this longtime rejection of the party of Lincoln the peculiar historical circumstances within which the tradition began provide the decisive insight.

[69] Lucas, *Netherlanders in America*, pp. 529 ff. Daniels, "Immigrant Vote," table II and appendix A, lists the Iowa Dutch as strong Lincoln supporters. This conclusion resulted from an examination of the Hollanders of Black Oak Twp., Mahaska Co. Although the largest ethnic group in that township, these Dutch were outnumbered by native American voters by a more than two-to-one margin. It is likely, therefore, that the native Americans, rather than the Dutch, accounted for the heavy Republican vote there. The Black Oak Netherlanders represented a contiguous segment of the Pella colony.

[70] In gubernatorial races the township has voted Democratic in every election except in 1930. The Pella city wards, separated from the rural precinct since the turn of the century, remained consistently Democratic until 1928. Since then a two-party trend has emerged. All votes are in the yearly editions of the *Iowa Official Register*.

REJECTED REPUBLICAN INCUMBENTS IN THE 1866 CONGRESSIONAL NOMINATING CONVENTION: A Study in Reconstruction Politics

Lawrence N. Powell

"THE OLD FIRES OF 1856 and 1860 have been relit in this state," remarked a Pennsylvania Republican editor as the election campaign of 1866 got underway.[1] He was not indulging in hyperbole; the Congressional election of that year, involving the grave questions of Reconstruction, was one of the most heated in our history. By that time Andrew Johnson had broken with Congress, had thrown his prestige behind the newly-formed National Union Movement, and had aroused Republican hostility toward his patronage policy. And the New Orleans massacre, while over a month old, was still receiving fresh ink in the Union dailies. Only remaining in the future was Johnson's ill-advised speaking tour, his "swing around the circle."

This is a well-known scenario from a national campaign that has long attracted historians' attention. In the judgment of nearly all students of that period, it was a canvass that aggravated the entire North, stirred up remote hamlets, and left few indifferent. In historical legend it was a climactic moment in the radicalization of the Republican party and of the Nation. Of course historians have differed markedly in accounting for the turbulence of those years. William A. Dunning and Claude Bowers, in their different ways, discerned the devious hand of radical conspirators in the election's outcome, as did Howard K. Beale, though for other reasons. All assumed that a small band of determined Republican extremists, through fraud, misrepresentation, and a mountebank's regard for the passions, coerced their party and the northern electorate into opposing Andrew Johnson and endorsing a harsh southern policy.[2] Recent historians have disputed this argument. Though not fond of the radicals, Eric McKitrick has exonerated them of the common vilifications, pointing instead to Johnson's stubbornness, southern

---

[1] Johnstown *Tribune*, Aug. 31, 1866.

[2] William A. Dunning, *Reconstruction, Political and Economic, 1865-1877* (New York, 1962), pp. 45-47, 54-57, 80-83; Claude G. Bowers, *The Tragic Era* (Boston, 1962), p. 141; Howard K. Beale, *The Critical Year* (New York, 1930), pp. 6, 111-112, 141, 145,146.

intransigence, and northern demands for guarantees, to explain the 1866 election and its aftermath.[3] An English scholar, W. R. Brock, believes with McKitrick that "it is difficult to demonstrate a Radical plot in the rising tide of disquiet in the North." Neither "partisan passion" nor "material interest" can explain this critical moment in Reconstruction, he writes, "for the great moving power behind Reconstruction was the conviction of the average Republican that the objectives of his party were rational and humane."[4] The reason Republicans and the country moved as they did in 1866, McKitrick and Brock seem to argue, was because of a grass roots movement animated either by instincts of political survival or ideological commitment.

Despite the disparities in their conclusions, both of these broad historical schools share the conviction that national affairs intruded prominently into northern politics in these years, whether through the medium of a radical cabal or genuine issues that evoked a mass response. This was a time when events in the Capitol swept all else before them. Indeed, how could American politics not be touched by the controversies then convulsing Washington?

Surely one area where national influence on northern politics ought to have been reflected was in those Congressional districts which denied renomination to an aspiring Republican incumbent. In a day when editors announced "that the present Congressmen must be renominated to show that the party endorses their Congressional action,"[5] we should rightfully expect to discover Reconstruction issues figuring prominently in the retirement of Republicans wishing renomination. Indeed, given old and new Reconstruction historiography, we should anticipate one of two situations to have obtained, both relating to the alleged radicalization of the party. These Congressmen should have become either the victims of a national radical conspiracy to purge vacillating and conservative Republicans, or the casualties of local groundswell campaigns to send more reliable radicals to Congress. If either were a trend in 1866, we ought to be able to detect it in those seventeen districts where nominating struggles occurred.[6]

[3] Eric L. McKitrick, *Andrew Johnson and Reconstruction* (Chicago, 1960), pp. 448-485.

[4] W. R. Brock, *An American Crisis* (New York, 1963), pp. 43, 62.

[5] New Haven *Daily Palladium*, Feb. 14, 1867.

[6] It might be illuminating to know whether or not the Thirty-ninth Congress was unique with its seventeen Republican renomination failures, as compared with that of previous and succeeding Congresses. But it would take an enormous amount of research to determine this, since readily accessible sources, such as the *Biographical Directory of the American Congress*, are unreliable regarding the reasons why incumbents failed to return to Congress. I did not learn that nine of my sample had even lost renomination bids until after I did extensive research in local newspapers, and even now I cannot be sure that seventeen is a comprehensive figure. It is merely the best estimate available under the circumstances. For what it is worth, the *overall* Republican turnover rate for the Thirty-ninth Congress was not particularly high, and indeed at 37.3 per cent was lower than the rates for the Fortieth, Forty-first, and Forty-second Congresses. But even if the Republicans in the Thirty-ninth Con-

But this survey of Republican incumbents who lost renomination bids has turned up little evidence that the Republican party was radicalized by either means in 1866, if it were radicalized at all. The central fact in most of these districts was that Reconstruction had very little bearing on the nominations. In the overwhelming majority of cases the incumbents were replaced for entirely local reasons. Some of these Congressmen were the victims of local cabals and popularity contests, while others had to step down in deference to term rules and rotation customs. This pervasive localism seems to raise doubts that the Republican party was radicalized in 1866.

This is not to say that Reconstruction issues had no impact whatsoever, for there were at least two nominating episodes that had the earmarks of a grassroots movement to send more reliable Republicans to Congress. The Ohio Eighth District appears to have rejected James R. Hubbell's bid for renomination because of his irresolute conduct in Washington. Save for the Republican newspaper in his own Delaware County, the press throughout the district scornfully contrasted "his ability to hug his constituents before election" with his want of "zeal and ability in attending to their interests afterwards."[7] He had also gained the reputation of a "dodger" and a "weak kneed Congressmen" who had failed to stand up "manfully for the principles of the party that elected him."[8] A Republican conservative,[9] Hubbell was not helped by rumors that schemers intriguing to make the next Ohio delegation conservative were "anxious to retain Mr. H because they feel certain of being able to control him."[10]

Though outraged at what it deemed the "persistent determination to misrepresent" Hubbell merely because of "personal hostility," the Delaware *Gazette* was powerless to reverse the tide against its candidate.[11] All of the Delaware delegation save one favored his renomination, but other counties in the district endorsed favorite sons or remained ominously uncommitted.[12] At the convention it was "manifest" at an early hour that Hubbell's renomination chances were "decidedly doubtful."[13] After sixty ballots, the Delaware delegation holding out till the very

gress had a unique number of renomination denials, that fact would hardly alter the conclusions of this paper. If Reconstruction policy had slight influence on the failure of Republican incumbents to be renominated, as this article tries to demonstrate, then it is hard to imagine how it could have affected the rate of Republican incumbents in 1866 who lost renomination bids.

[7] Cardington *Reveille*, June 21, 1866.

[8] *Ibid.*; Delaware *Gazette*, Aug. 3, 1866; Mt. Gilead *Sentinel*, Aug. 27, 1866.

[9] John Lockhart McCarthy, "Reconstruction Legislation and Voting Alignments in the House of Representatives, 1863-1869" (Ph.D. dissertation, Yale University, 1970), Exhibit 3.1, 118.

[10] Cardington *Reveille*, June 21, 1866.

[11] Delaware *Gazette*, July 20, 1866.

[12] Marion *Independent*, Aug. 16, 1866; Marion *Democratic Mirror*, Aug. 16, 1866; Delaware *Gazette*, Aug. 24, 1866.

[13] Columbus *Morning Journal*, Aug. 23, 1866; Marion *Democratic Mirror*, Aug. 16, 30, 1866; Delaware *Gazette*, Aug. 10, 1866.

end, C. S. Hamilton emerged among Hubbell's four rivals as the party's new nominee. The conclusion to draw from the episode, allowed the Columbus *Morning Journal,* was that Hubbell's "constituency have determined to send [to Congress] a man. . . whose reliability should be beyond all question and above all suspicion." The casualty of a rank and file resolve that "there shall be neither doubt nor dodging upon the great vital issues now before the country," Hubbell was just too vulnerable before Hamilton's vocal radicalism.[14]

Much the same thing appears to have happened to Andrew J. Kuykendall in the Cairo District of Illinois. One of the most conservative Republicans in the Thirty-ninth Congress, Kuykendall must have reckoned that his political conduct was the safest policy in this notorious copperhead neighborhood. But the Republican party here, though only marginally in power,[15] expected greater firmness from their Representative. Reports had it that none in his district were "so poor as to do him reverence."[16] In the Gallatin County caucus not even a quarter of the delegates were willing to endorse him; the Williamson County delegation did not list him among its choices; and a Republican gathering in Cairo was so hostile as to keep him from participating.[17] His prospects were indeed gloomy. The convention nominated General Green B. Raum by acclamation, a move some believed just punishment for one "who has so clearly misrepresented his constituents."[18]

While it appears that Hubbell and Kuykendall fell before constituencies determined on Representatives more responsive to their feeling on Reconstruction, nothing of the sort can be said of Henry J. Raymond's demise. It had all the characteristics of a purge. An ally of the Weed-Seward forces, founder and editor of the New York *Times,* and since 1864 Republican Congressman and chairman of the National Union Executive Committee, Raymond was a frequent supporter in the Thirty-ninth Congress of Andrew Johnson, whose restoration policy was consonant with Raymond's strict interpretation of the Constitution.[19] This conduct earned him a certain amount of hostility, as did his occasional fence-straddling on the issues.[20] But it was not until Johnson persuaded him to work with the National Union Movement that Raymond jeopardized his political career. He joined the movement reluct-

[14] Columbus *Morning Journal,* Aug. 23, 1866. Neither side of the contest, it should be noted, detected any outside interference in the convention's choice.

[15] Kuykendall won by only 52 per cent of the vote, and then only because of the soldier vote. McCarthy, "Reconstruction," Ex. 3-15, 224; Cairo *Democrat,* Sept. 6, 1866.

[16] Chicago *Tribune,* June 10, 1866.

[17] Cairo *Democrat,* July 10, 1866, Aug. 12, 1866; Chicago *Tribune,* Aug. 4, 1866.

[18] Cairo *Daily Democrat,* Aug. 12, 1866; New York *Times,* Aug. 12, 1866; Chicago *Tribune,* June 10, 1866.

[19] Dorothy Dodd, *Henry J. Raymond and the "New York Times" During Reconstruction* (Chicago, 1933), pp. 38-39; Francis Brown, *Raymond of the Times* (New York, 1951), *passim.*

[20] Brown, *Raymond,* pp. 291-293, 295; Cairo *Daily Democrat,* July 20, 1866.

antly, unsure of its true purposes, and then because he saw in it the only real chance of nationalizing the Republican party, of making it more than a sectional organization.[21] But the risks were great, among them what Raymond considered Johnson's overly close identification with the Democrats. His misgivings were sound. At the Philadelphia Convention he failed to win endorsement for the Fourteenth Amendment, a measure he thought in the "direction of harmony and conciliation."[22] And even though the convention expelled the notorious Clement Vallandigham and Fernando Wood, it was apparent that the "Democrats had accomodated themselves to the movement by simply gobbling it up. . . ."[23]

The Republican party quickly rebuked Raymond's participation in the National Union Movement. Soon after the convention, his enemies on the National Union Executive Committee did not let the absence of a quorum prevent them from relieving him of his chairmanship.[24] The New York State Republican organization also had accounts to settle with Raymond. Rubbing salt in the wound, it appointed a long-time political rival, Horace Greeley, to succeed him on the National Committee. A more serious reproach was the alleged tampering with the enrollment books in Raymond's Sixth District. Ostensibly investigating the Republican registration in the Sixth, the New York State Central Committee set aside the enrollment instead of revising it, and saw to it that only Republicans who declared against Johnson and Raymond were registered, at least acording to the New York *Times*. Little wonder, commented the *Times*, that the anti-Raymond ticket carried the district easily in the Republican-Union primary elections. Despite the *Times*'s declaration that it would not "submit to such wholesale swindling," Raymond consulted his self-respect and presumably his political fortunes and announced he would not stand for re-election. Against such a determined effort to purge him he apparently decided resistance was hopeless. Besides, the *Times*'s circulation figures had declined precipitously, and given the political climate in Congress there was little influence he could bring to bear.[25]

Henry Raymond's purge seems to have been authentic and fits admirably the description of how radicals supposedly whipped their party into obedience. But about the purges of John Kasson, John Wentworth, and Roswell Hart there is room for skepticism.

The Representative of Iowa's Fifth District, John Kasson had won his two terms to Congress by substantial pluralities, and had gained much popularity and influence, first as the Republican party's State

21 Brown, *Raymond*, p. 295.

22 Quoted in McKitrick, *Andrew Johnson*, p. 358; Dodd, *Henry J. Raymond*, p. 57.

23 McKitrick, *Andrew Johnson*, p. 416.

24 New York *Times*, Aug. 29, Sept. 1, 4, 5, 1866; Dodd, *Henry J. Raymond*, p. 59-60; Brown, *Raymond*, pp. 307-308.

25 New York *Times*, Sept. 26, 27, 1866; McKitrick, *Andrew Johnson*, p. 420.

Chairman and then as the First Assistant Postmaster General in Lincoln's early administration. But Kasson's recent habit of conciliating Andrew Johnson had made him vulnerable in a district which defiantly called itself "as Radical as any in the State."[26] Thus, after touring the South in 1865 he circulated a public letter defending Johnson's restoration policy. He also spoke against the D.C. Suffrage Bill, even though he voted for it, in order to preserve his influence at the executive mansion.[27] The Republican paper in Des Moines, the seat of his district, refused to defend him because his conduct "could not be defended."[28] Kasson appeared to be in hot water with his constituents.

But in reality he was in deeper trouble with state politicos, and not simply because of disagreements over Reconstruction policy. Too aloof and distant to win firm loyalty from political managers, he had alienated the Des Moines clique of young, ambitious politicians by his handling of patronage and his meddling in the United States senate race.[29] Several of his lieutenants, miffed by his neglect of their ambition, deserted him for the movement forming around Grenville M. Dodge, the celebrated Civil War general and railroad builder, who was unhappy with his patron's alleged support for a rival railroad group in Des Moines.[30] Needing little coaxing, Dodge told Kasson that the Congressman's Reconstruction policy obliged them to sever their relationship.[31]

Since Kasson controlled the district's patronage and therefore most of its older politicians, the Dodge forces had to resort to duplicity. It was easy for them to exploit the marriage scandal that enveloped Kasson when his wife left him on grounds of infidelity. An indignant brother-in-law obligingly printed a vicious circular alleging, among other infelicities, that Kasson was "*a diseased man from dissipation.*"[32] By convention time many county delegations had passed resolutions condemning Kasson's "moral defection and political declension."[33] Despite the calumny, Kasson did not fall easily. Dodge finally won after three days of balloting, and then only because he used the promise of a job with the Union Pacific to persuade a candidate to throw votes in his direction.[34] The Dodge paper in Des Moines saw in Kasson's removal a determination "to add strength to the Republican cause."[35] But

[26] Iowa (Des Moines) *State Register*, May 22, 1866.

[27] *Ibid.*, May 24, 1866.

[28] *Ibid.*, May 22, 1866.

[29] Edward Younger, *John A. Kasson: Politics and Diplomacy From Lincoln to McKinley* (Iowa City, Iowa, 1955), pp. 179-180, 187-189.

[30] *Ibid.*, p. 195.

[31] Stanley P. Hirshson, *Grenville M. Dodge: Soldier, Politician, Railroad Pioneer* (Bloomington, Indiana, 1967), pp. 140-141.

[32] *Ibid.*, pp. 136-137; Younger, *John A. Kasson*, p. 205.

[33] Younger has found letters demonstrating, he argues, that "the circulars turned away from Kasson enough delegates to defeat him." Younger, *John A. Kasson*, p. 208; Iowa (Des Moines) *State Register*, June 12, 1866.

[34] Younger, *John A. Kasson*, p. 206; Hirshson, *Grenville M. Dodge*, pp. 136-137.

[35] Iowa (Des Moines) *State Register*, June 20, 1866.

though Dodge did prove more radical in Congress, it was by inadvertence and not design: his backers certainly did not promote him because of his Reconstruction radicalism. The fissures in the state organization arising from patronage and railroad disputes had more to do with Kasson's purge than his occasional courtship of Andrew Johnson. Grenville Dodge's most recent biographer sums it up well: "by far the most important issue at stake was who was going to get what."[36]

As in the Iowa Fifth, so in the Illinois First: a clique of political and business enemies engineered the incumbent's downfall. "Long John" Wentworth, the colorful Chicago Congressman, had accumulated a number of them during his many years on the political circuit, first as the aggressive editor of the Chicago *Democrat* and then as an independent Jacksonian with whom neither party felt entirely comfortable. He had already served four terms in Congress in the 1840's and '50's, and had been Chicago's first Republican mayor. But he seemed always embroiled in controversy. As mayor he was domineering, and irritated not a few businessmen by his strict enforcement of the anti-cluttering laws.[37] With the other Chicago newspapers he was endlessly in desperate competition for subscribers and advertisers, until libel suits in the early 1860's forced him out of business. The plaintiff in one of these cases, Norman B. Judd, never forgot or forgave Wentworth's unproven charges of peculation and intrigue against Lincoln's Senate campaign in 1858.[38] Nor did the Springfield Republican organization look kindly on his cooperation with the Democrats during the Civil War in drafting a new state constitution, an enterprise to which his Jacksonian bank sentiments attracted him.[39] Over the years his many enemies had grown accustomed to ambushing him, and they were not about to relent in 1866.

His personal habits, and not his political principles, were his major campaign liabilities.[40] The redoubtable Chicago *Tribune*, probably one of the most radical journals in the country, gave up the useless attempt to taint Wentworth with copperheadism. He was consistently on the radical end of the continuum in the Thirty-ninth Congress's First Session.[41] It concentrated instead on his intemperate habits.[42] Chicago had outgrown his peculiar style of electioneering, it intoned, and now desired "a Representative who will have some higher ambition than to

[36] Hirshson, *Grenville M. Dodge*, pp. 134-135.

[37] Don E. Fehrenbacher, *Chicago Giant: A Biography of "Long John" Wentworth* (Madison, Wisconsin, 1957), pp. 145-146.

[38] *Ibid.*, pp. 169-170.

[39] *Ibid.*, pp. 193-195.

[40] New York *Times*, Oct. 21, 1866.

[41] McCarthy, "Reconstruction," Ex. 3.1, 118.

[42] The *Tribune* also attacked his vacillating tariff position, his passivity during the Reconstruction debates, and his lukewarm support of soldier's bounties, but not nearly with the tenacity it devoted to Wentworth's clownishness. Fehrenbacher, *Chicago Giant*, p. 204.

create a horse-laugh in the House."[43] In addition, his Republican enemies in Springfield, who had not forgotten their uneasiness at his radicalism during the 1860 Presidential campaign, obliged his Chicago rivals by making the office of Police Commissioner a lifetime appointment, thereby removing the police force from politics and denying Wentworth control of the agency which for so long had contributed to his endurance in Chicago politics.[44] Prospects darkened for Wentworth after the *Tribune* faction chose as his successor the popular former minister to Berlin, Norman B. Judd, who in a revengeful mood accused Wentworth of persuading Andrew Johnson to withdraw his portfolio, a charge which may have carried weight in a heavily German city.[45] And when Wentworth attended a public meeting "in a state of 'offensive intoxication,' " an episode which the *Tribune* spared no ink in publicizing, he threw his nomination chances into grave peril.[46] Though he swept the rural districts in the primary election, he was swamped in the city. The subsequent convention nominated Judd easily on the first ballot.

Just as Wentworth's repudiation had nothing to do with Reconstruction policy, so was Roswell Hart's rejection the outcome of local party feuds. A middle-of-the-road Republican from the New York Twenty-eighth district,[47] Hart had slipped into office in 1864, having run well behind the state ticket. Moreover, the district organization, weakened by internal dissension and jealousy, was not solidly behind him.[48] Though he angered many by his opposition to the Soldier's Bounty Bill and his support for a Congressional pay raise, his older political colleagues in Rochester were more upset with his attempts to consolidate his own party place and power.[49]

From first to last the older party chieftains resisted Hart's candidacy. Because of a complicated system of choosing delegates, and the intrigue of both factions, every ward in Rochester as well as two of the four assembly districts sent rival sets of delegates to the district convention. With nearly every delegation contested, the meeting could not decide on machinery for sorting out credentials. The delegates split into two conventions, each claiming regularity and each nominating its own candidate, Hart and Lewis Selye, both of whom stood upon platforms affirming the Congressional plan of Reconstruction.[50] Efforts at con-

---

[43] Chicago *Tribune*, Sept. 20, 1866; Wentworth's comic antics, his biographer notes, kept him from ever occupying a chairmanship during his Congressional career. Fehrenbacher, *Chicago Giant*, p. 45.

[44] Chicago *Tribune*, Aug. 31, 1866; Fehrenbacher, *Chicago Giant*, p. 186.

[45] Chicago *Tribune*, Sept. 29, 1866; Fehrenbacher, *Chicago Giant*, p. 204.

[46] Fehrenbacher, *Chicago Giant*, p. 205.

[47] McCarthy, "Reconstruction," Ex. 3.1, 118.

[48] New York *Times*, Aug. 22, 1866.

[49] Rochester *Daily Union and Advertiser*, Sept. 19, 1866, Aug. 21, 1866, Oct. 15, 1866.

[50] *Ibid.*, Sept. 4, 1866, Oct. 18, 1866.

ciliation failed. The Hart men refused the offer of a compromise from the Selye faction, and zealous partisans from both camps almost disrupted the entire party slate in their attempts to force the uncommitted to choose sides. Not even the State Commitee's ruling in favor of Hart healed the breach.[51]

Hart's strategy was to corner the radical market. He embraced Frederick Douglass, his celebrated Negro townsman, and declared himself a victim of the Andrew Johnson conspiracy to defeat radical Congressmen.[52] Selye responded by abandoning his original Republican platform, presumably with the consent of the older organization, and made an open appeal for Democratic support. Unsure of their own prospects for victory, the Democrats fell in behind Selye, even though earlier in the canvass they considered him a "Radical above par."[53] In these circumstances a victory for Selye, so long as he endorsed the National Union platform of the Johnson-Republican-Democratic coalition, was preferable to running a Democrat who might split the Selye vote to give the election to Hart.[54] The addition of Democratic strength to the Republican faction which resented Hart's political ambition decided the contest; Selye won by a handsome plurality. But though the campaign, once underway, ostensibly centered around Reconstruction issues, it clearly had little to do with the realities in Washington. Such disputes over national policy as entered into the election were merely means to the end of winning. The long and the short of it is, it was simply a contest for control of the local party apparatus, which the older ring of politicians apparently had to compromise in order to maintain their ascendancy.

If Reconstruction had a diversionary and not a central role in the defeats of Kasson, Wentworth, and Hart, it did not even play a minor part in the retirements of John Longyear, Walter McIndoe, and Josiah Grinnell. The only Republican in the Michigan delegation not to be returned, the moderate John Longyear succumbed to a neighbor far more celebrated than himself. Austin Blair, the state's popular Civil War governor, had the nomination in his pocket before the convention opened, and Longyear "for the sake of harmony refused to allow his name to go before the convention."[55] The convention assuredly had no reservations about his politics. It unanimously endorsed Longyear's conduct in Washington, and Longyear found little difficulty in campaigning actively for Blair.[56]

Walter McIndoe encountered roughly the same predicament in Wis-

[51] *Ibid.*, Oct. 12, 1866.

[52] *Ibid.*, Oct. 15, 1866.

[53] *Ibid.*, Sept. 11, 1866.

[54] *Ibid.*, Nov. 5, 11, 1866.

[55] Lansing *State Republican*, Sept. 5, 1866.

[56] Harriet M. Dilla, *The Politics of Michigan, 1865-1878* (New York, 1912), p. 66.

consin's Sixth District, though his opponent was a future governor just returned from distinguished service in the war. Cadwallader Washburn, the brother of Congressmen Israel and Elihu, had served three terms in the House before the war called him away.[57] Although he early aspired to renomination, McIndoe apparently decided before the convention that his opponent was just too formidable; he let it be "understood that Hon. W. D. McIndoe will not be a candidate for reelection." Washburn was nominated by acclamation.[58]

The substitution in the Iowa Fourth District of William Loughridge for Josiah Grinnell seemed even further removed from disagreements over Reconstruction. A fiery Abolitionist who had once hosted John Brown, Grinnell had recently provoked a caning from a Kentucky Congressman, General L. H. Rousseau, for his disparaging remarks about the South. Things had certainly changed since Preston Brooks assaulted Charles Sumner. Grinnell's constituency was less outraged at Rousseau's ruffianism than it was at their Congressman's passivity. An Iowa paper declared that it was Grinnell's duty when assailed by a bully "to return scourge for scourge, burning for burning, caning for caning . . . , and shot for shot through all the varieties of defensive warfare."[59] According to his biographer, Grinnell lost considerable esteem because of his non-resistance.[60] But while we may doubt that the Rousseau incident was solely responsible for his replacement, there is nothing in the vocal issues of the contest to suggest that Reconstruction policy influenced Grinnell's forced retirement.

In the remaining eight Republican districts Reconstruction policy was inconclusive, but for different reasons. For at least seven incumbents there was an element of regularity, almost of predictability, involved in their removal. Unlike Kasson, Wentworth, and Hart they had no local cabal to blame; nor could they commiserate with Longyear and McIndoe's eclipse by popular figures. Neither chance nor intrigue put them on the casualty list. Their downfall, in the main, was owing to local custom and party usage. Having entered Congress under well-understood arrangements, the incumbents should rightfully have expected to leave because of them.

One party custom, which seems to have been in fairly wide practice, was the term rule, under whose provisions the Representative was expected (some believed obligated) to step down after a specified period in office.[61] Unwilling to grant any man a lifetime lease on political office because it might invite corruption, some Congressional districts customarily limited the length of time a Representative could spend in

[57] Gaillard Hunt, *Israel, Elihu, and Cadwallader Washburn* (New York, 1925), pp. 319-333.

[58] Chicago *Tribune*, July 25, 1866, Sept. 7, 1866.

[59] Iowa (Des Moines) *State Register*, June 23, 1866.

[60] Charles E. Payne, *Josiah Bushnell Grinnell* (Iowa City, Iowa, 1938), p. 231.

[61] See pages 25-26.

Washington. Besides, the democratic logic continued, no one deserved political hegemony when there were so many others equally qualified for the position. Oregon Republicans shared this sentiment; for almost twenty-six years it was their custom to change Congressmen every term.[62] J. H. D. Henderson, the Republican incumbent, cautiously attempted to return. He failed, even though two party journals thought the one-term rule silly, especially since Oregon had but one Representative. The state's influence in Washington was diminished "by sending a new man every two years."[63]

Oregon's policy towards incumbents was severer than most. Elsewhere party usage permitted generally four years of Congressional service.[64] The local organizations took these understandings very seriously. A Congressman could provoke heated commotion if he tried to defy political custom. Portus Baxter's experience in the Vermont Third District is illustrative. When Baxter won his first nomination in 1860 he had been an advocate of the two-term rule.[65] In 1864 he had managed to secure a third nomination from a reluctant convention by ingratiating himself with the soldiers, but only after pledging to retire in 1866. Now he had broken his promise, and, to the thinking of six of the seven district newspapers, was using his crew of venal politicians to fasten himself upon the district "for an indefinite period of time."[66]

He very nearly succeeded. The Custom House officials, the tax collectors, postmasters, and some of the party machinery were active in his behalf. The Vermont Central Railroad, the state's most powerful monopoly, as well as Justin Morrill, the popular candidate for United States Senator, were solidly behind him.[67] He seemed invincible. But the determined opposition would not relent. A promise was a promise, the Union papers thundered, and "we are of the old-fashioned class which believes that men's promises are sacred."[68] When it was learned that Baxter and his satellites had hired all the livery teams so as to prevent opponents from travelling to the distant village hosting the conven-

[62] Oregon had her first Congressman in the Thirty-fifth Congress. She changed him each term until the end of the Forty-seventh Congress (1857-1883). *Biographical Directory of the American Congress* (Washington, D. C., 1961).

[63] "Oregon has but one Representative in the lower House, and as soon as he becomes a little familiar with the duties which he is expected to perform he is discarded and a new man is sent in his place." Oregon (Eugene City) *State Journal*, Mar. 17, 1866; Oregon (Salem) *Statesman*, Mar. 26, 1866.

[64] A political humorist remarked that "It's bin understood since Congressmen were invented that in Konnecticut 2 terms is awl any kan have." Norwich *Daily Advertiser*, Feb. 8, 1867.

[65] Burlington *Free Press*, Aug. 7, 1866; "It was only on the ground of rotation in office that [Baxter] and his friends based their claims" in 1860. Quoted from the Lamoille *Newsdealer* in the Burlington *Free Press*, Aug. 11, 1866.

[66] "The wireworkers pulled the wool over the district and got Mr. Baxter nominated a third time in defiance of the two terms rule." Burlington *Free Press*, Aug. 7, 1866.

[67] *Ibid.*, Sept. 4, 1866.

[68] *Ibid.*, Aug. 11, 1866.

tion, the canvass against him erupted into a crusade. "The livery teams may be hired by Mr. Baxter's understrappers, but the farm wagons are not," rang the slogan of the righteous.[69] The nearly three thousand delegates who assembled at the stormy convention returned home as divided as when they arrived. Exchanging charges of irregularity and fraud, rival factions refused to surrender their preferences, and the Republicans had two men in the field, Baxter and Romeo Hoyt.[70]

Because of a Vermont law allowing election only by a majority vote, the balloting in early September failed to decide the issue. Baxter had led his Republican and Democratic opponents by a commanding plurality but fell short of the necessary majority. There were at least four thousand Republicans adamantly opposed to him, and that made all the difference. As it finally happened, both Republicans withdrew from the canvass, and a new convention unanimously agreed on a neutral candidate, C. Worthington Smith, who in a special election went on to an easy victory in a district noted for its overwhelming Republican majorities.[71] But Baxter's attempt to prolong his Congressional career risked a permanent party schism, "an era of bad blood."[72] Such might be the consequences of defiance of the term rule.

Geographical loyalty also stood in the way of aspiring incumbents. Sectional politics, it appears, had other dimensions than the familiar North-South, East-West, urban-rural conflict. County sectionalism was at times just as intense and indomitable as conventional partisanship, whether it be because of local pride, parochial interests, or the ambitions of minor politicians for office. Towns and counties had certain political prerogatives that had to be taken seriously. The example of Trempeleau County, Wisconsin is illustrative. "In 1879 county sectionalism became an open issue, and because the Republican party was unable to adjust satisfactorily to the claims of different areas within the county, it suffered substantial defeat."[73] This sort of fate also awaited Congressional tickets that failed to appease counties within the district.

As a complement to the term rule there evolved, in some of the districts where it was a realistic possibility, a system of geographical rotation.[74] According to its provisions incumbents had to step down periodically not just to accommodate other qualified aspirants, but to allow other counties to be honored with the nomination. Admittedly, a candi-

[69] Ibid., Aug. 6, 1866.

[70] Ibid., Aug. 17, 1866.

[71] Ibid., Sept. 25, 1866, Oct. 26, 1866, Nov. 7, 1866.

[72] Ibid., Sept. 21, 1866.

[73] Merle Curti, The Making of an American Community (Stanford, California, 1959), p. 330.

[74] Obviously, geographical rotation was impracticable in Wisconsin's Sixth District, to name one example. It would have taken forty-eight years to distribute terms to aspirants from each of its twenty-four counties. Districts practicing geographical rotation usually contained only two to four counties.

date had to have proper credentials and a satisfactory allegiance to party principles. But unless his geography was acceptable, he probably would have difficulty passing the inspection of men whose business it was to nominate candidates.

A case in point is the Congressional nominating convention of the New York Twenty-sixth, an up-state district of four counties. Giles Hotchkiss had already served two terms, and his county convention, having no misgivings over his Congressional behavior, was prepared to return him for a third. Other counties had different ideas, especially Tioga County, which believed it had "a claim for the nomination which the other counties will admit."[75] They did so. The convention selected William S. Lincoln of Tioga with little ado. Endorsing the party's choice, the Republican weekly in Broome County, Hotchkiss's residence, explained that though Hotchkiss's course "has given entire satisfaction, yet, in accordance with a common custom, another portion of the district has at this convention been accorded the honor of the nomination."[76]

Connecticut Republicans also observed the custom. When a Bridgeport daily learned that the Fourth District's two-term incumbent, James H. Hubbard, had announced for another nomination, it was moved to protest. "As it was definitely understood that the next nominee should be taken from Fairfield County," it argued, "we do not see how Mr. Hubbard can consistently make any claims for another term. The nomination belongs to Fairfield County, and the voters of this county will not willingly submit to any violation of the district understanding on this subject."[77] Not satisfied with narrowing the selection to one county, the editor went on to discuss the claims of different towns within Fairfield. Norwalk had received political recognition too often, and since "the people generally feel that the candidates for high office should be taken alternately from different towns," Bridgeport by all standards deserved the nomination.[78] At the convention it was common knowledge that the united sentiment of the Fairfield delegation would prevent Hubbard's renomination; and probably through some *quid pro quo* bargain, the convention conferred the nomination on Bridgeport's Phineas T. Barnum, a showman of wide notoriety who had spent his lifetime ransacking the world for curiosities.[79]

The settling of competing geographical claims was not always so

---

[75] New York *Times*, Aug. 22, 1866, Sept. 4, 1866.

[76] Binghamton *Standard*, Sept. 26, 1866.

[77] Bridgeport *Evening Standard*, Feb. 11, 1867.

[78] *Ibid.*, Feb. 13, 1867.

[79] *Ibid.*, Feb. 15, 1867; Barnum was the only successor to a dismissed incumbent who lost in the general election. Notorious in unfriendly circles as the "prince of humbug," Barnum and difficulty explaining away his wooly horse, bearded woman, and countless other eccentricities. E. L. Godkin's counsel to scratch his name apparently carried some weight with scandalized Republicans. *Nation* IV, Mar. 7, 1866.

harmonious, as the stormy proceedings in Connecticut's Third and New York's Twenty-second Districts demonstrate. By convention time in the Connecticut Third each county and major town had declared special rights to the nomination. Windham County believed it her turn, especially since she had delivered a handsome Republican vote in the close election last year. "Shall no laurels be left to Windham?" her faithful asked. The Windhamites might be "the children of Spartan mothers," New London men conceded, but she had the State Speaker's chair and the candidate for Lieutenant-Governor last year, and prior to 1862 she had furnished the Representatives for eight consecutive terms.[80] Her claim was spurious, and the larger delegation of New London would have none of it. Having resolved to keep the Representative in New London County, the convention then divided over the merits of rival towns. Augustus Brandegee, the two term incumbent, had the solid backing of the delegates from the town of New London. The Norwich delegation just as adamantly backed its own favorite son, Henry H. Starkweather, a postmaster recently martyred by Johnson's impolicy of removing unsympathetic federal officials.[81]

The convention debate was heated. Brandegee partisans emphasized his valuable legislative experience—as did the friends of most incumbents seeking another nomination—and warned of the danger of changing horses in such perilous times. To the Norwich delegation this reasoning was old spinach. They were not about to yield, even though Starkweather's only claim was that "Norwich had had nothing."[82] United in its determination to select Starkweather, and as a bloc large enough to obstruct another's nomination, by fair or foul means Norwich gathered enough neutral delegates to clinch the contest. The Third District had a new nominee.

Convention politics were more volatile in New York's Twenty-second District. Even before Sidney T. Holmes, the incumbent, began maneuvering for renomination, newspapers in his own Madison County were taking "strong ground" in favor of Oswego County's D. C. Littlejohn.[83] The Republican party paper in Holmes's village also blessed Littlejohn, as it acknowledged "the binding force of the rule of rotation, which has been in operation so long."[84] These expressions did not discourage Holmes's ambition. As the convention approached he succeeded in having at least two Madison County town caucuses instructed for his renomination.[85]

Most of the Oswego delegation moved rapidly at the convention to

[80] Norwich *Daily Advertiser*, Feb. 14, 1867; Norwich *Daily Bulletin*, Feb. 14, 1867.
[81] Norwich *Daily Bulletin*, Feb. 14, 1867.
[82] *Ibid.*
[83] Cazenovia *Republican*, Aug. 1, 1866.
[84] Morrisville *Volunteer*, quoted in *ibid.*
[85] Cazenovia *Republican*, Aug. 22, 29, 1866.

reaffirm long-standing district usage. Offering a resolution that mentioned the political custom "by which the Republican candidates for members of Congress. . . have been alternately chosen from Oswego and Madison counties," Oswego delegates not only declared it their turn in the rotation but proclaimed it their right exclusively "to select the name or names of candidates to be presented to this convention," provided none of their preferences were offensive politically or personally to Madison County.[86] Knowing beforehand Madison's coolness towards playing weak sister in the nomination process,[87] Holmes may have figured that his amendment affirming Madison's prerogative to participate in the selection might lead to a breach of the rotation principle. After all, he argued, "the principle of alternation had not always been observed."[88] He calculated poorly, even though his resolution passed, primarily because of the unexpected support of the Oswego Third Assembly District, which saw the proposal as an opportunity to retaliate for the dominance Oswego City had long exercised in the County.[89]

The Oswego caucus during the afternoon recess failed to unite, the Third Assembly District remaining implacable. Rather than surrender its principle, the majority of the Oswego delegation bolted the convention, thereby wrecking the chances of its favorite, D. C. Littlejohn, who probably would have won the nomination had the Oswego bolters conceded to the Madison delegation, which all along had been enthusiastic about him.[90] As it happened, an Oswego Third District delegate placed in nomination Oswego's John C. Churchill, whom the convention approved "unanimously, without debate";[91] the bolters were roundly condemned throughout the district; Littlejohn fell in behind Churchill's candidacy; and it became clear that the crafty Holmes had mistaken a distaste for Oswego's selection machinery for a willingness to repudiate rotation altogether.[92]

In districts without long and uninterrupted observance of the rotation principle, it appears, the custom operated more informally and less predictably. County delegations attended nominating conventions unanimously instructed for favorite sons, and prepared to fight for them tenaciously. The strength of one delegation might not permit it to have its way, but it could (and usually did) deadlock the convention. At the

[86] Ibid., Sept. 12, 1866.

[87] A Madison County newspaper had written prior to the convention that "the Republicans of Madison County, while acknowledging the binding force of the rule of rotation, . . . still feel they have a right to indicate their preference in the selection of a candidate." Quoted from the Morrisville Volunteer in the Cazenovia Republican, Aug. 1, 1866.

[88] Cazenovia Republican, Sept. 12, 1866.

[89] Ibid., Sept. 12, 19, 1866.

[90] Ibid., Sept. 19, 1866.

[91] Ibid., Sept. 12, 1866.

[92] Ibid., Sept. 12, 19, 1866, Oct. 3, 17, 1866.

very least a county delegation, though unable to nominate its own man, was determined that, in the way of political bargains, there had to be something. So, either before or during the balloting, bargains were struck and promises made, usually involving the pledge that, in the near future, a county would be honored if it released its votes to another delegation.[93] Only after appeasing local pride, and probably after allocating spoils—in short, only after an almost symbolic round of horse-swapping—could a selection be made.

This was the scenario by which Ithmar C. Sloan of the Wisconsin Second District had been rotated into office in 1862. He had won another nomination in 1864 only after his Rock County delegation had conceded support to Columbia County's favorite in 1866. Now with two terms under his belt, and only a loose understanding to deter him, he felt sufficiently fortified to adventure defiance of the bargain.[94] But he had more audacity than strength. He had disgusted many with his absenteeism in Congress,[95] and had alienated Columbia County beyond appeasement.[96] The convention raged on for over 100 ballots before Sloan's support began fading. But Columbia's determination reaped an incomplete harvest. The Dane County men were just as firmly behind Benjamin Hopkins, a rising power in the Madison regency,[97] and a Sloan delegate, who disregarded county directions, made all the difference in an exceedingly close race: Hopkins won on the 136th ballot.[98]

Under some conditions counties might agree to suspend the system temporarily, especially if the incumbent had barely squeaked by at the last election. This happened in the Pennsylvania Seventeenth District, whose custom it was for every county to nominate a candidate and then submit him to a district conference for selection. By all party usage Abraham Barker, only in his first Congress, was deserving of another term. But his narrow victory in 1864 had alarmed party stalwarts. He had won only 51 per cent of the vote, achieving victory only because of the vote of soldiers in the field, since the home vote in 1864, considered by itself, would have given the election to the Democrats. His county convention dropped him for a more popular figure, Daniel J. Morrell, an iron manufacturer, considered throughout the district as a

[93] In one of his brief acknowledgments of the subject, Frederick Dallinger noted that "The nomination of a congressional candidate is often determined in advance by a private agreement that the incumbent, after one or more terms of service, shall retire and aid the nomination of his principal rival in a former convention." *Nomination for Elective Office in the United States* (New York, 1897), pp. 88-89.

[94] Chicago *Tribune*, Sept. 13, 1866.

[95] Out of 146 Reconstruction roll calls in the First Session of the Thirty-ninth Congress he missed 69 of them. McCarthy, "Reconstruction," Exhibits 3-1 and 3.4, 118, 153.

[96] New York *Times*, Aug. 28, 1866.

[97] Helen J. and Harry Williams, "Wisconsin Republicans and Reconstruction, 1865-1870," *Wisconsin Magazine of History*, XXIII (Sept. 1939), 20.

[98] Chicago Tribune, Sept. 13, 1866; Wisconsin (Madison) *State Journal*, Sept. 7, 1866.

probable "tower of strength in the coming contest."[99] Chafing from the setback, Barker and his friends asked "why Cambria County should put her right to the Congressional nomination in jeopardy, and make probable the nomination by the conference of a candidate from some other county in the district?"[100]

The other counties, however, were equally alive to the need for increasing the vote, and just as prepared to suspend party usage. The Lewistown *Gazette* wrote that "we are first for Mifflin County. . . . [unless] it can be shown that Mr. Morrell can defeat the Copperheads."[101] To most everyone's satisfaction but Barker's, Morrell appeared to have the best chances for victory. The district conference, in a rare departure from rotation custom, swiftly confirmed his nomination.[102]

These districts with rotation customs, either of the term rule or geographical variety, were unique only insofar as their Representatives attempted defiance of established usage. They were therefore more conspicuous in their political affairs in 1866, but we may suspect, not altogether distinctive. Fugitive evidence suggests that some of the thirty-seven Republican incumbents who did not stand for re-election probably retired voluntarily in deference to rotation understandings.[103] Nor were Republicans alone in observing the rotation convention; the Democrats practiced it too.[104] Rotation also seems to have predated the Civil War.[105] And it certainly was neither peculiar to the North,[106] nor confined to Congressional nominations.[107] In fact there is good reason to conclude that rotation accounts largely for the amazingly high turnover rates that characterized the House of Representatives throughout most of the nineteenth century. From 1789 to 1877 the mean terms of service never approached three, and from the 1840's through the Civil War it

[99] Johnstown *Tribune*, June 8, 1866.

[100] *Ibid.*, June 22, 1866.

[101] *Ibid.*

[102] This may have been Andrew J. Kuykendall's fate as well, though there is no explicit evidence to support this suspicion.

[103] Thomas T. Davis of Cortland County, New York, for example, stepped down voluntarily after his two terms. Unhappily, his action did not avert a schism in the Twenty-third District: Onondaga County bolted the convention after Cortland managed to have another of her own nominated. Rochester *Daily Union and Advertiser*, Sept. 20, 1866; New York *Tribune*, Sept. 20, 1866; see also the Rochester *Daily Union and Advertiser*, Sept. 6, 1866 for a related episode.

[104] Follow, for instance, Democratic affairs in the Illinois Thirteenth District. Cairo *Daily Democrat*, July 21, 24, Aug. 13, 1866.

[105] Abraham Lincoln advocated it in 1843 as a means of reconciling political ambitions with party harmony. Rivals within the local organization agreed to succeed each other in Congress rather than risk an internecine and crippling struggle for party dominance. Benjamin P. Thomas, *Abraham Lincoln* (New York, 1968), p. 104.

[106] The antebellum South practiced it regularly, at least on the state and local level. Ralph Wooster, *The People in Power* (Knoxville, 1969), pp. 42, 92-93.

[107] Merle Curti discovered a startling fluidity of officeholding within Trempleau County, Wisconsin. *Making of an American Community*, pp. 343, 320; see also Dallinger, *Nominations*, pp. 67-68.

was more often under two terms than not.[108] Surely the practice of giving every county and every aspiring politician a turn had more than a casual bearing on this phenomenon.[109]

What the rotation custom demonstrates even more strongly than the experiences of incumbents who were the victims of local cabals and popularity contests is the largely parochial character of American politics in these years. Despite the grave policy controversies in Washington, politics at the grass roots continued its preoccupation with local issues and provincial affairs. Even when the Reconstruction debate did emerge in nominating contests it was not really decisive: it was a smoke screen used not to disguise sectional business interests but to conceal local vendettas. In fact, there was but one case of a national purge, which surely is embarrassing to the radical conspiracy theorists, and only two instances of rank and file retribution, which weakens the assumptions of the grass roots mobilization school, at least as regards the timing of the popular groundswell, if there were one.[110] Indeed, considering the diversionary uses to which Reconstruction issues were often put, one may be forgiven the speculation that even in these latter two cases disagreements over southern policy might not have been the real reasons for the incumbents's replacement.

This relative absence in 1866 of Reconstruction issues in the Republican nominating struggles, which it seems fair to infer were sensitive barometers of the political climate within the party, suggests a few speculations about the alleged radicalization of the Republicans.

---

[108] Compare this with the 5.65 mean terms of service of the Eighty-eighth Congress. Nelson W. Polsby, "The Institutionalization of the U.S. House of Representatives," *American Political Science Review*, LXII (Mar. 1968), 146-147.

[109] Rotation admittedly needs more study. Aside from fugitive remarks in studies devoted to other subjects, scholars have given it relatively little attention. (F. W. Dallinger is no exception.) It would be instructive to know when the custom arose, how widespread it was, where it was concentrated, how it may have affected legislative behavior, and when and why it declined. Its eclipse was certainly related to the nationalization of American politics in the late nineteenth century, and probably had something to do with Republican determination to prevent the South from reestablishing its alleged antebellum hegemony in national councile. These comments from the New York *Post* are apposite: "Much of the preponderance formerly obtained by the Southern States in the government was due to the fact that they did not so frequently send new men to Congress—Old members are sure to get the control in legislative bodies from their familiarity with the rules and machinery whereas new men are obliged to spend half the session in acquiring the requisite knowledge for the performance of their duties. If the constituencies of the Northern States had been so sagacious as their opponents in this respect, there would have been far less opportunity for complaint of Southern aggression in Congress." Quoted in the Delaware *Gazette*, July 20, 1868. "Depend on it," Horace Greeley advised New York Republicans, "our state must upset this fashion of giving every county 'its turn' and dismissing each member after four years of faithful service before she can have her due weight in Congress." New York *Tribune*, Sept. 21, 1866.

[110] There is the possibility, slight I think, that the rank and file radicalized the candidates during the election campaign, a phenomenon which this study would have overlooked since it addresses itself almost exclusively to the nominating episodes. But surely if this were the case, one would expect to have discovered local party chieftains preparing for the eventuality at the nominating conventions. Instead they seemed oblivious to it.

It may mean that if the party were radicalized in 1866, as has been commonly assumed, it was not accomplished through the elective process. Another possibility is that by this time there was such a widespread consensus throughout the party on Reconstruction policy that one's position regarding it was taken for granted, which points to a third explanation. The Republican party was not radicalized in the 1866 election but probably earlier, either in some previous election, or as seems more likely in light of the apparent imperviousness of American electoral politics to national controversies, through the dynamics of the legislative process.[111] But these are only tentative conclusions that other lines of research must establish.

In any event, any investigation of the problem of Republican radicalization will have to take into account the parochialism that pervaded American politics during this period. This is not to argue the absurdity that national issues counted for nothing in nineteenth century politics, but only to emphasize that the impact of national themes upon the local political process was of a much smaller magnitude than historians have casually assumed. At the very least, the inappreciable importance of Reconstruction in Republican nominations during the supposedly critical year of 1866 ought to caution historians against focusing exclusively on the national capitol in their attempts to explain nineteenth-century American political life.[112]

---

[111] It is instructive to note at this point that the most exhaustive study of the Reconstruction Congresses we are likely to have proves, contrary to historical legend, that the Fortieth Congress in a relative sense did not represent the apex of Congressional radicalism but instead marked its decline. McCarthy, "Reconstruction," 247-248, 327-328.

[112] Historians would be advised to consult Donald E. Stokes's illuminating article, "Parties and the Nationalization of Electoral Forces," *The American Party Systems: Stages of Political Development*, ed. William N. Chambers and Walter D. Burnham (New York, 1967).

THE ROUT OF RADICALISM:

Republicans and the Elections of 1867

Michael Les Benedict

WHEN HOWARD K. BEALE entitled his great analysis of Reconstruction politics *The Critical Year*,[1] he referred to 1866, when Andrew Johnson and the Republican Congress opened their bitter warfare over Reconstruction policy, a year which culminated in congressional elections in which northern voters endorsed Congress' position that the South was not yet entitled to full restoration of rights and privileges in the Union. The elections of this "critical year" decided the issue between the President and the majority in Congress and set the stage for congressional (usually termed *Radical*) Reconstruction. But historians generally have underestimated the importance of the elections of 1867 held in nearly every northern state to fill various state and local offices. If the elections of 1866 decided the issue between President and Congress, the elections of 1867 decided a similar issue between more radical and more conservative Republicans. The stakes of the elections of 1866 had been high: whether as part of the peace black Americans in the South would be conceded equal civil rights (and, as it turned out, political rights as well) with white southerners, and whether those rights would be protected by law. The stakes of the election of 1867 were nearly as important: whether the program embodied in the Reconstruction Act of 1867 would set the limit of postwar reform in the South, or whether Republicans would go further yet in changing southern political, economic, and social institutions.

Since the publication of Eric L. McKitrick's *Andrew Johnson and Reconstruction* in 1960, historians have come to recognize the essential conservatism of the reconstruction program Johnson opposed.[2] But few

[1] Beals, *The Critical Year: A Study of Andrew Johnson and Reconstruction* (N.Y. 1930).

[2]McKitrick, *Andrew Johnson and Reconstruction* (Chicago & London, 1960). See, for instance, LaWanda and John H. Cox, *Politics, Principle, and Prejudice, 1865-1866: Dilemma of Reconstruction America* (Glencoe, Ill., 1963); W. R. Brock, *An American Crisis: Congress and Reconstruction, 1865-1867* (N.Y., 1963); Avery Craven, *Reconstruction: The Ending of the Civil War* (N.Y., 1969). The nearly complete acceptance of this new insight is marked by its incorporation into history textbooks, surely the most conclusive sign the profession can offer of general concurrence in a point of view. See Richard N. Current *et al.*, *American History: A Survey* (2d ed., N.Y., 1967), 457-62; John M. Blum *et al.*, *The National Experience: A History of the United States* (2d ed., N.Y., 1968), 376-80; John A. Garraty, *The American Nation: A History of the United States* (2d ed., N.Y., 1971), 508-12.

historians have noted the conservatism of congressional reconstruction
policy as it emerged in the Reconstruction Act of 1867. That law required that southerners ratify the Fourteenth Amendment to the Constitution and agree to impartial suffrage for blacks and whites as conditions for restoration to the Union. McKitrick, David Donald, and William R. Brock recognize that this law was the result of compromise between radicals and conservatives, but only Larry G. Kincaid, in an as-
yet unpublished dissertation, clearly has asserted that the Reconstruction Act was far more satisfactory to conservative Republicans, like
William Pitt Fessenden, John Sherman, James G. Blaine, and John A.
Bingham, than it was to radicals, like Thaddeus Stevens, Benjamin F.
Wade, or Charles Sumner. Research in connection with my own dissertation has led me to agree with Kincaid.[3]

When Congress adjourned in March, 1867, and as the Democratic
and Republican parties girded for the elections to be held in northern
states from July through November, radical Republicans immediately
began agitating for new measures. Charles Sumner urged passage of a
national law (as distinguished from a constitutional amendment) to
require racially nondiscriminatory voting qualifications within all states.
Not only would this enfranchise blacks in northern states, but it would
enfranchise them in the border states of Maryland, Delaware, and Kentucky, where hundreds of thousands of freed slaves were not protected
by military authorities acting under the Reconstruction laws. Moreover,
it would guard against the possibility that southern states might repeal
impartial suffrage laws once they were restored to normal relations in
the Union.[4] Sumner also demanded that southern states be required to
offer free public schooling to children of both races. (He was noncom-
mittal about whether these schools must be integrated, but years earlier
he had argued that segregated schools were inconsistent with constitutional requirements of equal rights in Massachusetts.)[5] As Sumner

[3] McKitrick, *Johnson and Reconstruction*, pp. 476-85; Donald, *The Politics of
Reconstruction, 1863-1867* (Baton Rouge, 1965), pp. 53-82; Brock, *An American
Crisis*, pp. 175-203. Brock, however, concludes that conservative resistance to radi-
cal pressure gave way completely in the passage of the first Supplementary Recon-
struction Act in March, 1867. *Ibid.*, pp. 204-208. Kincaid's dissertation is entitled
"The Legislative Origins of the Military Reconstruction Act, 1865-1867" (Ph.D.
dissertation, Johns Hopkins University, 1968). My dissertation is "The Right Way:
Congressional Republicans and Reconstruction, 1863-1869" (Ph.D. dissertation,
Rice University, 1970).

[4] Sumner urged his measure as a necessity in a long letter to Theodore Tilton,
editor of the Radical New York *Independent*. Tilton published the letter in his
newspaper and endorsed Sumner's position. Sumner's proposition received further
support from the Border State Convention, meeting in Baltimore early in September,
1867. As the only national Republican meeting of 1867, it was given wide publicity
by the party press. Presided over by Tennessee congressman Horace Maynard,
many leading border-state Republicans attended, including Congressman Robert T.
Van Horn, former Senator John A. J. Creswell and Tennessee leader (soon to be
U.S. Representative) Roderick R. Butler. N.Y. *Independent*, May 2, 1867; Edward
M. McPherson scrapbook: Campaign of 1867, I, 68-73, in the McPherson Mss.,
Library of Congress; N.Y. *Times*, Sept. 13, 1867.

[5] *Roberts v. Boston*, 5 Cushing 198 (1849). Sumner proposed his educational

pressed for a national impartial suffrage law and free public schools for all in the South, Stevens, Benjamin F. Butler, and other radicals began for the first time since the war to exert vigorous pressure for confiscation and land redistribution in the former rebel states. Many radicals also demanded the complete dispersal of the southern state governments erected by presidential authority in 1865, governments the Reconstruction Act recognized as provisional. Like Stevens, most radicals wished loyal, radical governments to replace them, to govern the southern "states" as territories for an indefinite time. Wendell Phillips articulated the program many radicals favored at the annual meeting of the American Anti-Slavery Society in New York city early in May. Anti-slavery men, he said, "will believe the negro safe when we see him with 40 acres under his feet, a school-house behind him, a ballot in his right hand, the sceptre of the Federal Government over his head, and no State Government to interfere with him, until more than one-half of the white men of the Southern States are in their graves."[6]

Another issue closely related to Reconstruction emerged during the spring and summer of 1867. An interpretation of the Reconstruction Acts delivered June 12 by President Johnson's conservative Attorney-General, Henry Stanbery, so emasculated the powers of the military commanders to whom enforcement of the law had been entrusted that Republicans were forced to return to Washington in July to pass a new law to remedy the destruction. Arguing that Johnson could never be trusted fairly and fully to enforce the Reconstruction laws, radicals urged the President's impeachment and removal. They were outmaneuvered by their more conservative Republican allies, who passed floor rules prohibiting debate on the question. But by the time the July session adjourned, the impeachment issue had become completely entwined with the 1867 campaigns in the states, Democrats pointing to it as an example of Republican extremism.[7]

Conservative Republicans were not very sympathetic to the new radical demands. They had already scuttled Stevens' hopes for long-term military control of the South once, when they passed the Reconstruction Act.[8] They had joined Democrats to defeat Sumner's southern

---

requirement as an amendment to the first Supplementary Reconstruction Act, but it had been defeated by a coalition of Democrats and conservative Republicans. *Congressional Globe*, 40 Cong. 1 sess., 165-70 (Mar. 16, 1867). He renewed his efforts at the July, 1867 session, called to modify the Reconstruction laws to prevent presidential interference. Again the Democrats and conservative Republicans defeated him. *Ibid.*, 581 (July 11, 1867).

[6] N.Y. *Tribune*, May 8, 1867. Thomas Wentworth Higginson, the society's president, seconded the demand for land reform at the same meeting. N.Y. *Independent*, May 2, 1867. Stevens expressed his views on reconstruction in letters to Edward M. McPherson, widely published in the nation's press. Butler's endorsement of confiscation came in a letter to a Republican campaign meeting in Washington, D.C., reported in the N.Y. *Times*, June 7, 1867.

[7] Benedict, "The Right Way," 368-73.

[8] The Reconstruction Act, as originally reported from the Joint Committee on Reconstruction, was merely a military government bill, providing no means for

education proposals. Lyman Trumbull, the conservative chairman of the Senate Judiciary committee, through which any national suffrage legislation would have to pass, publicly proclaimed during the campaign that Sumner's suffrage proposition was unconstitutional.[9] As late as 1868, the Republican national platform would assure northerners that blacks could be enfranchised by law only in the South.[10] Nor were the implications of confiscation and land redistribution lost upon conservative Republicans. When Butler complained of a landed aristocracy in the South, the moderate Boston *Daily Advertiser* asked, "Why a *landed* aristocracy? This mode of argument is two-edged. For there are socialists who hold that *any* aristocracy is 'fatal to the advance of the cause of liberty and equal rights'—socialists who would not hesitate to say that General Butler's large income places him in the ranks of an aristocracy . . . . It is dangerous to prove too much." The conservative Cincinnati *Commercial* began to refer to Stevens and Butler as "The Red Rads."[11]

Moreover, conservative Republicans feared the impact of the confiscation issue on southern politics. They hoped to build a southern Republican party around the issue of accepting restoration under the Reconstruction Acts, requiring only ratification of the Fourteenth Amendment and impartial suffrage. Many Republicans believed white southerners who were tired of the political limbo in which they were placed, who had lost faith in President Johnson's ability to protect them from Republican legislation, might be willing to join the newly-enfranchised blacks in organizing new state governments in conformity with reconstruction legislation in order finally to win readmission to the Union. If conservative southerners opposed their efforts, these whites would have no alternative but to ally with the Republican party. Already many Republicans believed they saw this happening. Henry Wilson, who acted with conservative Republicans during 1867, sent glowingly enthusiastic letters from the South. Horace Greeley echoed him. "The harvest is white," exulted the Boston *Journal*, "and we trust that our sagacious men will see that it is not neglected."[12]

---

restoration at all. After a bitter battle conservative Republicans succeeded in adding provisions to enable southerners to organize new civil governments entitled to restoration. See McKitrick, *Johnson and Reconstruction*, pp. 478-85; Brock, *An American Crisis*, pp. 188-203; Donald, *Politics of Reconstruction*, pp. 70-82; Benedict, "The Right Way," 274-339.

[9] N.Y. *Times*, Sept. 2, 1867.

[10] Kirk H. Porter and Donald Bruce Johnson, *National Party Platforms, 1840-1956* (Urbana, Ill., 1956), p. 39.

[11] Boston *Daily Advertiser*, June 13, 1867; Cincinnati *Commercial*, June 15, 1867.

[12] Boston *Evening Journal*, May 24, 1867; Wilson in the N.Y. *Independent*, May 9, June 6, 1867; Cincinnati *Commercial*, July 8, 1867; Boston *Daily Advertiser*, July 4, 1867. Greeley travelled to Richmond to conciliate southern whites. See his speech there, reported in his N.Y. *Tribune*, May 17, 1867. Greeley was also influenced in part by political considerations in joining a group of northerners in raising bail money for Jefferson Davis. See the comment of his N.Y. *Tribune*, May 31, 1867. For enthusiastic reports of white southern acceptance of the Republican party, see

Radical agitation for confiscation and land reform could only alienate these budding converts. "The ultraists . . . are determined to build up a party in the Southern States fully in accord with themselves," the conservative Republican New York *Times* charged. "Their plan is to consolidate the negro vote with that of the 'original Union men' of the South. . . . And they rely upon confiscation to secure this result."[13] Confirming conservatives' fears, radicals opened a bitter campaign against their own conservative allies, accusing them of selling out the principles of the party. "For every broken heart and desolate home in the South, for every murdered black there, we hold Fessenden, Wilson . . . and their clan, responsible," the editors of the *Anti-Slavery Standard* railed.[14]

Intimately connected with these substantive issues dividing radicals from conservatives in the Republican party was the problem of selecting a presidential candidate for 1868. Although many important Republicans were occasionally mentioned in 1867 as possible candidates, there were only three leading contenders. One was Benjamin F. Wade, the radical senator from Ohio and president *pro tempore* of the Senate. Salmon Portland Chase, also an Ohioan and Chief Justice of the United States, was a second. Most political observers considered both Chase and Wade to represent the radical wing of the Republican party (although within Ohio politics, Wade was clearly the more radical). As of spring, 1867, it had appeared that one or the other would be the Republican presidential candidate in 1868. When conservative Republicans desperately looked for a candidate to oppose them they could find only one with the national following which would make victory possible—Lieutenant General of the Army Ulysses S. Grant.

Before the elections of 1867 radicals were by no means reconciled to Grant's nomination. The general had not even declared himself a Republican by summer, 1867, and his past politics made him suspect in Radical eyes. Before the war he had been apolitical, and many con-

---

the N.Y. *Tribune*, May 20, 21, 28, 1867; Gen. John Pope to Robert C. Schenck, May 20, 1867. Schenck Mss., Rutherford B. Hayes Library, Fremont, Ohio; John Sherman to William Tecumseh Sherman, Aug. 9, 1867, quoted in John Sherman and William Tecumseh Sherman, *The Sherman Letters: Correspondence Between General and Senator Sherman from 1837 to 1891*, ed. Rachel Sherman Thorndike (N.Y., 1894), pp. 292-94.

[13] N.Y. *Times*, May 2, 1867.

[14] N.Y. *National Anti-Slavery Standard*, Aug. 17, 1867. See Thaddeus Stevens' attack on conservative Republicans in a letter published in the Gettysburg *Star and Herald*, quoted in the N.Y. *Times*, May 29, 1867; Stevens' speech before the American Anti-Slavery Society, quoted in the N.Y. *Tribune*, May 8, 1867; N.Y. *National Anti-Slavery Standard*, Mar. 30, Apr. 6, Oct. 26, 1867; Wendell Phillips' attack on Greeley, discussed in Clyndon G. Van Deusen, *Horace Greeley: Nineteenth Century Crusader* (N.Y., 1964), pp. 352-56, and Greeley's reply in the N.Y. *Tribune*, May 24, 1867; Zachariah Chandler's biting attack on conservative Republicans in a campaign speech at Ashtabula, Ohio, in the McPherson scrapbook: Campaign of 1867, II, 135-36. McPherson Mss.; Sumner's assault on conservative Republican Senators Fessenden, George F. Edmunds, and Roscoe Conkling in an interview with James Redpath, quoted in the Boston *Daily Advertiser*, Sept. 4, 1867.

sidered him apolitical yet. In 1864 Republicans had feared the Democrats might nominate him for President. From 1862 until late in 1864 Radicals regarded his rising fortunes with misgivings.[15] Grant reinforced their suspicions by his conduct during the Reconstruction controversy. An optimistic report he delivered in 1865 regarding conditions in the South had provided Democrats and President Johnson with their most authoritative evidence of southern good intentions at that time. During the 1866 election campaign the general had accompanied Johnson on his ill-fated "Swing 'Round the Circle," allowing himself to be used on an obviously political junket. Although Grant never made his position clear, his biographer believes he generally supported Johnson's policies at least through 1866. And there is no doubt as to the position of his staff. Adam Badeau and John A. Rawlins, his intimate friends and aides, both endorsed Johnson.[16] Finally, when President Johnson suspended Secretary of War Edwin M. Stanton in August, 1867, renewing Republican fears that Johnson would obstruct enforcement of the Reconstruction laws, the President named Grant as Stanton's interim replacement, using the general's popularity to deflect criticism. "General Grant . . . ," worried the editor of the radical New York *Independent*, "appears to have become a cat's paw for the President."[17]

But Radicals found most ominous the men who were advocating Grant's candidacy. In Pennsylvania, conservative former Governor Andrew J. Curtin, defeated for the Senate by a coalition of pro-Stevens and Simon Cameron radicals, led the Grant movement. In New York, where the Grant boom progressed most rapidly, it was sponsored by the conservative Seward-Weed faction of the Republican party, abetted by their organ, the New York *Times*. At the same time the independent Democratic paper, the New York *Herald*, urged Democrats to join conservative Republicans in supporting Grant. "There will be a tremendous struggle in the republican camp for the Convention of 1868, between the radical Chase faction . . . and the republican conservatives supporting General Grant," it prophesized. "The result, in all probability, will be a split of the republican party into two distinct parties for the succession. In this event the Northern democracy will hold the bal-

15 In the House of Representatives leading Radicals had opposed the re-creation of the rank of Lieutenant General of the Army for him. Stevens, George S. Boutwell, James A. Garfield, William D. Kelley, George W. Julian, and Henry Winter Davis had tried to prevent it but failed. *Cong. Globe*, 38 Cong., 1 sess., 427-31 (Feb. 7, 1864); T. Harry Williams, *Lincoln and the Radicals* (Madison, 1941), pp. 334-37; William Frank Zornow, *Lincoln & the Party Divided* (Norman, 1954), pp. 87-88, 94.

16 Hesseltine, *Grant*, p. 61; Badeau to E. B. Washburne, Oct. 20, 1865. Washburne mss.; Rawlins to Mrs. Rawlins, Aug. 30, Sept. 1, 1866, quoted in James Harrison Wilson, *The Life of John A. Rawlins* (N.Y., 1916), pp. 334-36; Orville H. Browning, *Diary of Orville Hickman Browning*, ed. James G. Randall (Springfield, Ill., 1938), II, 103-104.

17 N.Y. *Independent*, Aug. 29, 1867. See also Phillips in the N.Y. *National Anti-Slavery Standard*, Aug. 24, 1867; N.Y. *Tribune*, Aug. 15, 1867.

ance of power, and by casting their weight into the scale of the Grant, or anti-radical party, they will carry the election."[18]

The leader of the anti-Seward and Weed forces in New York, Horace Greeley, complained privately to Radical Senator Zachariah Chandler, "All that is fishy and mercenary in the Republican ranks combines with everything copperhead to escort Grant as the man destined to curb Radicalism and restore conservatives to power."[19]

So before the election of 1867, most Radicals were at best lukewarm to the Grant candidacy.[20] Nonetheless, many despaired of being able to withstand the conservative onslaught. John W. Forney, owner of the Washington *Chronicle* and Philadelphia *Press*, expressed these fears in a letter to Sumner. "I shudder at the idea of another doubtful man in that post . . . ," he wrote. "I cannot tell you how this . . . has depressed me. If Genl Grant wants the nomination I presume with such agencies and his great military strength he will secure it. I fear his administration. God help us! Are we never to have the right man in that place?"[21]

Under these circumstances the elections of 1867 took on immense importance. To a large extent, they would decide a struggle between radicals and conservatives for control of the Republican party. They would test the political viability of radicalism for the first time.[22] If the

---

[18] Curtain to E. B. Washburne, Oct. 17, 1867. Washburne Mss.; N.Y. *Herald*, July 6, 1867; Thurlow Weed Barnes, *Memoir of Thurlow Weed* (Boston, 1884), pp. 457-58; Glyndon G. Van Deusen, *Thurlow Weed: Wizard of the Lobby* (Boston, 1947), pp. 327-28; Hesseltine, *Grant*, pp. 91-92; *N.Y. Times*, Oct. 17, Nov. 10, Nov. 27, 1867.

[19] Greeley to Chandler, Aug. 25, 1867. Chandler Mss., Greeley attacked Grant and his New York supporters in his N.Y. *Tribune*, Aug. 15, 1867.

[20] Curtain, in Pennsylvania, found he could not convince Republican leaders to endorse Grant as part of their 1867 campaign effort. Curtain to E. B. Washburne, Oct. 17, 1867. Washburne Mss. Republican Congressman Godlove S. Orth reported that Indiana Republicans were lukewarm to the prospect of Grant's nomination. William Henry Smith reported the same as true of Ohio radicals. The New York *Tribune* mobilized the Radical wing of the New York party behind Chase. Charles Sumner openly criticized Grant's reticence on the issues. Orth to Schuyler Colfax, [spring, 1867]. Orth Mss. Indiana State Library, Indiana Division, Indianapolis; Smith to James H. Barrett, Apr. 25, 1867. Smith Mss., Ohio Historical Society, Columbus; N.Y. *Tribune*, Oct. 15, 1867; Sumner in the Boston *Daily Advertiser*, Sept. 4, 1867; Phillips before the American Anti-Slavery Society, quoted in the N.Y. *Tribune*, May 8, 1867; N.Y. *National Anti-Slavery Standard*, Aug. 3, 1867; James G. Blaine, *Twenty Years of Congress: From Lincoln to Garfield* . . . (Norwich, Conn., 1884-1886), II, 531.

[21] Forney to Sumner, July 10, 1867. Sumner Mss., Houghton Library, Harvard University.

[22] During the 1866 elections conservatives had worked hard to restrain their Radical allies in the effort to defeat Johnson and the Democrats. Not only had Republican legislation been conservative, but on the stump they had emphasized its conservatism and reasonableness, at least implying that if southerners ratified the Fourteenth Amendment, their states would be restored to normal relations in the Union. They had abandoned efforts to enfranchise blacks or to disband the governments in the South erected by presidential authority. Radicals had played a slight role in the campaign. Not until the southern state legislatures rejected the Fourteenth Amendment did Republicans decide they could go further than they had indicated they would during the 1866 canvass. See McKitrick, *Johnson and Recon-*

Republicans succeeded in an election in which radicals had taken such a prominent part, radicals would argue that the people were ready for more thorough measures of reconstruction, and they might win support from other elements in the party who agreed with particular parts of their program. This would affect both the platform and the candidate in 1868. The conservatives were worried. James G. Blaine wrote afterwards, "I felt . . . that if we should carry everything with a whirl in '67 that such knaves as Ben Butler would control our National Convention and give us a nomination with which defeat would be inevitable *if not desirable* . . . ."[23]

The people of twenty states went to the polls from March to November, 1867, and Republicans lost ground in nearly all of them. In March, Connecticut had replaced its Republican governor with a Democrat and elected three Democratic congressmen and only one Republican. Republicans lost 12,000 votes in Maine. The Democrats swept California, with Republicans running 20,000 votes short of their 1864 pace. The Republican vote in New Jersey fell 16,000 short of that polled in 1865, with seven of the twelve counties which voted Republican that year returning Democratic majorities in 1867. In Maryland, the Republican vote was reduced from 40 per cent of the total to 25 per cent. In Massachusetts, Republicans had won 77 per cent of the vote in 1866; one year later they received only 58 per cent. Republican percentages were also reduced in Vermont, New Hampshire, Iowa, Minnesota, Rhode Island, and Wisconsin. Only in Michigan and Kentucky did the party improve upon its showings of a year earlier.[24]

Most ominous were the losses Republicans sustained in Ohio, Pennsylvania, and New York. All three "swing" states, all three carrying great weight in the electoral college, Republicans could not lose them in 1868 and expect to carry the presidential election. The Ohio contest had been especially important. It was the only populous, northern, swing state where voters had the opportunity to vote directly on the issue of black suffrage. A combination black enfranchisement-deserter disfranchisement amendment to the Ohio constitution was on the ballot. Throughout the campaign it remained the central issue in the contest. Moreover, Ohio played a critical role in presidential politics. Both Wade and Chase were Ohioans; the legislature elected in 1867 would name a Senator to fill the Senate seat held by Wade, whose term expired in 1869. Wade was a candidate for reelection, and his presidential ambitions could not very well survive the election of a Democratic state leg-

---

struction, pp. 442-54; Hans L. Trefousse, *The Radical Republicans: Lincoln's Vanguard for Racial Justice* (N.Y., 1969), pp. 348-51.

23 Blaine to Israel Washburn, Sept. 12, 1867, quoted in Gaillard Hunt, *Israel, Elihu and Cadwallader Washburn: A Chapter in American Biography* (N.Y., 1925), pp. 122-23. The letter seems to have been dated earlier than one would expect, in light of Blaine's confidence that Republicans were not to succeed at the polls. However, it is dated after the Maine elections, in which Republicans did less well than they had the previous year.

24 The statistics are from the *New York Tribune Almanac . . . 1868* (N.Y., 1868).

islature. As the Ohio correspondent of the New York *Times* pointed out before the elections, Ohio "gives the key-note of the entire central West. If Ohio give [*sic*] a decided vote, you need not expect any of the ten States, west and north of it, including Missouri and Colorado to go otherwise. These states give about one hundred electoral votes in the Presidential election . . . . If Ohio carries the Constitutional Amendment [extending suffrage to blacks] . . . and gives the Radical candidate . . . a decided majority, you may rely upon it, that these one hundred electoral votes will be given to an uncompromising Republican candidate for the Presidency. By that I mean a Republican, and one whose principles on important issues cannot be mistaken."[25] The hostile reference to Grant is clear.

The Republicans had expected victory in Ohio. William Henry Smith, the Republican Secretary of State and an important local politician, anticipated a two to one Republican majority in the state legislature, a 40,000 majority for the Republican candidate for governor, Rutherford B. Hayes, and a 5-10,000 majority for the black suffrage amendment. Instead the Democrats won the legislature, the black suffrage amendment lost by 38,000 votes, and the popular Hayes squeezed into the governorship by only 3000 votes of 484,000 cast. The Republicans lost 13,000 votes from their 1866 total, while the Democrats gained 27,000. Twelve of the 45 Republican counties returned majorities against Negro suffrage.[26] As the Democratic Chicago *Times* admitted, "Democrats as well as Republicans, are astounded at the result in Ohio."[27]

In Pennsylvania the Republican state ticket lost by 1000 votes, although the party retained control of the legislature by a slim margin. The previous year the Republican state-wide majority had been 17,000 votes. In New York Republicans also lost, the narrow 13,000-vote Republican majority of 1866 converted to a 50,000-vote deficit.

Actually, the elections of 1867 were not disastrous for the Republican party as a whole. Few major offices were lost; most states merely showed greatly reduced Republican majorities. Conservative Republicans were not despondent. As Blaine wrote, "[The losses] will be good discipline in many ways and will I am sure be 'blessed to use in the edification and building up of the true faith' . . . ."[28] But for the Radicals the defeat

[25] N.Y. *Times*, Sept. 2, 1867.

[26] Smith to S. R. Reid, Oct. 3, 1867; Smith to Murat Halstead, Oct. 2, 1867. Smith Mss., Rutherford B. Hayes Library; Schuyler Colfax to John A. J. Creswell, Sept. 28, 1867. Colfax Mss., Hayes Library; John Sherman to William Tecumseh Sherman, Aug. 9, 1867, quoted in Thorndike (ed.), *The Sherman Letters*, pp. 292-94; Rutherford B. Hayes, *Diary and Letters of Rutherford B. Hayes, Nineteenth President of the United States*, ed. Charles Richard Williams (Columbus, Ohio 1922-26), III, 48 (Oct. 6, 1867). The election statistics are from the *Tribune Almanac, 1868*.

[27] Chicago *Times*, quoted in the Cincinnati *Commercial*, Oct. 12, 1867.

[28] Blaine to Israel Washburn, Sept. 12, 1867, quoted in Hunt, *Washburn*, pp. 122-23.

was a disaster—"a crusher for the wild men," the conservative congressman, Nathanial P. Banks, wrote happily.[29]

There had been many side issues distracting Republicans in various states, yet the cause of the setbacks was clear. As John Sherman recognized, "The chief trouble is the [Negro] suffrage question. It is clearly right . . . . It is easy to convince people so, but harder to make them feel it—and vote it." Ben Wade, deprived of his Senate seat and his chances for the presidency, put it more simply: "We went in on principle, and got whipped."[30] The consequences were clear. The perceptive, conservative New York lawyer and political observer, John Binney, wrote hopefully, "The extreme Radicals must now open their eyes to the palpable fact, that they must moderate their impetuosity so as to carry the prudent conservative Republicans along with them." But the unhappy Wade put it another way: "I fear its effect will be to make the timorous more timorous and the next session [of Congress] more inefficient than the last."[31]

The elections' practical effects were felt immediately. The radical New York *Independent's* correspondent found the change in Congress "startling." "Our friends have an overwhelming majority," he wrote, "but with the people apparently against the Radical members, it will be impossible to secure Radical legislation." As the session opened, he gloomily assessed the prospects. "First, the impeachment movement is dead . . . .

"Second, all confiscation bills will fail . . . .

"Third, Congress will not pass a national Equal Suffrage bill till after the presidential election."[32]

All these predictions proved accurate. Neither confiscation nor suffrage bills passed, and less than one half of the Republicans in the House of Representatives supported the radical impeachment resolution in December, 1867.[33]

Finally, the results of the elections of 1867 made Grant's nomination for President in 1868 inevitable. As the observant French journalist, Georges Clemenceau, informed his readers, "The real victims of the Democratic victory are Mr. Wade and Mr. Chase."[34] Even in Ohio,

[29] Banks to Mrs. Banks, Nov. 13, 1867. Banks Mss., Essex Institute, Salem, Mass.

[30] Sherman to Colfax, Oct. 20, 1867. Colfax Mss., Rush Rhees Library, University of Rochester; Wade in an interview published in the Cincinnati *Commercial,* quoted in the N.Y. *Times,* Nov. 8, 1867.

[31] Binney to John A. Andrew, Sept. 13, 1867, Andrew Mss., Massachusetts Historical Society; Wade to Chandler, Oct. 10, 1867. Chandler Mss.

[32] N.Y. *Independent,* Oct. 24, Nov. 14, 1867.

[33] *Cong. Globe,* 40 Cong., 2 sess., 67-68 (Dec. 7, 1867). The impeachment resolution which finally did pass came in Feb. 1868, when the President apparently violated a law of Congress—the Tenure of Office Act—in what seemed to be a scheme to overthrow the reconstruction laws. See McKitrick, *Johnson and Reconstruction,* pp. 486-509; Benedict, "The Right Way," 418-35.

[34] Clemenceau, *American Reconstruction,* ed. Fernand Baldensperger (N.Y. & Toronto, 1926), p. 118 (Oct. 1867).

which both Wade and Chase had hoped to make the cornerstone of their campaigns for the nomination, opposition to Grant collapsed. In the presence of Governor-elect Hayes, who would dominate the Ohio delegation to the Republican national convention, Sardis Birchard, Hayes' uncle, announced to a Republican audience that General Grant was as good as nominated, "though no convention had been held."[35] From other states came similar reports. The other candidates are "good men as we all know," a correspondent wrote the general's campaign manager, Elihu B. Washburne, "but we can only win with Grant." Most Republicans agreed.[36]

Disheartened, the dejected Wade lamented, "[I]t is very strange that when men talk of availability, they always mean something squinting toward Copperheadism. They never think of consulting the Radicals . . . . Oh, no; we must take what we can get."[37]

The elections of 1867 marked a turning point in the history of the Republican party. They set the limits on reform in reconstruction. They confirmed leadership of the party in conservatives. They convinced Republicans that radicalism was not a viable political creed. They proved that no matter how deeply Republican leaders were committed to a moral, economic, social, and political reform of race relations North and South, the conservatism of the northern electorate set limits which the party dared not transgress.

[35] Cincinnati *Commercial*, Oct. 21, 1867.

[36] W. Ralph Thayer to Washburne, Oct. 10, 1867; Curtin to Washburne, Oct. 17, 1867; John Cochrane to Washburne, Nov. 9, 1867; John Meredith Read to Washburne, Nov. 7, 1867; E. H. Rollins to Washburne, Oct. 11, 1867, Washburne Mss.; William Pitt Fessenden to James W. Grimes, Oct. 20, 1867. Fessenden Mss., Bowdoin College Library; E. D. Morgan to C. E. Bishop, Nov. 17, 1867. Morgan Mss., New York State Library, Albany, N.Y.; Henry J. Raymond to Hugh McCulloch, Oct. 11, 1867. McCulloch Mss., L.C.; N.Y. *Times*, Oct. 17, 1867.

[37] N.Y. *Times*, Nov. 8, 1867.

REPUBLICANS AND BLACK
SUFFRAGE IN NEW YORK STATE:
The Grass Roots Response

Phyllis Frances Field

In 1860 free blacks in the United States enjoyed equal voting privileges with whites in only five New England states.[1] Ten years later not only were all blacks free but the nation had ratified the Fifteenth Amendment prohibiting exclusion from the suffrage on the basis of race, color, or previous condition of servitude. The Republican party had been instrumental in bringing about these changes; throughout the Civil War and Reconstruction it had furnished almost the sole support for emancipation, black suffrage, and the termination of various other forms of racial discrimination. Yet the conduct of the Republicans during the struggle for black suffrage continues to be a source of controversy among historians. Two contrasting images of the party have emerged. One is that of the Republicans as the vanguard of racial reform. Hans Trefousse, for instance, has shown Benjamin F. Wade to have been a man who overcame personal prejudice to support equal rights for humanitarian reasons.[2] The other image is less favorable—that of the Republicans as cynical opportunists seeking political advantage or as men with more than a taint of racism.[3] The mounting evidence of Republican reluctance to face racial issues squarely and their frequent

---

[1] Leon F. Litwack, *North of Slavery: The Negro in the Free States, 1790-1860* (Chicago, 1961), p. 263.

[2] H. L. Trefousse, *Benjamin Franklin Wade, Radical Republican from Ohio* (New York, 1963).

[3] John H. and LaWanda Cox, "Negro Suffrage and Republican Politics: The Problem of Motivation in Reconstruction Historiography." *Journal of Southern History*, XXXII (Aug., 1967), 303-330 is the most important historiographical survey of this literature. Relevant works since this article include Eugene H. Berwanger. *The Frontier Against Slavery: Western Anti-Negro Prejudice and the Slavery Extension Controversy* (Urbana, 1967); V. Jacque Voegeli, *Free But Not Equal: The Midwest and the Negro During the Civil War* (Chicago, 1967); and Eric Foner, *Free Soil, Free Labor, Free Men: The Ideology of the Republican Party Before the Civil War* (New York, 1970), ch. 8.

catering to white prejudice against blacks has led C. Vann Woodward to term the Republican commitment to equality as "lacking
in clarity, ambiguous in purpose, and capable of numerous interpretations."[4]

The study of the racial views of Republicans has primarily focused on the views of leaders. Relatively little effort has been made
to analyze the divisions among rank and file Republicans, the
sources of these divisions, the nature of the changes they underwent over time, and their impact on the party leadership. Perhaps
the conduct of the Republican party on racial questions could be
better understood if the base of the party pyramid received as
much attention as its apex.

Both before and after the Civil War a number of northern states
held referenda on discriminatory portions of their state constitutions. These referenda provide a rare opportunity to examine grass
roots responses to the question of racial discrimination and offer
a different context in which to view the actions of political leaders.
The following analysis is based upon three such black suffrage
referenda held in New York in 1846, 1860, and 1869.

New York, while not typical of the entire North, was a large
state, socially and economically diverse, and politically important.
Its three referenda permit a study of change and continuity in voter
reactions to black suffrage over time. The referenda were held at
moments of great analytic interest. The first, in 1846, occurred before the formation of the Republican party but after the injection
of the antislavery question into politics. The second, in 1860, took
place on the eve of the Civil War and the third, in 1869, at the
climax of Reconstruction, after the passage of the Fifteenth Amendment and its ratification by New York. County returns were available for all three referenda. In addition, township returns were located for a majority of counties in each referendum (over 80 percent in the last two).[5] Townships are smaller and more homogeneous than counties, and township returns reveal a more precise
view of group voting behavior in the referenda.

[4] C. Vann Woodward, "Seeds of Failure in Radical Race Policy," *Proceedings of the American Philosophical Society,* CX (Feb. 18, 1966), 3.

[5] The county canvasses were obtained from newspapers, county court houses,
and county boards of supervisors' proceedings. In 1846 township returns were
located for 35 counties; in 1860, 49 counties; and in 1869, 52 counties. There
were 60 counties in all. The counties for which the township returns were
available were compared to the state as a whole on all the variables used in the
analysis. In general they closely resembled the state as a whole. In 1846, however, slightly more of the population of the "township" counties (compared
to the entire state) did live in the eastern part of New York.

The discriminatory clause in New York's constitution at which the referenda were aimed had its origin in 1821. Before that date the state had made no distinction between white and black voters. However, the requirement that voters be free (gradual emancipation began in New York in 1799 and was not completed until 1827) and meet property qualifications ranging from $50 to $250, depending on the office contested, effectively disfranchised most blacks.[6] The more "democratic" constitution of 1821 made white male voter qualifications minimal (taxpaying, eligibility for militia or highway service); blacks, however, were required to be citizens of the state for three years (compared to one year for whites) and possess a freehold estate worth $250 above all debts.[7] Thus, all blacks were not disfranchised, but they were severely discriminated against in exercising the right to vote. The difference in suffrage qualifications became even greater in 1826 when the remaining limitations on white voters were removed.

The attempts in 1846, 1860, and 1869 to remove the property qualification ended in failure. Each vote had unique qualities. Yet in all three referenda black suffrage was revealed to be an issue to which voters were attuned. In each referendum approximately 80 percent of the voters at the polls (the referenda occurred at general elections) took a position on the suffrage question.[8] Although some did fail to vote on it, it should be noted that the rate of participation was close to the maximum in *any* referendum in this period and well above the average for *all* referenda.[9] In 1869, although not in 1846, the suffrage question actually outpolled new state constitutions being simultaneously submitted. Interest was widespread too. In all but a small fraction of townships (never more than 5 percent) at least a majority of those at the polls voted in the referenda.[10] Thus, the sensitivity of politicians to the issue of black suffrage was perfectly understandable. It was not a matter of indifference to most voters.

Analysis of the 1846 referendum reveals that before the formation of the Republican party, party polarization on equal suffrage

[6] Charles Z. Lincoln, *The Constitutional History of New York* (Rochester, 1906), I, pp. 171-72, 175.

[7] *Ibid.*, p. 199.

[8] The actual percentages were 76.4 percent in 1846, 80.5 percent in 1860, and 82.9 percent in 1869.

[9] In 1866, 84.8 percent of those voting for governor had expressed a view on the calling of a new constitutional convention. This was the maximum during this period.

[10] In 1846, 1.0 percent had less than a majority voting, in 1860, 0.9 percent, and in 1869, 4.7 percent.

was not pronounced.[11] This was particularly true at the grass roots level, in distinct contrast to the later referenda. Only the small Liberty party was apparently undivided in its insistence upon the abolition of the property qualification for black voters. At the Democratic controlled constitutional convention in 1846, which submitted the suffrage question to the voters, just over two-thirds of the Whig delegates voted in favor of equal suffrage at least once during the proceedings while slightly over half the Democrats favored disqualifying all blacks from the suffrage.[12] At this level, level, then, there was a clear central tendency within each party, although each had a significant dissenting element.

When the question was submitted to the electorate, however, a different pattern emerged. Equal suffrage was defeated by nearly a three to one margin (223,834 to 85,306).[13] In only ten of fifty-nine counties, mostly in western and northern New York, did it receive a majority of the vote. And in eleven others, all in the southeastern portion of the state, it was opposed by 90 percent or more of the electorate. At the same time the Whigs were winning the governorship with a plurality of 49.8 percent. The prosuffrage vote correlated with the Whig at the township level at a mere .07 and with the Democratic vote at only a slightly higher, -.37.[14] Even making the conservative assumption that three-quarters of the Liberty men voted in the referendum and 90 percent favored equal suffrage and that all the remaining support for equal suffrage came from Whigs, no more than 38 percent of the Whigs who voted for the Whig gubernatorial candidate could have favored equal suffrage. In fact, in the overwhelming majority of townships the number of votes against removing the property qualification was actually greater than the total Democratic votes, indicating definite Whig opposition to equal suffrage. In fully a quarter of the townships the antisuffrage vote was more than half again greater than the

[11] John L. Stanley, "Majority Tyranny in Tocqueville's America: The Failure of Negro Suffrage in 1846," *Political Science Quarterly*, LXXXIV (Sept., 1969), 434-35, also draws this conclusion.

[12] This observation is based on a Guttman scale of four votes on suffrage in which only those voting at least twice on the subject were included. *Debates and Proceedings in the New-York State Convention for the Revision of the Constitution*, Croswell and Sutton, reporters (*Albany Argus*, 1846), pp. 783, 790, 791, 820.

[13] The returns from all three referenda by county may be found in the *Tribune Almanac and Political Register for 1870* (New York, 1870), p. 53.

[14] All correlations unless otherwise noted are based on township level data. The township N in 1846 was 520.

Democratic vote. Assuming that every Democrat and Native American voted in the referendum against equal suffrage, at *least* 15 percent of the Whigs must have opposed it also.[15] As Table 1 indicates, the best predictors of a township's support for equal suffrage proved to be the strength of the abplitionist Liberty party there and the proportion of Yankees in its population. These two variables alone "explained" 51 percent of the prosuffrage vote. Democratic voting was also related to prosuffrage vote. Democratic voting was also related to prosuffrage support but at a much lower level.[16] The alignments in 1846, thus, were not basically political but instead cultural, apparently rooted in the reform consciousness characteristic of the New Englanders who settled western New York.

As long as the party alignment present in 1846 continued undisturbed, there was little incentive for the leaders of the major parties to reconsider the suffrage question. With the breakup of the Whig and Democratic parties in the 1850s, however, equal suffrage gained new life. Republican legislatures showed increased interest in pro-

Table 1

Partial Regression Coefficients for Variables
Related to Prosuffrage Voting, 1846
(520 Townships)

Variable	*Beta*
Percent Liberty Party	.36
Percent New England Born	.34
Percent Democrat/Nativist 1846	-.21
Percent Democratic, 1848	-.15
Percent for Temperance, 1846	.11

Percentage of Explained Variance: 60.2%

Sources: *Census of the State of New York for 1845* (Albany, 1846); New York State Assembly, *Documents,* 70th Session, 1847, Document 40. Political data are from sources listed in footnote 4.

[15] There were some divisions among the Democrats too. The vote in favor of equal suffrage exceeded the combined Whig and Liberty vote in about 2 percent of the towns, most of them in the prosuffrage counties.

[16] The variables entered in the regression were: percent Liberty vote 1844, percent black, percent born New England, percent churches Dutch Reformed, percent Democratic/Nativist vote 1846, percent Democratic vote 1848, percent against licensing the sale of liquor (i.e., for temperance), value of dwelling per capita, and area settled before 1790 (a dummy variable). Only variables which added at least 1 percent to explained variance in a stepwise regression were included in the table.

posals to remove the property qualification from the constitution. The amendment procedure was difficult, requiring the approval of two successive legislatures as well as voter ratification. Still, the question was considered in every legislature from 1855 through 1860. During these years black suffrage became increasingly a partisan issue and increasingly related to the national agitation over slavery. In 1857, for instance, Republican anger over the Dred Scott decision helped speed the passage of an equal suffrage resolution through the Assembly.[17]

Some Republicans began to ask such questions as, "With what consistency . . . can we wage war even against American Slavery, or endeavor to preserve our institutions from the touch of the foul monster, and yet allow in our Constitution the very principles upon which Slavery lives and breathes?"[18] In every legislative vote on equal suffrage after 1856, at least 90 percent of the Republicans favored it, while over 90 percent of the Democrats opposed it.[19] Yet the Republicans' support for equal suffrage was somewhat erratic. Black suffrage was never endorsed in a party platform although the Democrats denounced it twice.[20] And in 1857 the amendment procedure was set back a full year by the failure of a Republican governor to have a statement of the amendment published before the legislative elections.[21]

How sympathetic the Republican masses were to the proposed reform was a key problem. Certainly the Republican coalition drew much more heavily than the Whig upon the areas where sentiment for equal suffrage had been strong in 1846. Support for the Republican party during its formative years from 1856 to 1859 correlated at the county level between .5 and .7 with the prosuffrage vote in 1846, much higher than the Whig vote had ever done.[22] The Republican party was a coalition, however, whose growth was conditional upon incorporating within it diverse elements that were in disagreement on some points. Some voters, for instance, favored the party because they wanted to see the western territories pre-

[17]*Albany Argus,* Mar. 31, 1857; *New York Tribune,* Mar. 28, 1857.

[18] Albany *Evening Journal,* Feb. 18, 1857.

[19] New York State Assembly, *Journal,* 80th sess., 1857, pp. 862-64; New York State Senate, *Journal,* 80th sess., 1857, pp. 262-63; New York State Assembly, *Journal,* 82nd sess., 1859, p. 732; New York State Senate, *Journal,* 82nd sess., 1859, p. 701; New York Assembly, *Journal,* 83rd sess., 1860, p. 332; New York State Senate, *Journal,* 83rd sess., 1860, p. 468.

[20]*Albany Argus,* Sept. 14, 1857, Aug. 17, 1860.

[21] New York State Senate, *Documents,* No. 3, 81st sess., 1858, p. 11.

[22] These correlations were: 1856, .57; 1857, .54; 1858, .56; and 1859, .66.

served for free *white* men. They had little interest in equal rights. An upstate New York Republican paper in 1860 thought black suffrage would be defeated by an almost unanimous vote, "as it should be."[23]

The 1860 referendum exposed some of the fission lines within the Republican party. While Lincoln swept the state, equal suffrage was resisted by 63 percent of the electorate, about 10 percent less than in 1846.[24] Support for equal suffrage expanded in many parts of Yankee-settled western New York. Eighteen counties (about one-third) were favorable to the reform this time. But very heavy opposition continued to come from the older southeastern section of the state. In contrast to 1846, however, the parties were polarized on the suffrage issue. The basic partisan division of the vote was indicated by a high township level correlation (.78) between the Republican and prosuffrage votes.[25] But whereas the Democrats were completely united in opposing equal suffrage, the Republicans were pulled in different directions.

The Democrats were almost certainly heavily antisuffrage. Horace Greeley had estimated in 1857 that at least 99 percent of them would never agree to let more black men vote.[26] There was not a *single* township in the forty-nine counties whose returns were available for analysis in which the prosuffrage vote was larger than the Republican vote. The large measure of agreement among the Democrats against equal suffrage allowed them great freedom to attack the Republicans on the subject.

The Republican situation was quite different. Even assuming that all the support for equal suffrage came from Republicans, only slightly over half (54.5 percent) of the Lincoln voters could have favored equal suffrage. Assuming that every Democrat at the polls voted against equal suffrage, over a tenth (13.8 percent) of the Republicans must have voted to retain the property qualification. Thus, while a majority of Republicans would acquiesce to

---

[23] Berwanger, *Frontier Against Slavery*; *Montgomery Republican* (Fultonville), Sept. 14, Oct. 20, 1860.

[24] The actual figures were 345,791 to 197,889. These totals differ from those in the *Tribune Almanac* for 1870 which includes inaccurate or incomplete returns from Orange, Chenango, and Herkimer counties.

[25] The Republican vote is that for president; The supporters of Bell, Breckenridge, and Douglas in New York formed a "fusion" slate to oppose Lincoln. The fusion vote, of course, correlates with the antisuffrage vote at .78 also. The township *N* in 1860 was 885.

[26] *New York Tribune*, Sept. 26, 1857.

voting equality with blacks, there was a strong current of opposition to this.

The nature of these contending factions on equal suffrage is of some interest. Although Republican opposition to equal suffrage was widespread, it took different forms and was much more significant in some areas than others. Thus, definite Republican opposition to equal suffrage (i.e., where the antisuffrage vote exceeded the Democratic vote) could be established in 86 percent of all townships. In about half of these, however, there was no more than a 10 percent difference between the vote against suffrage and the Democratic vote. In another 3.7 percent, the difference was over 50 percent.

The poor showing of equal suffrage was not due solely to Republicans joining Democrats to oppose it. There were also massive Republican abstentions in some areas. Frederick Douglass complained after the referendum, "While the Democrats at the polls never failed to accompany their state and national tickets with one against the proposed amendment, Republicans—many of them—refused to touch a ticket in favor of the amendment. . . ."[27] The township data indicate that the more hostile an area was to equal suffrage, the more likely it was to have a lower than average rate of participation in the referendum. (The correlation was .53). That the abstainers were primarily Republicans is suggested by a high correlation (-.72) between the voter turnout in the referendum and the amount by which the Republican and prosuffrage percentages in a town varied. Where turnout was low, Republicans were simply not voting for equal suffrage.

The prosuffrage vote fell considerably short of the Republican vote in highly localized townships, mostly in southeastern New York. The most extreme case on the county level was Putnam, where 48 percent of the voters had backed Lincoln and only 7 percent favored equal suffrage. Table 2 further examines the characteristics of these areas.[28] Democrats tended to be strong there. Of the thirteen counties where the Republican and prosuffrage votes differed by 30 percent or more, eight were Democratic and five marginally Republican (none more than 52.6 percent Republican).

---

[27] *Douglass' Monthly*, Dec., 1860.

[28] The dependent variable for the regression was calculated by subtracting the prosuffrage vote in a township from the Republican vote and dividing this difference by the Republican vote. This, in effect, measures the maximum percentage of Republican voters who did not vote for the amendment, assuming that all the prosuffrage votes were cast by Republicans.

Table 2

Partial Regression Coefficients for Variables
Related to Republican Nonsupport of Equal Suffrage, 1860
(885 Townships)

Variable	*Beta*
Percent Born in New England	-.22
Percent Democratic, 1860	.21
Area Settled Before 1790	.19
Percent American Party, 1858	.18
Percent Black	.17

Percentage of Explained Variance: 42.7%

Sources: Nonpolitical data from the *Census of the State of New York for 1855* (Albany, 1857). Political data from the *Evening Journal Almanac*, 1859 and 1861.

This situation gave local Republican leaders good reason to soft pedal the suffrage question, especially since the Democrats used it unsparingly against the Republicans throughout the campaign.[29] It also meant, however, that these areas tended to be disproportionately underrepresented among Republican officeholders (in the state legislature, for example). They were far from being the heart and soul of the Republican party. Republican dissenters were also much less likely to come from areas of recent Yankee settlement than from the older, eastern region of the state where the influence of the old native Dutch stock was still felt and slavery had once flourished. Blacks tended to make up a larger share of the population there. Hostility in this instance was probably more an indication of the prior slaveholding tradition than of the actual fear of local blacks. Blacks made up 5 percent or more of the population in only two counties and about 3 percent of the townships in the study (no township was more than 15 percent black). The American party had also been strong as late as 1858 in many of the areas where Republicans opposed or abstained on equal suffrage. Since the Republicans eventually absorbed many of the American party members, it is possible that factional lines on race may have coincided to some extent with those on nativism.

With this type of division at the grass roots level the lack of clarity in the "Republican" attitude toward racial discrimination

[29] There were innumerable examples of such Democratic attacks during the 1860 campaign. See, for instance, *Sag Harbor Corrector*, Sept. 15, 1860; *Schenectady Democrat*, Nov. 1, 1860.

becomes more understandable. In New York in 1860 there was majority support among Republicans for pursuing the objective of equal suffrage for the state's blacks. Yet there was also a great deal of sentiment against this. Although much of the opposition came from the "fringe" areas of Republicanism, these areas could be very crucial under certain circumstances. For only once from its formation until 1869 did the Republican party win more than 53.7 percent of the vote in New York.[30] As the *New York Nation* observed in 1867:

the ardent Republicans are never sufficiently numerous to win an election. They have to secure their majority by the help of a few thousand who are only lukewarm Republicans, whose political feelings are not strong, who are affected in voting by diverse collateral considerations, and who, unless they are well looked after, are as likely as not to go over to the enemy on the day of battle. It is these men who decide political contests in nearly all the closely divided states.[31]

Thus, making equal suffrage a test of party fidelity might be fatal to the party. In this light, the schizophrenic behavior of Republican leaders in New York on suffrage becomes somewhat more comprehensible. In the 1860 referendum Republicans were deliberately evasive on the suffrage question. Horace Greeley, one of the most vocal advocates of equal suffrage in 1846, warned Republicans in 1860 to stick to the "main" issues—those in the platform—and not respond to the "bugaboo stories" on race put forth by their opponents.[32] His advice was largely heeded. Frederick Douglass lamented after the amendment's defeat, "We were overshadowed smothered by the Presidential struggle—over laid by Abraham Lincoln and Hannibal Hamlin. The black baby of Negro suffrage was thought too ugly to exhibit on so grand an occasion."[33] Even in endorsing equal suffrage the Republican press was inclined to defer to the prejudices of white voters. A Utica paper, for instance, insisted that the party was opposed to social equality with blacks and another in Buffalo reassured its readers that "there is no danger of his [the black man's] ever attaining positions of distinction in society or government. . . ."[34]

[30] Yearly returns may be found in the *Tribune Almanac* or *Evening Journal Almanac.*

[31] *Nation,* Sept. 19, 1867.

[32] *New York Tribune,* Sept. 15, 1860

[33] *Douglass' Monthly,* Dec., 1860.

[34] *Oneida Weekly Herald,* Oct. 23, 1860; *Buffalo Morning Express,* Oct. 24, 1860.

What complicates the problem of the relationship of the Republicans to equal suffrage still further is the fact that it was constantly changing over time, especially at the grass roots level. State Republican leaders continued to operate in the sixties much as they had in the late fifties. In the legislature they overwhelmingly supported resolutions favoring blacks (abolition, black suffrage in the District of Columbia, the Thirteenth through Fifteenth Amendments, etc.). In this, of course, they were often following the national party's lead. They also tried to avoid confrontation on racial issues at election time. They stressed, for instance, the military expedience of such measures as emancipation and the use of black troops and rarely challenged voters' prejudices directly. Horace Greeley frankly admitted at the end of the war,

we have . . . liberated him [the black] from galling and grinding bondage, not specially for *his* sake, not because we pitied him as weak, downtrodden and terribly abused, but because the life of the nation hung upon a course of simple justice to this long-suffering race—because it was for our advantage, our peace, our safety and our prosperity to acknowledge the manhood of the Black, who involuntarily has become the greatest benefactor of this nation, since through him we have been able to strike a blow at faction and to assert the supremacy of the Constitution.[35]

Even though a Republican controlled constitutional convention in 1867 voted to remove the property qualification from black voters and not a single Republican dissented from this position, a decision was also made to submit the question separately rather than risk the defeat of the constitution by incorporating equal suffrage within it.[36] The constitution, although completed in February 1868 was not submitted to the voters until November 1869. This delay prevented equal suffrage from coming before the electorate during a presidential election year, reserving it instead for a time when the highest office being contested was secretary of state.

Mass support among Republicans for black suffrage showed relatively greater change during the 1860s. The Civil War and its aftermath had served to put New York's black suffrage discrimination in a different perspective. Increasingly the struggle over suffrage was linked to the conflict with the South. Thus, one editor

[35] *New York Tribune,* June 14, 1865.
[36] New York State Constitutional Convention, *Journal of the Convention of the State of New York* (Albany, 1868), pp. 287-92, 303-306, 979-80. The Republicans' hesitancy is described in James C. Mohr, *The Radical Republicans and Reform in New York during Reconstruction* (Ithaca, 1973), ch. 8.

could write, "To vote that they [blacks] shall not vote is in effect to vote that the Southern Confederacy, which was avowedly and logically based on the natural and rightful subordination of Blacks to Whites, was the only rational, legitimate government ever set up in this country. . . ."[37]

Republican sponsorship of black suffrage in the South increased the recognition among Republicans that the issue was indeed a partisan one. Even the moderate *New York Times* admitted, "Support of Congress implies support of impartial suffrage, and the party which upholds it as a measure of justice and safety for the South cannot honorably shirk it in its application to this State."[38] By 1869 the *Albany Evening Journal* could observe that New York's suffrage discrimination "merely presented in distinct form an issue of national importance, concerning which the attitudes of Republicans and Democrats alike has been most clearly determined by the various aspects of the reconstruction controversy."[39]

When equal suffrage was once again submitted to the voters in 1869, it was defeated by a vote of 282,903 to 249,802. About 53 percent of the electorate wished to retain the property qualification, 10 percent fewer than in 1860. In western and northern New York only small pockets of resistance to equal suffrage remained. The correlation between the Republican and prosuffrage percentages at the township level was very high, .89. A multiple regression analysis similarly shows that an extremely high 79 percent of the variation in the prosuffrage vote could be predicted on the basis of the Republican vote alone; no other variable added as much as 1 percent to explained variance.[40] If all the prosuffrage votes came from Republicans, then over three-quarters (78 percent) of the party must have opposed the property qualification, a large gain over 1860. Unlike 1860, also, Republicans were no more likely than Democrats to abstain on the referendum. Assuming that both parties participated at the same rate (83 percent), as many as 93 percent of the Republicans voting in the referendum may have favored equal suffrage. Definite Republican crossovers on the suffrage question were apparent in only one-quarter of the townships and most of these were minor. In almost three-quarters of the town-

---

[37]*New York Tribune*, Oct. 4, 1869.

[38]*New York Times*, Sept. 25, 1867.

[39]*Albany Evening Journal*, Nov. 3, 1869.

[40]Variables entered were percent Republican; area settled before 1790; percent born Ireland and Germany; percent born New England; and percent non-evangelical of religious communicants. The township N was 954.

ships (72.5 percent) they amounted to no more than 5 percent of all Republican voters. Near unanimous opposition to equal suffrage, regardless of party, as had occurred in a number of lower Hudson counties in 1860 was a thing of the past.

The smaller scale of Republican defections made them that much harder to characterize than those in 1860. In only eight counties was the difference between the Republican and prosuffrage percentages in 1869 as much as 5 percent, in none more than 13 percent. Again the larger discrepancies tended to be located in southeastern New York, which had been the most consistently hostile area to black voting equality in all three referenda. However, this time only *some* of these counties were involved. In fact, none of a series of ethnic, economic, political, and social indicators correlated with the difference between the Republican and prosuffrage votes at a level of .2 or higher.[41] One might hypothesize that equal suffrage still tended to be relatively more unpopular with the same groups that had disliked it in 1860 but that Republican organization was more effective in some of these areas in marshalling support for the referendum.

Thus, as the sixties had progressed, Republicans had become more united on the subject of black suffrage. However, they had also become less potent politically. Republicans failed to carry New York in 1867, 1868, or 1869. The role of suffrage in these defeats has been more often taken for granted than demonstrated, but one of the reasons there were fewer Republicans opposed to equal suffrage in 1869 may have been because the Republican party was no longer as broadly based as it had been in 1860.

In retrospect it hardly appears strange that Republicans have acquired such a varied reputation on racial matters. In New York one gets a somewhat different view of them depending on whether one looks at national leaders, state leaders, newspaper editors, or the voting public. Our view also depends on the *time* at which we examine the party. While badly divided on black suffrage in 1860, Republicans were far closer to agreement in 1869. The size and character of the dissenting elements helped shape political responses to the suffrage issue throughout this period. Thus, if we are to understand fully the functioning of the Republican party on racial questions, we cannot afford to look only at the Charles Sumners and the Thaddeaus Stevenses. We must attempt instead to integrate

[41] These indicators were percent Republican; percent born Ireland; percent born Germany; percent born New England; percent black; percent landowners; and average value of dwelling per family.

our knowledge of what was going on at different levels within the party, because all were intimately interrelated. The situation was a complex one and deserves to be recognized as such.

How typical were New York Republicans of those of the North? Only further study can determine this. Eastern Republicans are usually credited with being somewhat more sympathetic to blacks than those in the Midwest or West.[42] Since many other northern states also held referenda on suffrage before and after the war, comparable analyses of these states are feasible and desirable.[43]

Black suffrage was clearly a difficult issue for Republicans whenever they faced it. It has been argued that one of the reasons moderate Republicans favored the Fifteenth Amendment was that it offered to solve some of their political problems by providing more black voters in the North.[44] Blacks were not sufficiently numerous to have this effect in New York, but perhaps one of the reasons the Fifteenth Amendment was welcomed there was that it removed the troublesome and divisive issue of suffrage from the local political arena once and for all.[45]

[42] See, for example, the comparison of the reactions of different sections to the Fifteenth Amendment in William Gillette, *The Right to Vote: Politics and the Passage of the Fifteenth Amendment* (Baltimore, 1965), chs. 4-8.

[43] A few quantitative studies of referenda have already appeared. See, for example, Stanley, "Majority Tyranny," pp. 412-35; Robert R. Dykstra and Harlan Hahn, "Northern Voters and the Negro Suffrage Question: The Case of Iowa, 1868," *Public Opinion Quarterly*, XXXII (Summer, 1968), 202-15; and Ronald P. Formisano, "The Edge of Caste: Colored Suffrage in Michigan, 1827-1861," *Michigan History*, LVI (Spring, 1972), 19-41.

[44] This is the thesis of Gillette, *Right to Vote.*

[45] Papers pointing out this advantage included the *New York Tribune*, Feb. 27, 1869; *New York Times*, Mar. 19, 1869; *Harper's Weekly*, Feb. 13, 186

PART III:

THE
"SPIRIT OF PARTY":
Congress and
Roll Call Voting

PARTY AND SECTION: The Senate and the Kansas-Nebraska Bill

Gerald W. Wolff

THE KANSAS-NEBRASKA ACT of 1854 was one of the most important bills ever passed by an American Congress. The legislative struggle surrounding it and succeeding events profoundly affected, not only the American party system, but also ultimately the very structure of the nation itself. The Whig Party was destroyed, the Democracy was seriously weakened, and intense animosities were created between northerners and southerners as a result of this piece of legislation.

The Kansas-Nebraska Bill was not only controversial and far reaching, but was also confusing and enigmatic. Roll-call material as it bears upon this legislative proposal in the Senate helps to unravel some of that mystery. By applying to these roll-calls a variation of a technique developed by sociologist Louis Guttman, it is possible to derive what amounts to rather sophisticated attitude patterns. These patterns, in turn, can be compared quite precisely with certain other factors, in this case, their relationship to party and sectional affiliation.[1] Put in another way, this paper will be mainly concerned with discovering the attitudes of Senators toward the Kansas-Nebraska Bill and the role played by party and sectional affiliation in shaping those attitudes.

The voting pattern or scalogram used in this analysis was derived by a method of trial and error. We first began with the final vote taken on the Kansas-Nebraska Bill and then attempted to scale with it every roll-call whose contents were directly related to the Nebraska struggle. This involved those votes concerned with parliamentary procedure, as well as the various attempts to amend the measure. In the end, the scale consisted of ten roll-calls and provided seven clear-cut scale types or attitudes on this issue. To facilitate discussion and comparison, however, the seven types were collapsed into three main attitude blocs in a way that would not distort the findings. These blocs could have been assigned several different labels, but it was decided that the following would be most useful: anti-Kansas-Nebraska Bill, moderates, and pro-Kansas-Nebraska Bill. The "moderate" category was the most useful and important of the three, and its meaning must be defined precisely. The term "moderate," as used here, has meaning and relevance only

---

[1] Of the many important works dealing with roll-call analysis, perhaps the best starting place for those interested in the subject is Lee F. Anderson, *et. al. Legislative Roll-Call Analysis* (Evanston, 1966).

within the context and perimeters of this particular scale, and is relative to the two more extreme classifications. For example, besides those who were very much for or very much against almost every aspect of the Kansas-Nebraska Bill, the scalogram indicates those who were less polarized in their attitudes toward it. These men were not extremists on the Kansas-Nebraska issue as defined by this scale, and hence can be labeled moderates or non-extremists on that issue. The types of moderate vary from scale to scale and within the scales and must be analyzed. From the standpoint of attitudinal analysis of roll-call material, however, the moderate classification provides a more meaningful and sophisticated approach than the dichotomous breakdown provided by roll-calls taken individually. In fact, it would seem that the major utility of the scalogram over individual roll-calls is that by using scales it is possible to obtain more than a simple yea-nay opinion from Congressmen on a given issue by using roll-call material.

Sectionalism was the first variable tested against these attitude blocs. All historians dealing with the Kansas-Nebraska question have recognized that it involved, to some degree, North-South sectionalism because of the slavery issue it enveloped. However, in interpreting that sectionalism, most scholars have concentrated largely upon the words and actions of the Senate leaders. The scale data, on the other hand, provide one type of opportunity to gauge systematically the magnitude and intensity of sectionalism, as it involved a large portion of the Senators. The voting patterns clearly revealed a North-South split, but the division was milder than was anticipated. While nearly 60 per cent of the southerners enthusiastically endorsed virtually every aspect of the Nebraska measure covered by the scale, over one-third were less vigorous in their support and voted as moderates. Similarly, although 45.8 per cent of the northern senators strongly opposed it, one-third appeared in the moderate category, and over one-fifth were actually strongly in favor of the bill. A similar pattern emerged when East-West sectionalism was tested (see Table One).

More can be shown about sectionalism, however, in this regard. Of all the northern senators, those from the Northeast manifested the greatest hostility toward the Kansas-Nebraska Bill. Almost three-fourths of them turned up in the anti portion of the scale, and not one appeared in the pro section. The most adamant opponents of slavery extension appeared here. The northwestern senators, on the other hand, reacted quite differently. Only 23.1 per cent of them were strongly antagonistic toward the measure, while 38.4 per cent were moderates, and a like percentage were actually very much in favor of the bill. So despite the demonstrations of public anger in the Northwest over the Kansas-Nebraska Bill, a rather small proportion of that section's senators strongly opposed the measure. There was then a rather severe contrast on this issue between the voting behavior of the northern senators from the East and those from the West.

As for the Southeast and Southwest, an interesting voting pattern emerged. While almost 80 per cent of the senators from the southern inland states gave solid support to the Kansas-Nebraska Bill, three-fourths of their colleagues from the South Atlantic coastal states were only moderates (see Table Three). The favorable response of so many of the southwesterners seems reasonable enough, but the moderate voting posture of such a high percentage of the senators from the Southeast is curious in some ways and merits further scrutiny.

At first glance, one is tempted to account for their position largely in terms of apathy brought on by the realization that the geographical position of their states would preclude their constituents from ever having a decent opportunity to take practical advantage of the repeal of the Missouri Compromise, popular sovereignty, and the economic opportunities that would result from the organization of Kansas and Nebraska. Yet this analysis is inadequate, for it ignores the complexity of the situation and the passion with which southeastern Senators so often defended state rights. It is virtually impossible to probe the motives of moderate Jackson Morton of Florida because he chose to remain silent during the Nebraska debates, and there are no other sources, as far as we know, which indicate why he took the position he did. With respect to the other five southeastern moderates, however, there is enough evidence to suggest an explanation for their voting behavior.

For some of these senators, a primary and dominant element in any interpretation of their moderate stance must involve intensity of feeling rather than indifference. Harboring an extreme position on the rights of slaveholders, they withheld unqualified support for the Kansas-Nebraska Bill. Believing that the bill did not go quite far enough in protecting slavery in the territories, they felt compelled to rationalize the bill's usefulness at great length before supporting it. Robert M. T. Hunter of Virginia and Andrew Butler of South Carolina, two of the most powerful members of the Senate, shared what one historian has called the common property doctrine regarding the authority of the federal government over the territories.

In its pure form, the common property position was that, although the federal government managed the territories, it governed only in the capacity of a guardian, subject to the desires of all the states, who owned the territories in common. As a guardian, the federal government must allow citizens from every state to move to the territories with their property, including slaves, if they wished. It must also ensure that territorial governments protected that property once the migrants arrived and had become residents. Therefore, not only was the Missouri Compromise unconstitutional, but also the principle of popular sovereignty, which would allow territorial legislatures to sanction or to disavow slavery. If the federal government could not exclude slavery in the public domain, then it was not possible, legally or logically, for the national government to grant that power to one of its own creatures, namely a territorial legislature.[2] This was the most extreme position to evolve in the South regarding the rights of slaveowners in the territories. In the process of reaching a final decision on the Nebraska question, Butler and Hunter adhered strictly to certain parts of the common property doctrine, while agreeing to compromise on other aspects of it. Because the position taken by these two senators is so important to a major portion of the thesis of this study, it is necessary to scrutinize their views carefully.

Both Hunter and Butler declared emphatically that the Missouri Compromise was unconstitutional and should be repealed, just as the Nebraska Bill proposed. To Hunter, the compromise impaired the constitutional guarantee of equality of the states.[3] Similarly, Butler declared that the South had never acknowledged any constitutional obligations under the Compromise of 1820. The government in Washington, as the agent of the sovereign states, had no constitutional right, either explicit or implicit, to run an arbitrary line through the common territories of the states in a calculated move to prohibit slavery and disfranchise an entire section. Given the northern majority in Congress, if the slave states continued to acquiesce in the reasoning and process of accommodation associated with the Missouri Compromise, then those states would ultimately fall victim to the most arbitrary, uncontrollable, and unlimited of all powers, namely legislative discretion.[4] The Missouri Compromise, in Butler's opinion, made a mockery of the constitutional concept of equality of the states in the name of majority rule and compromise. "Suppose a gallant crew," he asked,

trusting in each other's honesty and good faith, were to embark in a vessel at sea, under definite articles of equal copartnership, and that one portion should assume, in violation of the fundamental *principles—not terms only*—of equality, to construe the terms of the copartnership so as to give and distribute the fruits of the voyage to one recognized class in preference to another; what would be thought of such a proceeding? . . . Sir, rather than remain on such a ship—talked of as an equal, but spurned as an inferior—would not the weaker party be doing the highest office of duty and honor to quit the ship, and take to the boats, trusting to the winds and

---

[2] An excellent description of the common-property doctrine is contained in Robert Russel, "The Issues in the Congressional Struggle Over the Kansas-Nebraska Bill, 1854," *Journal of Southern History*, XXIX (May, 1963), 188. Russel also pulls together a great deal of material showing that the Kansas-Nebraska Act fell short of what the congressional advocates of this position wanted, despite a long list of painful concessions made to them by many northern senators. He does not recognize any of them as moderates, however, but states only that the supporters of the common-property doctrine accepted and voted for the bill in the end. See also Arthur Bestor, "State Sovereignty and Slavery: A Reinterpretation of Proslavery Constitutional Doctrine, 1840-1860," Illinois State Historical Society, *Journal*, LIV (Summer, 1961), 117-180.

[3] U. S. *Congressional Globe*, 33 Cong., 1 sess., XXIII, Appendix, 221 and 224. For the general views of Hunter and Butler see *ibid.*, 223, 225, 238-239; *ibid.*, Pt. 1, 423, 689, 690, 1307. Also see *ibid.*, 519, 1064-1065 and *Ibid.*, App. 648-653, 789-801.

[4] *Ibid.*, App., 232, 238.

the waves for their fortunes, and if the ship were to perish, would they not be justified?[5]

Despite their adamant common property stand on the Missouri Compromise question, both senators were willing to accept the doctrine of popular sovereignty as contained in the Nebraska Bill, but within certain strict limits. To Hunter, a territorial legislature should be given "all possible political power as long as it did not impinge upon the equal rights of the states as provided in the Constitution."[6] Butler went to much greater lengths to delineate his position. He refused to concede that "the first comers upon the soil of a Territory can appropriate it, and become sovereigns over it," but rather Congress controlled the territories from their conception until they reached maturity.[7] A territorial legislature, as a child of Congress, could not do what its parent was forbidden to do. If it was unconstitutional for Congress to approve the Missouri Compromise or other unfair territorial restrictions, then it was also unconstitutional for "clandestine squatters" to pass measures of this type.[8] He was willing, in the case of the Nebraska Bill and as a general principle, to trust the people; but he would never assent to "trust the simple despotism of a majority."[9] If the territorial governments of Kansas and Nebraska should act in any way contrary to the common principles of the Constitution both senators agreed that the federal courts should intervene.[10]

Despite all this rhetoric regarding the rights and future of slaveholders in the Kansas and Nebraska territories, both men steadfastly insisted that the Kansas-Nebraska Bill would bring no practical advantage to the South, only psychological satisfaction. "Slavery might go there for a time," declared Hunter, but "it could not survive the formation of a State Constitution."[11] Butler believed that the Nebraska Bill would not provide "anything but an advance to the sentiment of honor."[12] "The South," he concluded, "wants her heart lightened-not her power increased."[13]

Both these gentlemen offered a summary of sorts explaining why they finally decided to accept the Kansas-Nebraska Bill. According to Hunter, the measure was a step toward peace, removing from Congress a primary "cause of strife, disturbance, and collision," namely the slavery extension issue.[14] The Bill had accomplished this, moreover, simply by applying the Constitution "to the question of slavery in common with

[5] *Ibid.*, 238.
[6] *Ibid.*, 223-224, 226, 289.
[7] *Ibid.*, 239. See also *ibid.*, Pt. 1, 1307.
[8] *Ibid.*, App., 239, 240; See also *ibid.*, Pt. 1, 690, 1307.
[9] *Ibid.*, App., 240.
[10] *Ibid.*, 224, 240; *Ibid.*, Pt. 1, 423, 689, 690.
[11] *Ibid.*, App., 224.
[12] *Ibid.*, 292.
[13] *Ibid.*, 240.
[14] *Ibid.*, 226, 225.

all others . . . ," and all sections could now "live in the peace of conscious security."[15] Hunter seems to have convinced himself that the
demise of the Missouri Compromise, even with the subsequent substitution of popular sovereignty, had vindicated the common property
doctrine by providing constitutional justice for the slave states, as well
as the free states. He may have felt secure in this position because of
his narrow interpretation of the prerogatives of territorial legislatures
and of the role he envisioned for the federal courts as the arbiters of
territorial decisions on the slavery question.

Butler was less enthusiastic about the virtues of the measure; but
the alternative was to prolong the life of the Missouri Compromise.
"Under one," he declared, "it is certain we can have no rights; under
the other we may have some."[16] Even if no slaves ever entered Kansas
or Nebraska, this piece of legislation would be worthwhile, because it
recognized southern honor. In fact, he concluded, "even if I were perfectly certain that the bill would operate injuriously to the South, with
the convictions on my mind that the Missouri Compromise is unconstitutional, I should be bound to vote for the bill."[17]

Like Hunter and Butler, moderate Thomas Pratt of Maryland, although practically speechless during the debates, also favored, or at
least leaned toward favoring, the common property doctrine. He was
an avid state rights advocate and would barely admit after careful
questioning and prodding by several northern senators that under the
popular sovereignty principle a territorial legislature could actually
exclude slavery.[18]

William Dawson of Georgia also asserted that the territories were
the common property of all American citizens and that there should
be no obstacle to any of them settling there if they chose. The Missouri
Compromise was such an obstacle. That arrangement was unconstitutional, conceived and executed in perfidy by the North, and the South
was under no obligation to obey it. The Kansas-Nebraska Bill, by removing it, was performing an act of justice long overdue, and the people of the United States would receive it as such.[19]

Evidently, Dawson believed that under the Nebraska Bill there was
a good chance that slavery could be extended to Kansas and Nebraska,
and he displayed few if any reservations about the use of squatter sovereignty there. When a territory acquired enough population to become
a state, he declared that it should be allowed to "come into the Union
with a republican form of government, with or without slavery, as its
people may decide."[20] Dawson then accepted popular sovereignty as a

[15] *Ibid.*, 226.
[16] *Ibid.*, Pt. 1, 689; *ibid.*, App., 233, 239.
[17] *Ibid.*, App. 240.
[18] *Ibid.*, 937.
[19] *Ibid.*, 303-304.
[20] *Ibid.*, 304.

solution to the slavery question in Nebraska and Kansas much more willingly than the senators previously discussed. Because he seemed to have few objections to the Kansas-Nebraska Bill, it is difficult to explain his moderate voting posture. Perhaps a discussion of the position of George Badger of North Carolina, the last of these moderates, can shed some light on Dawson's motives.

Badger was the only southeastern moderate who definitely did not espouse the common property doctrine, and he did not believe that the Missouri Compromise or popular sovereignty in the territories were unconstitutional, although he disapproved of both. His moderate voting stance can be best explained, it would seem, by observing the structure of the scalogram. If Badger had reversed his votes on the last two roll-calls in the scale, it would have placed him in the pro category. One of those roll-calls was his own amendment.

Toward the end of the Nebraska debates in the Senate, it was suggested that, if the Missouri Compromise were repealed, it would revive the old Spanish laws, which had sanctioned slavery in the Louisiana Territory. Northern senators were aroused immediately. This would not only have given the South a marked advantage with regard to slavery extension, but also would have put many northern senators in the very embarrassing position of having legalized slavery there by voting to repeal the Compromise of 1820. Badger then offered an amendment which removed any such threat by stating that no law dealing with slavery in the Louisiana Purchase prior to the Missouri Compromise would be legal.[21] Later, many southern representatives chastised Badger for making what they believed to be a vital concession to the North. The North Carolinian did not mean his amendment to represent this, any more than did the southern common property advocates who voted with him, including William Dawson. It would appear, however, that Badger was operating under a different set of motives than the proponents of common property. The common-property men, if they truly believed in the tenets of their doctrine, had to vote for Badger's amendment. If all of them agreed that the Missouri Compromise was unconstitutional in terms of their doctrine, and some even had doubts about the constitutionality of squatter sovereignty, certainly a Spanish law, even though favorable to their interests, was also unconstitutional. Badger, on the other hand, introduced his amendment partly to soothe the sensitive feelings of his northern colleagues, but also because, as a lawyer of considerable reputation, he believed that the repeal of the Compromise of 1820 could not possibly activate any earlier provision regarding slavery in the Louisiana Purchase.[22]

Here then are at least a few plausible explanations for the moderate scale positions taken by these senators from the Southeast. However, before leaving this discussion of the relationship of sectionalism to the

[21] *Ibid.*, 291, 145-150, 289-296, 836; *ibid.*, Pt. 1, 250.
[22] *Ibid.*, Pt. 1, 689-691.

Kansas-Nebraska scale, it might be useful to scan briefly the broader pattern that emerges from the quantitative data (see Table Four). Of the various subsections, the Northeast and Southwest manifested extreme attitudes toward the various facets of the Kansas-Nebraska question embodied in the scale. The Northwest and Southeast, on the other hand, provided some rather subtle variations of opinion. These patterns make it very difficult to explain Senate attitudes toward the Nebraska question primarily in terms of a North-South split, although North-South sectionalism obviously did much to shape the views of senators on this piece of legislation.

If sectionalism was an important factor in the Congressional struggle over the Kansas-Nebraska Bill, so was party allegiance. Although, on the whole, Democratic senators tended to support the measure and the Whigs leaned toward rejecting it, there was no more of a clear cut division between the parties on this issue than between the North and South (see Table Five). Within the Whig Party, however, the slavery extension issue as it burst forth in the Nebraska debates, destroyed that organization along North-South lines. There was absolutely no cooperation between the northern and southern Whigs on this piece of legislation.[23] In the scale, 75 per cent of the southern Whigs appeared as moderates (see Table Six). All of these senators, however, with the exception of one, ultimately voted for the Kansas-Nebraska Bill, despite any reservations they may have harbored.[24] The northern Whigs were even more united on the other side of the Kansas-Nebraska spectrum of opinion. Every one of them appeared in the anti portion of the scale (see Table Six).[25] If there had been a substantial number of southern or northern Whig leaders in the Senate, or better still, a combination of both, who shared a less extreme attitude toward slavery extension, and who were willing to put the well-being of their party first, as had happened so often in the past, the Whigs might have had a much better chance to escape annihilation. But when the Nebraska question surged to the forefront, the Whigs became permanently polarized on the slavery extension issue, and those Whigs, once so famous for their ability to compromise and to harmonize critical issues, dwindled in number and finally disappeared into oblivion, as their party trailed after them.

[23] Arthur Cole, The Whig Party in the South (Washington, 1913), p. 305.

[24] Six men fell in this category; the motives of four of them, Pratt, Morton, Badger, and Dawson, have already been discussed, as far as possible. One of the remaining two, James Jones of Tennessee, was a common property advocate and expressed a point of view very similar to Dawson's. Cong. Globe, 33 Cong., 1 sess., XXIII, Pt. 1, 341-343; ibid., App., 1038-1039; ibid., 2 sess., Pt. 3, 1149; Mrs. Archibald Dixon, A True History of the Missouri Compromise and Its Repeal (Cincinnati, 1899), p. 443. John Bell of Tennessee was the only southern Whig in this scale who was moderately opposed to the bill. He believed, among other things, that it was simply not worth stirring up the slavery question again. Cong. Globe, 33 Cong., 1 sess., XXIII, App., 408-415, 938-948, 437, 755-758.

[25] Ibid., 764-765.

With respect to the Democrats, it is clear that the senators from the North reacted quite differently to the Nebraska struggle than those from the South. One-half of the northern Democrats were moderates, while nearly 80 per cent of the southern Democrats appeared in the pro part of the scale (see Table Seven).

The primary appeal of the Nebraska Bill to the southern Democrats was contained in a series of concessions to the rights of slave owners, which their leaders were able to wrest from their northern colleagues. Furnishing the hard core of this leadership were the members of the F Street Mess, a group of southern Senators who lived and dined in the same boarding house in Washington. Each held a powerful position in the Senate. James M. Mason, and Robert M. T. Hunter of Virginia and Andrew Butler of South Carolina headed respectively the foreign relations, finance, and judiciary committees. Missouri's David Atchison, president *pro tempore* of the Senate, was also an important part of this clique.[26] These gentlemen were convinced that President Pierce's patronage program had favored the free soil, "barnburner" faction over their interests, and so developed a plan to improve their position and, at the same time, promote the welfare of their party. According to one leading interpretation, the Mess was determined to save the Democracy from Pierce's blundering by assuming the leadership of the party, and reinterpreting the Baltimore platform of 1852. They would do this by making that interpretation a fundamental test, which the barnburners would be required to accept before the Senate would confirm barnburner appointments. Atchison's personal ambitions and the Kansas-Nebraska Bill were to be key elements in their strategy.[27]

In December, 1853, the bill to organize Nebraska was about to be introduced again without mention of slavery. Atchison had been grappling bitterly with Thomas Hart Benton in the Missouri political arena that past summer. During the battle Atchison had promised to obtain a Nebraska Bill which would not exclude slavery from the area or quit as a candidate for re-election.[28] The members of the Mess concluded that they could use the Nebraska question to aid Atchison against Benton and as a test of party loyalty. The "barnburners," like the President, had accepted the principle of popular sovereignty contained in the Compromise of 1850. The Mess believed that it was only reasonable that these principles should be accepted for all territories, even those, like Nebraska, protected from slavery by the Missouri Compromise. Both the Democracy in general and the barnburner faction in particu-

---

[26] Roy F. Nichols, "The Kansas-Nebraska Act: A century of Historiography," *Mississippi Valley Historical Review*, XLIII (Sept., 1956), 229-233; William E. Parish, *David Rice Atchison of Missouri: Border Politician* (Columbia, 1961), pp. 115-117; John A. Parker, "The Secret History of the Kansas-Nebraska Bill," *National Quarterly Review*, XLI (July, 1880), 111-112.

[27] Nichols, "Kansas-Nebraska Act," 201-203.

[28] P. Orman Ray, *The Repeal of the Missouri Compromise* (Cleveland, 1909), Ch. IV.

lar must be made to accept this formula.[29] These leaders rejected, once and for all, the exclusion of their states' citizens from the territories because of slavery. Atchison went to Douglas in December and reminded him that he needed at least four southern votes to pass any bill for the organization of Nebraska and that he would never get those votes unless he found some way of allowing slavery to enter the territory.[30]

This interpretation of the role played by the F Street Mess in the Nebraska controversy poses several problems from the standpoint of the motivation of those involved. There is ample evidence to support the contention that Atchison wanted the Missouri Compromise removed and that he believed popular sovereignty would provide an adequate solution to the slavery problem in Nebraska, once the 1820 restriction was eliminated. Yet there is no evidence to show that Atchison wished to promote these ideas for the sake of party unity or as a test of party loyalty. Moreover, he never indicated, either directly or indirectly, that he was aware that the F Street Mess had such a plan in mind.[31] In view of this, it would seem more reasonable to assume that Atchison demanded the removal of the Missouri Compromise, because as a southerner, he thought the measure was unfair, and because he believed it had to be voided to fulfill the promise he had made to his constituents, and so save his career.

But what of the rest of the Mess, namely Hunter, Butler, and Mason? It is true that as state rights, pro-slavery politicians, they were disappointed in the Pierce administration for having doled out patronage to barnburners. It is also true that as major Democratic leaders, they were convinced that they and their friends had been denied the party recognition they deserved. Finally, it is also true that these senators believed that the Missouri Compromise was unconstitutional and that the Nebraska Bill must destroy that measure. At least two of these gentlemen, however, shared another characteristic. They were extremely uneasy about the use of popular sovereignty as a territorial mechanism for resolving the slavery issue. Of the fourteen southern Democrats in the scale, only three fell outside the pro portion (see the Kansas-Nebraska scale). Two of these three were Hunter and Butler, both of whom were members of the Mess, and both of whom, as previously discussed, had serious qualms about popular sovereignty. As for Mason, he did not make clear his views on squatter sovereignty, but he was an advocate of the common property theory, and during the debates, asserted that there were "some provisions in the bill, which as a Southern man, I should be glad to see out of it."[32]

29 Nichols, "Kansas-Nebraska Act," 202-203.

30 Ibid., 203-204.

31 See Ray, Repeal of the Missouri Compromise, 189-193, 257 and Ch. IV; Fred H. Harrington, "A Note on the Ray Explanation of the Origin of the Kansas-Nebraska Act," Mississippi Valley Historical Review, XXV (June, 1938), 79-81.

32 Cong. Globe, 33 Cong., 1 sess., XXIII, App., 229. See also ibid., Pt. 1, 507.

All this tends to raise some doubts about the validity of the argument that the members of the Mess purposely devised a plan to unite
and to save their party by insisting that their fellow Democrats accept
the popular sovereignty formula of 1850 and include it in the Nebraska
Bill. It seems highly unlikely that these "true heirs of Calhoun" would
seize upon that strategy to foster party solidarity.[33] Otherwise, one
could reasonably expect their position on popular sovereignty to have
been more positive or favorable.[34] Any involvement of the members of
the Mess, as a group, in the creation of the Nebraska Bill can most
logically be attributed more to sectional and personal motives than to
party considerations.

This aside, Douglas realized that Atchison meant what he said, and
that he would have to deal with the slavery issue if he wanted the
Nebraska Bill passed.[35] Subsequently, before the bill finally became
law, Douglas, the F Street Mess, and several other Democratic leaders
worked through the Committee on Territories and various caucuses to
thrash out a series of compromises and concessions on slavery to meet
the demands of a constantly changing political climate. Certain of the
decisions made it easier for various northern Democrats to vote for the
measure, but because the leadership was largely southern, that section
gained the most.[36] One of those compromises involved an altered ver-

[33] Nichols, "Kansas-Nebraska Act," 201-203.

[34] It must be noted that Nichols does not offer any documentation for his assertion that the Mess devised such a plan. *Ibid.*, 203. The reports of Atchison's description of his confrontation with Douglas on this issue make no mention of any
discussion of popular sovereignty even though Atchison had long favored it as a
solution. The Missouri senator merely told Douglas, that as Chairman of the Committee on Territories, he would have to devise some way to cancel the Missouri
Compromise restriction, so that slaveholders could legally enter the Nebraska territory. See Ray, *Repeal of the Missouri Compromise*, 201-202 and 277-279. It is
not beyond the realm of possibility that Hunter, Butler, and Mason had convinced
Atchison to forget the popular sovereignty portion of his plan, and to concentrate
upon simply gaining the removal of the Missouri Compromise, which all the members of the Mess desired. Moreover, what these men desired to have included in
the Nebraska Bill with regard to slavery rights went considerably beyond the doctrine of popular sovereignty as set forth in the Compromise of 1850. See Parker,
"Secret History of Kansas-Nebraska Bill," 112; Ray, *Repeal of the Missouri Compromise* 230-232.

[35] Nichols, "Kansas-Nebraska Act," 204.

[36] For a generally excellent analysis and description of the slavery provisions of
the various versions of the Kansas-Nebraska Bill and the machinations necessary
to achieve them, see Russel, "Congressional Struggle Over the Kansas-Nebraska
Bill," 187-210 and Nichols, "Kansas-Nebraska Act," 204-208. Also see *Cong. Globe,*
33 Cong., 1 sess., XXIII, Pt. 1, 221-222, 175; *Report on Nebraska Territory, Senate
Reports,* 33 Cong., 1 sess., No. 15, Jan. 4, 1854; F. L. Burr to Gideon Welles, Jan.
5, 1854, Gideon Welles Papers, Library of Congress; New York *Times,* Jan. 6, 1854;
Detroit *Free Press,* Jan. 11, 1854, Washington Correspondent, Jan. 6, 1854; Pitts-
burg *Gazette,* Feb. 7, 1854, Washington Correspondent, Feb. 3, 1854; *ibid.,* Feb.
9, 1854, Washington Correspondent, Feb. 5, 1854; *ibid.,* Feb. 13, 1954, Washington Correspondent, Feb. 8, 1854; Detroit *Free Press,* Feb. 8, 1854, Washington
Correspondent, Feb. 3, 1854; Robert Toombs to W. W. Burwell, Feb. 3, 1854 in
U. B. Phillips (ed.), "The Correspondence of Robert Toombs, Alexander H. Ste-
phens and Howell Cobb," (Washington, 1913), II, 322.

For a description of the various pressures applied to Douglas, see Henry B.

sion of the bill, which Douglas presented to the Senate on February 7, and which was approved handily on February 15.[37] An earlier statement that the eighth section of the Missouri Compromise was "superceded by the principles of the legislation of 1850 . . . and is . . . declared inoperative" was replaced by the phrase "which being inconsistent with the principle of nonintervention by Congress with slavery in the States and Territories, as recognized by the legislation of 1850 . . . is declared inoperative and void."[38] The substitution of the words "inoperative and void" for "inoperative" is considered, by at least one historian, as a concession made to southerners.[39] There is reason to believe, however, that it was also a concession made by the southern extremists to their colleagues. The Washington correspondent of the Detroit *Free Press*, for example, wrote on February 5, two days before Douglas made his report, that he was convinced that the caucus had previously reached a decision to repeal the Missouri Compromise outright. "It was originally the intention," he declared,

to provide for the direct repeal, but the present provision [declaring the Missouri Compromise 'inoperative'] was adopted out of deference to the opinion of Senators who regard the Missouri Compromise as unconstitutional, and who would not therefore vote for its repeal, lest by doing so, they should acknowledge its constitutionality and binding force.[40]

It is plausible, therefore, that the closest thing to actual repeal these doctrinaire southerners would permit was the addition of the word "void."

At any rate, other concessions were made to the slavery interests in general, and they go far in helping to explain the consistently favorable voting pattern manifested by most southern Democrats on the Nebraska issue.[41]

Learned, "Relation of Philip Phillips to the Repeal of the Missouri Compromise in 1854," *Mississippi Valley Historical Review*, VIII (Mar., 1922), 308-311; Archibald Dixon to Henry S. Foote, Sept. 30, 1858 quoted in Henry M. Flint, *Life of Stephen Douglas* (New York, 1860), pp. 172-173; Mrs. Dixon, 445; George M. McConnell, "Recollections of Stephen A. Douglas," Illinois State Historical Society, *Transactions* (1900), 49.

37 *Cong. Globe*, 33 Cong., 1 sess., XXIII, Pt. 1, 421; Russel, "Congressional Struggle Over the Kansas-Nebraska Bill," 199.

38 Russel, "Congressional Struggle over the Kansas-Nebraska Bill," 199-200; *Cong. Globe*, 33 Cong., 1 sess., XXIII, Pt. 1, 353.

39 Russel, "Congressional Struggle over the Kansas-Nebraska Bill," 199.

40 Detroit *Free Press*, Feb. 10, 1854, Washington Correspondent, Feb. 5, 1854.

41 There are, of course, other factors which might aid in explaining their attitudes. The fact, for example, that the Pierce administration threw its full weight behind the bill may have been a major reason for their support. Or the bitter accusations and attacks emanating from the North may have raised their ire enough to vote for the measure. It is very difficult, however, to formulate a satisfactory explanation for their decisions because, in most cases, their individual feelings and attitudes toward this piece of legislation are not on record anywhere. For example, during the debates only three of these eleven southern Democrats uttered anything meaningful on the Nebraska question. Benjamin Fitzpatrick (Ala.), John Slidell (La.), and Josiah Evans (S.C.), said absolutely nothing during the Kansas-Nebraska debates. Three others, Robert Johnson (Ark.), Clement Clay (Ala.), and

The northern Democrats were less reticent on the subject, and their words assist greatly in fathoming why half of them voted as moderates. It would appear that these men were torn between two opposing and formidable forces. On the one hand, their own personal attraction and their party's commitment to popular sovereignty enticed them to befriend the Kansas-Nebraska legislation. The administration, although experiencing considerable difficulty controlling its members because of factionalism and the President's patronage policies, was far from impotent. It worked tirelessly through a number of devices to convince Democrats in both branches of Congress to stand by the bill. For example, Caleb Cushing, acting with the President's blessing, went so far as to offer Senator Hannibal Hamlin of Maine control of Democratic patronage in New England in exchange for his assistance in behalf of the measure.[42]

But there was also considerable pressure calculated to defeat it. The northern Democrats were being confronted with the angry protests of a large number of their constituents, who were insisting vehemently and in a variety of ways that they vote the bill down.[43] It may well be that the moderate voting position taken by these Democrats was, in large part, a product of their frustrating attempts to reconcile the conflicting and severe pressures thrust upon them as a result of this Nebraska question.

Senator Lewis Cass of Michigan, for example, was delighted to have squatter sovereignty applied to the Nebraska situation, since he was the originator of the doctrine. His only concern was that the principles of popular sovereignty not be misrepresented in the bill.[44] On the other

---

Stephen Adams (Miss.), made a few remarks and asked a few questions during the debates, but made no speeches. Lastly, William Sebastian (Ark.) and Thomas Rusk (Tex.) made speeches, but these speeches dealt only with a negligible number of aspects involved in the Nebraska struggle. Rusk spoke briefly about a motion to postpone consideration of the bill, and Sebastian made a few short speeches regarding the elimination of certain Indian treaties which would have affected the settlement of the territories. See *Cong. Globe*, 33 Cong., 1 sess., XXIII, App., 411 and *ibid.*, Pt. 1, 353-355. Moreover, there is no other evidence available regarding the opinions of these senators toward the Kansas-Nebraska Act. For these reasons, any attempt to determine the motivations in this situation, regardless of how logical or sensible, must be considered tenuous and incomplete.

[42] Claude Fuess, *The Life of Caleb Cushing* (New York, 1923), II, 192; Charles E. Hamlin, *Hannibal Hamlin* (Cambridge, 1899), pp. 264 and 268-271.

[43] See, for example, *Resolution on the Missouri Compromise by the New York Legislature, Senate Miscellaneous Documents*, 33 Cong., 1 sess., No. 22, Feb. 9, 1854; *Resolution Relative to the Nebraska Bill by the Maine Legislature, Senate Miscellaneous Documents*, 33 Cong., 1 sess., No. 28, Mar. 1, 1854; Edward Pierce, *Memoirs and Letters of Charles Sumner* (Boston, 1877-1893), III, 362-379; Fred Seward, *Seward at Washington* (New York, 1891), pp. 217-218, 222, and 356; Henry Hubbart, *The Older Middle West, 1840-1860* (New York, 1936), pp. 100-101; Grace Clarke, *George W. Julian* (Indianapolis, 1923), p. 150; Charles Hawley, "Whittier of Iowa," *Iowa Journal of History of Politics*, XXXIV (Apr. 1936), 133-141; G. W. Jones to Howell Cobb, Feb. 16, 1854 in R. P. Brooks (ed.), "Howell Cobb Papers," *Georgia Historical Quarterly*, VI (Mar. 1922), 150.

[44] *Cong. Globe*, 33 Cong., 1 sess., XXIII, Pt. 1, 333-344 and 456-458; *ibid.*, App., 270-279.

hand, however, he opposed the destruction of the Missouri Compromise right from the beginning. On January 14, the *Washington Sentinel* suggested that Cass should introduce an amendment to the Nebraska Bill negating the slavery agreement of 1820.[45] He made it clear in short order that he "could not make such an attrocious [sic] proposition, whatever others might do," and that "the measure was frought [sic] with evil."[46] But Cass did not push his opposition beyond this, for he was also a loyal Democrat of long standing.[47] It was reported as early as January 23 that Cass, although "he was not consulted and was decidedly against the renewal of agitation . . . will vote with the pro-slavery side."[48] The Michigan senator sat quietly during the debates until February 20, when he made his views public. He chastised the South for demanding the removal of the Missouri restriction and for its unreasoning attachment to the institution of slavery. Cass had an immense dislike for slavery, but believed that the only possible solution to the question in Nebraska lay in squatter sovereignty.[49] He also revealed the intensity of the public pressure being brought to bear upon him. "It requires but little exertion to swim with the current," he said,

while he who opposes it must put forth all his strength and even may become its victim. Popular feeling is a hard power to resist, and the reproach of being a dough face belongs to him who panders to it, and not him who strives to maintain the constitutional rights of all.[50]

In the end, Cass followed his personal convictions and his party's policy, ignoring both the will of a good portion of his constituents and his own antipathy towards the repeal of the Missouri Compromise, and voted for the Nebraska Bill.

Senator Isaac Walker of Wisconsin exhibited the same pattern of frustration, but could not persuade himself to go this far. There were too many slavery clauses in the Nebraska Bill that troubled him. Among them was the abrogation of the Missouri Compromise, which he believed would create widespread agitation throughout the nation and inflict tremendous damage on the Democratic party. He could not lend himself, he said, to a reopening of the slavery question. During the debates, however, he also revealed part of the deeper mental and emotional anguish he was experiencing in reaching these decisions. He grew extremely defensive and went to excessive lengths to answer Senator John Weller's charge that, because of his negative attitude toward the Nebraska Bill, he was being disloyal to his party.[51] At the same time,

---

[45] *Washington Sentinel*, Jan. 14, 1854.

[46] Quoted in the diary of Gideon Welles, June 29, 1855 in Gideon Welles Papers.

[47] Hamlin, *Hannibal Hamlin*, 268.

[48] Salmon P. Chase to E. S. Hamlin, Jan. 23, 1854 in "The Diary and Correspondence of Salmon P. Chase," 256.

[49] *Cong. Globe*, 33 Cong., 1 sess., XXIII, Pt. 1, 450-451; *ibid.*, App., 270-279.

[50] *Ibid.*, App., 277.

[51] *Ibid.*, 291.

it was clear that Walker also dreaded the probable reaction of his constituents if he failed to placate them on the issue of slavery extension.
In 1850, he had voted for only one of the several compromise measures,
and by doing so, he asked if any other Senator had "brought upon himself more of abuse, more of censure, more of condemnation, and involved himself in greater danger with his constituents . . ."[52] Here was
a man, sensitive to the desires and pressures of his party on the Nebraska question, but unable to comply completely for fear of voter
retaliation. When the final roll-call was taken on this controversial measure, he cast a negative vote.

Although no neat and clearly defined sectional or party cleavage developed on the Kansas-Nebraska question, both party and sectional influences played a major role in determining the voting behavior of
Senators on this issue. Of the two factors, sectionalism appears to have
been most potent. Even the moderate voting stance assumed by most
of the southeastern senators on the Nebraska legislation seems ironically to have been the product of an extreme interpretation of the rights
of slaveholders. Again a similar pattern emerged among the southern
Whigs, most of whom also voted as moderates on the roll-calls in question. In the heat of the Nebraska controversy, the party polarized along
North-South lines, and organized Whiggery disappeared forever. As
for the Democrats, the high percentage of southern senators who backed
the bill enthusiastically was the result, in large part, of the many concessions that were made to the sensibilities of the slavocracy. Within
the southern Democratic group, moreover, the powerful F Street Mess
promoted the measure, it would seem, more for sectional and personal
reasons than a desire to use the bill to strengthen the Democracy. For a
substantial number of northern Democratic senators, however, the
process of reaching a decision on this legislation involved a painful personal choice between party and sectional loyalty. The frustration entailed in this situation goes far in explaining why half of them voted
as moderates. In the end, for most of them, the urgings of the administration that they accept the bill, combined with their own attraction
for all or part of the measure, held sway over the demands of their
constituents that they reject it. But this partial triumph of party allegiance over sectional considerations was exceptional when Senate
voting behavior on the Nebraska question is viewed as a whole. The
pattern did not augur well for the future of the Union.

[52] *Ibid.*, 294-296; Also see *ibid.*, 285-286 and 288; *ibid.*, Pt. 1, 344 and 692.

TABLE ONE

The Relationship Between Sectional Membership and Voting Positions on the Kansas-Nebraska Act in the Senate of the Thirty-Third Congress.

	North		South		East		West	
	No.	%	No.	%	No.	%	No.	%
Anti	(11)	45.8	(1)	4.5	(8)	42.1	(4)	14.8
Moderate	(8)	33.3	(8)	36.4	(9)	47.4	(7)	25.9
Pro	(5)	20.8	(13)	59.1	(2)	10.5	(16)	59.3
Total	(24)	99.9	(22)	100.0	(19)	100.0	(27)	100.0

North—Conn., Me., Mass., N. H., R. I., Vt., N. J., N. Y., Pa., Ill., Ia., Ind., Mich., O., Wis., Calif. *South*—Del., Fla., Ga., Md., N. C., S. C., Va., Ala., Ky., Miss., Tenn., Ark., La., Tex., Mo. *East*—Me., Mass., N. H., R. I., Vt., N. J., N. Y., Pa., Del., Fla., Ga., Md., N. C., S. C., Va., Conn. *West*—Ill., Ind., Mich., O., Wis., Ia., Mo., Ala., Ky., Miss., Tenn., Ark., La., Calif., Tex.

TABLE TWO

The Relationship between Northern Sectional Membership and Voting Positions on the Kansas-Nebraska Act in the Senate of the Thirty-Third Congress Controlling for East-West Sectionalism.

	East		West	
	North		North	
	No.	%	No.	%
Anti	(8)	72.7	(3)	23.1
Moderate	(3)	27.3	(5)	38.4
Pro	(0)	0.0	(5)	38.4
Total	(11)	100.0	(13)	99.9

TABLE THREE

The Relationship Between Southern Sectional Membership and Voting Positions on the Kansas-Nebraska Act in the Senate of the Thirty-Third Congress Controlling for East-West Sectionalism.

	East		West	
	South		South	
	No.	%	No.	%
Anti	(0)	0.0	(1)	7.1
Moderate	(6)	75.0	(2)	14.3
Pro	(2)	25.0	(11)	78.6
Total	(8)	100.0	(14)	100.0

TABLE FOUR

The Relationship Between North-South Sectional Membership and Voting Positions on the Kansas-Nebraska Act in the Senate of the Thirty-Third Congress Controlling for East-West Sectionalism.

| | East | | | | West | | | |
| | North | | South | | North | | South | |
	No.	%	No.	%	No.	%	No.	%
Anti	(8)	72.7	(0)	0.0	(3)	23.1	(1)	7.1
Moderate	(3)	27.3	(6)	75.0	(5)	38.4	(2)	14.3
Pro	(0)	0.0	(2)	25.0	(5)	38.4	(11)	78.6
Total	(11)	100.0	(8)	100.0	(13)	99.9	(14)	100.0

TABLE FIVE

The Relationship Between Membership in the Major Parties and Voting Positions on the Kansas-Nebraska Act in the Senate of the Thirty-Third Congress.

| | Democrats | | Whigs | |
	No.	%	No.	%
Anti	(4)	13.3	(6)	42.8
Moderate	(10)	33.3	(6)	42.8
Pro	(16)	53.3	(2)	14.3
Total	(30)	99.9	(14)	99.9

TABLE SIX

The Relationship Between Whig Party Membership and Voting Positions on the Kansas-Nebraska Act in the Senate of the Thirty-Third Congress Controlling for North-South Sectionalism.

| | North | | South | |
| | Whigs | | Whigs | |
	No.	%	No.	%
Anti	(6)	100.0	(0)	0.0
Moderate	(0)	0.0	(6)	75.0
Pro	(0)	0.0	(2)	25.0
Total	(6)	100.0	(8)	100.0

TABLE SEVEN

The Relationship Between Democratic Party Membership and Voting Positions on the Kansas-Nebraska Act in the Senate of the Thirty-Third Congress Controlling for North-South Sectionalism.

| | North | | South | |
| | Democrats | | Democrats | |
	No.	%	No.	%
Anti	(3)	18.7	(1)	7.1
Moderate	(8)	50.0	(2)	14.3
Pro	(5)	31.2	(11)	78.5
Total	(16)	99.9	(14)	99.9

Key to Votes on Legislation to
Organize the Nebraska Territory,
Thirty-Third Congress, First
Session, Senate.

Scale
Number   Issue and Vote

1. Chase amendment, to make the Nebraska Territory one instead of two sec-
    tions. March 2, 1854. Def. 8-34. Vote no is pro.
2. Chase amendment, to provide for the immediate popular election of officers
    for the Nebraska Territorial Government. March 2, 1854. Def. 10-30. Vote
    no is pro.
3. Chase amendment, to allow the people of the Territory to prohibit slavery if
    they wished. March 2, 1854. Def. 10-36. Vote no is pro.
4. Douglas amendment to strike out in section 14 the words "which was super-
    ceded by the principles of the legislation of 1850, commonly called the Com-
    promise Measures" and inserting: which being inconsistent with the principle
    of nonintervention by Congress with slavery in the States and Territories, as
    recognized by the legislation of 1850, (commonly called the Compromise
    Measures) is hereby declared inoperative and void; it being the true intent
    and meaning of this act not to legislate slavery into any Territory or State,
    nor exclude it therefrom, but to leave the people thereof perfectly free to
    form and regulate their domestic institutions in their own way, subject only to
    the Constitution of the United States." February 15, 1854. Carried 35-10.
    Vote yes is pro.
5. Motion by Seward that the Kansas-Nebraska Bill should be engrossed for a
    third reading. March 2, 1854. Carried 29-12. Vote yes is pro.
6. Motion by Hunter that the Kansas-Nebraska Bill should be engrossed for a
    third reading. May 25, 1854. Carried 35-13. Vote yes is pro.
7. Douglas amendment, to strike out in section 14, the words "was superceded
    by the principles of the legislation of 1850 commonly called the Compromise
    Measures." February 6, 1854. Def. 13-30. Vote no is pro.
8. Motion by Cass calling for a vote on the question of whether or not the Kan-
    sas-Nebraska Bill should pass. March 3, 1854. Carried 37-14. Vote yes is pro.
9. Motion by Wade to postpone consideration of the Kansas-Nebraska Bill from
    then (Friday, February 3, 1854) until Monday, February 6, 1854. February
    3, 1854. Carried 23-17. Vote no is pro.
10. Badger amendment, that nothing in the Kansas-Nebraska Bill will be thought
    to revive any law before the Missouri Compromise "protecting, establishing,
    prohibiting, or abolishing slavery." March 2, 1854. Carried 35-6. Vote no is
    pro.
    Anti   = Scale scores 4, 5, 6.
    Moderates = Scale scores 2, 3.
    Pro   = Scale scores 0, 1.

Kansas-Nebraska Bill Scale

Senator	Party	Score	State	Anti. YYYNNNYNYY 12345678910	Pro NNNYYYNYNN 12345678910
S. Chase	FS	6	O.	XXXXXXXXOO	
W. Fessenden	W	6	Me.	XXXOXOOXOO	
S. Foot	W	6	Vt.	XXXXXXXXXX	
H. Hamlin	D	6	Me.	XXOXXXXXXX	
W. Seward	W	6	N.Y.	XXXXXXXXXX	
T. Smith	W	6	Conn.	XXXXXOXXXX	
C. Sumner	FS	6	Mass.	XXXXXXXXXO	
B. Wade	W	6	O.	XXXXXXXXXX	
P. Allen	D	5	R.I.	OXOXXXXO	OO
H. Dodge	D	5	Wis.	XXXXXXXX	XX
H. Fish	W	5	N.Y.	XXXXXXXX	OO
S. Houston	D	4	Tex.	XXOOXXX	XXX
J. Bell	W	3	Tenn.	OX XXX	XXXX X
L. Cass	D	3	Mich.	X XO	OOOXOX X
C. Stuart	D	3	Mich.	X X XX	XXXXX X
I. Walker	D	3	Wis.	XXXXOX	OOXO
G. Badger	W	2	N.C.	XX	XXXXOXXXX
R. Brodhead	D	2	Pa.	XX	XXXXXXXX
A. Butler	D	2	S.C.	XX	XXOXXXXX
W. Dawson Jr.	W	2	Ga.	XX	XXXXXXXX
W. Gwin	D	2	Calif.	XX	XXXXXXXOX
R. Hunter	D	2	Va.	OX	XXXXXXXX
G. Jones	D	2	Ia.	OX	XXXXXXXX
J. Jones	W	2	Tenn.	XX	XXXXXXXX
J. Morton	W	2	Fla.	OX	XXXXXXXX
M. Morris Jr.	D	2	N.H.	X XX	X XXXXXX
T. Pratt	W	2	Md.	OX	XXXXXXXX
J. Williams	D	2	N.H.	XX	XXXXXXXX
D. Atchison	D	1	Mo.	X	XXXXXXXXX
J. Benjamin	W	1	La.	X	XXXXXXXXX
C. Clay Jr.	D	1	Ala.	X	XXXOXXXXX
A. Dixon	W	1	Ky.	X	XXXXXOXXX
A. Dodge	D	1	Ia.	X	XXXXXXXXX
S. Douglas	D	1	Ill.	X	XXXXXXXXX
J. Evans	D	1	S.C.	X	XXXXXOXXX
B. Fitzpatrick	D	1	Ala.	X	XXXXXXXXX
J. Mason	D	1	Va.	X	XXXXXXXXX
J. Pettit	D	1	Ind.	X	XXXXXXXXX
W. Sebastian	D	1	Ark.	X	XXXXXXXX X
J. Shields	D	1	Ill.	X X	X XOXXXXX
J. Slidell	D	1	La.	X	XXXXXXXXX
J. Weller	D	1	Calif.	X	OOXXOXXXX
S. Adams	D	0	Miss.		XOXXXOXXXX
A. Brown	D	0	Miss.		XXXXXXXXXX
R. Johnson	D	0	Ark.		XXXXXXOXOX
T. Rusk	D	0	Tex.		XXXOOXOXOX

Thirteen Senators are not included because of absences, vacancies, or ambiguous voting records.

Reproducibility=98.9%

THE UNCONSCIOUS "SPIRIT OF PARTY" IN THE CONFEDERATE CONGRESS

Richard E. Beringer

DESPITE THE LONG YEARS which have elapsed since the Civil War, historians remain remarkably uninformed about Confederate politics in general and the Confederate Congress in particular.[1] The feeling seems to persist that since the Confederacy was only a wartime phenomenon, its politics were unimportant; and, since the Confederacy lost the war, it is assumed that southern congressmen had little to do and did that poorly.

In reality, the politicians in the Confederate Congress had much to do. The legislative branch existed before the new nation was fully established; it created a constitution, raised and supplied armies, levied taxes, provided a circulating medium of exchange, borrowed money, and encouraged new industries. Even contemporaries were silent on these achievements, usually attributing them to the Executive or else forgetting them altogether,[2] but important contributions were nonetheless made toward the creation of a modern national state. This new state lacked a system of political parties, however, and this remarkable absence is one of the most neglected aspects of Confederate politics. There were no party organizations, no caucuses, no party committee system with channels of communication from grass roots to capital and back. Partisan labels were still important, along with the personal loyalties and antagonisms that went with them, but more in reference to what a man had been rather than to what he was. The normal process of political development, including conception of proto-parties, and

---

[1] Wilfred Buck Yearns, *The Confederate Congress* (Athens, 1960) is the only general study, but a detailed analysis of congressional roll-call behavior may be found in Thomas B. Alexander and Richard E. Beringer, *The Anatomy of the Confederate Congress: A Study of the Influences of Member Characteristics on Legislative Voting Behavior, 1861-1865* (Nashville, 1972). E. Merton Coulter, *The Confederate States of America, 1861-1865* (Baton Rouge, 1950), has a good background chapter on Congress, and Eric L. McKitrick's essay, "Party Politics and the Union and Confederate War Efforts," in William Nisbet Chambers and Walter Dean Burnham (eds.), *The American Party Systems: Stages of Political Development* (New York, 1967) is a thought-provoking comparison of the Union and Confederate congresses. This article develops further some of the tentative suggestions offered in *Anatomy of the Confederate Congress*; figures pertaining to biographical characteristics are compiled from Appendix I.

[2] An exception is found in the unpublished Memoirs of W. S. Oldham, Confederate Senator, 1861-1865 (Barker Library, University of Texas), which, while devoted primarily to an account of the last days of the Confederacy and to problems of military strategy, does have a number of interesting observations on Congress.

their nurture in the womb of crisis, has therefore been ignored. A baby never having been born, the doctor has too often assumed that none was ever conceived.

Most mid-nineteenth-century southerners, indeed many Americans of the time, viewed political parties so negatively that the deviation from previous experience was looked upon with approval. The institution was considered to be a vehicle of personal ambition, and therefore antagonistic to national welfare. Most Confederate congressmen would have agreed with the 1852 evaluation of Ezra C. Seaman, a nineteenth-century American commentator on law, politics, and economics. "Devotion to the party," Seaman wrote, "is regarded as a substitute for patriotism; the principal object of party leaders seems to be, not to promote the interest and welfare of the nation, but the party . . . the chief inquiry is, what will be popular and strengthen the party, and not, what will benefit the country."[3] In this vein, a North Carolinian in 1857 urged his fellow Tarheels "to throw off party ties" in state elections, contending that "the prime cause of all our backwardness and neglect of precious and valuable interests and advantages" was that state politics "have almost uniformly been of a partisan and political character."[4] Thus Howell Cobb, in his final speech as President of the Provisional Congress, told the approving delegates that "the spirit of party has never shown itself for an instant in your deliberations," and expressed the hope that the same would be true of future congresses.[5]

Nevertheless, the party concept did exist; when southerners denounced parties, as they constantly did, they protested too much. Certainly there was a bountiful crop of divisive issues, such as conscription, habeas corpus suspension, impressment, taxation, and military policy, all fertilized by the disaster of an unsuccessful war. Long casualty lists aggravated the situation and created a war weariness in the South which eventually exceeded that of the North. Some degree of party behavior becomes even more plausible in the light of the lawmakers' diverse backgrounds. Not only did they differ in previous political affiliation, but also in other characteristics peculiar to the time, such as stand on secession and the location of their constituencies in relation to the Union army. Any one of these attributes, or any combination of them, could have provided the wedge for political cleavage into formal parties. That parties did not emerge could be due solely to the fact that the Confederacy did not exist long enough for the developmental process to have been completed.

If we may assume that party development would be generated by

[3] Ezra C. Seaman, *Essays on the Progress of Nations, in Civilization, Productive Industry, Wealth and Population* (New York, 1967 [1852]), p. 112 (original in italics).

[4] Quoted anonymously in J. G. de Roulhac Hamilton, *Party Politics in North Carolina, 1835-1860* (Durham, 1916), pp. 205, 206 (in reverse order).

[5] *Journal of the Congress of the Confederate States of America, 1861-1865* (Washington, 1904-1905), I, 846; hereafter referred to as *Journal*.

dissent, it seems highly likely that this embryonic partisanship sprouted as early as the secession crisis. Nowhere is this more obvious than in North Carolina, where historians of the period, such as Wilfred B. Yearns and E. Merton Coulter, as well as a number of contemporary observers, have seen some peculiar behavior.[6] The secession crisis there revealed strong dissent and a striking lack of public enthusiasm as the state entered upon the uncharted course of independence. In the balloting of February 28, 1861, voters narrowly defeated the convention movement and made a "sweeping victory for the unionists," who composed a majority of the delegates elected to serve in the event the convention proposal had been successful.[7] Even after Lincoln's call for troops, North Carolina lagged behind her Confederate sisters. When the state convention was finally called it contained strong pro-Union elements, some of whom even denied the legality of secession.[8]

Being less enthusiastic for secession than the citizens of other states, North Carolinians might well be expected to display strong disenchantment and war weariness. An 1863 protest meeting roundly condemned conscription, the tax-in-kind, habeas corpus suspension, supposed currency repudiation, and appointment of general officers from other states to command North Carolina troops. The partisan nature of this protest is illustrated by the charge that when general officers had been appointed from North Carolina, they were "almost invariably of the same politics [Democratic] with the administration."[9] By August, 1863, even the state treasurer, Jonathan Worth, was "for peace on any terms not humiliating. . . ." "The masses," he added, "are for peace on *any* terms."[10] This popular feeling was reflected in the congressional elections of that year. The North Carolina delegation to the First Congress was split between those who had favored secession and those who had not, and between former Democrats and former Whigs. After the 1863 elections, however, the composition of the North Carolina contingent included ten Union Whigs and only two Secession Democrats (one a holdover senator).[11]

[6] However, Coulter, *Confederate States of America*, makes surprisingly little mention of North Carolina's leading role in political dissent. See pp. 115, 389, 534-536. Georgia Lee Tatum, *Disloyalty in the Confederacy* (Chapel Hill, 1934), pp. 107-135, is detailed, but more useful for understanding the political effect of North Carolina disaffection upon Congress is Yearns, *Confederate Congress*, especially pp. 52-54, 171-183, 220-226, and Yearns' earlier article "North Carolina in the Confederate Congress," *North Carolina Historical Review*, XXIX (July, 1952), 359-378.

[7] Estimates of delegate strength vary, but indicate about 80 unionists and 40 secessionists. See Ralph A. Wooster, *The Secession Conventions of the South* (Princeton, 1962), p. 193.

[8] *Ibid.*, pp. 198-199.

[9] *American Annual Cyclopædia . . . 1863* (New York, 1867), p. 691.

[10] Worth to Joseph A. Worth, Aug. 13, 1863, J. G. de Roulhac Hamilton (ed.), *The Correspondence of Jonathan Worth* (Raleigh, 1909), I, 256-257 (emphasis Worth's).

[11] According to Josiah Turner, the sole surviving North Carolina Democrat in the

With good reason, loyal Confederates came to be quite uncomfortable about North Carolina. In January, 1864, Congressman Caspar W. Bell of Missouri wrote that in North Carolina "the people are almost ready for a second revolution. . . . Much concern is felt here in official circles on account of recent demonstrations there, which are interpreted as leading to reconstruction."[12] By January, 1865, Representative Jehu A. Orr of Mississippi reported that North Carolina was "prepared to follow the lead of any state" toward calling a convention of the states,[13] and in March, Governor William Smith of Virginia, a former Confederate congressman and proponent of the desperation policy to arm slaves, pointed with alarm to a North Carolina senator who had threatened that if a policy of using black soldiers were adopted, his state "would no longer have a motive to continue the struggle."[14]

Such apparent disloyalty within the very bosom of the would-be nation might have reflected or been instrumental in the creation of incipient parties—not real parties but rather factions of the type which are way-stations to party. We may assume that such factions would be organized to secure office and establish policy, and that their members would act in concert to achieve those ends. They would undoubtedly leave behind them traces of their behavior, which would enable investigators to uncover their presence. It seems useful, for this purpose, to turn to the roll-call record for a more precise understanding of Confederate political growth than other evidence is able to provide. The underlying assumption of this paper is, therefore, that if incipient party behavior developed in the Confederate Congress, the application of two types of clustering technique to the divisions of the House of Representatives will reveal it.[15]

The first of these techniques is Guttman scaling, a procedure which allows identification of roll calls legislators thought had strong attitudinal relationships to each other, arrangement of them in ordinal ranking, and discovery of factions or cliques of like-minded men by comparison of individual votes on the issues composing a given attitude scale.[16] When applied to a content area embracing all the major subjects

---

Second House won his seat by a majority of only sixteen votes. *American Annual Cyclopaedia . . . 1864*, p. 214.

[12] Bell to Sterling Price, Jan. 9, 1864, Eldridge Collection, Huntington Library.

[13] Orr to L. Q. C. Lamar, Jan. 21, 1865, quoted in Orr, Reminiscences (Miss. Dept. of Archives and History).

[14] Smith to Senate of Virginia, Mar. 6, 1865, Brock Collection, Huntington Library. Quotes from Eldridge Collection (n.12) and Brock Collection by permission.

[15] The literature discussing or employing these methods is extensive. See Lee F. Anderson, Meredith W. Watts, Jr., and Allen R. Wilcox, *Legislative Roll-Call Analysis* (Evanston, 1966); Charles M. Dollar and Richard J. Jensen, *Historian's Guide to Statistics: Quantitative Analysis and Historical Research* (New York, 1971); and Duncan MacRae, Jr., *Issues and Parties in Legislative Voting: Methods of Statistical Analysis* (New York, 1970).

[16] Any examination of the literature of Guttman scaling should begin with Mac-Rae, *Dimensions of Congressional Voting: A Statistical Study of the House of Representatives in the Eight-First Congress* (Berkeley and Los Angeles, 1958). Also

voted upon by the Confederate Congress, however, the most notable result produced by scaling is a remarkable lack of scalability.[17] No reliable scales are uncovered in the first three years of the Congress' existence, except in the first two sessions of the First Congress, February 18, 1862 to October 13, 1862, where a few roll calls dealing with conscription fit into a scale pattern. It is as if congressmen simply could not see any logical relationship between any of the pressing issues which confronted them—taxation, manpower, martial law, impressment—or often between roll calls on the same issue.

In American politics this is not typical legislative behavior.[18] The explanation might simply be that a lack of scalar relationships among roll calls in multi-subject content areas could be characteristic of a non-party legislative situation, at least in American political experience. If this is so—the suggestion must eventually rest upon more evidence than the Confederate Congress alone can provide—then if cross-content scalability increases, it could be an indicator that a party system was developing.

This hypothesis is supported by the Second Confederate Congress (May 2, 1864 to March 18, 1865), in which two very substantial and meaningful scales are discovered. One reason for a dramatic change of voting behavior in such a short time was the turnover resulting from the 1863 elections, which brought into the Congress a massive influx of former Whigs and Unionists.[19] Furthermore, Congress now had a num-

---

helpful is MacRae's *Parliament, Parties, and Society in France 1946-1958* (New York, 1967), which discusses on pp. 91-95 the specific procedures used here. (Using Yule's Q, the minimum criteria employed in this article to determine presence of a scale were six roll calls with a strength of association of Q=.7.) Two useful articles are George B. Belknap, "Scaling Legislative Behavior," and Charles D. Farris, "A Scale Analysis of Ideological Factors in Congressional Voting," both reprinted in John C. Wahlke and Heinz Eulau (eds.), *Legislative Behavior: A Reader in Theory and Research* (Glencoe, 1959). Examples of scaling by Civil War historians are Edward L. Gambill, "Who Were the Senate Radicals?" *Civil War History*, XI (September, 1965), 237-244; Joel H. Silbey, *The Shrine of Party: Congressional Voting Behavior 1841-1852* (Pittsburgh, 1967); Allan C. Bogue, "Bloc and Party in the United States Senate: 1861-1863," *Civil War History*, XIII (September, 1967), 221-241; Thomas B. Alexander, *Sectional Stress and Party Strength: A Study of Roll-Call Voting Patterns in the United States House of Representatives, 1836-1860* (Nashville, 1967).

[17] Since the programs used for this article effectively handle a maximum of 150 roll calls, only a limited number of votes could be analyzed at once. Roll calls which are duplicates, obviously unimportant, nearly unanimous, or strictly procedural have been eliminated, and care has been taken to insure that those selected included a reliable cross section of congressional business. The result is a universe of content in which all important subjects brought to a vote are eligible for inclusion in a cross-content scale. An alternative procedure, used in many scale analyses, is to examine each subject content area separately. This method will uncover more scales and produce more reliable determination of individual attitudes on specific issues, but it is not as likely to expose attitudinal relationships common to a variety of legislative topics. Both methods are useful, depending upon the purpose for which they are employed.

[18] See, for example, Silbey, *Shrine of Party*; Alexander, *Sectional Stress*; and Gambill, "Senate Radicals."

[19] In the First House, Democrats and Secessionists outnumbered Whigs and

ber of legislators who were said to be of the "peace party," and who
brought into Congress something new in the way of an ideology. Many
of them sincerely yet naively thought that peace could be won at the
conference table even though it could not be won on the battlefield,
and that full civil rights could be maintained while fighting an all-out
war with half-hearted measures.

These changes were symptomatic of profound war weariness, as a
would-be nation which craved resounding and immediate victory apparently could achieve only a long, drawn-out stalemate. The shocks of
the casualty lists were clearly reflected in the electoral seismograph.
It was even contended that prisoners paroled by General Grant after
the fall of Vicksburg had used their votes to defeat some of the staunchest supporters of the Confederate President.[20] Disastrous events
brought a new Congress, which behaved in a radically different manner
from its two predecessors.

This turnabout was noted by contemporaries. Edward A. Pollard,
wartime editor of the Richmond *Examiner*, remarked that "it was astonishing how, in the last periods of the war, it [Congress] threw off its
servile habit to the President," and went on to contend that a "peace
party" had gained strength "in exact inverse proportion" to steadily
deteriorating military conditions.[21] Senator Williamson S. Oldham of
Texas portrayed more graphically the political and behavioral effects
of accelerating military disaster. He noted a deeper gloom among congressmen than citizenry as the last session of Congress opened, and felt
a marked change of attitude after the unsuccessful peace conference
at Hampton Roads on February 3, 1865. This failure "had a different
effect upon different members of Congress. . . . Some were aroused to
the highest point of defiant determination. . . . Upon others the effect
was the reverse. Already conquered, they were willing to accept the
terms of the conqueror." More specifically, wrote Oldham, the determined members "set themselves to work to continue the struggle. There

---

Unionists nearly two to one, but the balance was even in the Second House, where
the fifty freshman representatives were about two-thirds Unionist and three-fifths
Whig.

[20] See W. T. Walthall to G. W. Lay, Aug. 6, 1863, *Official Records of the Union
and Confederate Armies*, Ser. IV, Vol. II, 726-727. Walthall contended the elections in east central Alabama had "been generally carried by an opposition known
as the 'Peace Party.'" One of the newly elected congressmen from Alabama was
former U.S. Congressman Williamson R. W. Cobb, who voluntarily passed into the
Federal lines and was eventually expelled from Congress without ever having
bothered to claim his seat (*Journal*, VII, 12, 125, 275-277; *Biographical Directory
of the American Congress 1774-1971* [rev. ed., Washington, 1971], p. 758. There
was also conjecture that a peace society had been strong enough to affect Confederate fortunes at both Missionary Ridge and Vicksburg. See statement of Jefferson
Faulkner and Abner R. Hill, undated, but probably spring 1864, in *OR*, Ser. IV,
Vol. III, 398. For further information of similar import, see Tatum, *Disloyalty in
the Confederacy*, Ch. VI, which deals with the especially interesting case of North
Carolina.

[21] Edward A. Pollard, *Life of Jefferson Davis* . . . (Philadelphia, 1869), pp. 417,
460.

were some who abandoned their seats and went home in despair, there were others who did worse, turned factionists, and as far as in their power did what they could to destroy public confidence and crush out hope."[22] It is quite likely that this remarkable terminal polarization of individual views signaled an unconscious evolution of parties which never matured due to southern collapse.

Something of the nature of this change may be determined by the second clustering technique, Rice-Beyle cluster-bloc analysis. This device compares the voting record of every congressman with that of each of his colleagues and attempts to isolate blocs by using an index of agreement (usually a percentage) which indicates the extent to which each possible pair of congressmen voted alike.[23] The most useful threshold for the study of the Second Confederate Congress seems to be 70 per cent agreement for bloc membership, with a fringe defined as those who agree on at least 70 per cent of their mutual divisions with at least 50 per cent of the bloc members. To be called a bloc, a group of like-minded legislators must be at least four in number.[24] At this level three clusters may be discerned. The first two overlap, as may be seen in Table 1. The third is quite distinct, having not a single member with a pairwise agreement score of 70 per cent or more with any member of the other two clusters. It is not surprising that this bloc is composed of eight North Carolinians in the Second House, plus one bloc member and two fringe members from other states. All eleven of these men had been Union Whigs, and nine of them came from areas not yet occupied or seriously threatened by the Union army at the start of the Second Session of the Second Congress.

The other two clusters are more diffuse. They overlap each other (many pairs missed 70 per cent agreement only by slim margins), and both are composed of two blocs which also overlap. The result is rather amorphous; four such indistinctly defined blocs can supply only imprecise notions about the parameters within which some congressmen operated. In direct contrast to the totally Union Whig nature of the

22 Memoirs of W. S. Oldham, pp. 297, 301, 305.

23 For an early example of cluster-bloc analysis see David B. Truman, *The Congressional Party: A Case Study* (New York, 1959). Unlike Guttman scaling, cluster-bloc analysis has been relatively ignored by historians. Some exceptions are Bogue, "Bloc and Party in the United States Senate," and Sheldon Hackney, *Populism to Progressivism in Alabama* (Princeton, 1969). "Interpretating roll call votes," says Hackney (p. 371), "is dangerous business, but it is better to err than to ignore."

24 The poor attendance which so marked the Confederate Congress was at no time more prominent than during the Second Congress. Only one of the eight Missourians cast any votes at all in the First Session, and on the last day of the Congress' existence, Mar. 18, 1865, one division had only 42 responses. Not all silent lawmakers left Richmond, although many had, but they frequently declined to vote. This high absence rate, plus the lack of a pair system, made it necessary to establish one additional criterion: no pairwise agreement score would be considered if it were based on fewer than ten mutual divisions. In the House of Representatives of the Second Congress, only 700 of approximately 6,000 pairwise comparisons of individual congressmen's votes are based on as many as 100 of the 139 divisions in the cross section selected for analysis.

North Carolina bloc and fringe, however, these clusters contain more Secessionists and Democrats than Unionists and Whigs (these attributes are unknown for some members). But all twenty men who compose the "Border South" cluster represented Exterior constituencies by November, 1864, and fourteen of them came from the potential Confederate irredenta of Kentucky, Missouri, or western Virginia.

Fifteen of the nineteen congressmen in the "Virginia" cluster also were from Exterior constituencies, but ten men represented Virginia and an eleventh, from New Orleans, was practicing law in Washington, D.C., on the eve of the war. The distinction between these two clusters was closely associated with intra-Confederate sectionalism, and may be summed roughly as Border South *versus* Virginia (significantly, Johnston and Funsten, who appear most frequently, came from the border areas of western and northern Virginia). But the primary division in the Upper South was not between the Border and Virginia. The Upper South was rent more surely by the dissimilarity between these two clusters and the North Carolina assemblage.

The odd thing is that relatively few Lower South congressmen joined either the North Carolinians and their followers on the one hand or the Upper South clusters on the other. Of the 42 legislators in these three clusters, 74 per cent came from Kentucky, Missouri, Virginia, or North Carolina, although the delegations from these states embraced only 40 per cent of the Second House membership. Eleven additional bloc and fringe members came from Alabama, Mississippi, Tennessee, and the New Orleans area; none came from Arkansas, Florida, Georgia, South Carolina, Texas, or the rest of Louisiana. The development of voting blocs, of whatever persuasion, was therefore much further advanced in most of the Upper South than in the Lower South. Obviously this pattern did not appear because Upper South congressmen were in substantial agreement. Probably it occurred because the war was closer to them, forcing them to be more decisive and to behave in a more consistent manner than their colleagues from the Lower South.

These observations, based on the general run of congressional business, should be supplemented by an examination of those special issues which defined principles and attitudes. It is common orientation which creates parallel voting behavior by individual congressmen and which influences them to combine into parties. The influences behind factional allegiance should become apparent from more detailed analysis of the Guttman scales found in the House of Representatives of the Second Congress.

The longer of the two includes a wide range of issues covered by twenty-one roll calls. At the weak, "anti-Confederate" end, two partially associated divisions indicate the close relation of this scale to the peace movement. The first of these implied acceptance of the principle of peace without independence and the other looked to the establishment of an "American diet," in which Union and Confederacy would each have one vote.[25] Other extreme issues included a convention of the states, blanket conscription exemptions for newspaper editors (to insure a free press), and restriction on the use of state troops outside their states. Issues on which there was less dissent embraced centralization of control over transportation and communication, borrowing coin to purchase army supplies, and the expulsion of Representative Henry S. Foote after he was arrested crossing Confederate lines in a personal bid to initiate peace discussions with Lincoln. More widely accepted issues included mandatory payments for impressed goods at inflated local market prices and weakening of the tax-in-kind. Divisions concerning the suspension of the writ of habeas corpus are found throughout the scale.

In order to categorize lawmakers by their positions on the two scales, scores were assigned to them based upon the extent to which their roll-call votes indicated they agreed with the attitude represented. Since the subject matter of the scales was similar, the scores were then cross tabulated (see Table 2).[26] The implied and quite reasonable assumptions are that men with high scores on two similar scales belonged to a faction which would eventually have evolved into one political party, while those with low scores would have evolved into another; and that parties will generally be composed of men with similar backgrounds and ideas—at least in the initial stages. The largest cluster in Table 2 is composed of congressmen who scored high on both scales, and the second largest is formed by those with low scale positions on both.

The most important observation is to confirm that polarization had occurred in the last months of the Confederate Congress which, given the general lack of scalability, had not occurred before. Perhaps we see here the nuclei of parties which might have evolved if the Confederacy had been in existence longer, a suggestion which is verified by examining the personal characteristics of the congressmen in the largest two scale clusters (see Table 3).

The low-score group illustrates the advantage of using scaling procedure to filter out from the general business of a legislature those votes which outlined basic dimensions. This group includes all eleven of the

[25] These two roll calls were not scored, since they narrowly missed the scale criteria established. They are included here for discussion only.

[26] The content of the other scale included a presidential veto of an officer promotion bill, adjournment, use of slave and free black soldiers, the Hampton Roads Peace Conference, conscription exemptions for overseers, Confederate use of state-chartered shipping, and exemptions from the tax-in-kind. The Spearman rank-order correlation for these two scales is $r_s = .51$. While this shows a meaningful degree of association, it nevertheless understates that degree — as is often the case when one attempts to associate one set of rather complex phenomena with another. Computation of the correlation coefficient depends on determining, for each individual case, the difference between rank on one scale and rank on the other, then squaring that difference. Squaring increases the weight of outlying cases, such as those in the lower left quadrant. This cluster would be worth separate discussion if space permitted. It must suffice to say that its appearance is not surprising. A single figure index is an unreliable substitute for visual inspection of the scatter diagram.

lawmakers in the North Carolina bloc and fringe, and adds three more who were apparently in frequent disagreement with that bloc on general business—but not on those important issues which defined their dominant political attitudes. Only three had been in the First Congress, and eight of the fourteen were from the Tarheel state. Twelve of them had been Unionists and Whigs, while eleven still represented safe Interior constituencies at the start of the last session of Congress (by which time two-thirds of the whole house came from occupied or threatened areas).

These fourteen low-scoring congressmen evidently had an absolute loathing of the extreme sacrifice necessary to maintain Confederate existence. They formed a significant portion of what less precise analyses have called a state rights faction and what men in 1865 often labeled the "peace party." Some idea of their ideological orientation and their basic defeatism may be obtained by an examination of their postwar amnesty petitions.[27] James M. Leach of North Carolina illustrated his colleagues' steadfast determination, for he not only claimed that he had opposed "for ten years in the Legislature, & for more than *twenty* on the hustings, the execrable political heresy of *Secession* . . . ," but also vied with his namesake, James T. Leach, for the honor of being the first man in his state to advocate reconstruction.[28] John A. Gilmer, also of the Old North State, revealed the loneliness of tenacious Unionism, asserting that he did his "utmost to keep down the rebellion, until after hostilities actually commenced and until all my near relatives & my only Son left me . . . and until it seemed no friends would be left to keep me company."[29]

Other members of the peace faction also indicated their basic lack of enthusiasm for war. Thomas C. Fuller, North Carolina, claimed that he "was morally and physically compelled to enter and remain in the army . . . ," and that he was elected to Congress by the Conservative party.[30] George W. Logan, North Carolina, an alleged leader of the secret antiwar organization known as the Red Strings, claimed that his undeviating unionism caused him to be threatened with violence, and that he went into Congress "for the two fold purpose of opposing *tyranny* [as Davis' war policies were sometimes called] & keeping *out*

[27] From a twentieth-century point of view, we might expect these petitions to be as self-serving as possible. However, the fact that the most ardent secessionists frequently made no attempt to hide or even apologize for their earlier activities seems to indicate that, except for an occasional touch of self-righteousness, the petitions of Unionists and peace men may be taken at close to face value.

[28] Pardon petition of James M. Leach, Amnesty Papers, North Carolina, Records of the Adjutant General's Office, Record Group 94, National Archives (emphasis Leach's); hereafter referred to as Amnesty Papers. Leach (no relation to James T. Leach) was one of the few southerners who denied that a right of secession even existed; he considered it to be revolution (*Congressional Globe*, 36 Cong., 2 sess., Appendix, p. 197).

[29] John A. Gilmer petition, Amnesty Papers, North Carolina.

[30] Thomas C. Fuller petition, *ibid*.

of the rebel army."[31] Williams C. Wickham of Virginia apparently held similar views. John Minor Botts, a staunch Virginia Unionist, supported Wickham's amnesty petition, informing President Johnson that throughout the war the Confederate brigadier and congressman had been "*at heart*, and in the *conviction of his judgment*, an earnest and loyal union man," who was, in effect, forced into the army, and who "was voted for, and elected to Congress by the Union men of his district. . . ."[32]

For men like Fuller, Logan, and Wickham, Congress functioned partly as a personal alternative to fighting,[33] but it could also provide a forum for opposition to policies which supported the war effort. Thus James M. Leach wrote after the war that he "never supported a measure asked for by Jeff Davis,"[34] and Thomas J. Foster of Alabama confessed an attempt to support the interests of his state "with an honest fidelity" while opposing vital war measures such as conscription, military exemptions for overseers, and other policies which he "conceived to be violent or oppressive or in the least tending to overthrow or compromise the rights of the People."[35]

James G. Ramsay, North Carolina, went further, for he directed his opposition not only against war measures, but against the war itself. Not only had Ramsay opposed secession and the arming of his state, he had also looked upon his election to the Second Congress as "the result of a great reaction in popular sentiment, because I stood upon a peace platform and opposed the Administration." He wrote that he "favored every feasible scheme for the restoration of peace upon the basis of the Constitutional, the inalienable and hereditary liberties and rights of the people."[36] James T. Leach, who was one of the first legislators to accept peace without independence in the public forum of congressional debate, later claimed to have been the first man in North Carolina to call for a settlement "by negotiation subject to the decissions [*sic*] of the people regardless of geographical lines. . . ."[37] Thomas C. Fuller was more specific: "I uniformly acted and voted with the party which labored for reconstruction. The journals will show that I voted with the Leachs [*sic*] of N.C., with Boyce of S.C. and Wickham of Va."[38] Williams C. Wickham also reflected the transformation which

[31] George W. Logan petition, *ibid.*, J. G. de Roulhac Hamilton (ed.), *The Papers of Randolph Abbott Shotwell* (Raleigh, 1929-1931), II, 294-295.

[32] Botts to Johnson, June 15, 1865, enclosed in Williams C. Wickham petition, Amnesty Papers, Virginia (emphasis Botts').

[33] Even Sen. William T. Dortch, a North Carolina Secession Democrat who was not a member of the peace faction, claimed that he remained in Congress because he feared conscription. Dortch petition, Amnesty Papers, North Carolina.

[34] James M. Leach petition, *ibid.*

[35] Thomas J. Foster petition, Amnesty Papers, Alabama.

[36] James G. Ramsay petition, Amnesty Papers, North Carolina.

[37] James T. Leach petition, *ibid.*; *American Annual Cyclopaedia . . . 1864*, p. 213.

[38] Thomas C. Fuller petition, Amnesty Papers, North Carolina. James M. Leach also named some of his fellow factionists: "My Colleagues in Congress Messrs. Turner, Fuller, Dr. [James T.] Leach Ramsay & Logan were all *peace* men . . . Gov.

occurred in the complexion of Tarheels and others during the last two years of war. In his application for amnesty, this Virginia delegate, who traded a general's commission for a seat in Congress, pleaded that upon election he "at once and assiduously devoted myself to the endeavor to bring about a termination of the bloody strife that was being waged."[39] Jehu A. Orr of Mississippi added—as most of the ascertained members of the peace faction could have done—that during his 1863 campaign for Congress he

distinctly took the ground that the people were heartily sick of the war & that I should gladly avail myself of the earliest practicable opportunity to restore peace to the Country on any honorable terms. I was then satisfied that secession was a terrible mistake & there has been no subsequent time when if in my power I would not have terminated the war by a reconstruction of the Union.[40]

Cluster-bloc and scale analysis do not combine in so complementary a fashion for other congressmen as for the North Carolina faction. The coterie of exterior legislators at the opposite extreme from the peace party, as the North Carolinians and their followers from other states were called, is delineated almost as imprecisely by scaling as by the cluster-bloc technique. However, scaling does isolate a group of fifteen legislators who sought victory even in the Confederacy's darkest hour. All except four were to be found in either the Border South or Virginia clusters revealed by cluster-bloc analysis (see Table 1). These congressmen, who constitute the high-scoring segment of Table 2, are not so relevant to the hypothesis of the emerging party as their counterparts. If they formed a faction which was also developing into a party they were further from that consummation, and, in any case, their background was not so homogeneous (see Table 3). Most were from the Upper South. Although party is unknown for five, seven were Democrats and only three had been Whigs. Eleven had been members of the First Congress. Seven were Secessionists, but it is uncertain whether any had been Unionists since this information is lacking for eight. What appears to be the most important determinant of voting behavior for these fifteen fire-eaters is the fact that twelve came from localities which were occupied by Federal troops by late 1864 and ten represented the previously mentioned potential Confederate irredenta. We need not delve further into this faction; but it bolsters the conclusion that if incipient party-building was a phenomenon of the late Confederate Congress, it took place along the lines of former party affiliation, secession stand in 1861, and the relation of a congressman's constituency to the Federal army.

Examination of voting records, biographical characteristics, and postwar amnesty petitions of Confederate congressmen leaves no doubt

---

Graham [Senate member of the faction] & Hon. Mr. Gilmer, *not quite so conservative*, were and are, nevertheless, *true men*." James M. Leach petition, *ibid.*

[39] Williams C. Wickham petition, Amnesty Papers, Virginia.

[40] Jehu A. Orr petition, Amnesty Papers, Mississippi.

that, although the "peace party" was not a full-fledged party, neither was it a mere political expression. When members wrote about a "peace party" they knew exactly what—and whom—they were talking about, and their political positions in relation to that "party" were a matter of conscious decision. This is not to say that a true party actually existed or that members necessarily looked to the formation of one in the future.[41] It is simply to assert that the legislators knew what they were doing, that some of them did create a faction revolving around peace, military, and civil rights issues, that others formed a loose opposition, and that the action was so open that other congressmen were fully aware of what their colleagues had done.

In this manner Confederates created foundations for a party system which might have emerged if the would-be nation's existence had been prolonged. Had the "peace party" been correct in its basic assumption that independence could be won at the negotiating table when it could not be won on the battlefield, the North Carolina representatives and their allies from other states might well have formed the nucleus of a future political party. The basis of postwar politics in the Confederate States of America might then have been the divisions created by the willingness of politicians to engage in negotiations with the Union and upon the degree to which they were unwilling to depart from normal governmental involvement in the lives of citizens.

A comparative study of other non-party periods in American history might help to substantiate this conclusion. It is not too much to expect that had the Confederate experiment been allowed to continue, it would have followed much the same pattern as that of the Union eighty years earlier. The political leaders of the Federalist period had been part of the independence movement of the 1770's, just as Confederates had been states' righters in the 1850's. Uniting for the purpose of achieving separation, in both cases the independence movement split, thereby influencing the character of future politics.

The parallel may be illustrated by William Nisbet Chambers' work on the early national period, in which he examines the development of the Federalist and Republican parties and applies his findings to the development of parties in general.[42] "Viewed in historical analysis and against the retrospect of American faction politics in the 1770's and 1780's," writes Chambers, "the emergence of the Federalists reveals a transition from the older 'connexions' of fluid factions, family cliques, or juntos to the newer, modern connection of party."[43]

Family cliques and fluid factions were also important in Confederate

---

[41] Some Confederates did have this in mind. A Mar., 1864, investigation of the Peace Society in Alabama revealed that one of its goals was the "organization of a political party opposed to the present government." OR, Ser. IV, Vol. III, 397.

[42] William Nisbet Chambers, Political Parties in a New Nation: The American Experience, 1776-1809 (New York, 1963). See especially pp. 44-51.

[43] Ibid., pp. 44-45.

voting behavior.[44] But the progression from faction to party may be illustrated by Chambers' model. A party, he says, needs a "regularized relationship between leaders and followers" (structure), functions (as nomination, formation of agreements between groups, and public appeal), a broad base of support (enough to encompass a wide range of opinions), and an ideology.[45] A faction might have some of these characteristics, and the most distinctive faction of the Second Confederate Congress displays some of these attributes to a striking degree.

While there was no national party structure, in isolated local areas the old labels and sometimes even the framework of the old parties remained. This is especially true in North Carolina, where "for practical reasons the old political organizations were retained as the most convenient method of supporting candidates" for the convention elections in 1861.[46] Old political groupings continued to exist in the Old North State after secession, but under new labels. Union Democrats and Whigs combined to form the Conservative party, while the rest of the Democrats with perhaps a few Whigs joined together in the Confederate party.[47] A number of peace societies were also formed, and engaged in political action in state and local elections, notably in 1863 when some of them seem to have served the purpose of nomination and public appeal. Furthermore, the base of popular support for one of the factions under discussion was widening as peace sentiment grew—widening geographically because the peace societies spread from several areas of origin to cover large parts of the South, and widening politically as the peace issue became related to habeas corpus, impressment, and conscription and exemption. Most of all, the peace faction of the Second Congress had an ideology. Strongly pro-state rights where that principle was involved, it also opposed those measures which were necessary for the vigorous prosecution of the war effort.

The superficially non-partisan politics of the Confederacy had far-reaching implications, not only for the South, but for representative government in general. Informal and transitory combinations replaced party discipline and ideology. Lacking these guides, congressmen turned too easily to the support of administration policy; presidential proposals often won by default, rather than by superior virtue tested in the marketplace of ideas. Without party, there was no automatic device for the mobilization of legitimate opposition, and legitimate op-

---

[44] The role of family cliques in the civil and military politics of the Confederacy is currently being studied by Archer Jones and Thomas L. Connelly.

[45] Chambers, *Political Parties in a New Nation*, pp. 45-48.

[46] Yearns, "North Carolina in the Confederate Congress," p. 360.

[47] Hugh T. Lefler and Albert R. Newsome, *The History of a Southern State: North Carolina* (rev. ed. Chapel Hill, 1963), pp. 437-438; Richard E. Yates, "Zebulon B. Vance as War Governor of North Carolina," *Journal of Southern History*, III (Feb., 1937), 46; Clement Eaton, *A History of the Southern Confederacy* (N.Y., 1965) p. 258; and Horace W. Raper, "William W. Holden and the Peace Movement in North Carolina," *North Carolina Historical Review*, XXXI (Oct., 1954), 495-496.

position is what parties are all about.[48] Dissenters from executive policy therefore appeared, on the surface, to be questioning personalities rather than programs.[49] Soldiers and even congressmen eventually voted with their feet, but dissent of that sort hardly makes possible a dynamic political opposition.

On the other hand, if Davis' opponents did not possess an organization with which to mobilize an alternative program, the Confederate President lacked an important device for the generation of vital support. Basing his congressional power, as Wilfred Buck Yearns points out, "primarily on an agreement of ideas, not on party discipline,"[50] Davis found that when the vital prop of consensus had been knocked out there were no others to rely upon. Unfortunately for both parties to this dialogue, "goaded by the demands of 'modern,' total war, the Confederate government abandoned the political system which it was called into being to defend."[51] The political party was vital to that discarded system. Toward the end, some Confederates seemed to have understood that the fatal deficiency was not opposition, but rather an effective and acceptable means of directing it.[52]

[48] For recent study of the gradual emergence and acceptance of this concept, see Richard Hofstadter, *The Idea of a Party System: The Rise of Legitimate Opposition in the United States, 1780-1840* (Berkeley and Los Angeles, 1969); and Michael Wallace, "Changing Concepts of Party in the United States: New York, 1815-1828," *American Historical Review*, LXXIV (December, 1968). The matter is briefly discussed, with specific reference to the Confederacy, in McKitrick, "Party Politics and the Union and Confederate War Efforts."

[49] Thus, to a degree, the commonly over-simplified analysis of the Confederate Congress in terms of a pro- and anti-Davis dichotomy has some validity. This is the approach taken by Yearns throughout his *Confederate Congress.* Other writers also see a basic split in Congress between pro- and anti-Davis forces. Eaton, *History of the Southern Confederacy,* saw a conflict of realists and doctrinaires, but also stated that Congress was weak because "it was torn by a conflict between the Davis supporters and the opposition" (see pp. 63-66; quote on p. 63). Charles P. Roland, *The Confederacy,* pp. 61-62, 98-99, 179-180, agrees, going so far as to say with great exaggeration (p. 99), "By 1864 every representative from the state of South Carolina was hostile to Davis; and thus it went throughout the South." Similar points of view are less explicit in Coulter, *Confederate States of America,* Ch. VII; Frank E. Vandiver, *Their Tattered Flags* (New York, 1970), pp. 265-272, 295-299; and Vandiver, *Basic History of the Confederacy* (Princeton, 1962), pp. 90-91. Immediately after the Civil War, Edward A. Pollard set the tone of future interpretation. Legislation which Davis opposed Pollard labeled "the faint shadow of a counterrevolution," and he observed that the passage of an 1865 law for the appointment of a general-in-chief indicated that Davis' "party had dwindled down to an insignificant number." It was "scarcely anything more than that train of followers which always fawns on power and lives on patronage," and was opposed by a "Congressional party" supposedly under the leadership of Texas Senator Louis T. Wigfall. See Pollard, *The Lost Cause; A New Southern History of the War of the Confederates . . .* (New York, 1866), pp. 653, 656-657. Pollard made the same point in a later work, writing that Congress was a "servile appendage" to the Davis autocracy, but that opposition to the executive developed toward the end. Pollard, *Life of Jefferson Davis,* pp. 162, 417.

[50] Yearns, *Confederate Congress,* p. 234.

[51] Emory M. Thomas, *The Confederacy as a Revolutionary Experience* (Englewood Cliffs, New Jersey, 1971), p. 78.

[52] See, for example, Memoirs of W. S. Oldham, pp. 138-139. Apparently other Confederates had second thoughts about the widespread condemnation of parties.

It was probably inevitable that the Confederacy, sharing other American traditions and institutions, would also have claimed for its own the party system to which it was heir. If this is so, it is appropriate to consider the parties which would have developed. First, it is apparent that both significant factions, or proto-parties, exhibited the tensions of men gaming for high stakes, with all the frustration and intensity of emotion to be expected of those on the losing side. Congressmen who suffered most under the pressure of war, those who took their duties most seriously (whether conceived in terms of fighting or surrendering), could have been expected to form the nuclei of these political clusters. In their initial moments, therefore, any new partisan combinations would have partaken as much of the nature of stress groups as of issue-oriented parties.

Second, Confederate parties would have had familiar aspects. They would doubtless have operated much like any other parties of American history, and they would have had a direct lineage from prewar political antagonisms. Although the Confederacy did not have a functioning party system, neither did the immediate prewar South.[53] In 1860 the region was poised for realignment regardless of secession and war. Certainly a long and cruel civil war might be expected to have had a wrenching effect upon partisan behavior, but this realignment, insofar as it had taken place by 1865, did not show a great divergence from the past. Far from the "marked shifting of old party lines,"[54] which Charles W. Ramsdell expected to see, the most noteworthy characteristic of Confederate congressional-level politics was the extent to which they followed old patterns. In a victorious Confederacy new political parties doubtless would have resumed rivalry along old Whig-Democratic lines, with some significant switching of loyalties directed by wartime experience with enemy occupation and other, as yet undetermined, influences.

This analysis adds additional support for the theme of continuity developed by Thomas B. Alexander;[55] the deviant years of war hinged nicely with the prewar past and the postwar future—at least as far as the development of parties is concerned. The crumbling of partisan cohesiveness which marked the South in the late 1850's continued into the war, and the resurgence of the Whigs and of party development during the year or two prior to Appomattox was continued after the

---

"By 1864 the Richmond *Whig* was agreeing that parties were 'necessary to good government' and that to erase all party lines was 'to create a one-man power' " (Coulter, *Confederate States of America*, p. 115). See also note 41 above.

[53] Alexander, *Sectional Stress*, p. 126. As measured by the voting behavior of southerners in the 35th and 36th U.S. House of Representatives, the party system below the Ohio River was dead. Roll-call votes were cast more in accordance with sectional than partisan considerations.

[54] Charles W. Ramsdell, "Some Problems Involved in Writing the History of the Confederacy," *Journal of Southern History*, II (May, 1936), 145.

[55] Alexander, "Persistent Whiggery in the Confederate South, 1860-1877," *Journal of Southern History*, XXVII (Aug., 1961), 305-329.

surrender. That political growth of a partisan nature did take place in the Confederacy seems fairly certain. It is the interpretation of this event which remains open, pending further investigation into the mechanics of party formation.

The preceding analysis contributes to the irony of one phase of Southern history. Engaging in what they thought of as a conservative revolution, Confederates eventually realized they had instead accelerated full-scale social and economic change. Seeking to preserve localism, they built a unitary state more powerful than the one they had abandoned. Shunning the political labels of their fathers, they nevertheless thought of each other as Whigs or Democrats. Avoiding political parties, they unwittingly began to develop new parties much like the old ones they claimed to detest. They attempted to transfer their loyalties to a new nation and found themselves taking oaths of allegiance to the old one. The results prove simply that Alphonse Karr was right: "plus ça change, plus c'est le même chose."

BLOC AND PARTY IN THE
UNITED STATES SENATE: 1861-1863

Allan G. Bogue

As HE FOUGHT FOR ELECTION in 1854, James Harlan explained how he would conduct himself if elected to the Senate of the United States: ". . . in all *Constitutional* questions . . . I would expect to be guided in my action by the decisions of the Supreme Court and the well-settled principles of Constitutional Law—in all questions of *Legislative Expediency*, by the views and wishes of the Legislature and people of Iowa—and in all questions of *Conscience* by the Bible."[1] To understand court, constituency and holy writ was to understand the legislative behavior of Senator Harlan, or so he said. The fact is that it is rather difficult to understand Senator Harlan at times in these terms or by any other simple formula and this is also true of his colleagues in the Senate. Led, some time ago, to the Thirty-seventh or first Civil War Congress by my interest in the great economic legislation of that body, I soon found myself trying to understand the major forces that were reflected in the voting of the congressmen. This paper is an outgrowth of that rather frustrating endeavor—a case study of general voting behavior in the Senate during the second session, the longest and most important of the three legislative sessions of the Thirty-seventh Congress.

The historian who seeks for understanding can, of course, usually find other historians willing to guide him. We are all familiar with the interpretation which pictures a beleagured Lincoln, struggling during the Civil War to maintain his leadership against the determined onslaughts of the Radical faction that dominated his party and the Congress. This organizational theme has been rewarding and, indeed, the authors of some of the historical classics of the Civil War have used it. But recently David Donald has argued that historians have overstressed the difference between Radical and Moderate Republicans and suggested that the importance of party bonds should be emphasized instead.[2] T. Harry Williams, however, continues to

---

[1] Johnson Brigham, *James Harlan* (Iowa City, 1913), p. 87.
[2] David Donald, "Devils Facing Zionwards" in Grady McWhiney (ed.), *Grant,*

believe that the distinction is an important one.[3] If we exclude the executive branch from our discussion and focus on the congressional aspects of the Radical-Moderate controversy it is clear that the problem can be stated more precisely. Did party or did factional groups within the Republican party more significantly influence the voting of Republican senators and representatives during the Civil War years? More recently still, Professor Donald has suggested that the congressional district played a major part in determining the votes of members of the House of Representatives when they were considering reconstruction legislation.[4] Thus in a sense he joined Senator Harlan in emphasizing the importance of constituency in helping to determine congressional voting patterns—a factor which may have accounted for the presence of Moderate and Radical factions among the Republicans, if indeed they did exist.

We remember also that Frederick Jackson Turner had something to say about the relation of constituency to legislative behavior. "A study of votes in the federal House and Senate from the beginning of our national history reveals the fact," wrote Turner, "that party voting has more often broken down than maintained itself on fundamental issues; that when these votes are mapped or tabulated . . . a persistent sectional pattern emerges."[5] The Thirty-seventh was of course the first congress of the Civil War and unusual in that most of the representatives of one great section were missing. Although the empty seats render this and the next congress unique in the history of national legislative behavior, Earle Ross and others have maintained that sectionalism, particularly that of East against West, continued to influence the actions of legislators during the Civil War.[6] In the *Congressional Globe* we can easily find proud affirmations of loyalty to constituency, frank declarations of sectional interest, and the appeals of Republican leaders to their colleagues to shun factionalism and cleave to party. But oratorical flourishes can be deceiving; in the end it was the votes of the senators that counted. And what do the votes tell us of geographical bloc, of party faction and of the bonds of party?

When I began this research I selected for analysis all of the sub-

Lee, Lincoln and the Radicals: Essays on Civil War Leadership (Evanston, 1964), pp. 72-91.

[3] T. Harry Williams, *"Lincoln and the Radicals: An Essay in Civil War History and Historiography," ibid.*, pp. 92-117.

[4] David Donald, *The Politics of Reconstruction: 1863-1867* (Baton Rouge, 1965).

[5] Frederick Jackson Turner, "The Significance of the Section in American History," *Wisconsin Magazine of History*, VIII (1925), 270.

[6] Earle D. Ross, "Northern Sectionalism in the Civil War Era," *Iowa Journal of History and Politics*, XXX (1932), 455-512; Jacque Voegeli, "The Northwest and the Race Issue, 1861-1862," *Mississippi Valley Historical Review*, L (1963), 235-251.

stantive votes which were concerned with slavery and confiscation measures, both broadly defined; the tariff and the internal revenue tax bills; legal tenders; the agricultural college bill; the homestead law; the department of agriculture bill; the Pacific railroad act; northern civil liberties and the general conduct of the war, as well as a few important procedural votes that seemed related to such measures. Most of these votes fell into one of three broad categories. Eighty-seven dealt with the confiscation of rebel property or the status of slavery; fifty-one emerged from the debate on the Internal Revenue Act of 1862; and the debates on other major economic legislation of national interest produced thirty-five votes. During the course of the research I broadened the scope of the study to include 368 roll calls of this session, excluding only those that related to appointments.[7] These votes are the major source for the scholar seeking evidence of patterns in the voting of the thirty-one Republicans, eleven Democrats, five Border Unionists and one northern Unionist who sat in the Senate during most of the second session of the Thirty-seventh Congress.[8]

In the following pages I have used a few simple devices that describe legislative behavior in quantitative terms.[9] An index number of cohesion shows the extent to which a political party or group is united in a particular roll call on a scale running from one to one hundred. Similarly, an index number of agreement or likeness measures the degree to which the members of two parties or groups vote alike in a division, and the obverse of such a number can be called an index of disagreement. Thus, if Democrats and Republicans agreed on a particular vote to the amount of 40 per cent of the maximum agreement which would result when all Republicans and all Demo-

[7] This included votes in the Senate proper, in committee of the whole and in executive session. Tallies used are those recorded in the Senate *Journals*, supplemented occasionally by those in the *Congressional Globe*.

[8] In the Border Unionist category I included five senators of Whig origins from the Border States. I have used the term Northern Unionist to describe Senator Joseph A. Wright of Indiana. A prominent Democrat prior to the Civil War, Wright was selected by Governor Morton to replace Senator Bright and abjured party politics for the duration of the war. See his letter to the Indiana State Union Convention, *National Intelligencer*, June 23, 1862. However, Kenneth Stampp lists him as a War Democrat in *Indiana Politics During the Civil War* (Indianapolis, 1949), p. 237.

[9] These are described in more detail in Lee F. Anderson *et al*, *Legislative Roll-Call Analysis* (Evanston, 1966) and in Samuel C. Patterson, *Notes on Legislative Behavior Research* (Iowa City, 1965). An index of cohesion may be calculated by subtracting the per cent yea of a party's vote (if the smaller) from the per cent nay (if the larger) or vice versa. When 83 per cent of Republicans voted yea and 17 per cent voted nay on a bill the index number of cohesion is 83 - 17 = 66. If 75 per cent of the Democrats and 50 per cent of the Republicans voted yea in a roll call the index of likeness or agreement is 100 - (75 — 50) = 75.

crats voted alike, the index of likeness would be forty and the index of disagreement would be sixty.

Other techniques help us to identify groups of legislators that act in concert, or relative differences in attitude among legislators. If we record the number of times that each legislator votes with every other legislator we can find groups of like-minded individuals by fitting the pair-agreement scores into a matrix with the highest agreements in the upper left corner. Legislative groups derived by this process are often called cluster blocs. The Guttman scale deals with association among the senators in a different way. In effect, this variety of scaling procedure isolates a roll call in which a small group of legislators vote against the rest of the chamber and then adds to this roll call others in which the members of the small group are in agreement but are joined, roll call by roll call, by other legislators who vote with the original minority on subsequent votes added. Because they could find few who shared their opinion on the original roll call the members of the initial small group are assumed to have held an extreme or radical position on a particular subject. The added roll calls express increasingly moderate views on the same area of legislation until the last roll call added may perhaps contain only a small group in opposition to the original minority—a group whose members are utterly opposed to any legislative concession whatsoever on the subject at issue. Roll calls arranged in this way, therefore, form a scale which ranks congressmen according to their attitude on legislative proposals dealing with a particular problem.

The cluster bloc technique may not reveal the shifting patterns of agreement among legislators over time and gives no hint of the relative extremeness in attitude of group members in comparison with the positions taken by the members of other groups. It may require the researcher to make arbitrary decisions concerning the outer limits of the groups or clusters. The scalogram masks but does not completely destroy temporal relationships, does not isolate the members of self-conscious groups, and discards roll calls that will not scale. There also is involved in scaling the assumption that legislators will vote for measures which in their minds represent only half a loaf because half is, after all, better than none. Not all representatives and senators are so logical; some, in frustration, vote against bills because they deem them too weak and there are instances of such behavior in the Thirty-seventh Congress. But in general the principle holds. Indeed, John Sherman stated it neatly on one occasion in this Congress, "It is always better, in a legislative body . . . to do the best you can. It is a principle by which I have always been governed. . . ."[10]

---

[10] *Congressional Globe*, 37 Cong., 2 sess., p. 2999.

Neither the index number approach, the cluster bloc technique, nor the Guttman scale is perfect or all revealing but used together these methods can reveal a great deal about legislative behavior. We should, of course, avoid imposing unreasonable standards in evaluating the behavior of political groups or individual legislators. To expect voting blocs or factions to maintain the same membership over long periods of time is unrealistic. Wayne Morse, no matter what he would like to think, is hardly a unique creation of this harried age. It is similarly unrealistic to suppose that all legislators will maintain exactly the same ideological position over a period of two or more sessions, or even during one session. It is unreasonable to assume that group feeling must be reflected by agreement across a number of different kinds of issues or that all members of a group should reflect the same intensity of attitude concerning even those issues on which they most strongly agree. The crucial defection or the betrayal of friends provides us with the high drama of political history but such acts must be viewed in the general perspective of voting frequencies and it is with these that we are mainly concerned here.

"We" [of the Northwest], said Senator Grimes, "are the only portion of all the loyal States that feel the effect of this war oppressively. . . . Whilst men who own the railroads in the Northwest are making fortunes out of this war by the transportation of our produce, we are receiving nothing in fact from it."[11] Later in the session, Ten Eyck of New Jersey spoke for the East when he asked: "Now what inducement is there for a Senator from an Atlantic State to vote an appropriation of large sums of money, even in the shape of a loan, to construct a variety of [rail] roads for the advantage of the western States?"[12] These were the oratorical flourishes of eastern and western sectionalism. We can quite easily design a procedure that will reveal the presence of sectional determinants in voting divisions.

In examining the roll calls of the Senate, I assumed that a disagreement index of forty or more represented substantial disagreement between eastern and western Republicans. Western Republican senators included all of those from Ohio or states to the west and eastern Republicans, those members of the party from the states east of Ohio. The states represented by Democrats were few and widely spread; I did not, therefore, use Democratic votes in my search for roll calls that revealed the sectionalism of East and West. By these definitions there was substantial sectional disagreement among eastern and west-

11 *Ibid.*, p. 114.   12 *Ibid.*, p. 2805.

ern Republican senators in forty-six of the 368 votes of the second session.[13]

The sectionalism of East and West appeared most frequently in voting on economic measures of national significance.[14] In the original selection of eighty-seven roll calls relating to slavery and confiscation and eighty-six that were linked to major economic legislation only 7 per cent of the slavery and confiscation roll calls showed substantial sectional disagreement between the eastern and western Republicans, in comparison to 25 per cent of the votes on economic policy. Consideration of all 368 roll calls does not change the generalization. In voting on slavery and confiscation measures, the Republican senators divided on the basis of East and West in seven substantive votes and in three procedural votes. The same pattern appeared in two roll calls concerning the possibility of expelling Lazarus Powell, senator from Kentucky. Among the votes on economic legislation we find a division between eastern and western Republicans on eight roll calls during the debates on the internal revenue bill; on eight votes in the discussion of the land grant college bill; on three concerning greenback issues; on three during the Pacific railroad debates; and two divisions concerning the tariff. Sectionalism appeared also in three votes relating to the judiciary, three concerning appropriations for the armed forces, and in five roll calls on miscellaneous matters.

Western Republicans ranged themselves against the eastern members of their party most sharply when they voted on the land grant college bill. Eight of the nine roll calls, generated in discussion of this bill, showed substantial disagreement between East and West; the index of disagreement between the sections ranged from seventy-one to eighty-five in the roll calls on the major amendments. In the end both Wisconsin senators and one Republican senator from Iowa, Indiana, and Kansas actually voted against the bill. They were joined by Senator Wright, the northern Unionist from Indiana, whose Republican colleague supported the most severe amendments proposed by the westerners but did not vote on the bill itself. No other economic measure inspired such consistent and strong antagonism between eastern and western Republicans in this session.

Indices of likeness or disagreement do not reveal whether the representatives of a section were more united in their approach to certain categories of legislation than were the legislators of another section. But this was indeed the case among the Republican senators of the

13 A list of these roll calls is available on request from the author.

14 Of course, much of the legislation, passed or proposed, concerning the South was "economic" in both its short-run and long-run implications, but for the sake of convenience I will distinguish between legislation on slavery and confiscation (or southern legislation) in contrast to national economic legislation.

Thirty-seventh Congress. The average voting agreement among all possible pairs of western senators was 61 per cent (with absences deleted) in the roll calls on the major national economic legislation and 59 per cent in the votes on the internal revenue bill.[15] In contrast, the eastern Republicans had mean agreements of 76 and 65 per cent. The differences between the two groups of senators would have increased still more had I dropped the senators from the Middle States from the comparison. Six New England senators, Clark (N.H.), Collamer (Vt.), Fessenden (Me.), Foot (Vt.), Foster (Conn.), and Morrill (Me.) were in particularly strong agreement in the votes on economic legislation. Minimal mean agreement among these men was 73 per cent and Clark and Fessenden voted together in 97 per cent of the roll calls on major economic legislation. There was no western group comparable either in numbers or in the strength of agreement among its members.

Among the 368 roll calls of the second session there were ninety-one in which the cohesion indices of eastern and western Republicans differed by as much as forty points. In fifty-nine of these roll calls it was the easterners who showed the greater solidarity. The western Republicans were more cohesive in voting on only thirty-two roll calls of this type. Of the 105 votes in this session which were apparently related to economic measures of national interest, thirty-five, or 33 per cent, showed a marked difference in the cohesion of eastern and western Republicans. Of 120 roll calls linked to slavery, confiscation and the general conduct of the war, only eighteen, or 15 per cent, revealed a similar pattern. Thus, economic issues provoked more sectional response between eastern and western Republicans than did legislation concerned with slavery and confiscation, and it is clear also that the eastern Republicans were in greater agreement on the national economic legislation of this Congress than were their western colleagues.

The most striking sectional alignment in Congress during the years before the Civil War had reflected the divergent interests of North and South.[16] During most of the second session of the Thirty-seventh Congress senators represented five slave states. This group, containing both Democrats and former Whigs, guarded the southern heritage insofar as they considered it appropriate and feasible—which was sometimes a good deal further than the Republicans liked. An index

[15] Absences of individual senators are disregarded in the calculation of these percentages.
[16] In "The Civil War Synthesis in American Political History," *Civil War History*, X (1964), 130-140, and in *The Shrine of Party: Congressional Voting Behavior, 1841-1852* (Pittsburgh, 1967), Joel Silbey cautions against overemphasizing sectionalism in these years.

of disagreement which compares the voting of the senators from the slave states with that of the senators from the free states shows substantial disagreement on 154 of the 368 Senate roll calls of this session. Sixty-seven of these votes appeared in the original selection of eighty-seven roll calls, related to slavery and confiscation legislation. The slave-state delegation was so small that this bloc's voting was sometimes masked by other voting determinants, but the group could be of major importance when Radical and Moderate Republicans disagreed.

To examine the conflict of Radical and Moderate Republicans is more difficult than it is to examine sectional manifestations in Congress, as we have no ready-made categories to use. But the documentary evidence suggests that the distinction had real meaning among the legislators. In December, 1861, Timothy Howe of Wisconsin predicted factional strife in the party when he wrote:

Everything about us portends the coming of a rupture in the ranks of the war party and if so, a fierce struggle between the two factions. The organization of a party designing either to rule the administration or to supplant it has I think already commenced. Emancipation—the utter extinction of slavery will be the watchword & the effort of one faction. Where the other faction will plant itself is not so certain.[17]

And if one reads only the debates on the confiscation bills of the next spring one finds the senators describing, explicitly or implicitly, the differences among Republicans. Some opponents of a harsh confiscation bill invoked the Constitution against those who maintained that Congress should exercise war powers and advocated "legislative encroachment upon the prerogatives of the other departments."[18] But men who complained in this fashion, retorted Senator Wade, were contending for "the irresponsible power of the Chief Magistrate in time of war," a doctrine which he characterized as "most slavish and un-American."[19] Senator Dixon, who feared that the powers of the states might be diminished, maintained that the rebel states were still within the Union and their residents, therefore, were entitled to the guarantees of the Constitution if they were to be punished. He also implied that the chairman of the Judiciary Committee was an "opponent of this Administration."[20] To this the chairman, Lyman Trumbull, responded by suggesting that Dixon was a "courtier" and a "sycophant" who did "not mean to be in opposition to the Administration

---

[17] Timothy O. Howe to Grace Howe, Dec. 13, 1861. Timothy O. Howe Papers, Wisconsin State Historical Society.
[18] *Congressional Globe*, 37 Cong., 2 sess., p. 2919.   [19] *Ibid.*, p. 2930.
[20] *Ibid.*, pp. 2924-2928, 2973.

let what will happen. . . ."[21] In this exchange we find support of the administration used to distinguish one Republican from another.

Senator Cowan referred to "the ultra school of the Republican party," whose members had decided that the rebellion of "some of the slave States" should be "put down by main force, and by an utter disregard of the will of the whole people of the slave States," and were insisting on measures "utterly obnoxious and distasteful" to every senator from the slave states.[22] More personally still, Wade described himself and his friends as "the earnest, up and down, through thick and thin Republicans of this body," leaving the character of recusant Republicans to the imagination.[23] But on one occasion, Fessenden, in exasperation with Wade and his friends, spoke of "certain gentlemen on this floor," who "seem to think that they are the representatives of all righteousness . . . and that if anybody differs from them he is either a fool or a knave."[24]

Expression of such differences appeared in the correspondence of the senators. Writing to Chandler after the close of the second session and as the election of 1862 neared, Wilkinson worried only about the success of ultra-Radicals like himself.[25] Trumbull, as he reviewed the Illinois election for Chandler's benefit a few weeks later, remarked sarcastically: "Do you think it will be any loss to exchange Browning for a responsible Democrat?"[26] To Browning, after the Thirty-seventh Congress had ended, Harris lamented that the President had "been drawn into the views" unfortunately "of a miserable lot of politicians"; a "lot" of which the New Yorker obviously did not consider himself a member.[27]

Most of the eighty-seven roll calls on slavery and confiscation motions fit into six Guttman scales. Beginning at the end of these scales which, judging by the content of the motions, represented the most extreme position relative to slavery and confiscation, I calculated the mean percentile positions of the senators in each scale and then prepared a weighted average of each senator's various scale positions. The average mean-percentile score of both Wilmot and Wade was nineteen, but the score of Senator Powell, a slave state Democrat at the other end of the political spectrum, was eighty-two. The other senators ranged between these poles, Radical Republicans presumably giving way to Moderate Republicans and War Democrats until

21 *Ibid.*, p. 2973.   22 *Ibid.*, p. 2993.   23 *Ibid.*, p. 3002.
24 *Ibid.*, p. 2203.
25 Morton Wilkinson to Zachariah Chandler, Oct. 20, 1862. Zachariah Chandler Papers, Library of Congress.
26 Lyman Trumbull to Zachariah Chandler, Nov. 9, 1862, *ibid.*
27 Ira Harris to Orville H. Browning, May 30, 1863. Orville H. Browning Papers, Illinois State Historical Society.

finally the most conservative representatives of the border slave states were reached.[28] Table I presents the scale pattern found most frequently in the votes on slavery and confiscation.

Table I

A Voting Pattern on Slavery and Confiscation Measures

Senator	Party	State	Type	N 1	N 2	N 3	Y 4	N 5	N 6	Y 1	Y 2	Y 3	N 4	Y 5	Y 6
Powell	D	Ky.	6	°	°	°	°	°	°						
Kennedy	BU	Md.	6	°	°	°	0	°	0						
Davis	BU	Ky.	6	°	°	°	°	0	°						
Wilson, R.	BU	Mo.	6	°	°	0	°	°	°						
Carlile	BU	Va.	6	°	°	°	0	°	°						
Wright	NU	Ind.	6	°	—	°	°	°	°			X			
Saulsbury	D	Del.	5		°	0	0	°	°	0					
Stark	D	Ore.	5		°	0	0	°	°	0					
Willey	BU	Va.	5		°	°	°	°	°	0					
Henderson	D	Mo.	4			°	°	°	°	°	°				
Cowan	R	Pa.	4			°	°	0	°	°	°				
Browning	R	Ill.	4			°	°	°	°	°	°				
Anthony	R	R.I.	3				°	°	°	°.	°	°			
Doolittle	R	Wis.	3				°	°	°	°	°	°			
Collamer	R	Vt.	3				°	°	0	°	0	°			
Sherman	R	Ohio	3				°	°	°	°	°	°			
Foster	R	Conn.	3				°	°	°	°	°	°			
Ten Eyck	R	N.J.	3				°	°	°	°	°	°			
Fessenden	R	Me.	3				°	0	°	°	°	°			
Lane, H. S.	R	Ind.	3				°	°	°	0	°	0			
Simmons	R	R.I.	3				°	°	°	°	°	°			
Howe	R	Wis.	3				°	°	°	°	°	°			
Harris	R	N.Y.	2					°	0	°	°	°	°		
Foot	R	Vt.	2					°	°	°	°	°	°		
Clark	R	N.H.	1						°	°	°	°	°	°	
Hale	R	N.H.	1						°	°	°	°	0	0	
Wilson, H.	R	Mass.	1						°	°	°	°	°	°	
Sumner	R	Mass.	1						°	°	°	°	°	°	
Morrill	R	Me.	1						°	°	°	°	°	0	
Lane, J. H.	R	Kan.	0							°	°	°	°	°	°

[28] Some students have tried to summarize the voting positions of legislators by summing or averaging their scale type positions in a number of appropriate scales. Unfortunately, such procedure disregards the fact that Guttman scales are ordinal scales and we cannot be sure that the scale types in various scales are equivalent units of measurement. Here, therefore, I have calculated the number of percentiles that the legislators of each scale type occupied and allocated the mean percentile score to each man in the scale type. Such percentile values can, of course, be averaged with those derived from other scales. Actually, the rank ordering of senators derived in this way did not vary greatly from the rank order which resulted when I summed the scale types of the various legislators, although there were some minor differences. But one should not assume that the rank order derived by summing scale types in some published research is inaccurate simply because of the methods used. The results may or may not be correct. I am indebted to Professor Aage Clausen of the Political Science Department of the University of Wisconsin for assistance with this problem.

Name	Party	State			1	2	3	4	5	6
Harlan	R	Ia.	0		*	*	*	*	0	0
Pomeroy	R	Kan.	0		0	*	0	*	*	*
Grimes	R	Ia.	0		*	0	*	*	*	*
Chandler	R	Mich.	0		*	*	*	*	*	*
Wilkinson	R	Minn.	0		*	*	*	*	*	*
Trumbull	R	Ill.	0		*	0	*	*	*	*
King	R	N.Y.	0		*	*	*	*	*	*
Wade	R	Ohio	0	x	*	*	*	*	–	*
Wilmot	R	Penn.	0		*	0	*	*	*	0

* = pattern vote; –x = deviant vote (error); 0 = absent. Forty-six other roll calls from the original selection fitted into this scale. Missing senators voted in less than half of the divisions shown here. Coefficient of reproducability = .99.

Voting Key: 1—Final vote on S. 351, supplementary to the act for emancipation in the District of Columbia.

2—Final vote on S. 394, to amend the act calling forth the militia.

3—Sumner's motion to amend S. 351 by inserting, "That in all judicial proceedings . . . there shall be no exclusion of any witness on account of color."

4—Sherman's amendment to S. 394, inserting, "who . . . shall owe service or labor to any person who, . . . levied war or has borne arms against the United States . . ."

5—Sumner's amendment to S. 365, providing for emancipation in the state of West Virginia.

6—King's amendment to the confiscation bill, S. 151, inserting, "persons in the present insurrection levying war against the United States or adhering to their enemies . . ."

A rank-order list of this sort derived from Guttman scaling tells us (if we accept the assumptions of the scaling technique) that one senator was more extreme in his approach to a category of legislation than was another, but it does not divide the legislators into self-conscious groups. Some scholars have tried to solve this problem by dividing scale rankings into thirds or by designating one or more votes within a scale as boundaries. Both systems are arbitrary and I have instead worked out cluster blocs, using the percentages of agreement between every possible pair of senators in the voting on the eighty-seven roll calls on slavery and confiscation in my original selection. Such agreement scores showed considerable harmony among senators like King, Wilmot, Wilkinson, Chandler, and Wade, who stood at the Radical end of the scalogram rank order, and a considerably lower agreement among these men and a group which included Fessenden, Foster and a few other New Englanders who also agreed among themselves very strongly and appeared in the center of the scaling rank order. We can regard these two groups in a sense as the nuclei of the Radical and Moderate Republicans, with other senators forming an outer fringe in both factions. The boundaries of these groups suggested a cutting point in the scale ranking that yielded seventeen Radicals and fourteen Moderates. In this division the marginal Radicals agreed in their voting with the other Radicals substantially more than with the Moderates.[29]

Table II

Republican Radicals and Moderates

Radicals		Moderates	
Chandler (Mich.)	Morrill (Me.)	Anthony (R.I.)	Foster (Conn.)
Clark (N.H.)	Pomeroy (Kan.)	Browning (Ill.)	Harris (N.Y.)
Foot (Vt.)	Sumner (Mass.)	Collamer (Vt.)	Howe (Wis.)
Grimes (Ia.)	Trumbull (Ill.)	Cowan (Penn.)	H. S. Lane (Ind.)
Hale (N.H.)	Wade (O.)	Dixon (Conn.)	Sherman (O.)
Harlan (Ia.)	Wilkinson (Minn.)	Doolittle (Wis.)	Simmons (R.I.)
Howard (Mich.)	Wilmot (Penn.)	Fessenden (Me.)	Ten Eyck (N.J.)
King (N.Y.)	Wilson (Mass.)		
J. H. Lane (Kan.)			

Having divided the Republicans into Radicals and Moderates by using the scales and cluster blocs found in the original selection of eighty-seven roll calls on slavery and confiscation, I could then compute the index of disagreement of each of the 368 roll calls under study. In all there were fifty-eight roll calls in which the disagreement

[29] Some Radical and Moderate Republican Agreement Scores*

	King	Wilmot	Wilkinson	Chandler	Wade	Morrill	Sumner	Collamer	Foster	Anthony	Simmons	Fessenden
King												
Wilmot	97											
Wilkinson	96	98										
Chandler	94	90	91									
Wade	93	93	96	90								
Morrill	89	91	94	88	89							
Sumner	89	86	89	90	81	92						
Collamer	69	63	66	67	74	78	69					
Foster	68	62	68	69	71	81	72	95				
Anthony	68	64	65	69	72	74	71	92	91			
Simmons	55	58	59	55	60	74	61	90	91	93		
Fessenden	68	67	68	67	68	85	74	87	90	86	95	
Cowan	42	36	34	46	39	44	48	69	65	77	71	63

*Per cent agreement in 87 votes on slavery and confiscation; absences are ignored. The cluster-bloc pairing suggests that the Radical who was closest in his voting to the Moderates was Senator Clark, whose average agreement with the men above him in the matrix (the other Radicals) was 83 per cent, and with the Moderates 77 per cent. The scalogram percentile rankings drop Howard below Clark. Howard's mean pairing score with other Radicals was 80 per cent and with the Moderates only 65 per cent. Such variation is attributable to the fact that absences are handled somewhat differently in the cluster bloc and scaling procedures and to the fact that the mean percentile method of ranking is by no means precise since large numbers of tie scores are involved. The only senator

ranged between forty and one hundred.[30] These fifty-eight roll calls delimit the areas of major conflict between Moderate and Radical Republicans in the Senate during the second session.

Much of the disagreement between Radical and Moderate Republicans was, of course, related to emancipation and to the methods by which this might be achieved. During the discussion of Senate Bill 108, providing for the emancipation of slaves in the District of Columbia, Davis of Kentucky proposed that all individuals who were freed under this act should be colonized and that an appropriation should be made for that purpose. Doolittle moved to amend this, allowing all of the freed men of the District to choose whether or not they wished to emigrate. His amendment specified Haiti or Liberia as the destination of the emigrants or "such other country . . . as the President of the United States" might detemine, and limited the expenditures in each individual case to $100. The vote on both the Doolittle amendment and on the amended Davis amendment provoked substantial disagreement between Radicals and Moderates.

In the debate on Senate Bills 384 and 394, to amend the act calling forth the militia, Grimes offered an amendment designed to free the mother, wife and children of those of African descent who served the Union under the amended law, as well as the colored soldier or laborer himself. Moderate colleagues and Border State men opposed this amendment, suggesting that it should apply only to the slaves of traitors, that it should not touch the slaves of loyal slaveowners, or at least that loyal owners in the Border States should be recompensed for losses under it. Eight roll calls on various aspects of this matter produced disagreement of considerable strength. In a more direct blow at the institution of slavery in the Border States, Sumner tried to amend the West Virginia admission act by striking the limited emancipation clause, which provided that all children were to be born free, and substituting the provision that there should be neither slavery nor involuntary servitude in the new state except as criminal punishment. The ringing language of the Northwest Ordinance and

---

to present a real problem in classification was Senator Dixon. Historians usually consider him a Moderate, as he apparently did himself, but both scaling and clustering procedures ranked him among the Radicals. When a cluster-bloc matrix was prepared that counted absences as a third way of agreement between legislators, Dixon's average agreement with the Radicals fell to less than 60 per cent, although it was still somewhat higher than his average agreement with the Moderates. Dixon apparently absented himself on some embarrassing roll calls and I have therefore counted him among the Moderates, although this imparted a slightly conservative bias to the calculation of the index of disagreement between Radicals and Moderates.

[30] A list of these roll calls is available on request from the author.

of the Wilmot Proviso may have stirred proud nostalgia in many a Republican heart but not one Moderate voted for it.

Various divisive motions related to the disabilities of color, although the implications of the roll calls doubtless ran deeper on occasion. As Senator Clark tried, by amendment, to substitute the select committee version of the confiscation bill in place of the confiscation bill from the House, Sumner attempted to add the words "and in all proceedings under this act there shall be no exclusion of any witness on account of color," to one clause of the senate bill. Almost a full complement of Radicals supported Sumner's amendment and the Moderates massed in opposition to it. When Sumner also tried to attach this amendment both to House Bill 390, "in relation to the competency of witnesses in trials of equity and admiralty," and to a senate bill relating to the judiciary, he encountered strong Moderate opposition in the first instance and less in the second. Radical faced Moderate again when the senators voted on the Border State proposition to amend a naval appropriations bill by barring the use of slaves on the works of the naval service.

The Republican senators disagreed sharply among themselves in the debates on confiscation during the last four months of the session. The discussion focused first on the Trumbull bill, S. 151, which the Illinois senator reported from the judiciary committee. A compromise measure, S. 310, which a select committee under the chairmanship of Senator Clark drafted was considered next and then House Bill 471. Due mainly to the efforts of Moderates, aided by votes from the Border States, the Senate used the amendment process to substitute S. 310 for the bill from the House. Two major questions were involved in the debates: (1) Could Congress reach the property of rebels under powers opened to it by the war crisis or must it be bound by constitutional restrictions on the punishment of treason? (2) What categories of southerners ought to lose their property under the law? The Radicals in general supported the broad application of a law based on the war power; most Moderates fought for judicial processes which they believed were in accord with the treason clause of the constitution and wished to specify limited categories of southerners to whom the law was to apply. Senators introduced various major amendments during the debates and the parliamentary maneuvering was reflected in numerous disagreements between the Radicals and Moderates on procedural matters. In sum, the members of the two groups disagreed substantially in eleven roll calls during the debates on confiscation and the conflict persisted even into the vote on a motion that the Senate withdraw its amendment to the House Bill after the House had asked for a conference committee.

The division between Moderates and Radicals sometimes was revealed in the discussion of matters that at first glance do not relate directly to slavery or confiscation. A bloc of Moderates supported Senator Davis when he tried to amend House Bill 371, "to prescribe an oath of office . . .," so as to exempt congressmen from its operation. Moderates in some number also supported Henderson's amendment to the same bill, changing the affirmation, ". . . I have never voluntarily borne arms against the United States . . .," by striking "borne arms" and replacing it by the phrase "levied war." When Sumner tried to amend the internal revenue bill by inserting an additional section that taxed slave holders at the rate of $5.00 for each slave between the ages of ten and sixty, his action inspired a flurry of opposition and counterproposals which generated substantial disagreement between the Republican factions. So, too, did the effort of John Sherman to win reconsideration of a 50 per cent reduction in the cotton tax and Sumner's attempt to strike the tax on book-making materials.

The Radicals and Moderates disagreed in four votes dealing with the seating of Benjamin Stark, the Copperhead senator who replaced Baker of Oregon. A similar division appeared in four roll calls relating to the organization, or emoluments, of the armed forces. It was seen also when Senator Harris attempted to have Senate Bill 200, to establish provisional governments in certain cases, made a special order; on an amendment of Senator Grimes to Senate Bill 89, changing the boundaries of Federal judicial districts; in the case of two votes relating to the water and gas utilities of the District of Columbia; on Trumbull's motion to strike the second section of the extradition treaty with Mexico; and on a motion of Hale concerning the dead letter office. Finally, as the legislators reached mid-June, 1862, the same pattern of Radical in opposition to Moderate appeared in seven votes concerning adjournment and the operation of the Senate rules.

The disagreement indices provide us with some evidence of the duration as well as the intensity of disagreement during the session. Three votes revealed substantial disagreement between Radicals and Moderates during January of 1862 but in June there were nineteen, and in considerably less than a month of debate during July, there were seventeen such confrontations. However, every vote in which the index rose to eighty-five or better occurred in July. Party harmony was obviously in serious jeopardy as the session closed. Although we are tempted to emphasize the confiscation issue and the emancipation of slaves in the District of Columbia in discussing the achievements of Congress during this session, the sharpest disagreement between Radicals and Moderates did not develop in the roll calls on these measures but rather when the senators voted on the emancipation clause of the bills to amend the act calling forth the militia and on Sumner's amendment to provide unlimited emancipation in the new state of West Virginia. The votes on these issues produced disagreement indices that ranged from eighty-five to one hundred.

Although the senators might have explained their differences in terms of constitutional interpretation or conscience, we, as historians, inevitably ask ourselves if the differences between Radical and Moderate Republicans are explainable in terms of the conditioning which these men experienced in the years before the Civil War. Ralph Waldo Emerson was playing this game when he wrote in his journal:

The Unitarians, born Unitarians, have a pale, shallow religion, but the Calvinist, born and reared under his vigorous, ascetic, scowling creed, and then ripened into a Unitarian, becomes powerful . . . So it is in politics. A man must have had the broad, audacious Democratic party for his nursing-mother, and be ripened into a Free-Soiler, to be efficient. . . .[31]

Emerson's "Law" does have some predictive value when applied to the Republican senators of this session. Of seven former Democrats among the Republicans, six were Radicals, including four of the most Radical complexion, and only Doolittle was a Moderate. Among the senators of Whig antecedents, men who had made some striking commitment to the antislavery cause before 1854 seem in general to have been more extreme than those who made their public commitment in 1854 or thereafter.[32]

In distinguishing between Radicals and Moderates you will remember that I have not arbitrarily selected one or several votes and posited that all who voted one way or another on this limited selection were Radicals or Moderates. Instead I have been concerned with voting frequencies over a rather considerable number of roll calls. This reflects my feeling that it is unreasonable to expect the members of even a closely knit faction to vote together all of the time. And the high disagreement roll calls provide numerous examples of deviation. Sherman, seldom, if ever, considered a Radical, pressed doggedly for the more severe House version of the confiscation bill in preference

[31] Edward W. Emerson and Waldo E. Forbes, *Journals of Ralph Waldo Emerson, 1820-1876* (Boston, 1913), IX, 407-408. Some of Emerson's illustrations do not actually fit his pattern but the hypothesis is an interesting one.

[32] Basic biographical data were drawn from the *Biographical Directory of the American Congress* (Washington, seriatim); Allen Johnson (ed.), *The Dictionary of American Biography* (New York, 1928+); *The National Cyclopedia of American Biography* (New York, 1892+). When a senator was not listed in the *Dictionary of American Biography*, state and local biographical directories were consulted. Periodical literature and book-length biographies dealing with the senators are uneven in both quantity and quality. There are no published biographies of some of the senators; others are the subjects of a number of studies. Such material has been used wherever possible.

to the select committee's compromise measure. Of the Radicals, only Wade joined the Moderates in opposition to Sumner's amendment to the West Virginia admission bill although he termed his vote "very harsh and unsavory."[33] The lion could on occasion lie down with the lamb.

Was there any relation between the sectionalism of East and West and the disagreement between Radicals and Moderates in the Republican party? We have already noted that east-west sectionalism was most apparent in the voting on national economic issues, but in a number of votes relating to the South there was some alignment of western Republicans in opposition to eastern Republicans. There are various ways of examining this question. If the Republican Radicals were primarily eastern or western in constituency, roll calls showing a high sectional disagreement between eastern and western men should also have a high index of disagreement between Radicals and Moderates. Ten roll calls are common to the list of forty-six votes in which eastern and western Republicans differed substantially and the group of fifty-eight roll calls that show substantial disagreement between Radicals and Moderates.

We can attack the problem more simply by examining the division of eastern and western Republican senators between the Radical and Moderate factions of the party. Table III shows that slightly more than half of the eastern Republicans were Moderates and a somewhat larger proportion of western Republicans were Radicals. Antislavery sentiment in the West is sometimes linked to eastern origins and Table IV presents place of birth as a possible variable.

For what it is worth, the Republican senator most apt to be extreme

Table III°
Sections and Radicalism

	Radicals		Moderates	
Eastern Republican Senators (17)	8	47%	9	53%
Western Republican Senators (14)	9	64%	5	36%

°The contingency coefficient gamma is −.34.

Table IV°
Birth and Radicalism

	Radicals		Moderates	
Republican Senators of Eastern Birth (26)	15	58%	11	42%
Republican Senators of Western Birth (5)	2	40%	3	60%

°Gamma is .34 again.

[33] *Congressional Globe*, 37 Cong., 2 sess., p. 3308.

in his views toward the South and its institutions was a western senator of eastern origins; seven of the nine senators who fitted this description were Radicals (78 per cent). The senator most apt to be a Republican Moderate on the other hand was a western senator of western birth; three out of five, or 60 per cent, in this category were Moderates. But given the relatively small numbers of men involved, the percentage differences that support a sectional interpretation of the disagreement between Radicals and Moderates are rather small.

The fact that there were proportionately more Radicals in the West has sometimes made it difficult for historians to decide whether the sectionalism of East and West or the division between Radicals and Moderates most influenced a particular vote. The sectional aspect of the voting on the colonization amendment to the bill providing for emancipation of the slaves in the District of Columbia has been emphasized recently but roll call analysis seems to show that we should more appropriately view the issue as an aspect of factionalism between Radical and Moderate Republicans in the Senate.[34]

Historians have toyed with the idea that the Republican Radicals not only agreed strongly among themselves on southern policy but that they were peculiarly the spokesmen of northeastern industrialism.[35] We have in general rejected this thesis in recent years and there is little support for it in this research. We can, however, argue that some Republican senators agreed strongly with each other during the second session of the Thirty-seventh Congress both in their voting on slavery and confiscation and on the national economic program of the Republican party. Men like Fessenden, Collamer, Foster, and Anthony tended to agree much of the time, whether the subjects under debate were slavery and confiscation or economic measures of national import. Agreeing strongly with them on economic matters were some of the marginal Radicals from New England, particularly Foot and Clark. If any group of senators can be described as consistently cohesive it was the nucleus of New England Moderates.

Having examined some of the dimensions of geographical bloc and party faction, we can return to the question of whether the historian is justified in emphasizing the internecine conflicts of the Republicans or whether he should stress rather the importance of party and the basic agreement among Republicans. We have seen that eastern and

[34] See Voegeli, "Northwest and the Race Issue," 235-251. I discuss this matter in more detail in an unpublished paper, "Senators, Sectionalism and the 'Western' Measures of the Republican Party."

[35] See Donald, "Devils Facing Zionwards," pp. 72-73. I find it difficult to interpret T. Harry Williams', *Lincoln and the Radicals* (Madison, 1941), in this light, but it is applied explicitly to the reconstruction years by Howard K. Beale in his article "The Tariff and Reconstruction," *American Historical Review*, XXXV (1930), 276-294, especially 276.

western Republicans differed substantially in forty-six roll calls and that Radical Republican similarly opposed Moderate Republican in fifty-eight votes, with some overlap in the categories. By comparison, the Republican and Democratic parties differed by 40 per cent or more of the total disagreement possible in 161 roll calls. Restating the matter in slightly different terms, a majority of Republicans opposed a majority of Democrats in 180 of the 368 voting divisions. Of the eighty-seven roll calls in my original selection of votes on slavery and confiscation, sixty-five showed a majority of Republicans opposed to a majority of Democrats, and only twenty-one revealed a disagreement index between Moderate and Radical Republicans of substantial size. In these crude terms party was indeed more important than factionalism.

We cannot leave the matter there, however. Howard W. Allen and Jerome M. Clubb calculated the amount of party voting in a total of some twelve hundred votes on the most controversial issues considered in the senates of the Sixty-first, Sixty-second and Sixty-third Congresses, 1909-1915, when the winds of progressivism were blowing strongly. Since Allen and Clubb sifted out some votes on less controversial matters and I considered all roll calls the comparison cannot be exact, but the percentage ranged from 60 to 79 per cent in those congresses, with a mean of 71 per cent.[36] In the second session of the senate of the Thirty-seventh Congress the percentage of party votes in the selection of eighty-seven roll calls on slavery and confiscation issues was seventy-five but this figure drops to 50 per cent when all 368 roll calls are considered. Relatively speaking, party was apparently less significant in the voting of this session than on the more important issues of Progressivism. On the other hand, "party votes," as a percentage of all Senate votes, represented only 45 per cent on the average during the Eighty-fourth through the Eighty-eighth Congresses, 1955-1964.[37]

Yet, if party lines were drawn very sharply on the issues of slavery and confiscation during the second session of the Thirty-seventh Congress, one out of every four roll calls on such matters did reveal substantial disagreement between Republican Radicals and Moderates. Traces of this division appeared in many other votes as well. Basically, the differences between Radical and Moderate structured the voting of Republicans in one major category of legislation and also affected

[36] Jerome M. Clubb and Howard W. Allen, "Party Loyalty in the United States Senate in the Taft and Wilson Years." (Mimeographed, Inter-university Consortium for Political Research, Ann Arbor), pp. 1-29. See particularly pp. 7, 8 and fn. 8, p. 28.

[37] Ibid., p. 8, drawn by Clubb and Allen from the Congressional Quarterly Almanac.

a number of other types of legislative action that were only indirectly related to the southern question. Nor should we forget that the division between Radical and Moderate was a more important one than was the distinction between eastern and western legislators.

The relative cohesion of the Democrats and the Republicans has some bearing on the significance of party among the Republicans. In a recent article Leonard Curry has argued that the Democrats were more cohesive during the Thirty-seventh Congress than were the Republicans.[38] My voting analysis of the second session Senate supports his conclusion. The mean Democratic cohesion in my original selection of slavery and confiscation votes was sixty-nine and that of the Republicans was sixty-three. In eighty-six divisions on the major national economic legislation of this session, Democratic cohesion was sixty-six and that of the Republicans was thirty-eight. We have to discount this finding somewhat, however, because the Democratic group was small and absenteeism among its members much more marked than among the Republicans, even after adjustment is made for the illness of several Democratic senators.

To divide the roll calls of this session into those that show sectionalism, those that illustrate the conflict of Radical against Moderate Republican, and those that illustrate party differences is to disregard a considerable number of votes. There were 132 roll calls (again with some overlapping of other categories) in which Republican cohesiveness was sixty or below and in which the likeness indices of East against West and of Radical versus Moderate were quite high. In these divisions, apparently, the idiosyncracies of the individual constituency or senator were asserted or subregional voting patterns became important. Although it is possible to build some scales from these roll calls, the scalograms include a relatively small number of votes and it is difficult to identify underlying continua of attitude. As I move further into the task of calculating correlations between the various scales I may be able to refine my description of these votes.

In this session of the Civil War Senate, party obviously was an important voting determinant but we cannot disregard the significance of geographical bloc or party faction either, nor the importance of the individual senator and his constituency. And, of course, the decision to vote in sectional grouping or party faction may have come only after much agonizing deliberation. Obviously there is much to be said in support of the interpretations of both David Donald and T. Harry Williams concerning Republican factionalism, but we will profit, I believe, in the future by treating the houses of Congress dur-

[38] Leonard P. Curry, "Congressional Democrats: 1861-1863," *Civil War History*, XII (1966), 220-221.

ing the Civil War as political systems in which a variety of determinants of voting behavior were interacting.

This particular senate was hardly a classic illustration of the two-party system at work, with its strong Republican majority, its reeling Democracy, its homeless border Unionists and the unusual pressures of constituency and public opinion that played upon the senators. Comparison with a one-party legislature or a multi-party system may be more revealing than exposition of the conventional two-party model. But party objectives were by no means forgotten; Democrats hoped for a comeback and many Republicans had both the present and the future in mind as they labored during this session. The doctrinaire Hale scoffed that the department of agriculture bill was not the wish of the men who leaned "upon their plow-handles; but . . . the men who want them to take their hands off the plow-handle and vote for them at the ballot-box."[39] The more practical politicians of the new party prevailed against such criticism and the Thirty-seventh Congress bequeathed a formidable legislative legacy to the people of a reunited nation.

[39] *Congressional Globe*, 37 Cong., 2 sess., p. 2014.

WHO WERE THE SENATE RADICALS?

Edward L. Gambill

HISTORIANS' ATTEMPTS TO deal coherently with congressional Radical Republicans during the "Critical Year"—1866—illustrate the inadequacies often produced by traditional historical analysis of American political behavior. Specifically, they reveal the lack of attention devoted by political historians to systematic classification, and how this inattention can, in turn, produce misleading generalizations. They also point up the opportunities for applying research techniques developed by other disciplines.

Scholarly investigation of Radical Republicanism in 1866 dates from the turn of the century and the work of James Ford Rhodes.[1] For Rhodes, the Radicals were a handful of men, typified by Charles Sumner in the Senate and Thaddeus Stevens in the House, who stood well in advance of northern opinion in their demands for political reconstruction of the South. Rhodes did not endow these men with the cohesion of a cabal. While they essentially sought the same basic goal of Negro suffrage, he said, they displayed marked differences at the outset of the Thirty-ninth Congress about the extent to which this goal might be realized and how it might best be achieved. That the majority of northerners eventually endorsed the Radical goal was not the result of a highly disciplined political offensive but rather stemmed from the blunders of President Andrew Johnson and southern leaders.

With the publication in 1930 of Howard K. Beale's *The Critical Year*,[2] interpretation of the Radicals received a new emphasis which was to remain dominant for over two decades. The germ of Professor Beale's thesis was a concept of reality owed to the influence of Charles Beard. For Beale, as for other Beardians, historical reality was "hard," "hidden," and in the last analysis, economic. The factor which had

[1] James Ford Rhodes, *History of the United States from the Compromise of 1850 to . . . 1887*, V-VI (New York, 1909, 1915).
[2] Howard K. Beale, *The Critical Year: A Study of Andrew Johnson and Reconstruction* (New York, 1930).

brought the Radicals together was their common position as advance
agents for an incipient industrial order. Their basic goals were the
securing of tax benefits and protective tariffs for industry, the main-
tenance of the new national banking system, refunding of the federal
debt in hard money, and the commercial exploitation of southern and
western economic resources.

Beale's interpretation led him to view the Radicals as a conspiratorial group. As they could not and did not openly avow their "real"
aims in demands for political reconstruction of the South, they were
necessarily evolving their program in secrecy behind the scenes. This,
in turn, implied a high degree of cohesion and group discipline. Thus,
Beale maintained, the dynamics of the Critical Year lay in a "strongly
organized Radical minority hard at work to covert a passive but un-
convinced majority—a minority fully aware of the difficulties of the
task, but determined to win if indefatigable labor and earnestness of
purpose could bring victory."[3]

Beale's thesis has recently undergone searching criticism from a
number of historians. Professors Irwin Unger, Robert Sharkey, Stanley Coben, and Eric McKitrick have all argued that the Radicals could
not have been united by common economic bonds.[4] There were sharp
conflicts, these scholars observed, in economic interests among Radical
legislators and northern businessmen alike. High protectionist manu-
facturing interests in Pennsylvania and Ohio tended inevitably toward
a soft-money philosophy. New England proponents of hard money,
conversely, generally supported a low tariff program. Moreover, few
northern businessmen were interested in southern investments in the
early postwar years, and these few were hostile to Radical Republicanism.

With the attack on Beale's interpretation came renewed emphasis
on the political demands of the Radicals as the essential element distinguishing them from their northern colleagues. "The only common
denominator of 1866 that united the Radicals," asserted John and La-
Wanda Cox, ". . . was their determination that the South should not
be reinstated into the Union until there were adequate guarantees
that the slaves liberated by the nation should enjoy the rights of free
men."[5] McKitrick, in turn, found the Radicals of early 1866 distin-

---

[3] *Ibid.,* p. vii.

[4] Irwin Unger, "Businessmen and Specie Resumption," *Political Science Quarterly,* LXVI (1959), 46-70; Robert Sharkey, *Money, Class and Party: An Economic
Study of Civil War and Reconstruction* (Baltimore, 1959); Stanley Coben, "Northeastern Business and Radical Reconstruction: A Re-examination," *Mississippi
Valley Historical Review,* XLVI (1959), 67-90; Eric McKitrick, *Andrew Johnson
and Reconstruction* (Chicago, 1960).

[5] John and LaWanda Cox, *Politics, Principle and Prejudice, 1865-1866: Dilemma
of Reconstruction America* (New York, 1963), pp. 209-210.

guished by the promotion of Negro suffrage, their demands for the exclusion of the southern states, and their political opposition to Andrew Johnson.

The accent on Radical cohesion went the way of the economic interpretation. For McKitrick, "they were radical for different objects and for different reasons; they should not be endowed," he declared, "with too much retroactive solidarity or group purpose. We find no program, no unity, no 'grim confidence,' and certainly no 'fierce joy.' For anything more than a kind of irritable confusion the evidence is extremely sketchy."[6]

With this deemphasis came a downgrading of the Radicals as primary causal agents in the political drama of the Critical Year. Under the pens of McKitrick and the Coxes, President Johnson once again assumed a position at the center of the historical stage. Unlike Rhodes, however, McKitrick also elevated northern Democrats to a crucial role in undermining Moderate Republican proposals for the South. Implicit in McKitrick's idea of a Democratic offensive is a high degree of cohesion in that party.

With McKitrick's study, historiography on the Critical Year came full circle. Despite the profusion of old and new literature, however, meager attention has been devoted to several problems which appear crucial to the interpretations advanced. In the first place, emphasis has been given to explaining *what* the Radicals were, at the expense of determining *who* they were. Yet it would seem reasonably clear that these two matters are so closely interrelated that neglect of one raises serious doubts about conclusions regarding the other. Second, generalizations about the cohesion of various political groups in 1866 often appear to be postulated in a vacuum. Meaningful statements about supposedly tightly knit political units can hardly be made when the frame of reference is some abstract standard rather than the specific attitudes of the individuals involved.

To determine who the Radicals were—and only then their cohesiveness relative to other groups—requires the construction of some form of attitude scale against which the various degrees of political opinion can be measured. Speeches, reminiscences, editorials, and private correspondence are materials ill-suited for this task, since the distribution of such records among the persons under study is at best uneven. Furthermore, the difficulties involved in determining group relationships from these conventional sources are practically insurmountable.

In contrast, congressional voting records offer a fund of material readily adaptable to the problem. Even members of Congress who seldom gave speeches demonstrated their attitudes toward issues by

[6] McKitrick, *Andrew Johnson and Reconstruction*, p. 54.

their votes. Thus, a series of roll call votes is the most complete source available on the range of congressional attitudes. Such statements of opinion are also in a form amenable to systematic investigation.

The problem then resolves itself into how a variety of roll calls can be sorted out with respect to the issues and how they can then be ordered to delineate degrees of opinion on each issue. The "Guttman scalogram" method now commonly used by political scientists provides a solution. With this technique, related roll calls can be grouped, and when the respective votes are arranged in a scale the variations of opinion on a given issue become clear. The positions of individual congressmen, in relation to their colleagues, can thereby be easily observed.[7]

Before applying the Guttman scale to this problem, however, some criterion must be established to isolate the issues which separated Radicals from other congressmen. The criterion adopted here is that traditionally used as a test of Radicalism: political reconstruction. It might be noted that even Beale worked within the context of political issues and only assumed the economic base; thus he also defined Radicalism by the "ephemeral" reconstruction controversy.

To determine the attitude spectrum of senators on reconstruction during the Thirty-ninth Congress, roll call votes recorded in the *Senate Journal* were employed. These votes, in turn, produced nine "scales" covering such issues as southern representation, Negro rights, the Freedman's Bureau, civil law, control over political appointments, and the Reconstruction Act of March 2, 1867.[8] The "scores" of individual senators on each scale were then added and the total divided by the highest possible Radical response. The end result, as depicted in the table below, is a single attitude index which gives average percentage ratings for those senators who appeared on more than half the scales. Extreme Radicals appear at the beginning of the list; Republican Conservatives and Democrats are at the end; Republican Moderates are in the center.[9]

As the index indicates, there is no clear breaking point which separates Radical and Moderate Republican "blocs." The picture is somewhat clearer, however, as one moves toward the other end of the list. There is a steady progression away from Radicalism through the cen-

---

[7] For a full discussion of the Guttman scale technique see George M. Belnap, "A Method for Analyzing Legislative Behavior," *Midwest Journal of Political Science*, II (1958), 377-402.

[8] Further technical information on these scales is included in the appendix to this article.

[9] Thirteen senators, who appeared on less than half of the scales, are not included in the index. These are Cattell, Collamer, Edmunds, Fogg, Foot, Fowler, Frelinghuysen, Patterson (Dem.), Ross, Stockton (Dem.), Thayer, Tipton, and Wright (Dem.).

TABLE I

Senator	N*	%	Party	Senator	N*	%	Party
Wade	9	.967	R	Clark	7	.725	R
Sumner	9	.950	R	Grimes	8	.722	R
Chandler	9	.900	R	Creswell	5	.706	R
Pomeroy	9	.883	R	Foster	8	.701	R
Yates	9	.867	R	Sherman	9	.683	R
Morrill	8	.852	R	Lane (Kans.)	5	.649	R
Wilson	9	.850	R	Morgan	9	.633	R
Anthony	9	.833	R	Henderson	9	.617	R
Howard	9	.833	R	Willey	9	.567	R
Ramsey	9	.833	R	Van Winkle	9	.467	R
Trumbull	9	.817	R	Dixon	6	.465	R
Howe	9	.817	R	Doolittle	9	.317	R
Sprague	8	.807	R	Norton	7	.267	R
Fessenden	7	.804	R	McDougall	8	.204	D
Poland	9	.800	R	Hendricks	9	.100	D
Brown	6	.789	R	Johnson	5	.077	D
Nye	7	.784	R	Guthrie	8	.059	D
Conness	9	.783	R	Buckalew	9	.050	D
Lane (Ind.)	9	.783	R	Nesmith	7	.043	D
Cragin	7	.761	R	Riddle	7	.039	D
Stewart	9	.750	R	Davis	9	.017	D
Harris	7	.745	R	Cowan	5	.000	R
Kirkwood	7	.739	R	Saulsbury	8	.000	D
Williams	9	.733	R				

* The number of scales on which the individual's name appears.

ter of the index until Waitman T. Willey of West Virginia is reached. Below Willey there are two points which serve as possible divisions between Moderate and Conservative Republicans. It might also be noted here that James McDougall, a Democrat, was close to the Conservative Republicans while Edgar Cowan, a Republican, was at the extreme conservative end of the index.

Additional light is shed on the problem of the Republican Radicals when this index is compared with subjective conclusions derived from secondary material. The following are the names of senators assumed to be Radicals by several leading historians of the period:

Beale	*Randall and Donald*[10]	*McKitrick*
Wade	Wade	Wade
Sumner	Sumner	Sumner
Chandler	Chandler	Chandler
Wilson	Wilson	Wilson
Howard	Howe	Howard
Fessenden	Brown	Brown
Brown		

The number of discrepancies is substantial. If B. Gratz Brown, for example, can be classified as a Radical, then so can eight of his colleagues not mentioned by these historians. A partial explanation for the large proportion of omissions lies with the nature of the source material employed. There seems to be a definite tendency for these historians to cite those "Radicals" who frequently occupied the Senate floor while ignoring others who spoke infrequently. This is demonstrated by the number of pages in the *Congressional Globe* (first session) in which the senators appeared as speakers on reconstruction issues.[11]

TABLE 2

Senator	pages	Senator	pages
*Wade	120	*Howard	137
*Sumner	192	Ramsey	15
*Chandler	8	Trumbull	488
Pomeroy	72	*Howe	119
Yates	46	Sprague	2
Morrill	30	*Fessenden	268
*Wilson	234	Poland	16
Anthony	20	*Brown	12

* Designated as Radicals by Beale, Randall and Donald, and/or McKitrick.

Omissions, moreover, were not confined to the Radical end of the spectrum. Professor McKitrick, for example, overlooked two senators in identifying the Conservative Republicans. "In the Senate," he asserted, "of all the Republicans who might have held such a position only three actually did: James R. Doolittle of Wisconsin, Edgar Cowan of Pennsylvania, and James Dixon of Connecticut."[12] There is little reason to dispute the names cited, but the index indicates that Daniel Norton of Minnesota and Peter Van Winkle of West Virginia would then also have to be cited.

There are also several cases of overlapping classifications. Profes-

[10] James G. Randall and David Donald, *The Civil War and Reconstruction* (Boston, 1961).

[11] Debates on the admission of western territories to statehood are excluded.

[12] McKitrick, *Andrew Johnson and Reconstruction*, p. 81.

sors Beale, Randall and Donald, and McKitrick all depicted Lyman Trumbull as a Republican Moderate, and yet the Illinois senator occupies a more extreme position on the spectrum than B. Gratz Brown, who all four historians consider a Radical. The inclusion by Randall and Donald of Lot M. Morrill and William P. Fessenden in the Moderate camp provides additional conflicts with their list of Radicals. McKitrick also designated Fessenden as a Moderate but failed to cite Morrill.

What then can be said about where the dividing line between Radical and Moderate Republicans might be drawn? In the first place, any such decision would have to consider the commonly accepted assumption that the bulk of Republican senators were Moderates. If this assumption is correct, then Brown of Missouri would be a poor choice. Alexander Ramsey, on the other hand, meets the requirement while providing a minimal amount of conflict with senators historians have cited as Moderates. The breakdown of the groups would then be as follows:

TABLE 3

Radical Republicans	Moderate Republicans		Conservative Republicans	Democrats
Wade	Trumbull	Kirkwood	Van Winkle	McDougall
Sumner	Howe	Williams	Dixon	Hendricks
Chandler	Sprague	Clark	Doolittle	Johnson
Pomeroy	Fessenden	Grimes	Norton	Guthrie
Yates	Poland	Creswell	Cowan	Buckalew
Morrill	Brown	Foster		Nesmith
Wilson	Nye	Sherman		Riddle
Anthony	Conness	Lane (Kans.)		Davis
Howard	Lane (Ind.)	Morgan		Saulsbury
Ramsey	Cragin	Henderson		
	Stewart	Willey		
	Harris			

The problem now raised is the relative degree of cohesion of the designated groups. The following is a mathematical statement of the average divergence between senators in each congressional "bloc":

TABLE 4

Radical Republicans	.013 per cent
Moderate Republicans	.010 per cent
Conservative Republicans	.093 per cent
Democrats	.023 per cent

As the table indicates, Moderate Republicans were the most cohesive group in the Senate. Radical Republicans were less cohesive than the Moderates but demonstrated more unity than either Conservative Republicans or Democrats. It should be noted, however, that James McDougall alone accounted for much of the divergence among the Democrats and if he is excluded their cohesion would equal that of the Radical Republicans (.013 per cent). Edgar Cowan's extreme conservative position also exerted a similar effect on the Conservative Republicans, but if Cowan is excluded their degree of diversity (.050 per cent) would still remain much higher than that of the other groups. In any event, the group division suggested in Table 3 holds up well under the test of attitude cohesion.

Guttman scalogram analysis of the Senate's voting record in 1866 would seem to have provided an answer to the question, "Who were the Senate Radicals?" It also suggests the feasibility of a similar analysis of the House, and the technique might conceivably provide a fresh perspective on the relationship of congressional Radicalism to northern economic interests. Certainly the historiography of the Critical Year has reached a point where only such quantitative research may produce effective guidelines for further interpretation.

APPENDIX

SCALES USED

1. Southern representation, 10 roll calls, 9 scale types, C.R.=.967
2. Negro rights, 12 roll calls, 10 scale types, C.R.=.993
3. Negro rights, 11 roll calls, 9 scale types, C.R.=.994
4. Negro rights, 11 roll calls, 9 scale types, C.R.=.988
5. Freedman's Bureau, 14 roll calls, 7 scale types, C.R.=.991
6. Freedman's Bureau, 11 roll calls, 7 scale types, C.R.=.996
7. Civil law, 6 roll calls, 7 scale types, C.R.=.992
8. Political appointments, 7 roll calls, 7 scale types, C.R.=.992
9. Reconstruction Act of March 2, 1867, 10 roll calls, 4 scale types, C.R.=1.000

"RADICAL" POLITICAL AND ECONOMIC POLICIES:

The Senate, 1873-1877

Glenn M. Linden

SINCE THE LATE 1930's historians have shown an increased interest in the reconstruction period. Beginning with articles by Francis B. Simkins and Howard K. Beale and continuing with the work of C. Vann Woodward, T. Harry Williams, and David Donald, there has been much new evidence concerning the nature and achievements of reconstruction.[1] Slowly but surely the older traditional view as developed by James F. Rhodes, Charles W. Burgess, and William A. Dunning and popularized by Claude Bowers in *The Tragic Era* has been modified.

In no area of reconstruction is this revision more evident than in the increased attention being given to Radicals and Radicalism. In 1956, David Donald wrote a provocative essay in *Lincoln Reconsidered* in which he called for a reexamination of Radical Republicans and a reevaluation of their significance. "The Radical Republicans," he said, "were only one of the many factions that pulled for control of the Lincoln administrations. . . . Perhaps, then, it is time to discard the Malevolent Radical, along with the Copperhead Democrat and the Diabolical Southerner, as a stereotyped figure of evil."[2] In 1960, Eric McKitrick, in *Andrew Johnson and Reconstruction*, concluded that the Radical legend was the result of political partisanship and that it "once signified little more than the extreme position on any given issue, one which men could and did move in and out of with

---

[1] Francis B. Simkins, "New Viewpoints of Southern Reconstruction," *Journal of Southern History*, V (February, 1939), 49-61; Howard K. Beale, "On Rewriting Reconstruction History," *American Historical Review*, XLV (July, 1940), 807-827; C. Vann Woodward, *Reunion and Reaction; the Compromise of 1877 and the End of Reconstruction* (Boston, 1951); T. Harry Williams, "An Analysis of Some Reconstruction Attitudes," *Journal of Southern History*, XII (November, 1946), 469-486; David Donald, "The Scalawag in Mississippi Reconstruction," *Journal of Southern History*, IX (November, 1944), 447-460.

[2] David Donald, "The Radicals and Lincoln," *Lincoln Reconsidered* (New York, 1956), pp. 126-127.

surprising ease."[3] In 1963, the English historian W. R. Brock, in *An American Crisis*, attempted to divide Radicals from Moderates on the basis of a key vote in the House of Representatives on the Reconstruction Act of 1867. He found that "If Pennsylvania is left out of the account Radicalism appeared as the political programme of the more recently settled and rural areas; old settled areas, especially those with a number of developing towns and diversified economic activities, tended to be anti-Radical. Here perhaps is a hitherto unsuspected influence of the frontier upon American history."[4]

In 1965, David Donald, in *The Politics of Reconstruction 1863-1867*, attempted to identify Radicals and Moderates by the use of selected roll call votes in the House of Representatives. He found that a congressman's votes ". . . were determined less by abstract ideas than by the degree of strength and security each felt in his home district."[5] Thus the degree of Radicalism was proportionate to the strength of the Republican party in a congressman's constituency.

Harold Hyman's volume, *The Radical Republicans and Reconstruction* (1967), covered the years 1861-1870. It was Hyman's contention that Radicals remained true to certain basic principles throughout the entire period, especially protection and support of the Negro and his political condition. He stated that most Americans supported the Radicals in the 1860's but were unwilling to support them in the 1870's. "The altering concerns of their countrymen left the Radical remnant seriously out of phase with newer political currents. Radicals did not lose principles; most white Americans lost interest in those principles."[6]

While most of the research in the reconstruction period has been on its earlier years, it is becoming increasingly clear that many commonly accepted ideas about reconstruction may not be true for its later years. It is at least debatable whether Radicalism, once established as a program in the 1860's, did not change in the 1870's; whether the Radicals of earlier days were still committed to the same reconstruction program; and whether Radical strength remained constant in certain areas or if it did not begin to shift its base as a result of economic and political factors of the 1870's.

The traditional view of the last years of reconstruction, a view typi-

[3] Eric McKitrick, *Andrew Johnson and Reconstruction* (Chicago, 1960), p. 53.
[4] W. R. Brock, *An American Crisis: Congress and Reconstruction 1865-1867* (London, 1963), p. 73.
[5] David Donald, *The Politics of Reconstruction, 1863-1867* (Baton Rouge, 1965), pp. 81-82.
[6] Harold Hyman (ed.), *The Radical Republicans and Reconstruction 1861-1870* (Indianapolis, 1967), p. 522.

cal of the writings of many historians, may be briefly summarized as
follows:[7] As the mood of the nation changed, Radicals gradually lost
support for their economic and political policies. Those Radicals who
remained in Congress were under constant pressure and not only
were they unsuccessful in pressing for more legislation, they were
also unsuccessful in maintaining the programs already written into
law. Even the leadership of the Radicals changed. Charles Sumner
and Thaddeus Stevens, champions of Negro rights and of firm treatment of the South, were replaced by new leaders, like Roscoe Conkling and James Blaine, who were more concerned with economic gains
and the holding of political office than in idealistic programs. As Harold
Hyman has described this process: "Resting on oars or trying to back
water, Radical Republicans of prewar antislavery vintage observed
the new breed of recent recruits into Radicalism, 'regulars' within the
Grant forces in Congress, pick up the ways and means and even
some goals that Radicals had worked out since Sumter."[8] These new
leaders, we are told, were often political bosses or representatives of
various business interests, and their main concern was to complete
the organization of the Republican party around their own economic
interests. The idealism of the earlier period was replaced by a new
blend of cynicism and political realism. "With the decline," writes
Kenneth Stampp, "of the idealism and the disappearance of the realistic political and economic considerations that had supported it, radical reconstruction came to an end."[9]

This view of reconstruction, widely held by many historians, departs
from the interpretations of other writers, notably Charles A. Beard,
Howard K. Beale, and George Woolfolk. Beard, Beale and Woolfolk
consistently placed emphasis upon economic motives and policies as
being of primary importance throughout the period.[10] They focused
their attention not upon a decline of idealism or a loss of crusading
fervor, or even upon the changing leadership within the Republican
party. Rather they explained the developments of the 1870's in terms

[7] For some examples of his view, see: James Ford Rhodes, *History of the
United States from the Compromise of 1850 to the End of the Roosevelt Ad-
ministration* (1893-1906); Robert S. Henry, *The Story of Reconstruction* (1938);
Paul Buck, *The Road to Reunion* (1937); E. Merton Coulter, *The South During
Reconstruction, 1865-1877* (1947); John Hope Franklin, *Reconstruction after the
Civil War* (1961).

[8] Hyman (ed.), *The Radical Republicans,* p. 505.

[9] Kenneth Stampp, *The Era of Reconstruction, 1865-1877* (New York, 1965),
p. 213. Professor Stampp describes this process in detail on pp. 189-192 and 211-
213.

[10] Charles A. and Mary Beard, *The Rise of American Civilization* (New York,
1927); Howard K. Beale, *The Critical Year: A Study of Andrew Johnson and
Reconstruction* (New York, 1930); George Woolfolk, *The Cotton Regency: the
Northern Merchants and Reconstruction, 1865-1880* (New York, 1958).

of the Northeast imposing and maintaining economic controls upon the South until these policies were firmly established; then, and only then, was the South fully restored to the Union. It was their contention that economics triumphed over politics. A brief summary of their ideas will help to illustrate these points in more detail.

Beard, in his *The Rise of American Civilization* (1927) described reconstruction as a continuation of the Second American Revolution, —especially in the area of social and economic policies. He referred to a Radical minority in Congress which "sought to guard themselves as long as possible against the expected reaction."[11] Further, he stated that even in the 1870's there remained Radicals who sought to keep the surviving members of the planting aristocracy in complete subjection and that they were uniformly successful.

Beale, in *The Critical Year* (1930), continued this line of reasoning, arguing that the danger of the southern states returning to political prominence was that they would oust the new industrial class from power. In order to avoid this possibility, the South was kept out of power until the New England economic and social system and standards were firmly implanted. By the time the Radical domination of the South had spent itself, the new economic order was established beyond attack, and, as a result, the industrialized Northeast was triumphant over the agrarian South and West.

Woolfolk, in *The Cotton Regency* (1958), argued that northeastern business allied with midwestern business to exploit the South, and to fasten a system of credit controls upon it which "made the South open territory for the commercial ambitions of North and West."[12] The congressional Radicals provided a smokescreen behind which business consolidated itself. After 1880 the story was complete. . . . "industrial exploitation matured, and thus opened another story."[13]

From the foregoing summary it seems clear that there are fundamental differences of emphasis and interpretation about the nature and success of Radicalism in the last years of reconstruction. It is also evident that little direct attention has been given to these years except as an adjunct to the earlier period.[14]

It is the purpose of this paper to examine these years through the use of quantitative methods—a series of political and economic roll call votes of senators from March 4, 1873, to March 3, 1877. (The

---

[11] Beard, *Rise of American Civilization*, p. 121.
[12] Woolfolk, *Cotton Regency*, p. 9.   [13] *Ibid.*, p. 8.
[14] There is much useful research going on in the early years of reconstruction. It is indeed strange that so little attention is given to its later years. It would seem that changes during the last four years are significant enough to warrant careful analysis and it is obvious that these changes are of great relevance to later developments in both the North and South.

Forty-third and Forty-fourth Congresses). The votes on political measures will be examined first, then votes on economic measures, and finally a summary and comparison of the results with the views of the historians already discussed.

A total of forty-seven votes on political measures were examined (thirteen final votes and thirty-four votes on amendments).[15] Fifteen "Radicals," ten "Non-Radicals," and eight "Unaligned" senators who were still in the Senate were examined to determine their voting behavior and these results were compared with the position of their respective parties.[16] Those who remained in the Senate are listed in Table I.

TABLE I

Radicals		Non-Radicals	
Cameron, S.	Pa.	Bayard, J. A., Jr.	Del.
Carpenter, M. H.	Wisc.	Davis, H. G.	W.Va.
Chandler, Z.	Mich.	Hamilton, W. T.	Md.
Cragin, A. H.	N.H.	Hitchcock, P. W.	Nebr.
Edmunds, G. F.	Vt.	Kelly, J. K.	Ore.
Ferry, T. W.	Mich.	McCreery, T. C.	Ky.
Frelinghuysen, F. T.	N.J.	Saulsbury, W.	Del.
Hamlin, H.	Me.	Stevenson, J. W.	Ky.
Morrill, J. S.	Vt.	Stockton, J. P.	N.J.
Morton, O. H. P. T.	Ind.	Thurman, A. C.	Ohio
Patterson, J. W.	N.H.		
Pratt, D. D.	Ind.		
Ramsey, A.	Minn.		
Sherman, J.	Ohio		
Windom, W.	Minn.		

Unaligned	
Anthony, H. B.	R.I.
Conkling, R.	N.Y.
Howe, T. O.	Wisc.
Logan, J. A.	Ill.
Morrill, L. M.	Me.
Scott, J.	Pa.
Stewart, W. M.	Nev.
Wright, G. G.	Iowa

The results show that Radicals voted together on 401 out of 431 votes, or 93 per cent agreement; Non-Radicals 271 out of 303 votes, or 89 per cent agreement; and the Unaligned 225 out of 234 votes, or 96 per cent agreement. This high degree of unity would suggest an impressive degree of voting solidarity among each of the groups. However, when these results are compared with the party position on

[15] These measures include the Civil Rights Bill of 1874; Election and Count Act; Enforcement Acts; and the Electoral Votes of South Carolina.

[16] For a complete list of Radical, Non-Radical and Unaligned Senators, see Glenn M. Linden, "Radicals and Economic Policies, 1861-1873," *The Journal of Southern History*, XXXII (May, 1966).

the same measures, they do not seem so striking. The Republican senators voted together on 816 out of 894 votes (93 per cent agreement), while the Democratic senators voted together on 524 out of 549 votes (96 per cent agreement). From these roll call votes, it seems that senators voted most of the time in agreement with members of their own party and, secondly, that there is no significant difference in voting behavior to be found among Radical, Non-Radical, and Unaligned groups. It is also clear that the Republican party controlled the voting on both amendments and final votes, while the Democratic party was consistently outvoted. On the forty-seven votes, the Republican party was in the majority forty-three times, while the Democratic party was in the majority only ten times (on six roll calls the two parties voted together). It is apparent that the Republican senators consistently controlled voting on political measures and that they maintained a high degree of unity, while the Democratic senators also voted together but were unable to pass many of their measures.

In an effort to determine the extent and significance of possible politico-economic relationships, a total of fifty-five roll calls on a series of economic measures were analyzed with special attention to the Radicals, Non-Radicals, and Unaligned groups.[17] The results showed that Radicals voted together on 330 out of 493 individual votes (15 senators on 55 roll calls), or 67 per cent of the time; Non-Radicals on 270 out of 337 votes (10 senators on 55 roll calls), or 77 per cent; and Unaligned 223 out of 291 votes, or 77 per cent (8 senators on 55 roll calls). On these same measures the overall position of the members of the Republican party was 73 per cent, or 6 per cent higher than the Radicals, while the position of the Democratic party was 77 per cent, the same as the Non-Radicals and Unaligned. These figures indicate that there was less agreement among Radicals on economic policies than there was on political issues; there was a somewhat higher degree of unity among the Non-Radicals and Unaligned. This analysis of votes did not reveal a significant relationship between voting on political lines and voting on economic lines, whether in terms of groups or parties.

To see if there was a more pronounced pattern, the same fifty-five votes were rearranged according to the geographical area represented. In these terms, the New England senators voted together on 287 out of 332 individual votes, (11 senators on 55 roll calls), or 86 per cent; the Mid-Atlantic 166 out of 212 votes (7 senators on 55

---

[17] These measures include the Redemption Act of 1874; Inflation Act of 1874; Resumption of Species Bill of 1874; Sinking Fund Bill of 1875; Public Lands Disposition Bill of 1876; and the Pacific Railway Bill, 1877.

roll calls), or 78 per cent; the Midwest on 516 out of 700 votes (21 senators on 55 roll call votes), or 74 per cent; the Border region 281 out of 391 votes (12 senators on 55 roll call votes), or 77 per cent; the Pacific Coast 183 out of 238 votes (7 senators on 55 roll calls), or 77 per cent; and the South on 533 out of 672 votes (22 senators on 55 roll calls), or 79 per cent. These figures present a more consistent pattern. In particular, the New England senators appear to have voted alike on economic measures to a significant degree—86 per cent. This is in marked contrast to the voting of Radicals on the same measures—67 per cent. Also, the senators from the Midwest and South voted together more often than did the Non-Radicals or Unaligned, though by a narrow margin.

In an effort to find a more definite voting pattern, the same fifty-five votes were arranged according to party within each geographical section. On this basis, New England Republicans voted together 86 per cent of the time; Mid-Atlantic Republicans 81 per cent and Democrats 100 per cent; Midwest Republicans 75 per cent and Democrats 82 per cent; Border Republicans 68 per cent and Democrats 75 per cent; Pacific Coast Republicans 83 per cent and Democrats 86 per cent; and southern Republicans 85 per cent and Democrats 82 per cent. In four of the sections the pattern of voting was clearly more consistent, while in New England it was the same and in the Midwest it was slightly less.

One last step was taken in examining the fifty-five economic votes. The total votes of each section were compared with the final votes on measures and amendments in order to determine which senators and sections were controlling the voting on these measures. The results showed that the senators from New England supported the majority position nineteen times, the Mid-Atlantic twenty times, the Border senators twenty-four times, and the Pacific Coast seventeen times. In marked contrast, the midwestern senators agreed with the majority position forty-five times and the southern senators thirty-nine times. It is clear, therefore, that senators from the Midwest and South controlled over 70 per cent of the economic votes of the period while the other sections were consistently in a minority position and regularly outvoted.

The fact of midwestern and southern control of economic votes in this period came as a surprise to this writer. He had expected to see more evidence of New England and Mid-Atlantic influence and control. This finding obviously conflicts with the views of many historians who tend to explain economic legislation in this period by reference to northeastern senators.[18] In order to compare this fact of midwestern and southern control of economic votes during the period from 1873 to 1877 with those of the earlier periods, the writer examined the voting behavior of each section in the years from 1861-1873. The results are listed in the following table:[19]

TABLE II

	Apr. 1861- Apr. 1865	May 1865- Nov. 1866	Dec. 1866- Mar. 3, 1873	Mar. 4, 1873- Mar. 3, 1877
New England	21-7	5-3	30-29	19-36
Mid-Alantic	16-12	4-4	30-29	20-35
Midwest	18-10	5-3	41-18	45-10
Border	11-17	4-3	37-22	24-31
Pacific Coast	10-14	6-2	43-16	17-38
South				39-16

This table reveals clearly the changing patterns of economic sectional voting in the Senate from 1861 to 1877. During the Civil War years there was substantial agreement among the senators from the New England, Mid-Atlantic, and midwestern states, with the Border and Pacific Coast senators in the minority. During moderate reconstruction the picture is not as clear, perhaps because of the few roll call measures available. In any case, there was no longer substantial agreement. However, in the period December, 1866-March 1873, the pattern of Midwest dominance emerges. Allied with the Border and Pacific Coast sections, midwestern senators controlled the economic measures 70 per cent of the time. The New England and Mid-Atlantic sections barely maintained a 50 per cent support of the amendments and final votes. In the last period, March, 1873-March, 1877, the dominance of the Midwest is even more striking. United with the South, this section had over 80 per cent agreement with the economic votes as finally recorded, while the New England and Mid-Atlantic states had only 35 and 36 per cent respectively.

A number of conclusions are evident from an examination of 102 roll call votes in the Senate in the period March 4, 1873-March 3, 1877:

1. There was no longer a marked division within the Republican party in the Senate on political measures. The remaining Radicals and Republican Non-Radicals voted together as did other members of the same party. (In the period December, 1866-March, 1873, they

[18] If this finding is correct, it would seem that more attention needs to be paid to the policies and actions of midwestern and southern senators.

[19] The first figure is the number of times the senators from a section voted with the majority position; the second figure is the number of times they opposed the majority position.

were in constant opposition.) The Unaligned also voted with their party.

2. The Democrats who were Non-Radical before 1873 voted as a unit with other Democrats against the Republican party. Within the Democratic party there were no significant differences on political measures.

3. The most important characteristic in the area of political voting behavior appears to be that of party. Whatever their earlier activity, senators voted with their party on all measures concerning reconstruction of the South and treatment of the Negro.

4. In the areas of economic voting it is difficult to find a consistent political-economic relationship. There is little agreement among Radicals (67 per cent), with a somewhat higher degree of correspondence among Non-Radicals (77 per cent) and Unaligned (77 per cent).

5. A pronounced economic voting pattern emerges along geographic lines, though it is not as high as in earlier days of reconstruction. Senators from the same area tended to vote together regardless of party affiliation. A somewhat higher degree of voting cohesion is evident when each geographical section is analyzed in terms of party.

6. Finally, during the last four years of reconstruction, the midwestern and southern senators were able to control the voting on economic issues with the other sections being consistently in the minority. (Also, the Midwest was the only section in the majority during each of the four periods from 1861 to 1877).

From the foregoing analysis of votes during the last four years of reconstruction, it is clear that the Senate had returned to its normal voting habits in the realm of political and economic measures. The Republican and Democratic parties had achieved an impressive degree of unity and cohesion on political measures concerning support of the Negro and severity toward the South. In the economic area, the parties were sharply divided along geographical lines. Some economic voting patterns were evident within geographical areas, probably along the interests of various agricultural and business interests. Also, a new pattern of Midwest control with the help of the South was becoming evident.

In conclusion, it is clear that a systematic voting analysis of economic measures in the Senate in the years from 1873-1877 casts doubt upon some of the ideas of Beard, Beale, and Woolfolk. There is little evidence to support the contention that Radicals were powerful enough to guard themselves against a reaction from the South as Charles Beard has argued. The South was quite successful in having many of its economic ideas put into effect, with the cooperation of midwestern senators, and its opponents were singularly unable to defeat its economic measures. It is also doubtful that New England economic and social standards were firmly implanted in the South following the Civil War as Beale has argued. According to voting evidence, New England was barely able to maintain its economic interests during the years from December, 1866 to March, 1877, and this was also true of the Mid-Atlantic section.[20] Finally, there is little evidence in the economic roll call votes in the Senate to suggest any substantial cooperation between northeastern and midwestern businessmen as Woolfolk has maintained. The senators from the Midwest and the Northeast (New England and Mid-Atlantic areas) were in constant opposition to each other during the period from December, 1866 to March, 1877. While it is possible that the business interests of the two sections were able to control or direct many senators, voting evidence directly contradicts the supposition of extensive cooperation between senators from the Northeast and Midwest. Such a coalition may have existed during the war but there is little voting evidence to suggest its existence in the following years.

Much of the traditional view of reconstruction, as summarized earlier, cannot be adequately checked by quantitative methods. It requires the use of other materials and often requires a thorough qualitative analysis. It is clear, however, that part of the substantial change in reconstruction during its last years can be studied, through the use of quantitative evidence. Voting records make it possible to examine the plans and programs of those Radicals who still remained in Congress and to assess their success or failure. A similar examination of the "new" Radicals would help to pinpoint their policies and differentiate them from the "older" Radicals. Furthermore, a closer look at the relationship of the senators to their constituents—the relative security or insecurity of their seats—may yield fresh information relevant to a reappraisal of this period. As noted earlier, Professor Donald has argued that ". . . a Congressman's Radicalism during Reconstruction varied in proportion to his political security in his district."[21] Further work is needed to determine if this statement is accurate for the Senate during the last years of reconstruction.

There are still many unanswered questions about reconstruction. Where there are sufficient roll call votes available and the issues are clearly defined, an analysis of these records can be useful. Often such an analysis may help to resolve outstanding differences of emphasis and interpretation.

[20] These sections were outvoted 65 and 64 times respectively on the 114 votes examined for the period from Dec. 1866 to March 3, 1877.

[21] David Donald, *The Politics of Reconstruction, 1863-1867* (Baton Rouge, 1965), p. 49.

PART IV:

PATRONAGE, RELIGION, AND RACE:
The Ethnoreligious Dimension of Politics

POLITICAL PATRONAGE AND ETHNIC GROUPS: Foreign-born in the United States Customhouse Service, 1821-1861

Leonard Tabachnik

THE USE OF POLITICAL PATRONAGE BY POLITICAL PARTIES in America has had two major functions: to reward with favors and jobs loyal workers already in the party, and to attract the political allegiance of new voters.[1] During the early nineteenth century, with the arrival of more than five million immigrants into the country, both the Whig and Democratic parties sought to attract these immigrants through political patronage. This was especially the case in the major cities where the immigrant came to represent a major portion of the population. For example, in New York and Boston the alien population represented only 4 percent of the total population in 1820; by 1860, they represented from one-third to one-half of the population.[2] The story was the same in other cities. Aliens constituted only 2 percent of Philadelphia's and Baltimore's population in 1820, but, by 1860, they constituted approximately one-third of the total population of these cities. Considering the numerical importance of the immigrant in American politics at this time, his share of political patronage has been a neglected field of historical investigation, and what is available is highly impressionistic and often unreliable.

The neglect of the subject is rather surprising, in view of the fact that during this period there existed a widespread belief that the foreign-born were monopolizing patronage positions. This belief led to the creation of a major political movement in the form of the Native American party. Organized in some cities as early as 1835, the Native American party was to become a formidable political force in the urban areas by the forties and fifties. The party elected mayors, members of local governing bodies, state legislators, and congressmen. In Philadelphia, where the party was especially strong, it had a continuous existence for fourteen years, winning elections and maintaining a per-

---

[1] James Q. Wilson, in his article "The Economy of Patronage" *Journal of Political Economy*, Vol. 69, (1961) 371, lists four functions of patronage. While I do not disagree with his particular categorization, it seems to me that the four functions he lists can be subsumed under the two general categories which I have listed.

[2] For population statistics refer to the published United States Census reports for the respective states.

246 BEYOND THE CIVIL WAR SYNTHESIS

manent organization and leadership.[3] The fears most commonly expressed by the nativists were that members of the new ethnic groups were unqualified to hold elective and appointive political offices; that the foreign-born, even after naturalization, continued to maintain loyalties to their country of birth, and, therefore, represented a danger to the country, especially when placed in political office; and finally, that patronage jobs were given to the foreign-born at the expense of the native-born.[4] With the belief that the patronage practices of both major parties represented a serious threat to the country's security, nativists proposed two means of circumscribing the political influence of the immigrant. First was the extension of the naturalization period from five to twenty-one years, with the intent of delaying the immigrant's entrance into the political arena; and second, the exclusion of all foreign-born from elective and appointive office. If properly understood, then, the study of patronage and ethnic groups is important for a better understanding of the patronage practices during this period as well as a challenge to nativist mentality.

In spite of its importance, among the numerous histories dealing with the immigrant and the nativist reaction to the immigrant for this period, only two discuss the problem of political patronage and ethnic groups at any length.[5] In his study of the roots of American nativism, Ray A. Billington writes that, "Both Whig and Democratic parties were denounced for truckling to aliens appointing the foreign-born to profitable state and local governments."[6] Although Billington was mainly interested in attitudes held by contemporaries toward the immigrant, there was no attempt at verifying what the actual situation was in regard to the foreign-born holding patronage jobs. Robert Ernst's discussion of the same problem in his *Immigrant Life in New York City, 1825-1863*[7] is the most detailed account available in the historical literature. Relying on statistics provided by the *Irish Citizen*, a contemporary immigrant newspaper, Ernst concluded that: "Whether for Federal, state, or municipal jobs, the Irish were the most leading aspirants among the immigrants. One tenth of the seven hundred and fifty custom house officials in 1865 were Irishmen, mostly in the lesser and poorly paid posi-

[3] This is based on the author's dissertation, near completion, which is a study of the Native American party in Philadelphia.

[4] The nativist position is adequately discussed by such contemporary nativist historians as John Sanderson, *Republican Landmarks*, (N.Y., 1855); Thomas R. Whitney, *A Defense of American Policy*, (N.Y. 1855); and, John Hancock Lee, *The Origin and Progress of the American Party*, (Phila., 1855).

[5] Among the numerous immigration historians to neglect ethnic patronage are: Oscar Handlin, *Boston's Immigrants*, (Cambridge, 1959); Marcus Lee Hansen, *Atlantic Migration, 1607-1860*, (Cambridge, 1940); and, Carl Wittke, *We Who Built America*, (N.Y., 1939). Some studies of the Native American party are: Lawrence F. Schmeckebier, *History of the Know-Nothing Party in Maryland*, (Baltimore, 1899); Louis Dow Scisco, *Political Nativism in New York State*, (N.Y., 1901); and, *Nativism in the Old Northwest*, (Washington, D.C., 1936).

[6] Ray A. Billington, *The Protestant Crusade*, (New York, 1948 ed.) pp. 198-99.

[7] Robert Ernst, *Immigrant Life in New York*, (New York, 1948), p. 165.

tions." Assuming that the above figure for the year 1856 is accurate, it is insufficient information to warrant generalization about the condition of the immigrant in the customhouse. Without comparative data for other years there is no way of knowing whether or not this year was typical. Furthermore, the source, an Irish newspaper, may be unreliable for such information. This, however, is the most empirical knowledge historians have at their disposal on this particular subject.

Even historians dealing specifically with the question of customhouse patronage completely ignore the ethnic element. This absence is conspicuous in two basic books in the field: Leonard D. White's *The Jacksonians*, and Carl Russel Fish's *The Civil Service and the Patronage*.[8] A recent study of patronage in the higher civil service by Sidney Aronson, *Status and Kinship in the Higher Civil Service*,[9] does deal with the ethnic backgrounds of office holders in a meaningful way. Unfortunately, the book's concern is the higher civil service, and there is nothing comparable for the lower civil service.

Unlike many other questions in political history, it is possible to count the number of foreign-born holding federal office and arrive at an exact answer. Since one of the largest areas of political patronage was in the various customhouses, I have chosen to analyze of the number of foreign-born holding positions there from 1821 to 1861. Beginning in 1817, as a result of a law passed by Congress in the previous year, a biennial list of federal employees, the *United States Official Register*,[10] was published. The list includes such vital information as the employee's name, salary, type and location of work, and in some cases, as in the customhouse listing, place of birth. It is therefore possible to know exactly how many foreign-born were employed in the customhouse service. Because of the nature of the data, this study deals only with first generation immigrants. It is virtually impossible to verify the ethnic background of second generation immigrants from the sources used here.

For this study I have selected for analysis those reports closest to each quinquennial year. Since the reports were published biennially, in every odd year, there was the choice of using either the year before or after the decennial year. In most cases it would not have made very much diffence which year was used, except that by using the reports after the decennial year the administrations of William H. Harrison and Abraham Lincoln, a Whig and a Republican, are included. The only drawback to this approach is that the southern states are not included in the 1861 report because of the Civil War. Although this results in lower figures for that year it does not appreciably affect the total re-

---

[8] Leonard D. White, *The Jacksonians*, (N.Y., 1954 ed.); Carl R. Fish, *The Civil Service and the Patronage*, (N.Y., 1905).

[9] Sidney Aronson, *Status and Kinship in the Higher Civil Service*, (Cambridge, 1965), p. 113.

[10] *United States Official Register, 1821-1861*, (Washington).

sults since most foreign-born lived in the North and were appointed to positions there.

Appointment to the United States customhouse service was usually secured and held as a political favor of the party holding the presidential office. The President, or his adviser, appointed a collector for each port, and the collector in turn filled the numerous minor posts. During most of the period under discussion both Whigs and Democrats used the federal patronage to tie local politics to a unified national party system. At election time the office holder was expected to work for and help finance the party's campaign. Ultimately, the success or failure of a party's discipline and internal organization was based on the extent to which it was capable of rewarding its friends and punishing its enemies.[11] In the New York customhouse, for example, it was common knowledge that, "If the individual did not pay the amount he was taxed with, the collector would remark, you will be reported to the general committee—and everybody understood that proscription would follow."[12] The need to purge disloyal officeholders, whether they were of the opposite party or of a different faction within the party, turned the system into a cannibalistic ritual. William L. Marcy, a veteran practitioner of the "spoils system" captured its savageness when he remarked that under Buchanan's tenure "Pierce men are hunted down like wild beasts."[13]

Under such a tightly controlled system of appointments the number of foreign-born in the customhouse service was strictly regulated and ought to have reflected the political importance of the foreign-born vote. For a variety of reasons the immigrant supported the Democratic party and his support, in part, contributed to the virtual dominance of the party in American politics during this era. Though the Whig made a number of attempts to court the immigrant, they failed primarily because many Whig leaders openly sympathized with the principles of nativism. The corollary to this has been the acceptance of the idea that the foreign-born were rewarded with patronage. The only group to maintain that the foreign-born were insignificant and underrepresented in the customhouse were the foreign-born themselves.

On the surface it appears that the foreign-born made gains in the customhouse during the forty-year perod under discussion. An analysis of the customhouse reports in the *United States Annual Register*, which

[11] Robert V. Remini, *Martin Van Buren and the Making of the Democratic Party*, (N.Y., 1954). In reference to the Albany Regency Remini writes: "So carefully did the members consider the prejudices and feeling of local communities to be affected by their appointments, so thoroughly did they investigate the petty details connected with the distribution of patronage, and so precisely thought out was each authorized removal that they steadily advanced over the years toward the full establishment of state-wide machine politics," p. 9. See also Roy F. Nichols, *The Disruption of the Democracy*, p. 74.

[12] *United States Congress, House Document 13*, 15 Cong., 3 sess., Dec. 10, 1838).

[13] White, *The Jacksonians*, p. 313.

appears in Table I, shows that the number of foreign-born holding positions in the customhouse more than tripled from 45 in 1821 to 169 in 1861, with a high of 203 in 1855. This increase, however, is slightly mis-

TABLE I

Number and Percentage of Foreign-born in
the Customhouse Service, 1821-1861

YEAR	1821	1825	1831	1835	1841	1845	1851	1855	1861
Total ♯ of Positions	1097	1195	1464	1156	1434	1357	1751	2146	1988
♯ Of Foreign-born	45	62	66	70	56	111	98	203	169
% Foreign-born	4.0	5.0	4.5	6.0	3.9	8.0	5.5	9.0	7.0

leading because it fails to account for an increase (almost double) in the total number of positions in the customhouse for the same period. On a percentage basis the gain is less impressive. During this forty-year period the foreign-born held from 4 to 9 per cent of the positions with a 5.8 per cent average.

While there was a slight and perhaps inconsequential increase of foreign-born in the customhouse for the forty-year period, the gains never kept pace with the increase of the foreign-born population. When the percentage of foreign-born positions in the customhouse is correlated with the percentage of foreign-born population, as in Table II,[14] there

TABLE II

Foreign-born in the U.S. Population and in
the Customhouse Service (per cent)

YEAR*	1820-21	1830-31	1850-51	1860-61
Foreign-born Pop.	.05	.8	12.4	14.8
Customhouse	4.0	4.5	5.5	7.0

* The U.S. Census did not enumerate foreign-born for 1840.

was a relative decline in representation. In 1820 and 1830, though the foreign-born held a smaller percentage of positions than at a later period, they were overrepresented in comparison to their number in the population. In 1850 and 1860, however, when they represented a much larger percentage of the population they were underrepresented in the customhouse.

[14] Material for these correlations are taken from the published U.S. Census reports and the *U.S. Official Register*.

This phenomenon is greatly magnified when the four major port cities of Boston, New York, Philadelphia and Baltimore are studied separately. During the 1820's and 1830's, as shown in Table III, the foreign-born were under represented only in Boston. In Philadelphia and in Baltimore they were overrepresented; and, in New York the difference was small. After 1850, however, there was an actual and relative decline in every city except New York. And in New York the foreign-born were significantly underrepresented.

TABLE III

Foreign-born in the Population and Customhouse
Service of Four Major Cities (per cent)

	1820-21		1830-31		1850-51		1855°		1860-61	
	Pop.	Ch.	Pop.	Ch.	Pop.	Ch.	Pop.	Ch.	Pop.	Ch.
Boston	4.1	.8	5.6	2.6	34.3	.8	38.8	2.6	35.8	2.0
New York	4.3	6.4	8.7	6.2	46.7	7.9	52.2	10.9	47.1	13.3
Philadelphia	1.9	20.0	2.3	12.3	28.8	10.4	–	–	29.1	12.5
Baltimore	1.8	15.9	2.2	10.3	18.7	26.5	–	–	24.9	5.8

° Only New York and Massachusetts conducted a state census for 1855.

When each ethnic group is analyzed separately similar results are achieved, though the British have the least and the Germans the most underrepresentation. In Table IV, in each of the three years for which data is available for individual ethnic groups in the four major port cities, the percentage of foreign-born holding positions in the customhouse in relation to the total number of positions for each ethnic group is much smaller than the percentage of each ethnic group in the total population of the city. When the figures are translated into a ratio, as in Table V, the evidence is most compelling. Correlating the percentage of foreign-born in the customhouse service with the percentage of foreign-born in the population a perfect relationship would equal 100 percent, while a figure above that would mean overrepresentation. Except for one year, when the British showed a 140 percent representation, all ethnic groups were underrepresented from the low of zero to a high of 51 per cent. And, except for Philadelphia in 1850 and New York in 1855, the British showed a higher ratio of representation than the Irish.

The Irish, however, even though they were underrepresented in relation to their numbers in the population, held a significantly larger number of positions than any other ethnic group. Except for one year, as seen in Table VI, the Irish held the largest share of positions given to all ethnic groups, and for two-thirds of the time, they held over 50 per cent of these positions. It is quite possible that this disproportionate share of Irish in patronage positions was responsible for the myth of immigrant domination.

For an explanation as to why the Irish did so well in comparison with other ethnic groups, one touches upon the heart of patronage practice in

TABLE IV

Irish, British, and Germans in the Population and Customhouse
Service of Four Major Port Cities. (per cent)

	1850-51					
	Irish		British		German	
	Pop.	Ch.	Pop.	Ch.	Pop.	Ch.
Boston	25.7	.4	2.9	.4	1.2	–
New York	26.0	4.0	6	2.8	10.8	.6
Philadelphia	17.7	9.1	5	1.6	5.5	–
Baltimore	10.2	2.1	1.5	2.1	11.6	10.2

	1855					
	Irish		British		German	
	Pop.	Ch.	Pop.	Ch.	Pop.	Ch.
Boston	28.8	.2	3.2	.4	2.1	–
New York	28.8	8.65	5.0	1.2	15.4	.4
Philadelphia	–	–	–	–	–	–
Baltimore	–	–	–	–	–	–

	1860-61					
	Irish		British		German	
	Pop.	Ch.	Pop.	Ch.	Pop.	Ch.
Boston	25.8	.6	3.1	.3	1.8	1.0
New York	27.7	7.2	4.5	2.1	14.7	2.3
Philadelphia	16.5	4.3	3.8	5.4	7.6	2.7
Baltimore	7.3	.8	1.2	.8	14.3	2.5

TABLE V

Ratio of Irish, British, and Germans in the Population and
Customhouse Service of Four Major Port Cities

	1850-51			1855			1860-61		
	Irish	British	German	Irish	British	German	Irish	British	German
Boston	1.5	13.7	–	.6	12	–	.2	.9	5
New York	15	46	5	30	24	2.5	25.6	46	16
Philadelphia	51	32	–	–	–	–	26	142	35
Baltimore	20	140	87	–	–	–	10	66	17

TABLE VI

Number and Percentage of Positions Among Four Ethnic
Groups in the Customhouse Service

Year	Irish #	Irish %	British #	British %	German #	German %	French #	French %
1821	24	56	17	37	1	02	2	04
1825	26	43	15	31	6	10	7	11
1831	32	46	17	25	6	09	6	09
1835	28	40	30	42	6	08	3	04
1841	31	55	16	28	4	07	4	07
1845	77	69	18	15	9	08	2	01
1851	55	56	28	29	8	08	2	02
1855	148	72	25	11	7	03	5	02
1861	86	58	40	26	34	22	1	006

American politics. The only possible explanation for the Irish success was their political activism. After the Irish immigrant landed here he was literally guided through the labyrinth of American political life by the various immigrant leaders who informed him of his political rights as an alien, the procedures necessary for naturalization, and advised him on how to vote once a citizen. Already during the thirties and forties an Irish political leader had emerged and was invariably typed by native Americans as either "Murphy" or "Blarney O'Democrat."[15] Their success was certainly not due to their social and economic position. One writer has concluded that the social rank of the Irish was only slightly above that of the Negro,[16] and antipathy toward the Irish, when manifested in violence, was often stronger than that towards the Negro. When one compares the famous anti-Irish riots in Philadelphia in 1844 with anti-Negro riots in the same city at about the same time, one must conclude that in terms of loss of life and property the outrages committed against the Irish were far greater than those committed against Negroes.[17] Nor were the Irish considered trustworthy. American opinion of them, as a group, was highly unfavorable. "Indolence and vaga-

[15] Oscar Handlin, "Foreign influences in American politics," in William F. Bowers, *Foreign Influences in American Life*, (1952). Anony. "Blarney O'Democrat" (New York, 1838).

[16] Max Berger, "The Irish Emigrant and American Nativism as Seen by British Visitors, 1836-1860," *Pennsylvania Magazine of History and Biography*, Vol. 70, pp. 146-160 passim.

[17] Sam Bass Warner, Sr., *The Private City: Philadelphia in Three Periods of its Growth* (Phila., 1968), ch. 7.

bondism," wrote one nativist in 1851, "appears to be, in some measure, a national characteristic of the Irish."[18]

In comparison, the German immigrant had a far better image. As a group, the Germans were thought of as "industrious" "hardy," "kindly," and a "quiet people."[19] But, the Germans were as yet not active in national politics, and, therefore, did not share significantly in the distribution of the patronage until 1860 when they supported Lincoln's campaign. It does not appear to have been the language barrier which prevented them from acquiring patronage jobs, for how does one explain the sudden jump of the number of Germans in the customhouse from three-tenths of a percent in 1855 to 22 per cent in 1861. Their facility for the English language was certainly not that much improved in six years. The only exception to this was in Baltimore in 1851 where they did exert themselves as a political force and where they shared a substantial number of the patronage positions.

A question closely related to ethnic patronage is whether the foreign-born did better under a Democratic or Whig administration. In practice, the Democratic party represented the foreign-born and should have been active in their behalf; the Whig and Republican parties, which sympathized with the nativist position and which had a large nativist faction, should have proscribed the foreign-born from office. The statistics, as shown in Table VII, are revealing. During Andrew Jackson's first administration the percentage of foreign-born in the customhouse service was lower than those of his predecessor, John Quincy Adams, whose campaign in 1828 was avowedly antiforeign.[20] Jackson's second administration was a slight improvement, but it represented no breakthrough. Under two Whig and one Republican administration the number of foreign-born positions declined from previous Democratic administrations at most by 2.5 per cent. This hardly warrants the generalization that the Democrats were the only party to give the foreign-born patronage.

When the appointments of each ethnic group are viewed separately, as in Table VII, some modifications are necessary. Not all ethnic groups did uniformly well under Democratic administrations. Whereas the Irish did well under Presidents Polk and Pierce, they received the lowest percentage of the foreign-born appointments during Jackson's second administration, even lower than under John Quincy Adams. The English benefited most from Jackson, while the Germans made their most impressive gain under Lincoln.

There can be little doubt from the evidence presented in this paper that contrary to many widely held views the immigrant did not significantly share in patronage jobs during this period of mass immigration.

18 *The American Banner*, July 21, 1851.

19 John Gerow Gazley, *American Opinion of German Unification, 1848-1871* (New York, 1926), p. 33.

20 Florence Weston, *The Presidential Election of 1828*, (1938).

Nor was there any appreciable difference in the patronage practices of the two major parties toward the immigrant. By the 1850's one could say that the Democrats were more inclined than the Whigs to reward the immigrant, but considering that most immigrants voted for the Democratic party, they were not fairly rewarded.

TABLE VII

Correlation of the Percentage of Foreign-born in the Customhouse
Service with Various Presidential Administrations

President	Political Party	Year	% F.B.	% Increase or Decrease over Previous Year	% Irish	% English	% German	% Scotch
Monroe	Republican	1821	4.0	—	56	24	02	13
J. Q. Adams	Republican	1825	5.0	+1	43	15	10	16
Jackson	Democrat	1831	4.5	— .5	46	19	9	6
Jackson	Democrat	1835	6.0	+1.5	40	32	8	10
Harrison	Whig	1841	3.9	—2.1	55	23	7	5
Polk	Democrat	1845	8.0	+4.1	69	13	8	2
Fillmore	Whig	1851	5.5	—2.5	56	19	8	10
Pierce	Democrat	1855	9.0	+3.5	72	8	7	3
Lincoln	Republican	1861	7.0	—2.0	58	19	22	7

As for the nativists, their position in regard to the immigrant in patronage positions was overdrawn, exaggerated, and distorted. The success of political nativism in the major cities in no way correlates with the number of foreign-born holding patronage positions there. Though the party appeared to be equally successful in Boston, New York, Philadelphia, and Baltimore, patronage positions held by the foreign-born in these cities varied. In Boston they were virtually excluded from the customhouse, holding from .8 to 2.6 per cent of the positions, while in Philadelphia they held from 10.4 to 20.0 per cent of the positions. Undoubtedly, there are other areas of patronage in the municipal, state and federal governments which this study does not cover, but which would probably yield similar results.

It would, however, be a mistake to dismiss nativism solely as an irrational response. As the nativists perceived the situation there was an actual increase in the number of foreign-born holding positions, no matter how small. Moreover, nativists opposed any foreigner in political office on principle, and could not tolerate even a small representation.

THE RELIGIOUS AND OCCUPATIONAL ROOTS OF PARTY IDENTIFICATION: Illinois and Indiana in the 1870's

Richard Jensen

"RELIGION COMES VERY LITTLE INTO THE AMERICAN PARTY," declared James Bryce. "Roman Catholics are usually Democrats. . . . Congregationalists and Unitarians . . . are apt to be Republicans. Presbyterians, Methodists, Baptists, Episcopalians . . . have no special party affinities. They are mostly Republicans in the North, Democrats in the South."[1] With these brief, tidy generalizations the foremost commentator on late-nineteenth-century American politics dismissed the relationship between religion and partisanship, and steered generations of scholars away from the topic.[2]

Bryce was wrong. One of the most accurate ways to determine a voter's choices in the late nineteenth century was to ascertain his religious preferences (except in the South, where one ascertained his race). Table 1, showing the partisanship of the inhabitants of the small northern Illinois town of Geneseo, indicates that over 90 per cent of the Congregationalists, Unitarians, Methodists, Baptists, Swedish Lutheraans and Swedish Methodists were Republican, and over 90 per cent of the Catholics were Democrats.[3] Table 2, which cross-classifies the old-stock voters in Geneseo (i.e. those not identifiable as immigrants or sons of immigrants) according to church membership and occupation, indicates that quite apart from his religion, a man's occupation also was related to his party preference. These patterns, which held for a sample

[1] James Bryce, *The American Commonwealth* (New York, 1894), II, 37; cf. Seymour M. Lipset, "Religion and Politics in American History," in Earl Raab (ed.), *Religious Conflict in America* (Garden City, 1964), p. 72. The author is indebted to George Shockey for coding the Illinois data analyzed in Tables 5-9.

[2] Although Frederick Jackson Turner and several of his students were aware of the ethnic basis of partisanship, recent interest dates from Samuel Lubell, *The Future of American Politics* (New York, 1952), and Samuel P. Hays, "History as Human Behavior," *Iowa Journal of History*, LVIII (1960) 193-206. See Richard Jensen, "American Election Analysis: A Case History of Methodological Innovation and Diffusion," in Seymour Martin Lipset (ed.), *Politics and the Social Sciences* (New York, 1969), pp. 226-43.

[3] Only men listed as Republicans or Democrats were tabulated in Tables 1, 2, 3 and 5, because the Illinois directories sometimes neglected to ask party identification. The nonpartisans are examined in detail later. Although Geneseo had a population of just 3000, only one-sixth of the inhabitants of Illinois and Indiana lived in larger cities.

of other towns and rural areas in Illinois and Indiana in the 1870's, and probably for the Midwest as a whole, are too strong to be dismissed with Bryce's vague assertions. Religion, and to a lesser extent occupation, constituted the basic roots of party identification for the average citizen.

TABLE 1

PARTY, BY ETHNIC-RELIGIOUS GROUPS, GENESEO CITY AND TOWNSHIP, 1877

Ethnic	Denomination	% Republican (of two-party total)	N
Old Stock	Congregationalist	96.5	74
	Unitarian	96.0	25
	Methodist	91.4	70
	Baptist	90.9	22
	Presbyterian	72.5	29
	Other	80.0	20
	No denomination given	69.0	400
German	Lutheran	66.7	60
	Other Protestant	52.2	67
	Roman Catholic	25.0	16
Irish	Roman Catholic	0.0	52
Other	Roman Catholic	7.7	13
Swedish	Lutheran, Methodist, and other	96.3	72
Total		70.1	920
Actual Vote (Governor, 1876)		68.1	827

TABLE 2

PARTY, BY OCCUPATIONAL AND RELIGIOUS STATUS, GENESEO OLD STOCK, 1877
(Per cent Republican of two-party total)

	Church Affiliated		Not Church Affiliated		All	
	% Rep.	N	% Rep.	N	% Rep.	N
Business & Professional	95.4	151	75.4	221	86.4	372
Urban Labor	72.7	11	55.3	74	57.6	85
Farmer	84.6	78	67.6	105	74.9	183
All	90.8	240	69.0	400	77.2	640

The data for Geneseo, and all the other places tabulated, comes from recently discovered county directories published in the mid-1870's. The compilers attempted to ascertain the name, address, occupation, nationality, religious affiliation and party identification of every voter and taxpayer. The value of many farm holdings in Illinois, and in Indiana information on age, birthplace and year of arrival, were also included. Each of the directories seems to have canvassed the population quite thoroughly. Probably unskilled workers and farm laborers were frequently overlooked, but the possible bias in this deficiency can be largely overcome by grouping the men into occupational categories.[4]

The overwhelming Republicanism of the old-stock denominations in Geneseo is striking, especially the 95 per cent level for the business and professional men. Equally impressive is the homogeneity of the Republican Swedes and the Democratic Catholics (occupation made little difference here!). Nor was this pattern confined to Geneseo; all the Swedish communities in the Midwest were heavily Republican, and all the Catholic settlements heavily Democratic. The Protestant Germans (mostly Lutherans) were the only religious group that was politically divided. Indeed, the German voting patterns across the Midwest were constantly in flux, except for the small number of German Methodists and Baptists, who were consistently Republican. Analysis of aggregate election returns suggests that whenever prohibition was the salient issue, the Germans voted heavily Democratic; whenever the money question was uppermost (as in 1896) they swung toward the G.O.P.

Church affiliation, as Table 2 shows, added 20 points to the Republicanism of old stock professionals and businessmen, and 17 points to the Republicanism of old-stock urban laborers and farmers. The partisan spread between high and low occupational status groups in each religious category was about 20 points, with farmers midway between the high and low groups. Thus church affiliation was as important a factor as occupational status among the old stock in this city.

The Geneseo patterns are quite similar to those in the nearby city of Princeton, Illinois, as displayed in Table 3. For Princeton the coding scheme was slightly different, with skilled workers (like carpenters and bakers) and clerks grouped with the laborers instead of with the businessmen as in Geneseo. (The problem was the difficulty in deciding whether skilled artisans owned their own shops.) Church affiliation added 15 points to the Republicanism of high status old-stock Princeton voters, and 19 points to the low status men, while high status itself added only 2 to 5 points to the Republicanism of each religious group. Church affiliation, therefore, was just as influential in Princeton as in Geneseo, but occupational status was less important. (The difference was not caused by the coding change, however.) The various denominations

---

[4] The directories, not to be confused with "mugbooks" that charged for inserting laudatory biographies, were: *The People's Guide: A Business, Political and Religious Directory of Hendricks Co., Indiana* (Indianapolis, 1874); *The History of Henry County, Illinois, Its Taxpayers and Voters* (Chicago, 1877); *The History of Logan County, Illinois* (Chicago, 1878); *The Past and Present of Rock Island County, Illinois* (Chicago, 1877); and *The Voters and Taxpayers of Bureau County, Illinois* (Chicago, 1876). At least a dozen more of these directories exist for Illinois and Indiana. Cf. Ronald P. Formisano, "Analyzing American Voting, 1830-1860: Methods," *Historical Methods Newsletter*, II (Mar., 1969), 1-12.

divided in Princeton much the same as they did in Geneseo, except that the Protestant Germans in each occupational category were 2:1 Democratic, in contrast to Geneseo where they were 3:2 Republican.

TABLE 3

PARTY, BY OCCUPATIONAL AND RELIGIOUS STATUS,
PRINCETON CITY OLD STOCK, 1876
(Per cent Republican of two-party total)

	Church Affiliated		Not Church Affiliated		All	
	% Rep.	N	% Rep.	N	% Rep.	N
Business & Prof.	83.0	88	67.5	200	72.3	288
Blue Collar	80.8	47	62.1	208	65.6	255
All	82.2	135	64.7	408	69.1	543

Partisanship in Illinois and Indiana will be analyzed further with fresh data (excluding Geneseo and Princeton), but first a theoretical explanation of the results so far obtained is necessary so that a hypothesis will be available for testing.

Religion was relevant to social and political behavior in three ways. First, different theological positions produced different interpretations of morality and of the behavior most appropriate for the Christian citizen. Second, organized religious bodies formed fundamental social groups of the highest importance to their adherents. The members of a particular congregation or denomination knew other members intimately—they worshipped together, intermarried, and probably discussed political issues with each other over long periods of time. Thus a strain toward political uniformity within a particular religious group would not be unexpected. If like the German Lutherans a particular religious group was sufficiently inwardly directed, they might be said to constitute a distinct subculture. This usually happened in the case of immigrant groups sharing a common religion.[5] Thirdly, the denominations as formal groups sometimes took active parts in political controversies. Thus the Methodists before the Civil War came to adopt a semiofficial antislavery stance through the actions of respected elders, ministers, bishops, educators and editors. These positions were transmitted to the general membership through voluntary associations, special meetings, regular sermons, and an influential network of church periodicals.[6] By working with denominations rather than specific congregations, the three modes of religious influence can all be incorporated into an interpretation of how religious differences generated political differences.

[5] See Frederick Luebke, *Immigrants and Politics: The Germans of Nebraska, 1880-1900* (Lincoln, 1969), for an excellent discussion.

[6] Donald G. Mathews, "The Methodist Schism of 1844 and the Polarization of Antislavery Sentiment," *Mid-America* LI (1968), 3-23.

The importance of religion in nineteenth-century America cannot be overestimated. In 1789 the United States was a largely de-Christianized nation. Wave after wave of revivals, from the 1790's to World War I, converted the major part of the population to Protestantism. The depth and breadth of the revivals forced a revamping of the fundamentals of Protestant theology. The revivalists, led by a few powerful intellectuals at Yale and Oberlin and hundreds of preachers in the field, rejected the orthodox Calvinist theory of predestination, and the Catholic-Anglican-Lutheran established church styles of theology which emphasized patience, gradualism and incrementalism and which made no allowance for massive and sudden revivals. The antirevivalists fought back bitterly and often brilliantly, producing major theological and liturgical renaissances in the Episcopalian, Presbyterian, Reformed, Lutheran and Catholic denominations. The result was a century-long conflict between the revivalist or "pietistic" outlook, and the antirevivalist or "liturgical" outlook.

While this conflict was not the only divisive force in American religion,[7] it was the most intense and long-standing. By the end of the century, when the revivalist circuit riders had dismounted and ministers searched for new methods to tend their flock, the pietistic-liturgican conflict rapidly faded in the major denominations. This in turn set off another wave of formation of new sects and denominations by men who felt the dimension was all-important.

The liturgical (or "ritualistic" or "high church") outlook stressed the institutionalized formalities and historic doctrines of the established churches of Europe—Calvinist, Catholic, Lutheran and Anglican. Salvation required faithful adherence to the creed, liturgy, sacraments and hierarchy of the church. The quintessence of liturgical style could be found in Catholicism's lavish use of ornamentation, vestments, esoteric languages, ritualized sacraments, devotion to the saints, and vigorous pursuit of heretics, all directed by an authoritarian (and after 1870 infallible) hierarchy. Comparable ritualism became firmly established among Episcopalians and Orthodox Jews. German Lutherans (of the Missouri Synod, especially) and orthodox Calvinists (the "Old School" Presbyterians and many Baptists) similarly fixed ritualistic practices, clung to old theologies, and rejected both revivals and the manifestations of pietism.

One key element in the liturgical outlook was particularism, the conviction that their denomination was the one true Church of God, and most outsiders were probably damned. This attitude was strong not only among Catholics, but also among orthodox Calvinists, who clung

---

[7] Anti-Catholicism was widespread among Protestants. Most Catholics were Democrats, but so too were most anti-Catholic German Lutherans and Southern Baptists. Thus the political overtones of anti-Catholicism were muted; see Clifton J. Phillips, *Indiana in Transition: 1880-1920* (Indianapolis, 1968), p. 463; Paul Kleppner, *The Cross of Culture: A Social Analysis of Midwestern Politics, 1850-1900* (New York, 1970), 103-29, analyzes the importance of anti-Catholicism in Ohio and Wisconsin.

to predestination, high church Episcopalians, Missouri Synod Lutherans and Landmarkean Baptists. For the liturgicals, moralistic social action groups that were not an integral part of the church structure were illegal, unscriptural and unnecessary; the church could attend to all matters of morality without outside help. Thus the orthodox Calvinists ejected half the Presbyterian membership in 1837; the Baptists split over missionary societies in the 1830's; the Catholics underwent a great crisis in the 1890's regarding missions to Protestants; and the Episcopalians ordered their Church Temperance Society to disband in the 1920's.

Heresy, pride and innovation, rather than impure behavior, were the cardinal sins for the liturgicals. Consequently they responded to pietism by stressing orthodox theology and developing seminaries and parochial schools to preserve their faith unchanged. Catholics and German Lutherans relied on their parochial schools to the exclusion of public schools, thus opening a line of political battle that climaxed in 1890 in intensely bitter elections in Wisconsin and Illinois. The courageous pursuit of duty was the highest virtue for liturgicals, and the most outstanding exemplar of this trait was the son of a Calvinistic Presbyterian minister, Grover Cleveland.[8]

The pietistic outlook rejected liturgicalism. It had little respect for elaborate ceremonies, vestments, saints, devotions, and frequently opposed organ music in church. Theologically the key to pietism was the conviction (called Arminianism) that all men can be saved by a direct confrontation with Christ (*not* with the Church) through the conversion experience. The revival was the basis of their strength—the preaching of hellfire, damnation and Christ's redeeming love, the anxious bench for despondent sinners, the moment of inner light wherein a man gained faith and was saved. While the liturgicals routinely baptized all the children in their community, and then went out to baptize heathens, the pietists insisted on the conversion experience before membership could be granted, and demanded continuous proof in the form of pure behavior. The Methodists, for example, did not hesitate to expel a member whose conduct was unbecoming to a true believer. Creeds and formal theology were of little importance, and heresy was not a major concern. Denominational lines were not vital either, and pietists frequently switched churches. The pietists fostered interdenominational voluntary societies to distribute Bibles, conduct missionary work, abolish slavery and promote total abstinence.

Every major denomination was torn by conflicts between liturgical and pietistic members in the nineteenth century. In most cases, one group or the other gained the upper hand, often after heresy trials, thus driving the minority to silence, schism, or transfer to another denomination. By the 1860's, the midwestern Congregationalists, Disciples of Christ, Methodists and Quakers were overwhelmingly pietistic. The

---

[8] Robert Kelley, *The Transatlantic Persuasion* (New York, 1969), is especially interesting on Cleveland. Woodrow Wilson was another good example.

Episcopalians and Catholics were predominantly liturgical, although a sort of pietism had considerable support among Catholic bishops and intellectuals. The Presbyterians were fragmented, with liturgicals concentrated in the "Old School" assemblies, and pietists in control of the "New School" and Cumberland groups. (The Old and New Schools merged in 1869, and Cumberland joined in later.) The Baptists were fragmented, too. The Free Will Baptists were pietistic, the Primitive Baptists liturgical. However, the largest group of Regular Baptists contained both elements, since there was no central authority to insure theological uniformity. Lutherans divided into three camps: liturgicals (led by the Missouri Synod Germans), pietists (Scandinavians and old stock), and a middle-of-the-road group of diverse membership. Likewise, the Jews divided into Orthodox, Reform and Conservative camps. Round after round of schisms, mostly based on the pietistic-liturgical dimension, produced a proliferation of smaller denominations.[9]

The bridge linking theology and politics was the demand by pietists that the government actively support the cause of Christianity by abolishing the sinful institutions that stood in the way of revivals. Specifically, midwestern pietists demanded that the government halt the spread of slavery (or even abolish it), overthrow the saloon and the sale of liquor, and (among many pietists) restrict the "pernicious" and "corrupting" flood of Catholic immigration. (Nearly all the abolitionists were prohibitionists, and most were anti-Catholic.) Antiliquor, antislavery and nativism were the immediate causes of the realignment of parties in the mid-1850's that produced the third party system, pitting Republicans against Democrats.[10]

Liturgicals, as a rule, opposed prohibition, denounced abolitionists (even if they disliked slavery), and avoided the nativist agitation. The intrusion of government into affairs of morality was, in their eyes, a threat to the primacy of the Church in the spiritual realm, and an unconstitutional abridgment of individual liberties. Although the liturgicals did not favor the pernicious evils of the saloon any more than did pietists, they did not demand total abstinence of their members, nor did they discipline their slave-holding adherents. While the major pietistic denominations each suffered a north-south rupture *before* the Civil War, none of the liturgical churches was divided. The liturgicals feared·

⁹ The few studies of nineteenth-century pietistic-liturgical conflicts are Winthrop Hudson, *Religion in America* (New York, 1965); Timothy Smith, *Revivalism and Social Reform* (New York, 1957); H. Shelton Smith, Robert T. Handy and Lefferts A. Loetscher (eds.), *American Christianity* (New York, 1963), especially vol. 2, ch. 12, 13, 15, 18; and Frank S. Mead, *Handbook of Denominations* (New York, 1965); statistical returns appear in H. K. Carroll, *The Religious Forces of the United States* (New York, 1896).

¹⁰ See Joel Silbey, *The Transformation of American Politics, 1840-1860* (Englewood Cliffs, 1967). On the state level, see Floyd Streeter, *Political Parties in Michigan: 1837-1860* (Lansing, 1918); Arthur C. Cole, *The Civil War Era, 1850-1873* (Springfield, Ill., 1919); and Emma Lou Thornbrough, *Indiana in the Civil War Era* (Indianapolis, 1965).

that "fanatical" (their favorite epithet) pietists would use the government to further their moralistic crusades.

The liturgical fears were well grounded. Beginning with the Maine Law of 1851, a wave of prohibition legislation swept the country, instigated by the pietists, first through the Whig party, and then through the Know-Nothings and Republicans. After 1854 the slavery issue became paramount, and the pietists of the North mobilized into the moralistic, crusading Republican party. The Democrats, who had always claimed the support of most liturgical voters, sought to blunt the Republican attack by vigorously defending a wet, antinativist, antiabolitionist position. During the Civil War itself, the pietists were the mainstay of the Union war effort, while the liturgicals held back. Catholics, both Irish and German, rioted against the draft and emancipation; Old School Presbyterians refused to fly the American flag at their 1863 convention; and not a few Episcopalians were denounced as Copperheads. The Episcopalian church in Indianapolis was even ridiculed as the "Church of the Holy Rebellion." The only appeal that finally gained liturgical support for the war was Lincoln's emphasis on loyalty, patriotism, and nationalism.

It seems reasonable to hypothesize that when party lines reformed in the 1850's, the great majority of pietists in the Midwest became Republicans, and liturgicals Democrats, and that the phenomenon of political inheritance through families and long-term stability of individual partisan identification maintained this basic division for the remainder of the century. This hypothesis has to be modified slightly in view of the fact that after 1869 and the victory of Radical Reconstruction, the temperance issue reemerged as the most salient political issue on the state and local level throughout the Midwest. In the mid-1870's, with the formation of the Woman's Christian Temperance Union, the prohibition movement again attained the status of a continuous crusade. Thus the religious-political correlation established before the Civil War was reinforced afterwards. (The Republicans, furthermore, used the "bloody shirt" issue, and the anger of Methodists about southern religious developments, to maintain the Civil War cleavages.)

The postwar temperance movement brought religious tensions sharply to the fore. Denouncing the wicked saloon as the father of drunkenness, the cause of disease, crime, poverty, and urban decay—and the base of power of Catholic politicians—the pietists opened a crusade that finally triumphed in 1919. As one Democratic leader complained:

The preachers of Iowa with the exception of those in the ritual churches and a few [Old School?] Presbyterians . . . have been on the stump for legal prohibition, declaring that the use of alcoholic drinks is the source of all sin.[11]

The liturgicals bitterly opposed the prohibitionists. The Episcopalian

[11] John P. Irish, former Democratic state chairman, quoted in Des Moines *Iowa State Register*, July 12, 1882.

bishop of Iowa sneered at "the disappointments and disasters, the illiberal fanaticism and unwarranted license, of the so-called temperance reform."[12] A leading German Catholic priest in Cincinnati sounded the liturgicals' favorite charges of fanaticism and hypocrisy:

The American nationality . . . is often the hotbed of fanaticism, intolerance, and radical, ultra views on matters of politics and religion. All the vagaries of spiritualism, Mormonism, freeloveism, prohibition, infidelity and materialism, generally breed in the American nationality. While the Irishman will get drunk and engage in an open street fight, and the German drink his beer in a public beergarden, the American, pretending to be a total abstainer, takes his strong drink secretly and sleeps it off on a sofa or in a club room.[13]

More loftily, the Missouri Synod found "the real principle involved in prohibition is directly adverse to the spirit, the method and the aim of Christian morals."[14]

The Republican party, responding to the demands of its rank and file, supported efforts to control the saloon. In 1886 and 1888, for example, Republican platforms endorsed temperance positions in twenty-seven states, and opposed them only in California. The Democratic party, nationally and in each midwestern state, repeatedly endorsed wet positions.[15] As one party leader explained, "The Democratic party has never posed as the great and only party of morality and temperance. The Republican party has."[16]

One by one the pietistic denominations moved from endorsements of total abstinence to demands for temperance legislation, soon including total prohibition of the manufacture and sale of all alcoholic beverages. The Methodists were the most vigorous, as their official declaration in 1888 suggests:

The liquor traffic is so pernicious in all its bearings, so inimical to the interests of honest trade, so repugnant to the moral sense, so injurious to the peace and order of society, so hurtful to the homes, to the church and to the body politic, and so utterly antagonistic to all that is precious in life, that the only proper attitude toward it for Christians is that of relentless hostility. It can never be legalized without sin. No temporary device for regulating it can become a substitute for prohibition.[17]

---

[12] *Twenty-Ninth Annual Convention, Diocese of Iowa* (Davenport, 1882), pp. 56-57.

[13] Anton Walburg, *The Question of Nationality* (Cincinnati, 1889), quoted in Robert Cross (ed.), *The Church and the City* (Indianapolis, 1967), p. 118.

[14] *Lutheran Witness* VII (Feb. 7, 1889), 131.

[15] For details of the temperance crusades, see Charles E. Canup, "The Temperance Movement in Indiana," *Indiana Magazine of History*, XVI (1920) 112-51; Ernest Bogart and Charles Thompson, *The Industrial State: 1870-1893* (Springfield, Ill., 1920), pp. 42-50, 139-47; and for dry detail, *The Standard Encyclopedia of the Alcohol Problem* (Westerville, Ohio, 1924-1930); for party platforms, see *Cyclopedia of Temperance and Prohibition* (New York, 1891), pp. 152-53, 592-93.

[16] From 1895 speech in Indiana Senate by John Kern (Bryan's running mate in 1908, and later majority leader in the United States Senate), in Claude Bowers, *The Life of John Worth Kern* (Indianapolis, 1918), p. 104.

[17] *Cyclopedia of Temperance*, p. 426.

In 1883 the Presbyterians officially denounced the liquor traffic as "the principle cause of . . . drunkenness and its consequent pauperism, crime, taxation, lamentations, war, and ruin to the bodies and souls of men," and advised its members to "persevere in vigorous efforts" for total prohibition.[18] The Scandinavian Lutherans insisted it was the "duty" of the Christian voter to abolish intoxicating drinks by law.[19] In some smaller denominations, and even among Methodists, many ministers switched out of the Republican party to support the Prohibition party candidates. In 1888 the annual conference of the small Free Methodist denomination went so far as to assert "that it is the solemn duty of the ministers and laymen . . . to give to the National Prohibition party our hearty support in every proper way, and especially to vote its ticket."[20]

The effect of the prohibition issue in differentiating liturgical and pietistic voters of similar background can be traced in aggregate election returns. Most Norwegians in Iowa were pietistic Lutherans and voted 90 per cent Republican year in and year out. In Winneshiek county, however, liturgical Norwegian Lutherans predominated. The three towns of Pleasant, Glenwood and Madison voted 93 per cent Republican in 1881, before the temperance issue became salient. In 1882, the same towns voted 55 per cent against a prohibition amendment to the state constitution and, as the temperance crusade continued, the Republican share of the vote slipped 33 points to 60 per cent in 1891. In 1893, after the prohibition issue had been temporarily resolved to the satisfaction of the liturgicals, the vote in the towns shot up to 76 per cent. In heavily liturgical-German Dubuque, where the Republicans had taken 50 per cent of the vote in 1881, the prohibition amendment received only 15 per cent of the vote, and the Republican vote plunged at the next election to 28 per cent. (Dubuque's ward five, a German center, which had been 63 per cent Republican, voted 94 per cent wet, and the Republican vote then plunged to 22 per cent.)[21] The professionals in the Republican party finally learned that support for prohibition meant defeat at the polls and after 1891 generally refused to permit the pietists to dictate dry platforms.[22]

Religious outlook seems also to have affected occupational status. The

[18] *Ibid.*, p. 494.

[19] See Henry E. Jacobs and John Haas, *The Lutheran Encyclopedia* (New York, 1899), p. 395.

[20] *Voice*, Sept. 27, 1888 (this was the prohibition party newspaper); see issues of Sept. 6, 27, Oct. 4, 25, 1888; *Cyclopedia of Temperance*, p. 186; and *One Hundred Years of Temperance* (New York, 1886), pp. 96, 98, 344, 351, 414, 423, for details of third party activity among Methodist, United Presbyterian, United Brethren, Church of God, Quaker, Swedish Baptist, Free Will Baptist, and Free Methodist clergy. In 1889 one pietistic Ohio Lutheran synod endorsed the Prohibitionist nominee for governor. *Lutheran Witness*, VIII (Nov. 21, 1889), 93.

[21] Election returns and ethnic details based on the *Iowa Census of 1885* (Des Moines, 1885) and the Dubuque *Herald*.

[22] See Richard Jensen, *The Winning of the Midwest: Social and Political Conflict, 1888-1896* (Chicago, 1971) for details.

pietistic faith, by placing heavy emphasis upon individual initiative and responsibility for salvation, attracted entrepreneurs, while the passive liturgical faith was more amenable to less adventuresome men. One study of the split between Old School and New School Presbyterians in Philadelphia shows that from 60 to 80 per cent of the merchants, manufacturers, professional men and retailers chose New School (pietistic) congregations, while 75 per cent of the artisans and laborers moved into Old School congregations. Furthermore, the New School artisans were significantly more economically secure than the Old School artisans.[23] As Seymour M. Lipset has observed, "The Arminian [pietistic] emphasis on the personal attainment of grace, perhaps even more than the Calvinist stress on the existence of an 'elect,' served as a religious parallel to the secular emphasis on equality of opportunity and achievement."[24]

Occupational status had a more direct connection with politics; the Republican party always offered a comfortable home to the businessman, while the Democrats throughout the century consistently attacked the wealthy and the privileged. For example, in 1876, the leading Democratic newspaper in Illinois, noting that the Republican candidate for governor "speaks of Mr. Seward, the democratic candidate, as the 'barnyard' candidate," retorted:

The men of the shops and of the farms, the laborers of the cities and towns, in short, the workingmen, are the real owners of the country. They fight its battles in war and support its revenues in peace; the man who works in his barn-yard has a better claim upon the suffrages of his fellow citizens than has the banker who clips off coupons and shaves notes.[25]

A few years later, a Republican newspaper in Indianapolis proclaimed, "In this community the majority of people who occupy the foremost walks of life, as preachers, lawyers, doctors, merchants . . . are republicans." The leading Democratic organ immediately denounced this "snobbery" as "insults to every honest wage-worker," and as "un-American, undemocratic and monstrous" to boot.[26]

So far, men without religious affiliations have not been accounted for. The very fact that they did not belong to a church in an age of revivals suggests that most of these men would either be young voters who had not yet been converted, or else were reluctant to join in voluntary organizations. It can therefore be expected that their partisanship would be weak. And since they lacked religious affinities toward either party, they should be located midway between pietistic Republicans and liturgical Democrats. Furthermore, the two parties were very closely matched before 1894 and election campaigns very intensely

[23] Robert Doherty, "Social Bases for the Presbyterian Schism of 1837-1838," *Journal of Social History* II (1968), 69-79.

[24] Seymour Martin Lipset, *The First New Nation* (New York, 1963), p. 185; Lipset has a valuable chapter on the importance of religion in the nineteenth century.

[25] Springfield *Illinois State Register*, Oct. 25, 1876, quoted in Bogart and Thompson, *Industrial State*, pp. 118-19.

[26] Indianapolis *Sentinel*, Oct. 18, 1888.

fought. As every extra vote counted, both parties probably endeavored to enlist these men, thus dividing them 50-50. If they were in business or professional occupations, however, they might be drawn to the Republicanism of their colleagues and repelled by the antibusiness animus of the Democracy. If they were factory workers, the Republican high-tariff position would be especially appealing. If they were laborers or farmers, they might have been drawn to the Democracy as the party of the common man. All of these possibilities can be explored with interview data.

✿   ✿   ✿   ✿

The detailed analysis of one urban and seven rural townships in northern and central Illinois, and six rural townships in central Indiana[27] reaffirm the patterns displayed in Geneseo and Princeton and support the hypotheses drawn from that data. Table 4 shows the partisan distributions by denomination for the Indiana townships, where the coverage was unusually good (in part because the editors lived in one of the townships); all names were included except for twenty-four (1.5 per cent) who failed to return any information on party or religion, and who usually had no age data listed. Less than 25 per cent of the eligible men were missed by the canvassers here and, according to aggregate election returns, they voted the same way as the men who were included. Table 5 shows the party breakdown by denomination for the Illinois data. In this case, only Republicans and Democrats listed in the directories were included; otherwise coverage was comparable to that in Indiana.

TABLE 4

PARTY, BY DENOMINATION, HENDRICKS COUNTY, 1874

Denomination	% Rep.	% Dem.	% None or other	N
Friends (Quaker)	96.4	1.2	2.4	83
Christian (Disciples)	73.6	23.7	2.7	291
Methodist*	72.8	21.9	5.2	232
Presbyterian	64.3	31.4	4.3	70
Missionary Baptist	57.4	38.6	4.0	101
Misc. Prot. denoms.	52.1	39.1	8.7	23
No denomination given	47.0	48.3	4.6	699
Regular Baptist	17.0	78.7	4.3	94
Roman Catholic	4.2	83.3	12.5	24

*Methodist Episcopal plus African Methodist

[27] Lincoln city, Elkhart, Sheridan, and Chester townships, Logan county, Illinois; Black Hawk, Buffalo Prairie, Port Byron and Rural townships, Rock Island county, Illinois; Liberty, Lincoln, Marion, Middle, Union and Washington townships, Hendricks county, Indiana. See note 4 for list of sources.

TABLE 5

PARTY, FOR PIETISTIC DENOMINATIONS, 8 ILLINOIS TWPS., 1877-78
(Per cent Republican of two-party total)

Denomination	% Rep.	N
Congregationalist	82.0	39
Methodist	75.2	289
Disciples, Christians & Cumberland Presbyterian	71.8	220
Lutheran (pietistic synods only)	60.5	38
Presbyterian	57.7	108
Baptist	55.7	61

The four most Republican denominations, Quakers, Congregationalists, Disciples and Methodists, were strongly pietistic in the Midwest. The Presbyterians were predominantly pietistic, but the traces of Old School liturgical Democracy were evident.[28] The Baptists present an interesting special case. The Missionary Baptists were pietists, while most of the "Regular" Baptists in Hendricks county clung to orthodox Calvinist views and were especially hostile to missionary and temperance societies.[29] Only 4.2 per cent of the Hendricks county men were independent—including several "Greeley Republicans," two Grangers, three Prohibitionists, and one "Old Whig." Occupationally, only half the independents were farmers, in contrast to over three-fourths of the partisans; the independents were also a bit younger, but the small N's prevent more exact conclusions. The "Civil War" generation (born 1832 to 1845) in Hendricks county was only slightly more Republican than other age cohorts, controlling for religion and occupation, although 189 of the 236 Union veterans in the county (80 per cent) in 1880 were reportedly Republicans, with Democrats outnumbering Greenbackers two to one among the remainder.[30] Sectional origins were not significant in Hendricks—the great majority of all the voters had been born in the South or had fathers born in the South. Southern origins, less than a decade after the Civil War, did not affect the partisanship of these Hoosiers; the effect in Illinois was very small.

The interview records do not, of course, specify whether a man was pietistic or liturgical in orientation. Some oversimplification is necessary: all members of predominantly liturgical denominations must be classified as liturgicals, and all members of pietistic denominations as pietists.

[28] Suppose half the Presbyterians had been pietistic New School members and had voted 90 per cent Republican, while the other half had ben liturgical Old School members and had voted only 40 per cent Republican. Then about 65 per cent of all the Presbyterians would be Republican, or about the same as the actual results in Tables 1 and 4.

[29] See John F. Cady, *The Origin and Development of the Missionary Baptist Church in Indiana* (Berne, Ind., 1942).

[30] "The number of Ex-Union Soldiers in Indiana and their Politics in 1880," manuscript poll in Benjamin Harrison Papers, Library of Congress (series 14, reel 143 of the microfilm edition).

Obviously some men will be misclassified, but the effect of this error will be to weaken the true patterns. That is, if the hypothesis is true, most of the true liturgicals misclassified as pietists would be Democrats, and the misclassification therefore lowers the observed proportion of pietists who were Republicans. If the errors of misclassification could somehow be rectified, the estimated proportion of Republicans among pietists (already high) would be further increased and the estimated proportion of Republicans among liturgicals (already low) would be further lowered.[31]

All members of Protestant denominations were classified as pietistic with the exception of Episcopalians, German Lutherans, Old School Presbyterians, Primitive Baptists, and Anti-Missionary Baptists. Everyone else, including the handful of Jews, was classified as liturgical. Table 6 shows the aggregate totals by religious and party groups for the eight Illinois townships. The small number (73) of liturgical Republicans were mostly (56 per cent) German Lutherans; possibly some may have actually belonged to one of the pietistic Lutheran groups. Of the 262 pietistic Democrats, a disproportionate number were farmers (56 per cent versus 43 per cent of other Democrats), or were born in eastern states (26 per cent versus 10 per cent of other Democrats). This suggests that pietistic Democrats were older men who had first been socialized into politics during the second party system and had never abandoned the Jacksonian Democracy. This hunch is partially confirmed by the age data in Hendricks county. Half the pietistic Democrats (50.6 per cent) were born before 1833 and thus came of voting age before the Republican party was formed; however, almost as many pietistic Republicans (44.5 per cent) had also been born before 1833.

TABLE 6

PARTY AND RELIGION, 8 ILLINOIS TOWNSHIPS, 1877-78

	Pietistic	Religious Grouping Not Affiliated	Liturgical	All
Republican	515	549	73	1137
Democrat	262	504	333	1099
No party, other	45	510	56	611
All	822	1563	462	2847

The Illinois returns for each religious and political group are shown by their occupational distributions in Tables 7 and 8. Bear in mind that low-status occupations probably were under-represented in the direc-

[31] The proportion of Republicans among pietists would be mistakenly exaggerated only if the true liturgicals misclassified as pietists were more than 80 or 90 per cent Republican, an extremely unlikely situation. Conversely the proportion of Democrats among liturgicals would be mistakenly high only if the true pietists misclassified as liturgicals were nearly 100 per cent Democrats, an equally implausible situation.

tories. Several striking patterns appear. An urban-rural split occurs on party identifications. The great majority (83 per cent) of independents were non-farmers, while Democrats were somewhat more likely to be farmers than Republicans (51 per cent versus 41 per cent). There was, however, no urban-rural difference between liturgicals and pietists, while non-members were slightly more likely to be non-farmers. Age probably accounted for this—young men, who had not yet been converted, were leaving the farms for the nearby towns.

TABLE 7

NON-FARM OCCUPATION, BY PARTY AND RELIGION, 8 ILLINOIS TWPS., 1877-78 (Read Down)

| | % All | Party | | | | Religion | |
		% Rep.	% Neither	% Dem.	% Piet.	% None	% Lit.
Professional	8.5	9.6	8.9	6.8	13.4	7.3	4.6
Business	21.1	24.0	25.5	13.3	23.3	21.6	15.3
White Collar	6.8	6.9	7.3	6.3	5.8	7.6	5.3
Skilled Blue Collar	32.7	36.0	30.4	30.9	33.8	35.2	21.4
Unskilled Blue Collar	8.2	5.8	7.1	12.0	3.1	8.2	16.5
Unskilled Common Labor	15.2	10.2	13.6	22.9	11.0	13.2	30.4
Unknown	7.5	7.5	13.2	7.8	9.6	6.9	6.5
Total	100.0	100.0	100.0	100.0	100.0	100.0	100.0
N	1717	669	506	542	447	1009	261

TABLE 8

FARM OCCUPATION, BY PARTY AND RELIGION, 8 ILLINOIS TWPS., 1877-78 (Read Down)

| | % All | Party | | | | Religion | |
		% Rep.	% Neither	% Dem.	% Piet.	% None	% Lit.
Farm Owners	75.2	76.0	73.3	74.9	78.9	70.5	81.5
Sons of Owners	9.7	10.5	8.6	9.3	9.6	12.3	3.0
Renters & Laborers	15.1	13.5	18.1	15.8	11.5	17.2	15.5
Total	100.0	100.0	100.0	100.0	100.0	100.0	100.0
N	1129	467	105	557	374	553	201
Farmers as % of All Voters	39.7	41.1	17.2	50.6	44.5	35.5	43.5

Among the non-farmers (not all of whom lived in towns or cities), the Republicans were especially strong and liturgicals weak. This was the age of the Yankee mechanic, and the Republican protective tariff. To scotch one old myth, blacksmiths (in Indiana) were just as religious and partisan as anyone else, though it is true that the only "naturalist" and the "free and easy" independent in Hendricks county were both blacksmiths. The pietists were especially strong among professionals and weak among unskilled labor, with just the reverse for liturgicals. The religious literature of late-nineteenth century is full of warnings that the Protestant churches had abandoned the lower classes to the "Romanists."

By removing the political independents (and non-responders) the relative party strength among occupational groups, controlling for religion, can be discriminated. Table 9 shows the Republican share of the two-party vote for each occupational group by religious subgroups.

TABLE 9

PARTY STRENGTH BY OCCUPATION AND RELIGION, 8 ILLINOIS TOWNSHIPS, 1877-78
(Per cent Republican of two-party total)
(N in parentheses)

Occupation	% Pietists	% Not Affiliated	% Liturgicals	% All
Professional	75.9 (N=58)	50.0 (34)	33.3 (9)	63.4 (101)
Business	81.4 (97)	62.8 (105)	51.5 (31)	69.1 (233)
White Collar	60.0 (25)	61.9 (42)	38.4 (13)	57.5 (80)
Skilled Blue Collar	73.1 (145)	55.6 (218)	30.4 (46)	58.9 (409)
Unskilled	65.0 (60)	48.0 (123)	8.0 (113)	36.1 (296)
Unknown	65.9 (38)	52.6 (38)	31.2 (16)	54.4 (92)
All Non-farm	72.9 (423)	55.1 (560)	22.8 (228)	55.3 (1211)
Farm Owner	59.1 (279)	49.1 (348)	13.1 (145)	46.1 (772)
Sons of Owner	70.6 (34)	41.0 (61)	0.0 (6)	48.5 (101)
Renters & Laborers	42.5 (40)	52.4 (84)	7.4 (27)	41.7 (151)
All Farm	58.4 (353)	48.7 (493)	11.8 (178)	45.6 (1024)
All	66.2 (776)	52.2 (1053)	18.0 (406)	50.9 (2236)

The basic pietistic-liturgical correlation with party holds true for every occupational group, with two exceptions. Among high-status businessmen, Republican liturgicals barely outnumbered Democrats. Among low-status farm renters and laborers pietistic Democrats outnumbered Republicans. The unchurched groups hovered around the 50-50 mark, except among businessmen, white collar workers and, inexplicably, among adult sons living on their fathers' farms. The unchurched fell midway politically between the pietists and liturgicals in every occupation except white collar workers (but the N is small), and among those farmer renters and laborers. (The reason here is that only 3 of 35 Republican farm laborers were pietists, in contrast to 14 of 28 renters.) Note also that farmers were 10 points less Republican than non-farmers (14.5 points for pietists, 6.4 points for nonmembers, 11.0 points for liturgicals). As far as age is concerned, a random sample (N=314) from Indiana gives a median age of 36 or 37 for the Republican farmers and non-farmers, and for the Democratic non-farmers, but a median age of 44 for Democratic farmers—indicating again the special affinity for Jacksonian Democracy among older farmers.

The four rows in Table 9 representing the largest nonfarm occupational groups, businessmen, professionals, skilled blue collar workers, and unskilled laborers, illustrate the complex relationship among party religion and occupation. (White collar clerks, for whom the numbers are small, are somewhat exceptional.) The Republican strength in the four groups ranged from 65 to 81 per cent among pietists, from 48 to 63 per cent among unaffiliated, and from 8 per cent to 52 per cent among liturgicals. Three factors account for these patterns, and for the similar patterns in Tables 2 and 3: religion itself, occupation itself, and the joint effect (interaction) between religion and occupation.

For each occupational group taken separately, the Republican strength depended greatly on religious grouping. Pietists were 30 points more Republican than liturgicals among businessmen, and a remarkable 57 points more Republican among the unskilled. Secondly, among men in the same religious group, there was a wide range between the most and least Republican occupation, with businessmen highest and unskilled lowest for each group. Among pietists, businessmen were 16 points more Republican than laborers, while among liturgicals the businessmen were 43 points more Republican. Occupation was thus more influential among liturgicals than among pietists or the unaffiliated. Clearly religion and occupation were both "real" factors that cannot be explained away by statistical controls. The independent effects of religion and occupation added together so that pietistic businessmen had the extra Republicanism of pietists added to the extra Republicanism of businessmen, and were an amazing 73 points more Republican than unskilled liturgicals. This immense range between two polar groups living in the same community was far greater than the average differences in voting patterns between different communities. Considering the farmers too, the 2236 voters in the eight townships who expressed a political preference were almost exactly divided between the parties (50.9 per cent Republican versus 49.1 per cent Democratic). In aggregate terms, therefore, the townships hovered around 50-50, yet the constituent groups typically hovered around the 75-25 level (except for the nonaffiliated group which was 50-50). Any analysis of the social correlates of partisanship that depends upon aggregate election returns will miss the most important dimension of midwestern voting patterns, the deep internal conflicts, because the votes of the various religions and occupational groups were usually mixed together in aggregate data.

The factors of religion and occupation interacted so that the liturgical concentrated in the heavily Democratic low-status occupations (see Table 7). Thus the non-farmer pietists, taken all together, were 50 points more Republican than the liturgicals (72.9 versus 22.8), which is larger than the spread in any occupation group except unskilled. It is impossible to explain the reasons for this interaction, but the theological and social group functions of religion were factors, along with positive anti-liturgical job discrimination. If the interaction had not existed and the pietists, liturgicals and unaffiliated had been proportionately represented in each occupation, then the pietists would have been 71.5 per cent Republican instead of 72.9 per cent, the unaffiliated would have been 54.8 per cent instead of 55.3 per cent, and the liturgicals would have been 29.8 per cent instead of 22.8 per cent for a range of 71.5-29.8 =42 points instead of 72.9-22.8=50 points.[32] Thus, different occupational profiles increased the political difference between pietists and liturgicals from 42 to 50 points, an increase of 20 per cent.

Conversely, if the religious profile of each occupational group had been identical, the businessmen would have been 67.1 per cent Republican instead of 69.1 per cent, and the unskilled would have been 46.4 per cent Republican instead of 36.1 per cent. Thus the different religious profiles of the occupations stretched the difference between businessmen and unskilled from 67.1-46.4=21 points to 69.1-36.1=33 points, an increase of over 50 per cent. Hence, the religious distribution produced relatively greater effects than the occupational distribution did or, in other words, religion exacerbated the political tension between high and low status occupations.

The 21 point spread between the Republicanism of businessmen and unskilled laborers which remains after correction for the lopsided religious distribution has been made stands in need of further explanation. Unfortunately, no profound insights can be squeezed out of the tables. A variety of hypotheses could explain the result. Perhaps the Republicans were simply the party of the classes and the Democrats the party of the masses. This may be true, but it merely restates the results and does not explain when, how, and why such a difference emerged. If the pattern first emerged after the Civil War, it could be best explained in terms of Reconstruction race and economic policies and, perhaps, the effects of the depression of 1873-1877. If the pattern first emerged during the war, emancipation policies, conscription, economic conditions and Republican appeals to patriotism would seem to offer the best leads. If the patterns first emerged before the war, a different set of explanations is required. Until the dating problem is solved, the occupational differences cannot be explained.

New data is also needed to settle conclusively whether the relationships among religion, occupation and party can be generalized for the entire country. Clearly a different framework of analysis is necessary to explain the racially-oriented patterns of partisanship in the postwar

---

[32] The first column of Table 7 shows the occupational profile of all 1717 nonfarmers; the last three columns show the profile for each religious group. If the occupational profile for each religious group had been identical, 8.5 per cent of the pietists, nonmembers and liturgicals would be professionals, of whom 75.9 per cent, 50.0 per cent and 33.3 per cent, respectively, would be Republicans (according to the first row of Table 9). Arithmetically, the proportion of pietists who would then be Republicans is: 8.5% x 75.9% + 21.1% x 81.4% + ... + 7.5% x 65.9% = 71.5%. This procedure, called "standardization," was repeated for each religious group, and a similar standarization by religion was computed for each occupational group.

South. The political history of the northern states was relatively uniform in the 1850's, 1860's and early 1870's, but the East differed sharply from the Midwest by its more industrialized occupational profile and the tendency in some denominations (Congregationalists, Quaker, Presbyterian) for liturgical elements to be stronger than they were in the Midwest. Congregationalists in New England in the 1850's, for example, were less committed to temperance and antislavery than their counterparts in the Midwest.[33] The tentative conclusion is that the strong links among religion, occupation and politics that existed in Illinois and Indiana were typical of the Midwest, and perhaps the Northeast too, but not the South.

[33] Charles C. Cole, *The Social Ideas of the Northern Evangelists: 1826-1860* (New York, 1954), pp. 196-197; Richard R. Wescott, "A History of Maine Politics 1840-1856: The Formation of the Republican Party" (Ph.D. dissertation, Univ. of Maine, 1966), pp. 13-14; Whitney R. Cross, *The Burned-Over District* (Ithaca, 1950), pp. 222-23; John Niven, *Connecticut for the Union* (New Haven, 1965), p. 7; Lewis Vander Velde, *The Presbyterian Churches and the Federal Union 1861-1869* (Cambridge, 1932), pp. 62-63; Gilbert H. Barnes, *The Antislavery Impulse, 1830-1844* (New York, 1933), pp. 91, 242 n.10.

NEGROES IN THE FIRST AND SECOND RECONSTRUCTIONS OF THE SOUTH

August Meier

"REVOLUTIONS NEVER GO BACKWARDS": so declared the editors of the first Negro daily newspaper, the New Orleans *Tribune*, late in 1864.[1] Northern troops had occupied the city and much of Louisiana as early as 1862, and the *Tribune* insisted that the logical second step, after crushing the slaveholders' rebellion, was that the national government divide their plantations among the freedmen. Washington failed to act upon this proposal, and seventy years later W. E. B. DuBois, in assessing the reconstruction experience, perceived it as a revolution that had indeed gone backwards. It had gone backwards, he held, mainly because Congress had failed to press forward to the logical corollary of its reconstruction program; the distribution of the former slaveowners' lands among the Negroes.[2] More recently, Willie Lee Rose, though starting from a different philosophy of history, arrived at rather similar conclusions. In her volume on the South Carolina Sea Island Negroes during the Civil War she describes how the military authorities divided many of the Sea Island plantations among the freedmen. President Andrew Johnson, however, returned the lands to the former owners, and Congress failed to intervene. Mrs. Rose pithily sums up this sequence of events by entitling the last chapter of her book "Revolutions May Go Backwards."[3] Nevertheless, in the face of such distinguished scholarly opinion, I would like to suggest that what occurred during reconstruction was really not a genuine revolution, not even an abortive one.

Consider the following example. In Georgia, in April, 1868, slightly a year after the passage of the Reconstruction Act of 1867, a constitution drawn up under the procedures required by Congress was ratified by the voters, and new officials were elected. The process of reconstruction was supposedly completed when, in July, the legis-

[1] New Orleans *Tribune*, Nov. 29, 1864. This paper was one of a series read at Roosevelt University in the fall of 1965, marking the centennial of reconstruction.
[2] W. E. B. DuBois, *Black Reconstruction* (New York, 1935).
[3] Willie Lee Rose, *Rehearsal for Reconstruction: The Port Royal Experiment* (Indianapolis, 1964).

lature ratified the Fourteenth Amendment, and military authority was withdrawn. The new state government, however, was no genuinely "radical" regime. Just six weeks later the legislature expelled its Negro members, on the grounds that Negroes, though guaranteed the right to vote, had not been specifically made eligible for office.[4]

Before they departed, one of the Negro representatives, Henry M. Turner, a minister of the African Methodist Episcopal Church, and formerly a Civil War chaplain and Freedmen's Bureau agent, delivered a ringing, sarcastic speech, defiantly expressing his vision of a democratic America. He would not, he said, behave as some of his thirty-one colored colleagues had, and attempt to retain his seat by appealing to the magnanimity of the white legislators. He would not, "fawn or cringe before any party nor stoop to beg them for my rights," like "slaves begging under the lash. I am here to defend my rights, and to hurl thunderbolts at the men who would dare to cross the threshold of my manhood. . . . I was not aware that there was in the character of the [Anglo-Saxon] race so much cowardice, . . . pusillanimity . . . [and] treachery." It was the Negroes who had "set the ball of loyalty rolling in the State of Georgia . . . and [yet] there are persons in this legislature, today, who are ready to spit their poison in my face, while they themselves . . . opposed the ratification of the Constitution. *They* question my right to a seat in this body."

Then, in rhetoric typical of the era, Turner stated the Negro's claims.

The great question is this. Am I a man? If I am such, I claim the rights of a man. Am I not a man because I happen to be of darker hue than honorable gentlemen around me? . . . Why, sir, though we are not white, we have accomplished much. We have pioneered civilization here; we have built up your country; we have worked in your fields, and garnered your harvest, for two hundred and fifty years. And what do we ask of you in return . . .? Do we ask retaliation? We ask it not. . . . but we ask you now for our RIGHTS. It is extraordinary that a race such as yours, professing gallantry, and chivalry, and education and superiority, living in a land where ringing chimes call child and sire to the Church of God— a land . . . where courts of justice are presumed to exist . . . can make war upon the poor defenseless black man. . . .

You may expel us, gentlemen, but I firmly believe that you will someday repent it. The black man cannot protect a country, if the country doesn't protect him; and if, tomorrow, a war should arise, I would not raise a musket to defend a country where my manhood is denied . . . . You may expel us . . .; but while you do it remember that there is a just God in Heaven, whose All-Seeing Eye beholds alike the acts of the oppressor and

---

[4] Ethel Maude Christler, "The Participation of Negroes in the Government of Georgia, 1867-1870" (M.A. thesis, Atlanta University, 1932), *passim*, is the best general treatment. See also C. Mildred Thompson, *Reconstruction in Georgia, Economic, Political and Social* (New York, 1915), chaps. vii, viii, and x.

the oppressed, and who, despite the machinations of the wicked, never fails to vindicate the cause of justice.[5]

The events just described epitomize two things: the aspirations and hopes of Negroes on the one hand; and the superficial character of the reconstruction process on the other. Pressure from Congress and the state supreme court did later secure a reversal of the ban on Negro legislators, and one Georgia Negro, Jefferson Long, sat in Congress for a term. Nevertheless, southern whites actually dominated the state's government, and by 1872 the Redeemers, or Democrats, had returned to power. Thus the period of so-called Radical or Black reconstruction can scarcely be said to have existed in Georgia; and what happened in that state can hardly be called a revolution, even a revolution that later went backwards. Most writers on the history of Negroes during reconstruction have dwelt upon developments in South Carolina, Louisiana, and Mississippi, where Negroes formed a majority of the population and therefore held more high offices than elsewhere. What happened in Georgia was, however, a good deal more typical of what happened in most of the southern states during reconstruction.

The failure of congressional reconstruction, the return of the southern states to white hegemony, and the subordination and oppression of the black man were due not only to southern white recalcitrance, but equally as much to northern indifference and to the limitations in congressional policy. Northern indifference to the Negro's welfare and the consequent inadequacies of Congress' program were deeply rooted in the historical racism of the American public They were thus fundamentally a continuation of a cultural tradition that had not only permitted the existence of slavery in the South, but had relegated free Negroes to second-class citizenship in the North.

In the opening months of the Civil War, for example, Negroes and the small band of white abolitionists had been far in advance of northern opinion in regarding the war as fundamentally a struggle for the emancipation of the slaves. From the day of the firing on Fort Sumter, Negroes had envisioned the situation as an irrepressible moral conflict between slavery and liberty, and a war for the rights of man in fulfillment of the genius of the American democratic faith. However, the President, the Congress and most of the nation at first regarded the war simply as a campaign to preserve the Union, and only slowly and reluctantly, and as a result of the exigencies of

[5] Henry M. Turner, *Speech on the Eligibility of Colored Men to Seats in the Georgia Legislature . . . September 3, 1868* (Augusta, 1868), *passim.*

a prolonged and difficult military conflict, did the Federal government come to emancipate the slaves and enlist Negroes in the armed
forces.[6] Moreover, the vast majority of northerners continued to
resist the idea that Negroes should be accorded the rights of citizens.
In 1863, at the thirtieth anniversary convention of the founding of the
American Anti-Slavery Society, Frederick Douglass excoriated those
abolitionists who felt that their work was accomplished when the
slaves were freed. Negroes, along with a handful of white abolitionists, formed the vanguard of those who insisted that with emancipation the struggle for Negro freedom had only begun. To Negroes the
issues were moral ones, based upon the promise of American life,
upon the assumptions of the American faith that were rooted in the
Declaration of Independence and the ethics of Christianity. As a
conclave of Pennsylvania leaders declared in 1868: "It is America that
you have to civilize, to Christianize, and compel to accept and practically apply to all men, without distinctions of color or race, the
glorious principles and precepts laid down in her immortal Declaration of Independence."[7]

Long before the war had ended, northern Negro leaders had
spelled out the specific program they deemed essential for the creation of a truly democratic America. In October, 1864, the race's most
prominent men met in Syracuse, New York, to organize an Equal
Rights League that would agitate for citizenship rights and racial
equality. At that time the slaves had not yet been freed in the loyal
Border States, and most of the northern states prohibited Negroes
from voting, from testifying against whites in court, from serving
on juries, and in some cases from attending public schools (even
segregated schools). The convention delegates were critical of the
fact that most northern states still refused to accord Negroes the
ballot, and they even denounced the Republican party for being ar-
rayed with the proslavery Democratic party in its support of racial
prejudice. Their two chief demands were abolition and political
equality. As Douglass pointed out in an address before the Massachusetts Anti-Slavery Society a few months later, Negroes wanted the
suffrage . . .

because it is our *right*, first of all. No class of men can, without insulting
their own nature, be content with any deprivation of their rights. Again,

[6] James M. McPherson, *The Negro's Civil War* (New York, 1965), chaps. ii
and iii; McPherson, *The Struggle for Equality: Abolitionists and the Negro in
Civil War and Reconstruction* (Princeton, 1964), chap. iii.

[7] *Proceedings of the American Anti-Slavery Society at Its Third Decade . . .
December 3, 4, 5, 1863* (New York, 1864), pp. 110-118; *Proceedings of the
Fourth Annual Meeting of the Pennsylvania State Equal Rights League . . .
1868* (Philadelphia, 1868), p. 35.

I want the elective franchise . . . because ours is a peculiar government, based upon a peculiar idea, and that idea is universal suffrage. If I were in a monarchical . . . or aristocratic government, where the few ruled and the many were subject, there would be no special stigma resting upon me because I did not exercise the elective franchise . . ., but here, where universal suffrage . . . is the fundamental idea of the Government, to rule us out is to make us an exception, to brand us with the stigma of inferiority, and to invite to our heads the missiles of those about us. . . .[8]

Douglass and other Negro leaders, while addressing the nation on matters of abolition and citizenship, advocated also a program of economic and moral improvement to be undertaken by Negroes themselves. The Syracuse convention exhorted the freedmen "to shape their course toward frugality, the accumulation of property, and above all, to leave untried no amount of effort and self-denial to acquire knowledge, and to secure a vigorous moral and religious growth." To men of the nineteenth century thrift and industry and the acquisition of property—especially land—were essential parts of the good life, along with citizenship rights. Moreover, a common school education was almost a *sine qua non* for securing a comfortable livelihood. It cannot be overemphasized that along with agitation for political and civil rights, Negro leaders stressed the cultivation of middle-class morality, the pursuit of education, and the acquisition of property. To use the phraseology of the time, these things, like the ballot, were regarded as essential for elevating the race and securing its inclusion in the "body politic."

Southern Negroes espoused the same program, and in some respects were more radical than the northern ministers, editors and artisan-businessmen who predominated at Negro conventions. Representative of the point of view of articulate southern Negroes was the New Orleans *Tribune*, which in 1864 and 1865 prefigured the outlook of most Negro spokesmen during the decade after the war. This journal denounced Lincoln's plan of reconstruction and endorsed that of the congressional Radicals. Only through congressional reconstruction would Negroes "secure the full enjoyment of our rights—not as a matter of gratuitous or benevolent grant, revocable at will—but as an embodiment of the principles set forth in the Declaration of Independence."[9] Highest among these rights was that of the franchise, for it was the only means by which Negroes could protect themselves from civil and economic discrimination.[10] To those who

[8] *Proceedings of the National Convention of Colored Men . . . 1864* (Boston, 1864); Frederick Douglass, "What the Black Man Wants," in William D. Kelley, Wendell Phillips and Frederick Douglass, *The Equality of all Men Before the Law* (Boston, 1865), pp. 36-37.
[9] New Orleans *Tribune,* Jan. 3, 1865.
[10] *Ibid.,* Aug. 5, 1865; Sept. 13, 1864.

argued that a time of preparation should elapse before the ex-slaves were enfranchised, the *Tribune* replied: "We do not know of a single reform, in the whole course of history, that was brought about by gradual and systematic preparation. In fact, how is preparation practicable without the free exercise of the right contended for . . .? Could the white man of America be prepared to the general exercise of the franchise, unless by going to the polls and voting?" Given the opportunity, the freedmen would show a comprehension of "their own interests" and a "Devotion to the Union" that should justify their immediate enfranchisement.[11]

The *Tribune* also gave pointed attention to the question of segregation. It opposed a bill introduced in the legislature, providing for separate schools,[12] and it continually protested against the system of "star cars" for Negroes in the city until the military authorities ordered the provisional governor to end this example of discrimination.[13] The editors regarded segregation as silly, since it was due to the white man's lust that miscegenation had proceeded to the point where "it would be a pretty hard thing to find a pure . . . Negro in the whole city of New Orleans, where seventy thousand persons of African descent are now residing."[14]

The journal devoted much space to economic matters, especially to the conditions under which the former slaves labored on the plantations. On this subject the *Tribune* went far beyond the thinking of most northern Negro leaders at this time, and beyond the thinking of many southern leaders as well. The editors boldly advocated what only the most radical of the Republicans and abolitionists were thinking of—the destruction of the plantation system. It criticized the United States government for not immediately confiscating and dividing the lands of the rebellious planters into five-acre lots, to be assigned to the "tillers of the soil" at a nominal price, so that the freedmen would be "thoroughly imbued with that . . . praiseworthy 'Yankee' idea, *that every man should own the land he tills, and head and hands he works with.*"[15] In calling for these steps the editors hoped to accomplish a democratic revolution in the South against the power of the antebellum slaveowning aristocracy: "The division of the lands is the only means by which a new, industrious and loyal population may be made to settle in the South. Large estates will always be in the hands of an aristocracy. Small estates are the real element of democracy."[16]

Broadly speaking, the Negro elite stressed above all the importance

[11] *Ibid.*, May 4, 1865.   [12] *Ibid.*, July 26, Dec. 24, 1864; Feb. 17, 1865.
[13] *Ibid.*, Feb. 28, May 21, Aug. 10, 1865.   [14] *Ibid.*, Aug. 15, 1865.
[15] *Ibid.*, Sept. 10, Sept. 24, 1864.   [16] *Ibid.*, Sept. 15, 1865.

of the franchise and civil rights. Next in order of importance, in the thinking of most of them, was the value of at least a common school education for the masses of the race. Finally, they were concerned with the economic problems of the freedmen. Most of them urged the masses to work hard, save their money, and acquire property; but some at least advocated a radical expropriation of the slaveowners' plantations and the creation, under Federal benevolence, of a numerous landowning yeoman peasantry. Such a policy would not only provide Negroes with an economic opportunity, but would supply the foundation for loyal and democratic governments in the southern states.

On the other hand, the evidence indicates that the masses had a scale of priorities that was precisely the opposite of that of the elite. Their primary interest was in land ownership. Close to this in importance for them was education. Though politics was of somewhat lesser value in their thinking, enfranchisement did initiate enthusiastic political participation on the part of the freedmen. Like the elite Negroes they displayed a profound awareness of the importance of political activity in American culture. The same is true of their interest in education. Old and young flocked to the schools opened by the northern missionaries and the Freedmen's Bureau. Especially notable were the freedmen's own efforts at self-help in education, establishing schools, hiring teachers, and erecting buildings.

Most of all, like oppressed peasants the world over, the freedmen wanted land. As Vernon Lane Wharton put it in his study of Negroes in Mississippi after the Civil War: "Their very lives were entwined with the land and its cultivation; they lived in a society where respectability was based on ownership of the soil; and to them to be free was to farm their own ground."[17] When President Andrew Johnson restored the Sea Island plantations to their former owners, he sent General O. O. Howard, head of the Freedmen's Bureau, to Edisto Island to inform the freedmen of his decision. The Negroes who crowded the church at which Howard spoke were disappointed and angry, and shouted "No, no!" to his remarks. Howard later recorded in his autobiography that one man called out from the gallery: "Why, General Howard, why do you take away our lands? You take them from us who have always been true, always true to the Government! You give them to our all-time enemies! That is not right!" The committee selected by the freedmen to meet with the representatives of the planters in order to arrange the details of the transfer of property informed Howard that they would not work for their old masters

[17] Vernon Lane Wharton, *The Negro in Mississippi, 1865-1890* (Chapel Hill, 1947), p. 59.

under overseers, though they were willing to *rent* the land if ownership was ruled out. The planters, however, were not interested in this
kind of arrangement and after a series of indignation meetings the
freedmen wrote a final appeal to the President. They insisted that it
was "very oppressing . . . [that] wee freemen should work for wages
for our former oners." They felt it was unfair for the President to
expect the freedmen to ask "for bread or shelter or Comfortable for
his wife and children" from men whom they had fought against "upon
the feal of battle." They had, they said, no confidence in their former
masters, one of whom had declared he would refuse to sell land to
freedmen, even at $100 an acre. Johnson, of course, remained un-
moved, and in the end the Negroes had to capitulate.[18]

A significant number of the freedmen attempted to buy their own
farms, even in the face of white reluctance to sell land to them.
Travelers from the North, Freedmen's Bureau agents and missionaries reported enthusiastically upon evidence of progress in this
direction. A New England cotton planter on the Sea Islands reported the case of "a black Yankee . . . [with] the energy" and eye
"for his own advantage of a born New Englander." His industry and
sharp dealing had put him ahead of the other on the plantation,
though half of them had fenced in their own gardens and were raising vegetables for the Hilton Head market.

Linus in his half-acre has quite a little farmyard besides. With poultry-
houses, pig-pens, and corn-houses, the array is very imposing. He has even
a stable, for he made out some title to a horse, which was allowed; and
then he begged a pair of wheels and makes a cart for his work; and not
to leave the luxuries behind, he next rigs up a kind of sulky and bows
to the white men from his carriage. As he keeps his table in corresponding
style . . . the establishment is rather expensive. So, to provide the means,
he has three permanent irons in the fire, his cotton, his Hilton Head
express, and his seines. . . . While other families "carry" from three to
seven acres of cotton, Linus says he must have fourteen. . . . With a
large boat which he owns, he usually makes weekly trips to Hilton Head,
twenty miles distant, carrying passengers, produce and fish. . . . I presume his savings since . . . the capture of the island amount to four or
five hundred dollars. He is all ready to buy land, and I expect to see him
in ten years a tolerably rich man.[19]

Only a few with exceptional ability or luck were able to become
permanent and substantial landowners. The plantation system remained intact. In fact, it may even have increased in extent. It simply
changed its form. Instead of slavery, the characteristic labor arrangement became that known as sharecropping.

[18] Rose, *Rehearsal for Reconstruction*, pp. 353-355.
[19] Elizabeth Ware Pearson (ed.), *Letters from Port Royal* (Boston, 1906), p.
37.

By the last quarter of the nineteenth century sharecropping, in combination with the crop-lien system, had become a system of gross exploitation, which reached its most extreme form in debt peonage. Here was a system in which the Negro tenant was almost at the complete mercy of the white planter. Yet, in its origins at least the sharecropping system was not something that was simply forced upon Negroes, but was in part a result of the freedmen's desire for independence, freedom and economic advancement. Much research on this subject remains to be done before the origins of sharecropping during the reconstruction period will be fully understood but recent studies suggest that what likely happened followed the general pattern outlined below.[20]

After the emancipation of the slaves and the close of the Civil War, planters generally attempted to employ Negroes as wage laborers with annual contracts. Under these contracts the freedmen were worked in gangs as they had been under slavery. In order to enforce the contractual obligation, it was common for planters to hold back part of the pay until the end of the cotton harvest. Such a system, characterized by gang labor and with its powers of coercion lodged in the planter's hands, smacked altogether too much of slavery and Negroes resisted working under it. Universally the freedmen wanted to own their own land; where this was not possible they preferred to rent land for cash if they could. But, as in the case of the Sea Islands, planters resisted such an arrangement because it did not give them as much control over the labor force as they desired. The sharecropping system thus seems to have emerged, in large part, as a sort of compromise. Under it, the tenants had their own plots, organized their own time, and were not subject to the *direct* discipline of the planters. On the other hand the system was beneficial to the planter in that it encouraged the tenant to stay on the land until the crop was harvested, and encouraged him to work hard since he kept a share of the crop. Nevertheless, as late as the 1880's it was common for planters in certain areas to complain about the sharecropping system.

Rudimentary sharecropping arrangements had appeared even before the close of the Civil War, but they received considerable impetus from the encouragement of the Freedmen's Bureau during the late 1860's. Negroes were never satisfied with the system; they always aspired to become cash renters or landowners. Moreover, what started

[20] The ideas developed in the following discussion owe a good deal to material in Martin Abbott, "Free Land, Free Labor, and the Freedmen's Bureau," *Agricultural History*, XXX (1956), pp. 150-156; and Joel Williamson, *After Slavery: The Negro in South Carolina During Reconstruction, 1861-1877*, chaps. iii and v.

out as a concession to the freedmen's desire for independence, quite rapidly became a system of racial repression.

The responsibility for the unsatisfactory resolution of the land question did not rest entirely with the southern whites. In large part it rested upon the actions of the northern whites. Despite the talk of confiscation, most political leaders—even many of the Radical Republicans and abolitionists—had too strong a sense of the importance of property rights to espouse confiscation of anyone's estates—even those of the rebels. In the end it was Congress and the Republicans as much as President Johnson who betrayed the freedmen on this crucial matter. The proposal was entirely too revolutionary for nineteenth-century America. The Republican leaders and the upper- and middle-class white abolitionists were for the most part simply too conservative to accept confiscation with equanimity. In fact, in their thinking, the right of an individual to his personal freedom and to his property were two closely interrelated rights, both of them founded in the values of individualism. For a similar reason there was a lack of unity among the friends of the freedmen regarding the degree to which the government should practice a parternalistic benevolence in uplifting the ex-slaves. Many thought that government assistance to the freedmen in the form of granting them land would discourage the individual initiative and independence which they hoped the freedmen, crushed down under slavery, would quickly develop.[21]

In some ways the land issue was the central or crucial issue in reconstruction as far as Negroes were concerned. As the New Orleans *Tribune* suggested, and as students as diverse as W. E. B. Du Bois and Gunnar Myrdal have maintained more recently,[22] it can be argued that the failure to confiscate the large estates and redistribute them in small plots among the freedmen, doomed Congress' plans for political reconstruction to failure and the black men to generations of oppression. Viewed more broadly, the North's failure to grapple seriously with the land question was simply part and parcel of the whole pattern of northern indifference to the status of Negroes in American society. To put the matter baldly, most of the people in a position of political influence were not really interested in the Negroes' welfare. Only a handful of Radical Republicans had any sincere desire to make Negroes full citizens. Citizenship rights and the franchise were provided almost as a by-product of political squabbling in Washington. The civil rights bills and the Fourteenth and

[21] For a suggestive discussion see Kenneth Stampp, *The Era of Reconstruction* (New York, 1965), pp. 28-30.
[22] DuBois, *Black Reconstruction, passim;* Gunnar Myrdal, *An American Dilemma* (New York, 1944), I, 224-227.

Fifteenth Amendments were passed reluctantly, and only as the result of long battles and many compromises. Recent research suggests that they would not have been passed at all if President Johnson and the Democrats had acted skillfully instead of pushing the moderate Republicans into accepting the proposals of the Radicals. Negro suffrage resulted mainly from the desire to protect southern white unionists and from northern fears about the disloyalty of the ex-rebels.[23]

Moreover, as noted above, at the end of the Civil War Negroes did not enjoy equal rights, even in a legal sense, in most of the North. The states of the Old Northwest rejected efforts to enfranchise Negroes within their borders, and outside of New England and New York Negroes did not obtain the franchise until after the passage of the Fifteenth Amendment. And because the Fifteenth Amendment was rejected by a number of northern states, it was ratified only with the votes of the reconstructed southern states. Jim Crow practices existed in most of the Old Northwest and the Middle Atlantic states. In Pennsylvania, for example, only a long fight led by Negro abolitionists finally secured a state law against segregation in public conveyances in 1867; and not until 1881 was school segregation abolished in that state.[24] The Fourteenth Amendment, now interpreted as making segregation unconstitutional, was actually extremely vague on the matter of Negro rights. For most congressmen, even the Radicals, granting protection to life, liberty and property, and equality before the law, meant nothing more than the right to own and dispose of property, to sue and be sued, and to testify in courts. It apparently did not imply desegregation of transportation and public accommodations—a lack rectified only with the passage, after several years' arduous agitation, of Sumner's Supplementary Civil Rights Act in 1875. This law, unfortunately, for the most part went unenforced. The Fourteenth Amendment certainly did not encompass the idea of school desegregation. All these things, however, have been read into the amendment by the Supreme Court during the last twenty years.

Whether one accepts the older view that politicians and capitalists desirous of continued Republican ascendancy brought about Negro enfranchisement in order to protect their interests, or whether one

[23] I have been greatly stimulated by Eric L. McKitrick, *Andrew Johnson and Reconstruction* (Chicago, 1960); LaWanda and John H. Cox, *Politics, Principle, and Prejudice, 1865-1866* (New York, 1963), and Stampp, *The Era of Reconstruction*, though none of these authors would necessarily fully agree with conclusions stated here and elsewhere in this paper.

[24] Leslie H. Fishel, Jr., "Northern Prejudice and Negro Suffrage, 1865-1870," *Journal of Negro History*, XXXIX (1954), 8-26; McPherson, *Negro's Civil War*, pp. 255-261; McPherson, *Struggle for Equality*, chap. x.

accepts the newer view that Negroes received suffrage and citizenship rights as a sort of by-product of the political factionalism in
Washington and the self-defeating tactics of Johnson and the northern
Democrats, one thing emerges quite clearly—responsible whites in
positions of influence were simply not listening to the Negroes. Negroes received their rights in the South for a few brief years during
reconstruction not because of the brilliantly worded resolutions, addresses and petitions of the Negro conventions and orators, or because of the deep-rooted desires of the mass of freedmen for economic
independence and dignity, but because of the activities of the northern whites, to whom the welfare of the Negroes was usually an incidental or secondary issue. What was true for the Republicans was
also true in modified form for the abolitionists. James McPherson,
in his recent volume, *The Struggle for Equality,* makes a good case
for attributing at least a part of the development of congressional
sentiment for Negro rights to the agitation of some of the old abolitionists who felt that their work was not done with the emancipation
of the slaves. Yet even the abolitionists were divided, many of them
asserting that once emancipated the southern freedmen should be
left to help themselves. Others, like the great orator, Wendell Phillips,
and certain of the northern school teachers who went south after the
war and made the education of the freedmen their life work, were
sincerely interested in bringing citizenship rights and real equality
for the Negroes. Even these idealists often had an unconscious pa-
ternalism about them. They sincerely believed in racial equality, but
they also believed that they knew what was best for the Negroes.
Willie Lee Rose records the shock that some of the white missionaries
on the Sea Islands received when Negroes wanted to make their own
decisions.[25]

There is little evidence that such people listened, at least very
much, to what the Negroes were saying. Rather, their views in favor
of citizenship rights and, in some cases, of land for the Negroes, were
not a response to Negro demands, but grew out of their own philan-
thropic ideals. McPherson carefully records the influence of Negro
abolitionists upon the white abolitionists during the Civil War and
reconstruction. But from reading his book it is clear that the only
Negro whom the white abolitionists really listened to in this period
was Frederick Douglass, a figure so Olympian that he commanded
respect; and it does not appear that they listened even to him very
much.

The granting of citizenship rights and the vote to Negroes came

[25] McPherson, *Struggle for Equality, passim;* Rose, *Rehearsal for Reconstruction,* p. 369.

about not because of what the Negroes were articulating, but because of what whites, for their own various reasons, decided to do about the Negroes. Even the most advanced and liberal journals did not deem it worth their while to report what Negroes themselves were thinking and doing about their status and their future. Since the white abolitionists and Radical Republicans were not, for the most part, genuinely committed to a belief in the essential human dignity of Negroes—much as many of them verbally protested that they did—it was easy for many of them to become disillusioned with reconstruction, to accept the southern viewpoint about corruption and black power and to wash their hands of the whole problem. This was even true of many who had once been enthusiastic about guaranteeing Negroes their citizenship rights.

It is thus clear how it was that Turner and his colored colleagues were so easily expelled from the Georgia legislature, and how it was that even though they were readmitted the following year, Georgia returned to the hands of the white supremacists in 1872. It also should be clear why Congress was really ineffective in dealing with the violence perpetrated by the Ku Klux Klan and other terrorist organizations, and why it was that, one after the other, the southern states were all permitted to return to white supremacy. The fact is that neither the North as a whole, nor Congress, nor even the majority of the white abolitionists were sufficiently concerned about Negroes to protect the citizenship rights which they had guaranteed them.

These attitudes, characteristic even of the Negroes' friends, afford some insight into the role which Negroes played in southern politics during the era of congressional or black reconstruction. We can spell out the numbers and names of prominent Negro officeholders, and at first glance the list is impressive. Two Negroes, Alonzo J. Ransier and Richard H. Gleaves, served as lieutenant-governor in South Carolina; three, Oscar J. Dunn, C. C. Antoine, and P. B. S. Pinchback, held this office in Louisiana, and Pinchback served briefly as acting governor; and one, A. K. Davis, was lieutenant-governor in Mississippi. South Carolina and Mississippi had Negro speakers of the house—Robert B. Elliott and Samuel J. Lee in South Carolina, and John R. Lynch in Mississippi. William J. Whipper was an associate justice of the supreme court of South Carolina. James J. Hill served as secretary of state in Mississippi; Francis L. Cardozo held both that post and that of state treasurer in South Carolina; and Jonathan C. Gibbs was first secretary of state and superintendent of education in Florida. Three other states also had Negro superintendents of education; Mississippi, Louisiana, and Arkansas. On the national level Mississippi sent two Negroes to the Senate—Blanche K. Bruce and Hiram R. Revels; and seven states elected Negroes to the House of Representatives during reconstruction.

No one has really yet investigated the question: exactly how did the Negro politicians function in the southern reconstruction governments?[26] Probably, just as their numbers were small in proportion to the number of Negroes in the southern states, so their influence was less than their abilities or numbers warranted. After all, even the white abolitionists, the most equalitarian group in American society, did not permit their Negro colleagues in the movement to play a significant leadership role. Douglass, the only Negro of real influence in the movement, had to establish himself as an independent force outside of the two major antislavery societies. It is therefore most unlikely that the mixed bag of northerners and southerners, idealists, opportunists and adventurers that composed the southern Republican party were willing to accord Negroes a vital role.

Only three states, South Carolina, Louisiana, and Alabama, sent more than one Negro to the national House of Representatives; four others—Georgia, Mississippi, Florida, and Louisiana—were represented by one each; while three southern states—Virginia, Arkansas, and Texas—sent no Negroes at all to Congress during reconstruction. Moreover, outside of Florida, where Gibbs was superintendent of education, only Arkansas and the three states with a Negro majority in their population selected Negroes for prominent state-wide office. Even taking these three states—Mississippi, Louisiana, and South Carolina—we find that never was a Negro elected governor; that Negroes were unable to send one of their number to the United States Senate from either Louisiana or South Carolina, despite efforts to do so; and that only one of the states, South Carolina, had a Negro on its supreme court. And only in South Carolina did Negroes form a majority in the constitutional convention or even for a brief period in one house of the state legislature.

We know practically nothing of the interaction among the Negro and white politicians, but it would appear that to a remarkable extent officeholding at the highest levels tended to be a symbolic function. Each of the three states with a Negro majority had Negro lieutenant-governors—a purely honorific post. The two Negroes who served in the United States Senate were both moderates. Revels, the first one, voted Democratic consistently after reconstruction, while the other, Bruce, became a large plantation owner. In post-reconstruction Mississippi, the Bruce-Hill-Lynch triumvirate, which dominated the

---

[26] For a thoughtful discussion of the Negro political leaders during reconstruction see John Hope Franklin, *Reconstruction: After the Civil War* (Chicago, 1961), pp. 86-92, 133-138.

state's Republican party, cooperated closely with the Democrats, making a deal known as fusion, whereby a few posts would go to Negroes in those sections of the state where they were in a heavy majority, though most of the posts and all the important ones remained in white hands. A similar arrangement obtained in the black counties of coastal South Carolina.[27]

The power of the Negro politicians in these states is revealed by what happened to the school system. A nonsegregated school system was an important issue raised in a number of the state constitutional conventions. But only South Carolina and Louisiana provided for mixed schools in their constitutions. Even in these two states, in fact, the schools were administered so that there was practically no integration. Only the New Orleans school system and the University of South Carolina were integrated.[28] Neither on this issue nor on land reform were the Negro politicians able to deliver—any more than they were able to control a fair proportion of the offices.

The foregoing should not be taken as suggesting that Negro politicians were powerless. They were not. In Florida, for example, Negroes exercised a balance of power between two white factions, and under the astute leadership of the state superintendent of education, Jonathan C. Gibbs, were able to obtain certain concessions and keep Florida in the ranks of the Radical states until 1877. In Louisiana and South Carolina the Negro majorities among the voters did exercise some power, and certain individuals, such as Robert Brown Elliott and Francis L. Cardozo, seem to have been men with a measure of influence. But not only was their influence far less than the prosouthern historians have insisted, but it was also considerably less than their numbers, education, and ability warranted. Neither southern white opportunists, nor paternalistically benevolent northern whites, were inclined to accord positions of real power to Negroes.[29]

If the states with Negro majorities experienced a relative lack of political power on the part of Negroes, it is clear why in other states Negro officeholders had even less of a role, beyond the symbolic one. Effective power stayed in the hands of the whites in all the southern states. Much of the responsibility for this situation rests with the Republicans in Congress.

As the North, the Republicans, and many of the abolitionists de-

[27] Wharton, *Negro in Mississippi*, pp. 202-203; George B. Tindall, *South Carolina Negroes, 1877-1900* (Columbia, S.C., 1952), pp. 62-64.

[28] Louis R. Harlan, "Segregation in New Orleans Public Schools During Reconstruction," *American Historical Review*, LXVII (1962), pp. 663-675; Williamson, *After Slavery*, pp. 219-223, 232.

[29] For a sharply contrasting view see Williamson, *After Slavery*, chaps. xii and xiii.

serted and betrayed the southern Negroes, the visions of the equal
rights conventions of the 1860's and the hopes of the rural black
masses remained only hopes. Sharecropping and peonage, mob violence and disfranchisement became the order of the day. By 1877
southern Negroes were left with only the shreds of their status during
the apogee of congressional reconstruction. And even these shreds
were destroyed in the wave of proscriptive legislation passed at the
turn of the century. Meanwhile, the Supreme Court turned the Fourteenth Amendment upside down. In 1883 it held the Civil Rights Act
of 1875 unconstitutional, and thirteen years later, in 1896, it enunci-
ated the separate-but-equal doctrine, justifying state laws requiring
segregation. And two years after that, in 1898, it sustained the provisions of the Mississippi constitution of 1890 with its subterfuges that
effectively emasculated the Fifteenth Amendment.

Yet these two amendments, passed during the first reconstruction,
are the constitutional basis of the new or second reconstruction of
the present decade. First of all they were the foundation for the
NAACP court victories which, starting in 1915, had by the 1950's so
undermined the legal underpinnings of the southern race system
that they produced a revolution of expectations among Negroes. And
that revolution in expectations is at the bottom of the civil rights
revolution of the 1960's. Secondly, it is largely in these reconstruction
amendments that the legislative and executive branches have found
constitutional sanction for increasing federal intervention in the South.

Although tactics differ markedly from those employed during the
first reconstruction, Negro demands today are remarkably similar to
those made a hundred years ago—civil rights, the franchise, and economic opportunity. Like prominent Negroes then, civil rights leaders
today are concerned with more than constitutional rights; and,
quite remarkably, in both cases there is the conviction that the Federal
government should undertake the responsibility of providing special
assistance to the Negro to compensate for the past. Yet there is a
striking difference in the dynamics of the two situations. A hundred
years ago whites were not listening to what Negroes were saying.
But in the 1960's Negroes, rather than whites, furnish the impetus
for social change.

A century ago, as in our own day, something of a moral revolution
was going on in the conscience of white America, a revolution forced
by the slavery question. It is true that the causes behind that moral
revolution were not themselves entirely moral. For one thing they
were largely military. Northerners who expected a short war were
shocked by military defeat into advocating the destruction of the
slave system; and this very practical and *amoral* consideration blended

inextricably with, and gave enormous stimulus to fervently moral antislavery doctrines. For the first time white northerners generally became convinced that slavery was a moral evil that had to be swept away; that the Civil War was God's punishment upon a transgressing nation that had condoned slavery for so long. But few came to believe that Negroes were inherently equal to whites.

In the 1960's again military exigencies have played their role in changing the moral climate—the country's leading role in world affairs, the Cold War, and the crucial position of colored nations in the international power system. Yet unquestionably more and more white Americans have become aware that Negroes have aspirations that should be respected. This new awareness has been manifested not only in the increasing concern for equal rights but also in the way in which whites have been paying attention to what Negroes are saying and doing.

Will the new reconstruction prove as temporary and evanescent as the old? The history of the first reconstruction suggests that revolutions—if indeed there was a revolution—can go backwards; that the white majority may grow disillusioned or just weary of idealism.[30] On the other hand, the recent changes in the attitudes of white Americans appear more deeply rooted than those of a hundred years ago. For one thing changing racial views are part of a long-term trend rooted in the New Deal period, in the moral sensitivities aroused as a result of the struggle with racist Nazi Germany, and the postwar international pressures. Moreover for the past couple of decades the northern Negro vote has been a decisive factor in many elections, and the weight of increasing numbers of registered Negro voters in the South will be felt, the current "white backlash" notwithstanding.[31]

Reforms can be reversed; revolutions may indeed go backwards. It is conceivable that the new reconstruction will be undone as was the old. Certainly, at best it will be accomplished in a halting and spasmodic manner, and every advance will be the fruit of costly and hard-fought struggles, involving compromises and even reverses along the way. Nevertheless, if one may hazard a prediction, the increasing sensitivity of whites to the Negroes' needs and demands—a growing concern for Negroes as *persons* as contrasted to concern about the *institution* of slavery—suggest that the new reconstruction is more likely to prove to be a permanent one.

[30] For sensitive discussion of such trends see C. Vann Woodward, "What Happened to the Civil Rights Movement?" *Harper's Magazine* (Jan., 1967), pp. 29-37.

[31] See, for example, Reese Cleghorn and Pat Watters, "The Impact of Negro Votes on Southern Politics," *The Reporter* (Jan. 26, 1867), pp. 24-25, 31-32.

PART V:

IDEOLOGY
AND POLITICS

SLAVERY AND THE SLAVE POWER:
A Critical Distinction

Larry Gara

IN 1847 A GARRISONIAN abolitionist wrote: "We believe slavery to be a sin—always, everywhere, and only, sin—sin, in itself, . . . All the incidental effects of the system flow spontaneously from this fountain head."[1] Garrison, himself, when accused of using harsh language towards slaveholders, retorted: "The whole scope of the English language is inadequate to describe the horrors and impieties of Slavery, and the transcendent wickedness of those who sustain this bloody system."[2] And in 1851, at their annual meeting in Salem, Ohio, western abolitionists resolved: "That we are not merely warring against the *extension* of new slave territory, . . . nor against any fugitive slave law constitutional or unconstitutional; nor for the writ of habeas corpus, or the right of trial by jury for recaptured slaves, but we are waging eternal war against the doctrine that man can ever under any possibility of circumstances, hold property in man."[3]

The Garrisonians thus viewed the struggle against slavery as a never ceasing moral crusade. Anyone who dealt with slaveholders or who compromised in any way with their institution—even to the point of voting under a slave-sanctioning Constitution—was committing mortal sin and extending aid and comfort to the sinners. Their concern about slavery included pity for the individual slave. At times it extended to the rights of free Negroes in the northern states, as when Garrisonians helped in the successful fight against racially segregated schools in Boston.

Not all Americans who became involved in antislavery activity placed the same emphasis on the moral aspects of the question as did the Garrisonians and other moral suasionists. When the issue became political, the question of southern power played an increasingly significant role in northern thinking. One observer, writing to Charles Sumner in 1858, contrasted American and Brazilian slavery, by saying "the fact is, that, in this country, Slavery is really fostered as a *source of*

[1] "What Abolitionists Believe," in the Salem, Ohio *Anti-Slavery Bugle,* Sept. 24, 1847. Research for this article was made possible by a research grant from the Kettering Fund made available to the author by the Wilmington College Tenure and Personnel Policies Committee.

[2] *The Liberty Bell. By Friends of Freedom* (Boston, 1848), p. 284.

[3] Report of the Executive Committee of the Western Anti-Slavery Society, Aug. 25, 1851 in "Minute Book of the Western Anti-Slavery Society," Library of Congress.

political power, & not as an economical or social desideratum."[4] A
friend commented to Congressman Horace Mann: "I have been aston-
ished for many years to see how the Slave power (not one fiftieth part
of the voters) manage to control the whole United States." He quoted
Theodore Parker who said: "The North can manage Steam & Water
Power but the South can manage Men," and wondered whether "their
business as Slave raisers and Slave drivers fit them for this?"[5] Speaking
in 1849 in Massachusetts, Salmon P. Chase noted that the

American aristocracy is held together and made a unit, not so much by its property
in slaves, as by the political power which the Constitution has deposited in their
hands as the representatives of slaves. They represent their slaves. They put into
the Houses of Congress, and into the Electoral College of the United States, the
political power which is the exponent of their slaves; and of course, they are bound
together, just as any other aristocracy could be, by the strongest of possible ties.
This power then came into existence, as a distinct, independent, aristocratic power
in the government, naturally opposed to the temper and spirit of our institutions."[6]

Though Chase and the other political abolitionists also regarded
slavery as morally wrong, the main thrust of their attack was against
the slave power. They feared the effect of continued national rule by
slaveholding interests on northern rights, on civil liberties, on desired
economic measures and on the future of free white labor itself. They
had the active support of many who were very little concerned about
the morality of slavery, the plight of the individual slave or the rights
of free Negroes, north or south. It was the power that they objected to,
referred to variously as the "slave oligarchy," the "slavocracy," and
most frequently as merely the slave power. This distinction between
slavery and the slave power is crucial to an understanding of the sectional tension which led to civil war. It also helps to explain how Americans could repress a rebellion led by a slave oligarchy and at the same
time perpetuate a racist bias which a century later still plagues the nation.

Although historians have never agreed about the causes of the Civil
War, in recent years there has been a strong tendency to emphasize
slavery. In part this is a reaction to the influential work of the so-called
Civil War revisionists of the 1930's and 1940's, scholars who rejected
some of the over-simplified earlier accounts and drew upon the experience of World War I, with its aftermath of disillusion, and the findings
of a newer psychology for their understanding of the past. One of the
leading revisionists, James G. Randall, saw the war as the culmination
of the efforts of a blundering generation, incapable of arousing a spirit
of consensus in a nation that should have been more united than divided as a result of continued economic development. To Randall the
war was a product of "emotional unreason," "bogus leadership," "fanat-

[4] Stephen Higginson to Charles Sumner, Feb. 22, 1858, Sumner Papers, Houghton Library, Harvard.
[5] Joseph Stevens to Horace Mann, Aug. 15, 1850, Mann Papers, Massachusetts
Historical Society.
[6] Boston *Daily Evening Traveller*, Aug. 28, 1849.

icism," and politics which dealt with shadow issues rather than basic problems. He said the Republican party "produced quarrels out of things that would have settled themselves were it not for political agitation."[7]

The well-documented and highly readable works of Avery O. Craven added considerably to this argument. In his *Coming of the Civil War*, one of the most influential of all revisionist works, Craven downgraded the importance of slavery as an irritant between the sections and alleged that the basic differences between North and South resulted from the inevitable rivalry between a fundamentally rural, agricultural section and one primarily urban and industrial. The differences, however, were not irreconcilable. To Craven the Civil War had been a repressible conflict and a national tragedy of overwhelming proportions.[8]

William B. Hesseltine, Frank Hodder, George Fort Milton, Roy Franklin Nichols and Kenneth Stampp, among others, made significant contributions to the historiography of revisionism. Although they differed in emphasis, they largely agreed on several points: that slavery alone did not cause the war; that extremists, the abolitionists in the North and the fire eaters in the South, had stirred up people needlessly over basically insignificant issues; that moderates such as Douglas and the other compromisers deserve credit for trying to prevent war, and that they nearly succeeded. Implicit in the writings of all the revisionists is the idea that the war could have been prevented.

Because the revisionists viewed the conflict as a tragedy rather than a crusade, they were at times accused of being pro-southern and some of their critics equated their contributions with those of E. Merton Coulter, Frank Owsley, Charles W. Ramsdell and Arthur Young Lloyd, historians whose sympathies were clearly with the Confederacy and the civilization of the Old South. In recent years, critics have tended to lump together the revisionists and the southern apologists.

Such criticism is made plausible because of the revisionists' refusal to take sides in the war. Civil war, they argued, was the worst possible way for the nation to resolve its internal differences, and symbolized a breakdown of the democratic processes of compromise. Some of them assumed that slavery would have died a natural death if left alone. In studying the tragic events of the mid-nineteenth century they tried to be objective. One of them, William B. Hesseltine, excoriated any of his graduate students who allowed moral judgments to enter his writing. In one instance he dashed off a short essay on morality which included the admonition that the historian "may not judge past acts in terms of present day morality: Morality is not immutable. The moral climate changes, and what is moral at one time may be immoral at another."[9]

---

[7] Thomas J. Pressly, *Americans Interpret Their Civil War* (New York, 1965), p. 315.

[8] Avery O. Craven, *The Coming of the Civil War* (New York, 1942; published in a revised edition by the University of Chicago in 1957).

[9] William B. Hesseltine, undated note to the author.

Although the revisionists would not all subscribe to Hesseltine's views on morality, throughout their writings there runs the theme that a historian should not pass moral judgment on a generation which lived a century earlier. It was precisely the revisionists' unwillingness to become morally involved or even to recognize the moral issues of the war that led still another generation of historians to reject their contributions and to undermine their influence. Early notice that a new viewpoint was emerging came with the publication of several articles by Bernard DeVoto in 1946[10] and in 1949 with Arthur Schlesinger Jr.'s article "The Causes of the American Civil War: A Note on Historical Sentimentalism." Schlesinger's essay received wide notice and has reached many readers through several reprintings. In it he accused the revisionists of a failure to feel moral urgency themselves and thus, "By denying themselves insight into the moral dimension of the slavery crisis, the revisionists denied themselves a historical understanding of the intensities that caused the crisis. . . . To reject the moral actuality of the Civil War," he said, "is to foreclose the possibility of an adequate account of its causes. More than that, it is to misconceive and grotesquely to sentimentalize the nature of history." Schlesinger argued: "Nothing exists in history to assure us that the great moral dilemmas can be resolved without pain; we cannot therefore be relieved from the duty of moral judgment on issues so appalling and inescapable as those involved in human slavery; nor can we be consoled by sentimental theories about the needlessness of the Civil War into regarding our own struggles against evil as equally needless." He did, however, distinguish between issues and men. Judgment must apply only to issues, he said, for we "must judge the men of the past with the same forbearance and charity which we hope the future will apply to us."[11]

Clearly, Schlesinger and some of the early anti-revisionists were influenced by the Cold War which they saw as a repeat performance, on a world scale, of the struggle between slavery and freedom, good and evil. The preoccupation of many Americans with the civil rights struggle of the 1950's and 1960's added new strength to the trend away from revisionism. Once again slavery was brought into focus as the crux of the argument between the sections and once again the issue was one of morality. A new generation of scholars re-examined slavery and the antislavery movement as well as reconstruction. Some of those who had been revisionists, like Kenneth Stampp, modified their earlier interpretations. Allan Nevins' multi-volumed history of the Civil War era became more pro-northern with each volume. Even such older scholars as Avery Craven changed some conclusions in light of the newer scholarship. Despite the disclaimers of Fawn Brodie and Harold Hyman,[12]

[10] Pressly, *Americans Interpret Their Civil War*, p. 341.

[11] Arthur Schlesinger, Jr., "A Note on Historical Sentimentalism," in Edwin C. Rozwenc (ed.), *The Causes of the Civil War* (Boston, 1961), pp. 187, 190.

[12] Fawn M. Brodie, "Who Won the Civil War, Anyway?" *New York Times Book Review*, Aug. 5, 1962; Harold M. Hyman (ed.), *The Radical Republicans and Reconstruction, 1861-1870* (Indianapolis and New York, 1967), introduction.

both of whom insist that the South has won the verbal Civil War, the predominantly pro-northern interpretation has become more firmly entrenched with many recent monographs. Today the abolitionists are seldom criticized for extremism or explained away by oedipus or other complexes. Rather they are recognized as legitimate exponents of a righteous though unpopular cause. Martin Duberman's *Antislavery Vanguard*[13] provides a wealth of material summarizing much of the newer viewpoint. James McPherson gave the abolitionists a good rating in their concern for civil rights for black people, possibly a better rating than they deserved.[14] Dwight Dumond's massive work, *Antislavery*,[15] might well have won the political abolitionists' seal of approval, if not that of the Garrisonians. One effect of the newer viewpoint is to swing the spotlight once again on slavery as a cause of the Civil War. In this the recent books and articles are a much needed corrective for that part of the revisionist contribution which virtually removed slavery from the list of the war's causes. In another respect, however, the impact of the new scholarship might prove more misleading than helpful. Moral indignation at racial injustice in the twentieth century does not necessarily provide the key to an understanding of the dispute between the sections in the nineteenth century. While some abolitionists were indignant at the slave system and what it did to black men, many more northerners became anti-southern and antislavery because of what the slave system did or threatened to do to them. A failure to recognize this can easily lead us into a blind alley of over-simplification, and to view the events of a hundred years ago as a morality play with heroes and villains rather than a plausible presentation of a human dilemma.

After abolishing slavery themselves, the northern states were vaguely antislavery, though to most residents of the North slavery was an abstraction, not touching directly on their lives. Lysander Spooner commented in 1853: "The North, with no very important exceptions, although not enthusiastic in the matter, are abolitionists at heart. It is a slander on human nature to assert that they are not."[16] Such sentiments could thrive in a section where slavery had been eliminated and where no one had a direct, vested interest in its existence. Another contemporary participant in antislavery activity placed a different emphasis on northern opinion. In 1854 Horace Greeley confided to Theodore Parker that he had "never been able to discover any strong, pervading, overruling Anti Slavery sentiment in the Free States." Greeley believed "that if every voter in the Free States were to have half a dozen negro slaves left him by some Georgia uncle or cousin's will, that a decided majority would hold on to their chattels and make as much as possible out of them." Because of this he did not think an independent, anti-

13 Martin M. Duberman (ed.), *The Antislavery Vanguard* (Princeton, 1965).
14 James M. McPherson, *The Struggle for Equality: Abolitionists and the Negro in the Civil War and Reconstruction* (Princeton, 1964).
15 Dwight L. Dumond, *Antislavery: The Crusade for Freedom in America* (Ann Arbor, 1961).
16 Lysander Spooner, *The Unconstitutionality of Slavery* (Boston, 1853), p. 290.

slavery political party feasible. "I believe," he said, "a large majority of the voters are impelled by interest rather than principle, and that any political movement which appeals wholly to the mind, ignoring material considerations, is doomed to failure." Among other things, Greeley argued for working within the existing political parties rather than outside them.[17]

Regardless of their partisan preferences, many northerners came to the conclusion that southern power based upon slavery proved a threat to their own interests and had to be opposed. Joshua Giddings, one of the first antislavery congressmen, admitted in 1845 that he was disappointed with the slow progress of the cause. "In order to arouse the people much is to be said and done before they will understand their rights and the abuses to which they have been subjected," he lamented. But he was not wholly discouraged because he saw signs that the people of all parties exhibited evidence of "improvement on the subject of our rights and of the rights of mankind." Two years later he noted that the Mexican War, which he believed was fought exclusively for the expansion of slave power, was awakening public sentiment. He commented, "I now see the mighty deep of public indignation called forth against this war and the encroachments of the slave power. I now for the first time in my life see the Slave power falter and tremble before the combined denunciation of northern democrats and northern Whigs."[18]

The issue of southern dictation was frequently in the minds of those actively interested in northern politics in the 1840's and 1850's. One of John P. Hale's constituents reported to him in 1846 that citizens of his town had formed "a political organization to oppose Southern dictation and the evils resulting from the institution of Slavery." In this case the association was independent of the Liberty party as well as of the two major political organizations.[19] Such sentiments were repeated with many variations after passage of the Kansas-Nebraska Act in 1854. Myriads of meetings were held and organizations formed in response to the legislation, for the bill sponsored by Stephen A. Douglas had proved a serious miscalculation of northern opinion. Political ambition was the most frequent explanation of Douglas' alleged subserviency to southern wishes. A New England minister suggested to Charles Sumner "a convention of the Free States . . . from which might *go forth a voice* which should convince the South that we *mean* something. Something *must* be done to put a stop to the defiant usurpations of the Slave Power and check the aspirings of that ambition which would mount to office, though every round of ascent were made of a freeman converted into a Slave."[20]

[17] Horace Greeley to Theodore Parker, May 23, 1854, Parker Papers, Massachusetts Historical Society.

[18] Joshua Giddings to David Lee Child, Dec. 5, 1845 and Feb. 12, 1847, Child Papers, Boston Public Library.

[19] Richard Farwell to John P. Hale, Dec. 2, 1846, Hale Papers, New Hampshire Historical Society.

[20] Rev. E. Smalley to Charles Sumner, Mar. 14, 1854, Sumner Correspondence.

Salmon P. Chase asserted that witnessing mob action against the abolitionists in Cincinnati made him a "decided opponent of Slavery and the Slave Power," though not technically an abolitionist. Unlike the Garrisonians, his course was political—to denationalize slavery and deprive it of the protection of the Federal government. Chase regarded political action as the most potent force available against the slave power and slavery itself. In the Senate he rejoiced at the contributions of Sumner and the other antislavery men there. After hearing Sumner's initial senatorial speech, Chase reported to Gerrit Smith: "It is the first stone from the sling of the young Independent Democracy against the Goliath of the Slave Power, and it struck square in the forehead." Such speeches in Congress contributed powerful ammunition in the war against the slave power though their effect on slavery, the root of that power, was only indirect.[21]

Arrogant southern abuses of power combined with constant threats of further usurpation evoked rising opposition in the northern states. In 1855 Charles Sumner suggested to Theodore Parker that he make a speech showing the composition of the existing congressional committees. Parker could thus expose the power of slavery "first in grasping the places of power, and secondly in excluding from those places the special and obnoxious friends of Freedom."[22] A Boston correspondent reported to Sumner that the arrest of Anthony Burns and the threats to Sumner following "the passage of the nefarious Nebraska bill, had done more than everything else to unite the good men of all parties in a common sentiment of hostility to the encroachments of the slave power."[23] And when Sumner himself was struck down on the floor of the Senate and became a martyr to the cause of free speech, hundreds of northern sympathizers sent him letters of condolence. The blow was aimed not only at Sumner, one constituent said. "It was aimed at Massachusetts, at every antislavery man in the country, and especially at free speech. This may be regarded as the crowning act of a series of aggressions of the Slave Power since 1850."[24]

A few months earlier another correspondent told Sumner of several articles he had recently published, including one on the "Ulterior Designs of the Slaveholding Interest." He could not agree with those whom he called the "fierce abolitionists" and their unmitigated damnation of everyone in the South who happened to own slaves. However, he did agree with Sumner that the only solution for the country was for the North to take possession of the government. He went against slavery extension and against slavery as an economic, social and moral curse. "I go for a great Free States party," he said, "for wresting the government from the Slaveholding power: & for using every constitutional power it gives for limiting . . . the curse. I go for every effort to bring the whole

21 Salmon P. Chase, autobiographical letter to "My Dear Sir," July 10, 1853; Chase to Gerrit Smith, Aug. 27, 1852, Chase Papers, Library of Congress.
22 Charles Sumner to Theodore Parker, Dec. 14, 1855, Parker Papers.
23 George Livermore to Charles Sumner, June 1, 1854, Sumner Correspondence.
24 Hebron Vincent to Charles Sumner, June 16, 1856, *ibid.*

South to this mind." If dissolution of the Union should come, however, he looked forward to the possibility of union with Canada.[25]

The opposition to the southern slave power was recognized in the South for what it was, a serious threat to their political influence. A moderate northern Whig, Robert C. Winthrop, commented in 1850: "The Southern men have worked themselves up into a real belief that their rights are invaded, & that their only redress is to be found in separation."[26] Similarly, Horace Mann was sure that keeping slaves out of the territories acquired from Mexico would not harm the cotton and rice interests of the older slave states. However, that was not what was bothering the spokesmen of the southern interests, said Mann. "It is a fear of losing the balance of power, as they call it; and no doubt, in some cases, a fear that this is only a beginning of a war upon slavery *in the States themselves.*" Declarations from the North would not pacify them on the latter point for "on this subject they *are not a reasoning people.*"[27]

Senator Jefferson Davis summed up southern concern when he charged that the Free Soilers had some ulterior motive for their policy. He said they admitted they were not in favor of emancipating slaves and yet they desired "to weaken the political power of the southern states of the Union; and why? Because you want, by an unjust system of legislation, to promote the industry of the New England States, at the expense of the people of the South and their industry."[28]

To purists among the abolitionists the politics of antislavery seemed to involve an attack on southern power rather than an attack on the institution from which such power stemmed. Wendell Phillips, Stephen Foster and the other Garrisonians refused to concede that any existing political party was truly antislavery. The Free Soil party refused to extend the protecting arm of the government over the three million men and women "that were recognized by the government of the country only as brute beasts." Even the Liberty party was indicted. Many of its leaders supported the American church, a bulwark of slavery; it sanctioned the American government in its support of slavery; and, it "would degrade the high and holy enterprise of 'preaching deliverance to the captive,' to a mere squabble in party politics, utterly unworthy its high character and design."[29] Wendell Phillips maintained that any antislavery ideas which found their way into politics came because of the groundwork laid by the moral suasionists.[30]

Although the antislavery argument underwent a basic shift when it

[25] C. S. Henry to Sumner, May 20, 1854, *ibid.*
[26] Robert C. Winthrop to Mrs. Gardner, Feb. 10, 1850, Winthrop Papers, Massachusetts Historical Society.
[27] Horace Mann to Mary Mann, Mar. 15, 1850, Mann Papers.
[28] *Congressional Globe*, 35 Cong., 1 sess., 441.
[29] Boston *Liberator*, June 3, 1853; "Minute Book of the Western Anti-Slavery Society," 1846, Library of Congress.
[30] See Wendell Phillips' speech to the annual meeting of the Massachusetts Antislavery Society in the *Liberator*, Jan. 27, 1853.

entered the realm of politics, some of the politicians acknowledged their indebtedness to the moral crusader. Congressman John G. Palfrey deplored the disunionist proposal of the Garrisonians but admitted their "noble courage, constancy and disinterestedness" as well as "the great value of their services in awakening the public mind to the enormity of the evil."[31] Salmon Chase told Theodore Parker that the end of slavery would come "when the mind of the Nation is penetrated by such thoughts as your writings inspire. . . . I work in the political field . . . because God seems to have better fitted me for it than for any other." "But after all," he continued, "what is our political work but the growth into substantial form of the great ideas which higher thinkers put forth, and the preparation for larger like growths."[32] Nevertheless, many of the moralists continued to shun politics. Lydia Maria Child rejoiced at antislavery election victories, but seldom entered the political world, which always reminded her "of the small, black, ravenous animals clutching and clawing each other in a magnified drop of water."[33] Lewis Tappan told his brother, a moderate antislavery senator: "I have little confidence in the abiding and true-hearted abolitionism of any devotee to politics. Party, party, party!—is the watchword, and moral questions are lost sight of too frequently."[34]

Although the antislavery politicians thought of themselves as reformers and some of them, like Horace Mann, used the vocabulary of the moralists, they spoke primarily of the effect of continued rule by the slave power on northern interests. Joshua Giddings reported the great effect of John Quincy Adams' 1842 speech on both northern Whigs and Democrats in Congress when he "showed up the manner in which the Slave interest has assiduously crept into our whole policy, subsidized our presses, affected our Literature, invaded the sanctity of the Post office, degraded our Patriotism, taxed the free labor of the north, frightened our Statesmen and controlled the nation."[35]

The baleful effect of the slave power's domination of the national government was an often-repeated and highly effective argument. In 1844, with Texas annexation under consideration, Joshua Giddings saw the matter as a clear question of "*slavery* or *liberty*. . . . To give the South the preponderance of political power" he asserted, "would be itself a surrender of our Tariff, our harbor improvements, our distribution of the proceeds of the public lands." To him the suggestion that the United States should annex Texas was "the most abominable proposition with which a free people were ever insulted."[36] One of Horace Mann's

31 John G. Palfrey to Samuel May, Jr., July 27, 1849, Palfrey Papers, Houghton Library.
32 Salmon P. Chase to Theodore Parker, Mar. 25, 1858, Parker Papers.
33 Lydia Maria Child to Sumner, Feb. 12, 1855, Sumner Correspondence.
34 Lewis Tappan to Benjamin Tappan, Feb. 13, 1839, Benjamin Tappan Papers, Library of Congress.
35 Joshua Giddings to his wife, Feb. 6, 1842, Giddings Papers, Ohio Historical Society.
36 Joshua Giddings to Joseph Addison Giddings, Apr. 28, 1844, *ibid.*

constituents reported that he would rather see "Olive leaves scattered than to hear the *whiz* of bullets," but that he was ready "to resort to almost any means to get rid of Southern oppression. Where is the tariff? Where is the liberty of free-colored Seamen? where the necessary river & harbor improvement?" he queried.[37]

Southern political power was partly a result of the constitutional provision giving the slave states representation in Congress and in the electoral college for a portion of the slave population. This provided a valid and bitter complaint in the North, and as the argument between the sections intensified it was heard more often. Reflecting on the popular northern reaction against the Fugitive Slave Law of 1850, one of John P. Hale's constituents saw it as a very favorable time to get rid of slaveholding rule. "If the legal voters of the north only knew how they were degraded by slave representation," he said, "and their own influence lessened thereby, and that they were taxed to pay the wages of the representatives that had their seats in congress, in consequence of a certain species of property," they would soon refuse to elect any person to office who was in favor of such injustice.[38] After 1850 more and more voters in the northern states arrived at the same conclusion. Increasingly, northerners came to resent southern influence, whether real or imagined, as in some instances it was. In 1856 a Michigan resident reported immense popular excitement over a circular issued by the commissioner of the general land office which required an oath that land purchased under the graduation act was actually settled and cultivated, a provision not included in the law itself. The Michigan resident was convinced that the land circular "had its origin in, and was dictated by the same Power that passed the fugitive Slave Law, repealed the Missouri compromise and that now disgraces itself by tyrannizing over the brave men of Kansas. 320 acres of land are not enough for a Slave Plantation; but makes a splendid farm for a freeman and increases the vote of the free states."[39]

Even more telling was the allegation that the slave power not only demanded protection for its own peculiar type of property but made slaves of white men, northern and southern alike. "The question of African Slavery sinks into insignificance compared with the enslavement of the people of Kansas, and the subjugation of all the free states to the principles of Dred Scott vs. Sanford," commented an Illinois resident in 1857.[40] Charles Sumner denied that admitting slaves to the newly-opened territories would merely give the South equal privileges with the North. "If Slavery is there," he charged, "the privileges are not 'equal.' The free black citizens of the North cannot go there. It might be said also," he continued, "that free whites cannot secure that dignity

---

[37] George Alden to Horace Mann, Feb. 22, 1851, Mann Papers.
[38] George Doughty to John P. Hale, Feb., 1851, Hale Papers.
[39] James Birdsall to William Seward, n.d. (postmarked Mar. 1856), Trumbull Papers, Library of Congress.
[40] F. S. Rutherford to Lyman Trumbull, Dec. 7, 1857, *ibid.*

and consideration for their labor, which is the life of their labor."[41] And when Salmon Chase and the other Free Soil Democrats published their appeal for popular opposition to the Nebraska Bill, they included the charge that the bill was "part and parcel of an atrocious plot to exclude from a vast unoccupied region immigrants from the Old World and free laborers from our own States, and convert it into a dreary region of despotism, inhabited by masters and slaves."[42]

Fear that first free territory and then the free states themselves would be converted into slave states, dominated politically by the minority which comprised the slaveholding interest, was a major ingredient in the upheaval over the new Fugitive Slave Law which came into being as a part of the Compromise of 1850. Of course there were valid moral as well as political considerations involved, for sending a suspected fugitive back to southern slavery was nasty business at best, and the law was designed to expedite the unsavory procedure. Both antislavery men and some southern apologists admitted that the law had more to do with constitutional matters and sectional pride than with the anticipated return of fugitives, but it was at this point that northerners were most affected. Many who had never seen a fugitive were infuriated by the demands of the law. They agreed with such writers as William C. Whitcomb who claimed that the law, if carried out, "will enslave you and me as well as the black man. IT WILL MAKE SLAVES OF US ALL. Talk not of the *Free States*! there are none such now! nor will there be until this 'odious' law is repealed."[43] Senator Wade of Ohio characterized it as "an unfortunate bill." Speaking in the Senate he said: "God knows your fugitive act, with all its terrors and penalties with which you thought to overawe a free people, has irritated their minds so much that prudence ought to induce you, at all events to forbear. . . . The whole free North is against you, and against you with a determined purpose, and with a strong hand, to repel every further invasion of their rights that you may propose to make."[44] Theodore Parker saw in the Fugitive Slave Law clear evidence that despotic power was just as real in the United States as in Russia. Reminding his congregation of the return of Anthony Burns to slavery and the bludgeoning of Senator Sumner he commented: "Both blows were dealt by the same arm,—the Slave Power; both aimed at the same mark,—the Head of Freedom; each came from the same motive, which I need not name."[45]

If any of the issues relating to abolition involved a concern for the plight of the victims of the South's peculiar institution they were those which grew out of the Fugitive Slave Law and its operation in the North. Yet the law was viewed as a threat to northern civil liberties and northern rights and as homage to the slave power as well as an im-

---

[41] Charles Sumner to John G. Palfrey, Dec. 29, 1847, Palfrey Papers.
[42] Quoted in Allan Nevins, *Ordeal of the Union* (New York, 1947), II, 111-112.
[43] William C. Whitcomb, *A Discourse on the Recapture of Fugitive Slaves. . .* (Boston, 1850), p. 8.
[44] *Congressional Globe*, 33 Cong., 2 sess., 214.
[45] Theodore Parker, *A New Lesson for the Day . . .* (Boston, 1856), p. 30.

moral and unchristian enactment. If the focus had been on the victim, some attention, at least, would have been given to the fate of the free Negroes in the North and South. Yet, except for a small minority of abolitionists, most people involved in the antislavery struggle paid little or no attention to this group. When northern Negroes asked Free Soilers what they thought should be done for them or what course they should follow, the recommendation was always the same: separatism, and usually colonization in some other country as well, though the Free Soil politicians were careful to point out that they meant voluntary separatism or colonization and not forced measures. The Negroes feared that such a program would inevitably become coercive and they regarded it as a threat rather than an opportunity.[46]

When the newly-formed Republican party created a truly northern political organization, there was pressure from those who wanted it to take an antislavery stance stronger than mere free soil, and from those who feared it would do just that. Many Republicans clung to the idea of colonization and for some, at least, it was basic to their policy. Colonization "is the *key* of the whole question," commented one. "The exclusion of slavery from the territories is only an incidental part of a general policy of which colonization is the corner stone." The Republicans might hope to appeal to non-slaveholders in the South as well as to northern voters if they presented the question properly as a "question of the white man against the Ethiopian."[47] Though the anticipated support from southern Unionists did not materialize, the narrow issue of slavery exclusion remained the sole antislavery plank in the Republican political program. The combination of anti-slave power and anti-Negro sentiment was a powerful attraction in both the Free Soil and Republican programs. As early as 1851 John Jay, grandson of the first Chief Justice, had commented on the desirability of eventually enlisting the support of slaveholders in abolishing slavery. However, he doubted that such support would develop and believed instead that emancipation would be accomplished by the people of the North, who were then rapidly increasing in numbers and influence. A feud between them and the slaveholding capitalists growing out of increased interference with the interests of slave labor seemed highly probable to Jay. "But even if this should prove the case," he lamented, "the poor negroes would be little benefitted by a movement originating not in benevolence—but in avarice," and embittered by the jealousy and hatred of free laborers.[48]

When abolition finally came, it was accomplished through emergency war measures growing out of the rebellion of the slave power. To those who supported that rebellion it was in part, at least, a reaction to the growing unification of the North and the threat it posed to the slave interests. The emergence of a self-conscious North was symbolized by

[46] For examples of antislavery congressmen's letters to a convention of Negroes in Ohio see Wilmington, Ohio *Herald of Freedom*, Jan. 23, 1852.
[47] H. C. Trinne to Lyman Trumbull, Dec. 15, 1859, Trumbull Papers.
[48] John Jay to John G. Palfrey, July 25, 1851, Palfrey Papers.

the growing influence of antislavery men in Congress in the years after 1848. Such men as Horace Mann, Joshua Giddings, Amos Tuck, David Wilmot, and George Julian in the House and Salmon P. Chase, Ben Wade, William Seward and John P. Hale in the Senate set about consciously to challenge southern or slave power at every point. Many northerners considered this challenge long overdue and were proud to support their congressmen in this work. One wrote to Hale: "I feel *proud* Sir, that we have a Senator from New Hampshire who is not afraid or ashamed, to stand up for the rights of the North."[49] When Ben Wade was re-elected to the Senate a constituent wrote that he and others were proud that Ohio "has taken her stand first among the states of the Union in favour of Liberty and against Slavery encroachment."[50] A Maine resident boasted in 1856 that his congressional district would "redeem itself and be represented in the coming Congress by a man with Northern principles and who dares assert the rights of his constituents and of freedom."[51]

It was a contagious doctrine. Many who could not be won over to strictly antislavery principles were very much concerned about checking the continued domination of the slave power. Joshua Giddings noted the trend as early as 1843 when the congressional Gag Rule was still in effect. "The truth is," he commented, "our northern men are beginning to think of northern rights and the south must come under. Thank God that I have lived to see those fellows begin to humble before northern influence."[52] Four years later John Jay took account of the same development. He noted that the controversial debates in Congress would have their effect on the country at large, and added, "I trust that the hour of Emancipation for the North from the degrading bondage in which they have so long been held is near at hand."[53] It was near at hand, despite the setback provided by the Compromise of 1850 and its brief acceptance by the northern population. When the struggle to defeat Senator Douglas' Nebraska Bill was at full tilt, many in the North asked along with Charles Sumner, "Shall we have a North?"[54] The answer was soon to be clear as the Republican party emerged as the instrument of a self-conscious sectionalism. Even though the new party lost its first bid for the presidency, it succeeded in creating a coalition of northern political interests. A Philadelphia abolitionist reported to Charles Sumner in 1856 that the Republicans were settling in the conviction that they had suffered a victorious defeat. "They have not yet got a President but they have what is better, a North."[55]

49 William Wallace to John P. Hale, Apr. 11, 1850, Hale Papers.
50 Jonathan Oldham to Benjamin Wade, Mar. 3, 1856, Wade Papers, Library of Congress.
51 J. W. Babson to W. P. Fessenden, Mar. 3, 1856, Fessenden Papers, Library of Congress.
52 Joshua Giddings to Comfort Giddings, Dec. 25, 1843, Giddings Papers.
53 John Jay to John G. Palfrey, May 2, 1848, Palfrey Papers.
54 Charles Sumner to Horace Mann, Mar. 6, 1854, Mann Papers.
55 W. H. Furness to Sumner, Nov. 9, 1856, Sumner Correspondence.

The northern party was made possible because of a steadily increasing opposition to the slave power rather than to any growth of pure antislavery sentiment or humanitarian consideration for the slave as an oppressed human being. It is important to distinguish between the two in attempting to understand the developments which led to the Civil War and its portentous aftermath. As early as 1842 a friend of Joshua Giddings clarified the issue when he noted that there was "a wide and deep feeling" on the matter of antagonism between the North and South "silently stealing upon the hearts of our people." At that time they still regarded themselves as friends of the South, and the uncompromising enemies of the abolitionists. "But alas!" he said, "agitate the question of Southern dictation and you see their eyes flash and their faces burn." He rejoiced that the sentiment was more common among the Whigs, but he continued, "it would require but little to annihilate party distinctions to cause this imperceptibly kindling flame to burst into a devouring conflagration."[56] More, much more, than a little was required, yet within a span of two decades party distinctions were annihilated, new political alignments appeared, and the conflagration came.

[56] Albert G. Riddle to Giddings, June 7, 1842, Giddings Papers.

WILLIAM LLOYD GARRISON AND
ANTISLAVERY UNITY: A Reappraisal

Bertram Wyatt-Brown

A RECENT BOOK on current racial tensions is entitled *Who Speaks for the Negro?* One thing is certain: insofar as historical figures are concerned, it is not William Lloyd Garrison.[1] Seldom in American history has any figure been so thoroughly lambasted, by historians and non-historians alike, as the founder of the abolitionist crusade. A popular journalist has called the contents of his *Liberator* "obscene, the sort of self-intoxicated invective that made Senator Bilbo notorious"; and a widely-used college textbook bluntly refers to him as "wayward" and "neurotic."[2] Other scholars have not been much kinder. Despite recent changes in the treatment of abolitionism, Garrison more often than not is still distrusted and sometimes damned,[3] and the cause he

[1] Robert Penn Warren, *Who Speaks for the Negro?* (New York, 1965); see, for instance, Warren's interview (p. 274) with Judge Hastie, who said: "There are certain stages . . . when persons like [Garrison] represent the spark to a movement and we can recognize their value as that, without having a necessary admiration for the intemperate, even violent, personality. . . ." This paper was presented at the May, 1966, meeting of the Organization of American Historians in Cincinnati. It is an amplification of the last third of a paper presented to the Society for Religion in Higher Education, Notre Dame University, August, 1963.

[2] J. C. Furnas, *The Road to Harpers Ferry* (New York, 1959), p. 307; Richard Hofstadter, William Miller, Daniel Aaron, *The American Republic* (Englewood Cliffs, N.J., 1959), I, 463.

[3] Louis Filler, book review, *Journal of American History*, LII (1965), 625, notes the lack of a Garrison chapter in Duberman's collection, *Antislavery Vanguard* (see below); see also Filler, "Garrison, Again and Again: A Review Article," *Civil War History*, XI (1965), 70; "Professors have agreed that Garrison was a detriment to the movement." Unfavorable views of Garrison's agitational methods are found in: Stanley M. Elkins, *Slavery, A Problem in American Institutional and Intellectual Life* (Chicago, 1959), Ch. IV; Howard R. Floan, *The South in Northern Eyes, 1831 to 1861* (Austin, 1958), pp. 1-10; Hazel Catherine Wolf, *On Freedom's Altar, The Martyr Complex in the Abolition Movement* (Madison, 1952), pp. 18-31; John L. Thomas, *The Liberator, William Lloyd Garrison, A Biography* (Boston, 1963), a most successful effort but not sympathetic; less critical but perhaps less stimulating is Walter M. Merrill's *Against Wind and Tide: A Biography of William Lloyd Garrison* (Cambridge, 1963); Arnold Whitridge, *No Compromise! The Story of the Fanatics Who Paved the Way to the Civil War* (New York, 1960), pp. 7-11, 85-148; Oliver P. Chitwood, Rembert W. Patrick, Frank Owsley, and H. C. Nixon, *The American People: A*

began goes marching on quite well without him. Since it is hard to make a hero of a Yankee editor with a nasal twang, steel-rimmed glasses, and a gift for making enemies, Abraham Lincoln has pre-empted most of the glory and, indeed, most of the monuments. For the Negro rights movement today, who needs a spokesman from history remembered for his disruptive influence in the cause he served?

According to some historians, Garrison's attacks on enemies and friends alike had grown so boisterous by 1840 that he had not only wrecked the movement's cohesiveness, but, by a process of self-combustion had exploded his own authority, too.[4] Other historians have condemned the abolitionists generally and Garrison in particular for being too limited in approach, even, perhaps, insufficiently egalitarian. According to one scholar, Garrison's myopic leadership carried his followers into a labyrinth of religious perfectionism, a fruitless wandering in the byways of extraneous reforms, moral absolutes, and pietistic dreams. As a result, in 1861, the North tragically went to war without a clear moral path to follow toward racial harmony, a path which he could have helped to find. Thus, when emancipation came, he had nothing left to say.[5]

To lay the racial failures of the Civil War generation at the feet of Garrison is not altogether fair, but there is no doubt that his philosophy of agitation was romantic, bizarre, and, for most Americans, indigestible. He spurned the churches because they admitted slaveholders to the altar rail; he denounced the Constitution because of its proslavery clauses. Oath-taking and voting acknowledged that northerners were politically and morally committed to protect the slave system, a complicity with evil which only a peaceful separation of the sections could absolve. According to Garrison, all means of force led to oppression; the only weapon against evil was the testimony of nonresistance. He opposed institutions because these engines of coercion hindered the search for individual perfection. Moreover, he was willing to see "the land filled with the horrors of a civil or a

---

History (Toronto, New York, and London, 1962), I, 483-485; David Donald, *Lincoln Reconsidered: Essays on the Civil War Era* (New York, 1961), pp. 19-36.

[4] Filler, "Garrison, Again and Again," 70; Gilbert H. Barnes, *The Antislavery Impulse, 1830-1844* (Gloucester, Mass., 1957), pp. 174-175; Dwight L. Dumond, *Antislavery: The Crusade for Freedom in America* (Ann Arbor, 1961), p. 174; Thomas, *Liberator*, p. 281; see David Brion Davis, "Abolitionists and the Freedmen: An Essay Review," *Journal of Southern History*, XXXI (1965), 165, on the abolitionists themselves helping to promote Lincoln's symbolic role.

[5] Thomas, *Liberator*, p. 408; see the challenge of Louis Ruchames, "William Lloyd Garrison and the Negro Franchise," *Journal of Negro History*, L (1965), pp. 37-49; also, Davis, "Abolitionists and the Freedmen," 166-167; William H. Pease and Jane H. Pease, "Antislavery Ambivalence: Immediatism, Expediency, Race," *American Quarterly*, XVII (1965), 682-695, claiming abolitionist equivocation on racial prejudice.

servile war" if slavery did not end peacefully. He would applaud the destruction of the American Union if its existence stood in the way of emancipation. While refusing to encourage rebellion, he tried to frighten southerners with their own nightmare, by probing slavery's instability and threatening God's retribution for the national crime.[6]

It was a hard-hitting, single-minded, and seemingly inflammatory program: dramatic enough to draw widespread attention; romantic enough to enlist the intellectual elite of Boston and Concord; and extreme enough to satisfy the restless urgings of his disciples. Few Americans of that day could imagine a more fanatical approach to the slavery question. Many historians, though by no means all of them, have agreed, stressing its radicalism, waywardness, and demoralizing effect on the antislavery host, most of whom wished to manipulate rather than reject political and ecclesiastical institutions.[7]

What ought to be considered, however, is the moderation by which the movement preserved a unity of agitational method, its factionalism and diversity of personalities notwithstanding. Garrison's opposition to slavery was religious, not political; he required only a theoretical disobedience to national and state government, not a belligerent refusal to obey the law. Even that conservative reformer, Judge William Jay of Westchester, finally understood the meaning of Garrisonian secessionism. In 1857, he declared: "I . . . rejoice in every exposure of the immoral influence exerted by the Union. I rejoice in such exposure, as tending, not to bring about dissolution, but to

[6] Quotation from Larry Gara, "Who Was an Abolitionist?" in Martin Duberman (ed.), *The Antislavery Vanguard: New Essays on the Abolitionists* (Princeton, 1965), p. 37. William Lloyd Garrison to Richard D. Webb, Feb. 28, 1843, William Lloyd Garrison MSS, Boston Public Library (BPL); MS speech before the American Anti-Slavery Society, May 7, 1856, *ibid.* On his reaction to the Nat Turner rebellion, see Wendell Phillips Garrison and Francis Jackson Garrison, *William Lloyd Garrison, 1805-1879: The Story of His Life Told by His Children* (New York, 1885-1889), I, 230-231, 249-250. On the annihilation of the Union, see his "No Compromise with Slavery," *Selections from the Writings and Speeches of William Lloyd Garrison* (Boston, 1852); Garrison and Garrison, *Garrison*, I, 269: "If we deemed it pleasing . . . [to] God . . . we would immediately put ourselves at the head of a black army at the South. . . . Yet, I am for leaving vengeance to God."

[7] Elkins, *Slavery*, pp. 158-164, condemns the New England abolitionists with particular vigor for their anti-institutionalism. It is not suggested that all historians have treated Garrison in this light. Howard Zinn, "Abolitionism, Freedom-Riders, and the Tactics of Agitation," in Duberman, *Antislavery Vanguard*, pp. 417-451, is the latest and most provocative analysis of antislavery policies of action; see also the balanced portrait found in Russel B. Nye, *William Lloyd Garrison and the Humanitarian Reformers* (Boston, 1955); Louis Filler, *The Crusade against Slavery, 1830-1860* (New York, 1960), pp. 120-122, 128-130, points out some interesting weaknesses and strengths of the Garrisonian position; see also David Alan Williams "William Lloyd Garrison, the Historians, and the Abolitionist Movement," *Essex Institute Historical Collections*, XCVIII (1962), 84-99.

render it unnecessary."[8] At times, Garrison thought that once northern protection was withdrawn from the slave masters, rebellion would follow; but generally he pursued its moral imperative, not its revolutionary implications.[9] Admittedly, such an oscillation displayed the romanticism of what Garrison himself called his "foolishness of preaching," but it served his purpose as an agitator—to arouse, alarm, and convert.

Nonetheless, nonviolent disunionism was far from being a concrete program of radical dissent. At it was explained to Adin Ballou in 1844: "*It is not organically political or revolutionary at all; it proposes only conscientious, peaceable, individual and social action.*"[10] Among the possibilities *not* explored were: sustained opposition to militia duty; abstinence from the use of government agencies; and refusal to pay taxes. All these things would have dramatized the rejection of proslavery government. Indeed, a few peace men challenged the militia laws, and Charles Stearns and David Cambell went to jail rather than submit. When Stearns asked Garrison to approve his course of action, however, he was advised to pay the requisite fine "rather than *seem* to be rebellious."[11] Subordination to unjust laws,

[8] William Jay to Garrison, Phillips, Higginson, Sept. 24, 1857, *Liberator*, Oct. 9, 1857; see also, *ibid.*, Sept. 22, 1843, Adin Ballou's interpretation of disunionism and its results; "Hints for the American People in the Event of a Dissolution of the Union," *ibid.*, Oct. 30, 1846. At first Maria W. Chapman and Garrison both thought political abolitionism was more likely to bring on civil war than moral disunionism; *ibid.*, Sept. 22, 1843, and Garrison's "Massachusetts Abolitionist," *ibid.*, Feb. 22, 1839; Edmund Quincy, "The Life-Taking Principle," *ibid.*, Oct. 30, 1840. "No Union with Slaveholders," was similar to "Immediate Emancipation," in its lack of precision and yet radical coloration; see David B. Davis, "The Emergence of Immediatism in British and American Anti-Slavery Thought." *Mississippi Valley Historical Review*, LXIX (1962), 209-230.

[9] Frederick Douglass, *The Anti-Slavery Movement, A Lecture . . . Before the Rochester Ladies' Anti-Slavery Society* (Rochester, 1855), p. 31, quoting Garrison; cf. Garrison to Elizabeth Pease, July 2, 1842, Garrison MSS, BPL, citing moral purpose of disunion. The nature of a future Yankee republic did not concern him; S. Mitchell to Garrison, October 29, 1856, *Liberator*, Nov. 7, 1856, and editorial reply; editorial, *ibid.*, Dec. 5, 1856; William Henry Channing to Garrison, May 12, 1844, *ibid.*, May 24, 1844; "Address to the Friends of Freedom and Emancipation in the United States," *ibid.*, May 31, 1844; and Garrison and Garrison, *Garrison*, III, 49, 56; Charles E. Hodges, *Disunion: Our Wisdom and Our Duty* (New York, n.d.).

[10] *Liberator*, Nov. 4, 1859, Ballou quoting from a verbal committee report of the American Anti-Slavery Society; also *ibid.*, Dec. 6, 1839, and *Practical Christian*, May 28, 1844: "Let all our friends, especially Non-Resistants, be careful to make this distinction between political, corporate State dissolution of the Union, which is left to take care of itself, and individual moral, peaceable withdrawal from political covenant with slaveholders. . . . The former may be construed as sedition; the latter is at once the duty and privilege of every conscientious man." It is doubtful, however, that even Garrison construed disunionism in quite so pietistic a manner by the 1850's.

[11] Editorial comment on Stearns to Garrison, Jan. 31, 1840, *Liberator*, Feb.

Garrison maintained, was the Christian way to behave. The question of military service was never fully exploited.

From the Stamp Act crisis to the demonstrations against the Viet Nam War, American agitators have sometimes refused to pay taxes to protest what they consider unfair authority. Under Garrison's leadership, however, the issue did not receive the attention it probably deserved. Declared Adin Ballou: "No unnecessary offense is to be given Caesar; but . . . his taxes quietly paid. . . ."[12] The pacifists were open, nevertheless, to the charge of inconsistency. They met their duties to the state, but would not vote or hold office. After his break with Garrison, Frederick Douglass supported Horace Mann's side of a debate with the disunionists by asking: "IS IT CONSISTENT WITH THE DOCTRINE OF 'NO UNION WITH SLAVEHOLDERS,' TO PAY TAXES, TO BUY OR IMPORT GOODS, OR TO USE THE POST OFFICE, WHILE THE DOING OF ANY ONE OF THESE THINGS INVOLVES THE MAN WHO DOES SO IN SUPPORTING THE U.S. GOVERNMENT?" Wendell Phillips gave the standard reply of the Garrisonians; voting was voluntary, taxpaying compulsory. "Suppose I refuse," he said: "Government takes my house, sells it and takes the money. Exceedingly voluntary this!"[13] Using the post office was also voluntary, but the Garrisonians ignored their critics because they felt it "was a most useful instrumentality," cheaper than private postal companies. Of course, their position made practical sense, but in those romantic days of reform "expediency" was more often cursed than applauded, especially on the antislavery rostrum.[14]

Occasionally, however, some isolated reformer tried to reconcile perfectionist thought with actual practice. In 1843, Bronson Alcott refused to pay the unpopular state poll tax; but the incident brought forth just one letter from his friend Charles Lane, published in the

---

14, 1840, petition of Cambell, *ibid.;* see also, "The Militia Laws," from *Mercantile Journal, ibid.,* Aug. 9, 1839, and resolutions against militia system at the annual meeting of the New England Non-Resistance Society, *ibid.,* Nov. 1, 1839; ". . . we deem it unlawful to bear arms, or to hold a military office," declared the signers of the "Declaration of Sentiments adopted by the Peace Convention. . . ." Garrison and Garrison, *Garrison,* II, 231, but outright disobedience was not required or encouraged; *ibid.,* II, 105, 225. There was, however, much grumbling.

[12] At the Non-Resistant Society convention of 1839, *Liberator,* Dec. 6, 1839.

[13] *Frederick Douglass' Paper,* May 6, 1853; *ibid.* (quotation from Douglass), Apr. 23, 29, 1853; Garrison's editorial, *Liberator,* Feb. 14, 1840.

[14] *Ibid.,* Nov. 14, 1856; *Frederick Douglass' Paper,* May 6, 1853. Although the post office was, so to speak, morally neutral, law courts presumably were not. Nonresistants were to settle their differences with others outside the "contaminated" halls of state and national justice; Garrison and Garrison, *Garrison,* II, 225, 232.

Liberator, before the example was forgotten.[15] Only Henry David Thoreau remembered. Some years after his night in the Concord jailhouse for the same offense, he renewed the tax question in his essay on "Civil Disobedience":[16]

I know this well [he said] that if one thousand, if one hundred, if ten men . . . ay, if *one* HONEST man, in this State of Massachusetts, *ceasing to hold slaves*, were actually to withdraw from this copartnership, and be locked up in the county jail therefor, it would be the abolition of slavery in America.

As far as antislavery strategy was concerned, Thoreau's proposal had no impact whatsoever.

Finally, in 1856, Moncure Conway, a young Unitarian clergyman, found the same inconsistencies in nonresistant theory which had worried Douglass and Mann, but he came to a different conclusion. "When we contribute to the treasury of the State," he contended, "we are supporting that which, as a State, supports a Union that is irretrievably given over to the spirit of slavery . . .," a position incompatible with the no-voting principle. Like Thoreau, he believed that a single individual could defy society and set an example which "would shake the whole community," and "a large number . . . would be utterly irresistible." Abolitionists were too "much given to routine, even at Anti-Slavery meetings," he observed. It was time for a new and dramatic approach.[17] No one seconded his motion.

Abolitionists rejected this form of protest for a number of reasons. First of all, none of these advocates was a professional agitator whose ideas could command attention where it counted. Nor were they themselves willing to disobey long and loudly enough to get a hearing. Besides, neither Alcott nor Thoreau were precise about *why* they refused to pay in the first place.[18] In any case, they were in good standing on the revenue books by 1849, if not sooner.[19] The poll tax, moreover, was not an effective device. Its collection was

15 Lane to Garrison, Jan. 16, 1843, *Liberator*, Jan. 27, 1843; Abigail May Alcott, Jan. 17, 1843, in Odell Shepard (ed.), *The Journals of Bronson Alcott* (Boston, 1938), pp. 150-151. Garrison was away part of Jan., 1843, but he could have commented on the event, had he so desired.

16 Carl Bode (ed.), *The Portable Thoreau* (New York, 1947), p. 121; cf. Elkins, *Slavery*, p. 169, for a different use of the quotation.

17 *Liberator*, June 6, 1856, at New England Anti-Slavery Society Convention.

18 F. B. Sanborn, *Recollections of Seventy Years* (Boston, 1909), II, 446, 447; John Haynes Holmes, "Thoreau's Civil Disobedience," *Christian Century*, LXVI (1949), 787-788. Lane's letter indicates Alcott had in mind the general coerciveness of government rather than slavery in particular; see fn. 15; also John C. Broderick, "Thoreau, Alcott, and the Poll Tax," *Studies in Philology*, LIII (1956), 612.

19 Shepard (ed.), *Alcott Journals*, pp. 150-151, 164-165, and note 179; Broderick, "Thoreau and Alcott," 623.

haphazard and the levy too small to arouse much indignation, although it was a political issue in the state for a number of years. While some abolitionists, especially during the Mexican War, denounced tax collections for promoting slavery expansion, they had little stomach for confronting lawful authority over an abstraction. The whole tradition of antislavery, once its basic creed was worked out, became primarily an emotional reaction to national events rather than an uninhibited trial of new methods.

Most important of all, however, was the indifference of Garrison and his friends. By the time Thoreau's essay appeared, they had long since ceased the hunt for novel programs, their complacency extending to the Civil War.[20] Using Christ as his measure, Garrison hinged his reformism on New Testament precept. The Romans collected revenues to support idolatrous religion, gladiatorial combats, and other vices, he noted, yet, Christ rendered his accounts to Caesar; and, by implication, so would he.[21] The point is not that such a program would have helped the cause, but rather that, in his hands, there was little experimentation and much more caution than is commonly thought. After his announcement of the disunionist plan in 1842, Garrison made no other innovations, and he discouraged new radical ideas, especially those involving physical force. But if he was unwilling to thrust his policy beyond the realm of stirring manifestoes, other abolitionists in the 1840's began to stir restlessly. Timid though these early signs of extremism were, they eventually culminated in a challenge to Garrison's nonviolence in the following decade.

Any insurrectionary plot had to include the slaves themselves, but, traditionally, the antislavery men, including Garrison himself, had denied any intention of reaching them directly.[22] In 1842, however, Gerrit Smith of New York suggested that abolitionists try to communicate with the slaves and help them to escape. A timid refusal to do so, he thought, would demoralize the cause. But even Smith did not advocate violence at this time. The following year, the New England Anti-Slavery Society issued an address to the slaves (which

[20] *Ibid.*, 617-620; Louis Ruchames (ed.), *The Abolitionists: A Collection of Their Writings* (New York, 1964), p. 24; Thomas, *Liberator*, p. 348 and Ch. XVI.

[21] *Liberator*, Apr. 18, 1856.

[22] See "Declaration of Sentiments of the American Anti-Slavery Society," Ruchames, *Abolitionists*, p. 79; also William Jay's disclaimer for the American Anti-Slavery Society of 1835 in Bayard Tuckerman, *William Jay and the Constitutional Abolition of Slavery* (New York, 1890), pp. 67-73; William Jay to Richard Habersham, Feb. 24, 1840, William Jay MSS, Special Collections, Columbia University Library.

few of them probably ever saw), but such sporadic innovations had little effect on abolitionist strategy.[23]

In the 1840's some Negro leaders made a still more militant plea for intervention in the South; but they had to meet the objections of their own people, led by Frederick Douglass, then a Garrisonian, as well as the nonresistant whites. At a colored convention in Buffalo, Henry Highland Garnet called for the violent overthrow of slavery. His resolution was narrowly defeated.[24] Taking up the challenge to white antislavery policy, Maria Weston Chapman, temporary editor of the *Liberator*, felt obliged to spell out for Garnet the chapter and verse of the nonresistant gospel in an offensively patronizing tone.[25] On several other occasions in the 1840's Negroes spoke out for aggressive action. They kept the debate alive, but found few supporters.

Once in a while a Garrisonian such as Francis Jackson protested the use of northern arms and men to protect the southerners' favorite institution, but seldom was there talk of physical resistance to governmental policy. Instead, the slaves were expected "to wait patiently" for peaceful deliverance; they were supposedly too docile to be effective rebels, even if warfare was the right weapon—which the nonresistants claimed it was not.[26]

[23] *Gerrit Smith and the Vigilant Association of the City of New York* (New York, 1860), p. 21, quoting from New York State Abolition Convention Proceedings of Jan. 19, 1842; *Liberator*, Feb. 11, 1842, quoting from *Friend of Man;* "The New England Anti-Slavery Convention Exhorts the Slaves to Direct Action," William H. Pease and Jane H. Pease (eds.), *The Antislavery Argument* (Indianapolis, 1965), pp. 212-223.

[24] Herbert Aptheker (ed.), *A Documentary History of the Negro People in the United States* (New York, 1951, 1963 ed.), I, 226-232; John L. Thomas, *Slavery Attacked: The Abolitionist Crusade* (Englewood Cliffs, N.J., 1965), pp. 99-104.

[25] *Liberator*, Sept. 22, 1843; *ibid.*, Dec. 8, 1843 (Garnet's spirited reply); Aptheker, *Documentary History*, I, 234-236; his "Militant Abolitionism," *To Be Free, Studies in American Negro History* (New York, 1948), pp. 55-56; and his *"One Continual Cry" David Walker's Appeal to the Colored Citizens of the World (1829-1830) Its Setting & Its Meaning* (New York, 1965), pp. 16-38, all of which find the abolitionists, both white and black, more revolutionary-minded than they really were.

[26] *Anti-Slavery Reporter*, II, Aug. 1, 1854, 171, speech of William H. Furness; Theodore Parker, *The Great Battle between Slavery and Freedom, Considered in Two Speeches Delivered before the American Anti-Slavery Society, at New York, May 7, 1856* (Boston, 1856), pp. 6-7; Garrison's reply, *Liberator*, May 23, 1856; Aptheker, *To Be Free*, pp. 57-58; and notes 56, 57, p. 205; see also "State Convention of Ohio Negroes, 1849," Aptheker, *Documentary History*, I, 278-280 and *Liberator* reprint from New York *Ram's Horn*, 290-291. Garnet continued to speak for insurrection, *Liberator*, Aug. 10, 1849; W. M. Brewer, "Henry Highland Garnet," *Journal of Negro History*, XIII (1928), 44-47; Howard H. Bell, "National Negro Conventions of the Middle 1840's: Moral Suasion vs. Political Action," *ibid.*, XLII (1957), 250-252; George W. Perkins, "Can Slaves Rightfully Resist and Fight?" in Julia Griffiths (ed.), *Autographs for Freedom* (Boston, 1853), pp. 33-39.

In the 1850's, however, a change of mood became apparent. The revolutions in Europe in 1848 and 1849, the passage of the Fugitive Slave Act and the celebrated cases arising from it, the Kansas-Nebraska dispute and other signs of sectional tension brought the Negro advocates of violence and their white allies closer together. Charles Sumner and other sporadic antislavery supporters grew eloquent on the necessity of physical defense of northern and Negro rights. In addition, Henry C. Wright, Charles Stearns, Theodore Parker, and S. S. Foster, all former pacifists, relinquished their condemnation of war, at least to meet these temporary crises.[27] If Garrison were to lead abolitionist opinion, rather than be left behind, his proper move, some might say, would have been to scrap his nonresistant convictions, claiming southern provocation as a convenient excuse. According to one historian, he was in fact guilty of "moral failure and unpardonable folly" in refusing to accept force as a means to abolish slavery, when he could have seen, at least by 1857, that alternatives had vanished.[28] Perhaps he was a dreamer; but so, too, then, were those men, wiser in the political arts than Garrison, who sought pacific solutions to the sectional crises from 1850 to the eve of war.

More importantly, however, what would have been the advantage of such a dramatic about-face after nearly two decades of pacifistic agitation? The unity of the movement would have gained very little. Lewis Tappan, William Goodell, and other leaders of the evangelical wing, hardly less committed to peace than Garrison himself, were also battling against the rising tide of violence. When, for instance, Frederick Douglass adopted Henry Garnet's position, Lewis Tappan, an influential New York abolitionist, threatened to withdraw his support from his journal. "How can I encourage the wider circulation of a paper . . . deserving in most respects as is the Editor, when I believe he is scattering 'firebrands, arson, and death,'" he asked in late 1856. Garrison's apostasy, then, simply would have added this sur-

[27] Henry C. Wright, "Death to Kidnappers," *Liberator*, Oct. 4, 1850; Stephen S. Foster, at "Anti-Slavery Convention at Valley Falls, R.I.," *ibid.*, Oct. 11, 1850; Theodore Parker had already proposed forcible resistance to the return of fugitives to the South, *ibid.*, Dec. 4, 1846; Parker to President Fillmore, Nov. 21, 1850, John Weiss (ed.), *Life and Correspondence of Theodore Parker* (New York, 1864), II, 100-102; Charles Sumner, senate speech of Aug. 26, 1852, *The Works of Charles Sumner* (Boston, 1870-1883), III, 191-196; even S. J. May, Garrison's closest supporter, contributed to Kansas arms collection, *Liberator*, May 16, 1856; Charles Stearns to Garrison (from Kansas), Apr. 27, 1856, *ibid.*, May 23, 1856; on the impact of the 1848 uprisings see Frank Preston Stearns, *The Life and Public Services of George Luther Stearns* (Philadelphia, 1907), pp. 70-71.
[28] Thomas, *Liberator*, p. 407.

render of principle to his other crimes, as far as the Tappanites were concerned.[29] They quarreled with his disunionism and his church views, not his nonresistance. Even if one admits that Garrison's influence in the 1850's had declined as his prestige grew, the conversion of the *Liberator* into an organ for Negro and white aggression would have increased the likelihood of more violence and confusion without clarifying the slave issue at all.[30] Paradoxically, Garrison would only have lost much influence by a shift of policy. By embracing conventional views of warfare, he would no longer have retained his reputation as a radical agitator and conservator of the antislavery heritage, which, he always boasted, resided in the old American Anti-Slavery Society. In the tension arising from this dual role, he had found a variety of "extremism" ideally suited to strike a responsive chord in the Yankee conscience—and a note of fear as well.[31]

Anxious to avoid further schisms within the American Anti-Slavery Society, Garrison did not precipitate a fight between the pacifist camp and those who favored the defense of Kansas and the fugitives by force of arms. Nevertheless, he tried to bring them back to traditional nonresistant theory by means of dispassionate argument. When Theodore Parker, as well as the non-Garrisonians Henry Ward Beecher and Gerrit Smith, raised money for Sharp's rifles for Kansas free soilers, Garrison reminded them of their duty as Christians to obey the "Prince of Peace." He also noted their loose grasp of constitutional law, and remarked on the unworthiness of the settlers themselves. The first argument was designed to shame Parker and Beecher, who, as ministers of the gospel, were obligated to reflect the precepts of Christian teaching. Parker, moreover, also misunderstood the nature of the American Constitution. Was the North really able to abolish slavery "peaceably if it can, forcibly if it must." Garrison asked: "does Mr. Parker contemplate an armed invasion of the South . . .?" The Constitution provided no such authority. In answer to Parker's call for a reconstructed Supreme Court, the abolition of slavery in the territories and the District of Columbia, the exclusion of slave masters from holding office, and the prohibition of the inter-

---

[29] See, for example, William Goodell to Gerrit Smith, Apr. 23, 29, 1856, American Abolition Society letterbook, Oberlin College Library; Lewis Tappan to Gerrit Smith, Aug. 3, 1857, letterbook, Lewis Tappan MSS, Library of Congress (LC); Lewis Tappan to Frederick Douglass, Dec. 19, 1856 (quotation), Frederick Douglass MSS, microfilm, LC; all attempts to preserve the peace principle; cf., *Frederick Douglass' Paper*, Dec. 12, 1856.

[30] C. Vann Woodward, review of Thomas, *Liberator, New York Times Book Review,* June 30, 1963, 6.

[31] Truman Nelson, "The Liberator," *Ramparts,* IV (1965), 21-29, polemical but interesting evaluation; see for example, Howard Zinn's telling example of Garrison at the Douglass speech, Duberman (ed.), *Antislavery Vanguard,* p. 427.

state slave trade, he countered that the "monster Slavery must have suddenly become a very gentle beast, whose roar is like that of a nightingale," if it were to acquiesce. In comparison with his own program, Parker's seemed bloodthirsty and impractical. Its implementation, Garrison warned, would necessitate "an act of usurpation that would lead to civil war, and deluge the land in blood."[32] As for the Kansas free soilers, he observed how inconsistent and even hypocritical these people really were. As he saw it, they cruelly and callously turned their backs on abolitionism, the rights of free colored men, and the fate of fugitives, pursuing "a shuffling and compromising policy throughout. . . ." If these free soilers deserved military aid, he continued, "are not the crushed and bleeding slaves at the South a million times more deserving of pity and succor? . . . Why strain at a gnat, and swallow a camel? . . . Who will go for arming our slave population?"[33] The sarcasm was heavy-handed, as events later proved.

One could argue that Garrison was much more in favor of a vindictive war against the South than his public professions indicated. Certainly there was a constant and intense struggle within his puritan soul between hopes for utopian peace and dreams of a destructive purge of evil. The conflict itself, however, was the very source of his dynamic agitation, and made his pacifism no less sincere. He meant every word when he said: "We have assailed no man unjustly or by violence; we have sought the injury of no slaveholder; we have been law-abiding, in the highest sense of the term; we have not been guilty of treason, nor plotted insurrection; we have sought only a peaceful and voluntary emancipation of those in bondage. . . ."[34] As far as he was concerned, the movement should not depart from this course until victory was achieved, no matter what other Americans chose to do.

Although Garrison remained faithful to his principles throughout the middle 1850's, the assaults against the pacifist citadel grew increasingly virulent. To be sure, such men as James Freeman Clarke, William H. Furness, and O. B. Frothingham supported him, the latter claiming that disunionism was nothing more than a righteous state

[32] *Liberator*, Apr. 11, 1856; *ibid.*, Apr. 4, 11, 1856. "You see that such men as Gerrit Smith, Ward Beecher, and Theodore Parker are finding in Sharp's rifles more than in the peaceful Gospel of Christ to aid the cause of right and freedom! They will cause many professed friends of peace to apostatize [sic] from their principles, and give a fresh stimulus to the war principle." Garrison to S. J. May, March 21, 1856, Garrison MSS, BPL; also *Liberator*, Apr. 25, May 3, 1856; Parker in New York *Post*, Mar. 7, 1856, *ibid.*, Mar. 14, 1856; Garrison v. Beecher, *ibid.*, Feb. 29, 1856.
[33] *Ibid.*, Apr. 4, 1856.
[34] Framingham 4th of July address, *ibid.*, July 11, 1856.

of mind leading to "no greater convulsion than is experienced in passing from one frame of temper to another."[35] Yet, Thomas Wentworth Higginson, S. S. Foster, and William Wells Brown, among others, demanded what Higginson called a "New Revolution." At the New England Anti-Slavery Society convention of 1857, Higginson said, "You cannot learn men to swim on a table. You have no chance to turn men into freemen by giving them a sense of duty, but by giving them something to defend." Abolitionists, therefore, should prepare to scrap their "disguises and feints," which kept them from the main lesson: the duty of "open" and defiant, not "secret" and passive, treason.[36]

Garrison, although not remembered for tolerating rival ideas, remained on good terms with these advocates of violence. Undoubtedly age mellowed him, and socially he basked in his role as dean of antislavery, a cause now respectable, in Massachusetts at least. Even if he did not always speak out for peace when others talked of force,[37] he did contribute to antislavery unity by welcoming dissent. "We invite persons of all opinions in regard to the matter of resisting evil by physical force," he said of the American Anti-Slavery Society. Surprisingly enough, the old firebrand had become one of the conciliators in the movement, even defending the Republican party against the attacks of his more radical allies.[38]

His task of holding together the diverse elements in the American Anti-Slavery Society, however, was all the easier because very few

[35] *Ibid.*, May 29, 1857; Andrew T. Foss, James Freeman Clarke, at Hopedale meeting, *ibid.*, Aug. 7, 1857; Garrison at same, Aug. 28, 1857; William H. Furness, *ibid.*, May 19, 1854, May 22, 1857.

[36] *Ibid.*, June 12, 1857; *ibid.*, May 22, June 5, 1857; see also Thomas Wentworth Higginson, *The New Revolution: A Speech before the American Anti-Slavery Society at their Annual Meeting, May 12, 1857* (Boston, 1857), pp. 1-16, and his speech in *Proceedings of the State Disunion Convention, Held at Worcester, Massachusetts, January 15, 1857* (Boston, 1857), p. 21, a comparatively mild statement, however.

[37] See disunion convention, for example, *ibid.*, pp. 31-33, in which Garrison did not challenge the warmongers, who were themselves less aggressive than one might have expected; also the oblique attitude in S. S. Foster, *Revolution: The Only Remedy for Slavery* (New York, n.d.), pp. 1-20, and Parker's *The Aspect of Slavery in America and the Immediate Duty of the North: A Speech Delivered in the Hall of the State House, Before the Massachusetts Antislavery Convention, on Friday Night, January 29, 1858* (Boston, 1858), pp. 41-42.

[38] *Liberator*, May 23, 1856; a few days later he said: "Every abolitionist utters his own thought, acts upon his own conviction, whether he has any body to sustain him or not. This it is which makes us strong, vital, fearless, invincible," *ibid.*, June 13, 1856; Thomas Wentworth Higginson, *Contemporaries* (Boston, 1899), p. 249: "I am ready to testify that, at the later period of the contest . . . he seemed wholly patient and considerate with younger recruits," although, he noted, it had not always been so.

of the new activists took up arms themselves.[39] Only one member of the antislavery group in Boston actually made plans for an uprising in the South. Always an individualist, Lysander Spooner had for years recoiled from the "tame, cowardly, drivelling, truckling course pursued by the abolitionists," who wasted their energies "talking to women and children about the churches and the clergy. . . ."[40] His ideas about the antislavery nature of the Constitution were very influential in some antislavery political circles, but his corollary, that slavery could be litigated to death, made no headway. Not only did he claim that the American Constitution provided the legal authority to sue slaveholders for assault and battery, damages, and even the freedom of slave clients, but also that slaves had the right to bear arms and serve in the militia. When Spooner learned that Joshua Leavitt was engaged in the project to get Bibles to southern slaves, he wrote his friend George Bradburn: "Tall business indeed! He had better unite with us in trying to secure to them their natural and constitutional right 'to keep and bear arms.'"[41] With such an active imagination, it was easy for Spooner to justify slave rebellion.

Drawn up in the form of a printed circular sometime in 1858, his plan called upon northerners to prepare for military operations in support of slave rebellions. Southern white nonslaveholders were also to render as much assistance as possible. First would come the creation of Yankee conspiratorial cells, the establishment of newspapers to support their work, the raising of a war chest, and the training of military bands. After gaining the confidence of slaves and white sympathizers in the South, these armed companies would execute a number of simultaneous invasions. With remarkable innocence, he predicted that as soon as this was done, slaveholders would immediately surrender, perhaps without a drop of blood being spilled. If, however, the fighting was not immediately successful, nonslaveholding whites would form "Leagues of Freedom," to punish masters by lynch law or force them to sign emancipation papers. Kidnapped slaveholders, held in mountain retreats, would be used as hostages, and threats of

[39] The exceptions were those in Kansas, acting with John Brown. Wendell Phillips later said: "I like . . . these speeches about insurrection," but he showed little interest in initiating slave rebellion; Higginson, *Contemporaries*, 262-263: "It is doubtful whether he [Phillips] was, in his very fibre, a man of action; but he never discouraged those who were such, nor had he the slightest objection to violating law where human freedom was at stake."

[40] Lysander Spooner to George Bradburn, Jan. 30, 1847, Lysander Spooner MSS, New York Historical Society.

[41] *Ibid.*, Mar. 5, Sept. 14, 1847; to Gerrit Smith, Mar. 14, 1847, Sept. 10, 1857; to S. P. Andrews, Mar. 31, 1847; Spooner influenced Smith as seen in *Letter of Gerrit Smith to S. P. Chase on the Unconstitutionality of Every Part of American Slavery* (Albany, 1847), esp. p. 3.

the destruction of plantation property would compel quick manumissions. Admitting that a general slave uprising would be dangerous without proper planning, he suggested that guerrillas, operating in small bands, "could build forts in the forests, and there collect themselves, and carry on their warfare upon the Slaveholders."[42]

The reaction to the plan was predictable. Wendell Phillips, although one of the leading platform-soldiers, pointed out that such activities "would be treason & the Govt. would at once move & array all its power to crush" it. Daniel Mann and Francis Jackson both repudiated the scheme on the grounds that they were faithful Garrisonian nonresistants, Jackson confessing that he was "loaded down to the gunwales with their apparatus. . . ."[43] Only Stephen S. Foster and Thomas Wentworth Higginson supported his idea. When it came to raising money for it, however, Foster had to decline because of illness in the family and the temporary loss of his "vocal power" owing to the "extraction of all my remaining upper teeth." Even Higginson hedged his enthusiasm. Spooner, he thought, had been too outspoken in announcing the goals of the "Leagues of Freedom." Garrison's opinion apparently was not sought.[44] Thus, while it can hardly be claimed that Garrison alone prevented a more favorable response to Spooner's idea, it is true that his agitational methods, his theories, and above all, his example as a fear-inspiring but pacifist agitator hardly encouraged this sort of innovation. In a sense, Garrison's views of war and the Union were just "radical" enough to dampen enthusiasm for Spooner's kind of extremism.

Even if Spooner found lukewarm support for insurrection in the quiet neighborhoods of Boston, however, John Brown and his band, out on the front lines, so to speak, in Kansas were setting a stirring example for militant abolitionists. His "rescue" of twenty Missouri slaves inspired Wendell Phillips, Parker Pillsbury, and R. J. Hinton of Kansas to speak for this type of action at an antislavery convention in early 1859. With his gift for the picturesque phrase, Pillsbury likened John Brown to Oliver Cromwell and announced that he "longed to see the time come, when Boston streets should run with blood from Beacon Hill to the foot of Broad street.' "[45] Garrison,

[42] "A Plan for the Abolition of Slavery," Lysander Spooner MSS, NYHS; Aptheker, *To Be Free*, pp. 62-67, giving a full account of Spooner's project.

[43] Wendell Phillips to Spooner, July 16, 1858; Jackson to Spooner, Dec. 3, 1858; Daniel Mann to Spooner, Jan. 16, 1859; Lysander Spooner MSS, BPL.

[44] S. S. Foster to Spooner, Jan. 8, 1859, *ibid.*; Theodore Parker to Spooner, Nov. 30, 1858; Higginson to Spooner, Nov. 30, 1858; see also Lewis Tappan to Spooner, Oct. 7, 1858; Hinton R. Helper to Spooner, Dec. 18, 1858; Boston *Courier*, Jan. 28, 1859, clipping in Spooner MSS.

[45] *Liberator*, Feb. 4, 1859, meeting of the Massachusetts Anti-Slavery Society, quoted by Holden, of Lynn, Mass.

angry and alarmed, defended nonresistance. In reply to Hinton's unqualified praise for Kansas free soilers, Garrison retorted, "They went
to make money . . . I do not see that Kansas has given us any lessons
of wisdom in regard to the management of the warfare against slavery. I am for going on as we have hitherto done."[46] Other pacifists
rallied around the fading Garrisonian banner, even as the spirit of
aggression reached its climax at Harpers Ferry.[47]

Platform oratory and Spooner's circulars paled into insignificance
with this first and only translation of militant words into direct action
against the South. Faced with the challenge and shock of Brown's
example, Garrison at first reacted by calling it "a misguided, wild,
and apparently insane, though disinterested and well-intended effort.
. . ."[48] The comment drew the instant criticism of Henry Thoreau,
long since an apostate from nonviolence. While beatifying John
Brown, Thoreau had nothing but contempt for "ye Garrisons, ye Bu-
chanans, ye politicians, attorney-generals. . . ."[49] Deserted by so many
former pacifists, Garrison was at this point in danger of becoming a
curious relic of the antislavery past. Understandably, he left all but
nominal adherence to nonviolence behind and quickly joined the
chorus praising Brown.[50]

It would not be the last time an American reformer abandoned
his hatred of war to support a crusade against tyranny. It is ironic,
however, that Thoreau would be much more influential in the history of nonviolent agitation than Garrison, who had served this cause
longer and better. For seventeen years, he had maintained a fairly
consistent, if often equivocal, attitude toward slave rebellion. Still,
a professional agitator, such as he, faced with issues demanding editorial attack, grasps at the shocking sentiment, the belligerent tone,
thereby nullifying objectivity and consistency. Self-righteous though
he was, he had sometimes compromised his position when he thought
it essential or expedient.[51]

[46] Ibid.
[47] See Holden's speech in defense of nonresistance, ibid., and debate between
J. Miller McKim and Adin Ballou, ibid., Sept. 30, Nov. 4, 1859.
[48] Ibid., Oct. 21, 1859.
[49] Bradford Torrey (ed.), The Writings of Henry David Thoreau (Boston,
1906), XII (Oct. 19, 1859, journal entry) 408.
[50] Garrison to James Redpath, Dec. 1, 1860, Garrison MSS, BPL; also Garrison to LeRoy Sunderland, Sept. 18, 1851, in Liberator, Sept. 18, 1857, and
Garrison to R. Wertz, Mar. 7, 1874, Garrison MSS, BPL; these examples reveal
his ambivalent feelings about rebellion, but certainly the Brown affair called
for his condemnation on principle, a pacifist duty he passed by; cf. other former
pacifists reversing themselves, George M. Frederickson, The Inner Civil War:
Northern Intellectuals and the Crisis of the Union (New York, 1965), pp. 36-41.
[51] Thomas, Liberator, pp. 388-389, for example of Garrison's change of views
about political action; but see Richard Hofstadter, The American Political Tra-

Nonetheless, Garrison's contribution to antislavery unity was his own respectability. Even though he broke with the evangelical and political-minded moderates early in antislavery history, for thirty years he was living proof that even the wildest American radical was seldom the plotter of outright violence. He never sent a *Liberator* to the slaves of the South. He never said: "Slaves, arise, you have nothing to lose but your chains." Nor did he urge military action against the South, until the Civil War came. Instead, his pacifist protests, uncertain as they sometimes were, helped to act as a brake against the use of physical force. Frederick Douglass later reminisced that nonresistance (along with women's rights) "had a depressing effect upon the whole movement."[52] Perhaps he was right; but that was just as well in the light of the grim alternatives.

Some historians might insist that Garrison's pacifism was a hoax, or at best, an obvious impossibility; that since the issue which he raised led to war, he must be held responsible for the consequences. His flaming words were just as dangerous as flaming swords. Certainly his contemporaries frequently said so. It should be remembered, however, that boisterous, uninhibited language was hardly confined to the columns of the *Liberator*, but pervaded the colorful and romantic rhetoric of the times. In addition, even a casual thumbing of the journal would demonstrate that Garrison's vituperative qualities have been somewhat exaggerated.

Of course, it can be said that extremism is a relative matter, and by the standards of his time Garrison qualified as a genuine fanatic. Yet, it was not so much the language he used but the subject to which he applied it that made him seem fanatical. At the end of the nineteenth century, Thomas Wentworth Higginson recalled a point too frequently forgotten: "What such critics overlooked, is that the whole vocabulary of Garrison was the logical result of that stern school of old-fashioned Calvinism in which he was trained." In other words, the same threats of divine judgment delivered from the pulpit would hardly have worried the gentlemen with gold spectacles, but when applied to a volatile and insecure institution it was inflammatory. Under these circumstances, Garrison may be considered a crank, but

---

dition (New York, 1949), pp. 135-161, on the role of the agitator in democratic society. On insurrections, see Garrison to Redpath, Dec. 1, 1860, Garrison MSS, BPL; Garrison and Garrison, *Garrison*, I, "Universal Emancipation," poem, 229-230, and 231, 250n.; *Liberator*, Sept. 18, 1857, Dec. 7, 1860; James M. McPherson, *The Struggle for Equality, Abolitionists and the Negro in the Civil War and Reconstruction* (Princeton, 1964), pp. 33-34; Frederickson, *Inner Civil War*, p. 42.

[52] Douglass to R. J. Hinton, Jan. 17, 1893, *Journal of Negro History*, XXXIII (1948), 471.

hardly outside the main currents of American reform; religious zeal, Biblical language, and Christian pacifism have often been associated with reform movements. In any case, his refusal to advance from pleas for national repentance and disunionist absolution to nonviolent resistance to law or to revolution limits the extent to which he can justly be called extremist. Adin Ballou wisely said: "Mr. Garrison hurts the feelings of the oppressors of men by an application of wholesome truth. Is that to be compared to slitting their ears, breaking their arms, or blowing out their brains?"[53]

Critics of his policy overlook the wealth of alternatives open to the abolitionists in the 1850's. They might have rejected Garrison's paper nullifications, no more outrageous than the public burning of the Fugitive Slave Act and the Constitution, and instead organized guerrilla bands, publicized antislavery among the slaves, or attempted assassinations, kidnappings, and lynchings of proslavery men. There were plenty of European examples to follow, particularly after the 1848 rebellions, and in this country filibusters against Latin countries were then enjoying an unusual vogue. It is remarkable that only a handful of abolitionists supported John Brown's raid, and even more astonishing that after thirty years of agitation, there was only *one* major act of violence against the South. As Abraham Lincoln pointed out: "That affair, in its philosophy, corresponds with many attempts related in history, at the assassination of kings and emperors. . . . Orsini's attempt on Louis Napoleon, and John Brown's attempt at Harpers Ferry were, in their philosophy, precisely the same."[54] The models for violence had long been available. Only the antislavery will and tradition were lacking.

Since that tradition was largely the work of Garrison himself, his unwillingness to go beyond the platform measures of disunionism helped to retain abolitionism within nonviolent bounds. Except for the various abolitionist riots over fugitive slave cases and the defense of Kansas, few abolitionists ever hazarded open civil disobedience. If, on the other hand, he had tried to convert the American Anti-Slavery Society chapters into carbonari or dedicated guerrilla companies, abolitionists might easily have brought on a martyrdom and persecution that would have shocked the nation into either an earlier and more bitter Civil War or an era of rampant tyranny in North and South. If the Garrisonians had been truly destructive, then American

53 Ballou at the Non-Resistance Convention, Worcester, *Liberator*, Dec. 12, 1856; Higginson, *Contemporaries*, p. 251.

54 Roy P. Basler (ed.), *Abraham Lincoln, His Speeches and Writings* (New York, 1946, 1962 ed.), Cooper Institute Speech, Feb. 27, 1860, p. 531; Higginson estimated that no more than a dozen abolitionists in Boston "had quite made up their minds to fight," *Contemporaries*, p. 296.

historians might have good reason to question their motives and their sanity.

Yet, it would be a serious mistake to attribute the comparative moderation of Garrison's policy to him alone. The American tradition of reform has generally avoided bloody deeds even if society has been frustratingly slow in righting its wrongs. Garrison and his friends were actors in the last great era of Christian faith, and their appeal naturally focused on the deeply entrenched feelings of a conservative but conscience-minded northern community. This skittishness of revolutionary action was recognized at the time and sometimes lampooned. The editor of the Baltimore *Patriot*, for instance, wrote in 1854: "Perhaps if civil war should come, Mr. Phillips would be surrounded by a life-guard of elderly ladies, and protected by a rampart of whalebones and cotton-padding."[55]

John L. Thomas, in his biography of Garrison, makes brilliantly clear his religious preoccupations, Quaker-like pacifism and his Biblical sense of American destiny. Primarily, however, he and his disciples were liberal nineteenth-century reformers, for all their heady talk of Christian perfection. They were not so very different from others of their kind—Richard Cobden, John Bright, and Daniel O'Connell. In fact, Wendell Phillips, in his famous address to the Harvard Phi Beta Kappa chapter in 1881, pointed out the Anglo-American spirit of nonviolent reform. "In all modern constitutional governments," he said, "agitation is the only peaceful method of progress. Wilberforce and Clarkson, Rowland Hill and Romilly, Cobden and John Bright, Garrison and O'Connell, have been the master spirits in this new form of crusade." Phillips did not rule out the necessity of violence, even in democracies, when free men had their rights disregarded, but he took pride in the lawful approach of Garrison and his small band of crusaders.[56]

Like their British colleagues of reform, whom they much admired, the Garrisonians addressed themselves to the great middle class. In reference to abolitionism, Garrison might have echoed the grand, subtle spirit of Richard Cobden's words about Corn Law repeal:[57]

55 *Patriot,* quoted by *Liberator,* June 2, 1854.

56 Wendell Phillips, "The Scholar in a Republic," June 30, 1881, in Carlos Martyn, *Wendell Phillips, The Agitator* (New York, 1890), pp. 584, 588.

57 Quoted by John Morley, *The Life of Richard Cobden* (London, 1903), I, 249. It could be argued that Corn Law repeal agitation derived techniques from abolitionism; see G.R.S. Kitson Clark, "The Romantic Element, 1830-1850," in John Harold Plumb (ed.), *Studies in Social History: A Tribute to G. M. Trevelyan* (London, 1955), p. 232; also, for Anglo-American parallels, Asa Briggs, "John Bright and the Creed of Reform," *Victorian People: A Reassessment of Persons and Themes, 1851-1867* (New York, 1955, 1963 ed.), pp. 197-231, esp. p. 203; Fanny Garrison Villard, *William Lloyd Garrison on Non-Resistance*

We have carried it on by those means by which the middle-class usually carries on its movements. We have had our meetings of dissenting ministers; we have obtained the co-operation of the ladies; we have resorted to tea-parties and taken those pacific means for carrying out our views, which mark us rather as a middle-class set of agitators. . . .

It was a painful, frustrating task to goad that good-intentioned but sluggish lump of consensus into some recognition of antislavery duty. By taking a rhetorically radical stand Garrison gradually helped force stronger antislavery postures among antislavery men outside his faction and, at a slower pace, more conservative Yankees. "He did the work," as Higginson phrased it, "of a man of iron in an iron age." He did not, however, see far enough beyond the extinction of slavery to the racial barriers ahead. As John Jay Chapman said: "That short-sighted element in the philosophy of Abolition . . . ended by putting Slavery to its purgation so quickly and so convulsively that many features . . . of slavery were left behind in the nervous system of the people." Indeed, Garrison offered no "after-cure," but the problems, sufficiently perplexing in our own time, were not easily remedied then.[58]

Even though he had helped to preserve traditional antislavery action in nonviolent channels, he is seldom remembered for it, but only for his intellectual vagaries and belligerent language. Leo Tolstoy, however, once declared that he had been one of the "greatest reformers and promoters of true human progress," and indeed "the first to proclaim" the principle of peaceful resistance.[59] In spite of Tolstoy's claim of indebtedness to his example, in spite of Gandhi's admission of Thoreau's influence, which was largely derived from Garrison, and in spite of Martin Luther King's claimed inspiration from this pacifist heritage, the author of American nonresistant theory has gained little esteem.[60] By remaining faithful, *almost* to the last extremity, to

---

Together with a Personal Sketch by His Daughter . . . and a Tribute by Leo Tolstoi (New York, 1924), p. 74, finding Garrison's work "wonderfully suited to the sturdy middle-class. . . ." On Anglo-American connections generally see Frank Thistlethwaite, *America and the Atlantic Community, Anglo-American Aspects, 1790-1850* (New York, 1963), pp. 103-133; G. D. Lillibridge, *Beacon of Freedom, The Impact of American Democracy upon Great Britain, 1830-1870* (Philadelphia, 1954), both of which are challenged by David Paul Crook, *American Democracy in English Politics, 1815-1850* (London, 1965).

58 John Jay Chapman, *William Lloyd Garrison* (Boston, 1921), p. 275; Higginson, *Contemporaries*, p. 256; McPherson, *Struggle for Equality* on later role of Garrison and other abolitionists; Willie Lee Rose, *Rehearsal for Reconstruction, The Port Royal Experiment* (Indianapolis, 1964), for sensitive appreciation of abolitionist difficulties with their preconceptions and Negro realities; see also Ruchames, "Garrison and Negro Franchise," cited fn. 5, above.

59 Leo Tolstoy, "What I Owe to Garrison," in Fanny Villard, *Garrison on Non-Resistance*, p. 55.

60 *Ibid.*; and, his "Garrison and Non-Resistance," *The Independent*, LVI (1904),

his Christian principles, Garrison contributed much to the American reform tradition, in his own day and for the future. It can only be hoped that this unity of action, effective for the most part in the trying times before the Civil War, will remain a lively heritage.[61]

Perhaps the time will come when abolitionists of the Garrison persuasion will earn our respect if never our affection. These cantankerous, incorrigible, self-satisfied, moralistic and irascible reformers were tough old birds. They enjoyed their unpopularity. As Garrison once said, "Hisses are music to my ears." Yet, he did expect more recognition than he so far has received: "I look to posterity," he said, "for a good reputation."[62] He still looks in vain.

881-883; "A Message to the American People," *Complete Works of Count Tolstoi.* (New York and Boston, 1904-1905), XXIII, 462; also *ibid.*, 122-123 and XX, 6, 12; Henry Raymond Mussey, "Gandhi the Non-Resistant," *The Nation,* CXXX (1930), 608-610; Wendell Phillips Garrison to L. N. Tolstoi, Mar. 1, 1905, Wendell Phillips Garrison MSS, Houghton Library, Harvard; Gopinath Dhawan, *The Political Philosophy of Mahatma Gandhi* (Amedabad, 1951), pp. 30-31; *The Collected Works of Mahatma Gandhi* (Amedabad, 1958-), VII, 217-218, 228-230, 304-305; George Hendrick, "The Influence of Thoreau's 'Civil Disobedience' on Gandhi's Satyagraha," *New England Quarterly,* XXIX (1959), 462-471; Clarence A. Manning, "Thoreau and Tolstoy," *ibid.*, XVI (1943), 234-243; Richard B. Gregg, *The Power of Non-Violence* (Amedabad, 1960), foreword by Martin Luther King; Mulford A. Silbey (ed.), *The Quiet Battle, Writings on the Theory and Practice of Non-Violent Resistance* (New York, 1958), pp. 76-78, 82-83, 177-178 on Gandhi, and p. 72 on Thoreau.

[61] The best articles on the romantic and religious content of American antebellum reform: John L. Thomas, "Romantic Reform in America, 1815-1865," *American Quarterly,* XVII (1965), 656-681; and his "Antislavery and Utopia," Duberman (ed.), *Antislavery Vanguard,* pp. 240-269; Ralph Henry Gabriel, "Evangelical Religion and Popular Romanticism in Early Nineteenth Century America," in Grady McWhiney and Robert Weibe (eds.), *Historical Vistas, Readings in United States History* (Boston, 1963), I, 407-419; William G. McLoughlin, "Pietism and the American Character," *American Quarterly,* XVII (1965), 163-186.

[62] Quoted by Russel B. Nye, *William Lloyd Garrison and the Humanitarian Reformers* (Boston, 1955), pp. 200-203.

THE AIM AND IMPACT OF GARRISONIAN ABOLITIONISM, 1840-1860

James B. Stewart

HISTORIANS GENERALLY HAVE HELD that after 1840 Garrisonian abolitionists contributed little to the sectional conflict. This interpretation, simple and blunt, pictures utopian, unrealistic William Lloyd Garrison presiding over a truncated version of the American Anti-Slavery Society bereft of members and lacking funds. Many of abolitionism's most talented operatives, put off by the Garrisonian insistence on overthrowing the government, non-resistance and women's rights, had deserted the Society in 1840 for direct political involvement, the Liberty party. After that date, according to most scholars, the American Anti-Slavery Society claimed the allegiance of only a few itinerant agitators, who assailed a hostile public with bitter attacks on all political parties, while broadcasting Garrison's anarchic doctrine of northern disunion. "Misled by Garrison's antipolitical point of view," one historian has concluded, radical abolitionists "failed . . . to appreciate the contribution of political friction to the growth of antislavery sentiment."[1] In general, students of the antislavery movement have agreed with Gilbert Hobbes Barnes' contention that the radicals were 'dead weights' who had an "even less negligible" effect upon sectional events during the 1840's and 1850's.[2]

Recently, however, certain scholars have cast some general doubt upon the foregoing interpretation. Several historians have charted some of the general crosscurrents between Garrisonian radicalism and political events, arguing that pure moral agitation and pragmatic political developments must not be rigidly separated.[3] A re-examination of the 1840's and 1850's suggests that the Garrisonian approach to northern politics was not nearly as unsophisticated and unproductive as historians have assumed.

To best understand these matters, one must return to 1840. In that

[1] Richard Hofstadter, "Wendell Phillips: The Patrician as Agitator" in *The American Political Tradition and The Men Who Made It* (New York, 1948), p. 149.

[2] Gilbert Hobbes Barnes, *The Antislavery Impulse* (Washington, 1933), p. 175.

[3] See especially Howard Zinn, "Abolitionists, Freedom Riders and the Tactics of Agitation" in Martin Duberman (ed.), *The Antislavery Vanguard: New Essays on the Abolitionists* (Princeton, 1965), pp. 417-451; Louis Filler, *The Crusade Against Slavery, 1830-1860* (New York, 1960); Aileen Kraditor, *Means and Ends in American Abolitionism: Garrison and his Critics on Strategy and Tactics* (New York, 1969).

year a large minority departed the American Anti-Slavery Society.
They disavowed the traditional program of moral suasion as well as
Garrison's new, "heretical" doctrines, and plunged into politics by establishing the Liberty party. The violent recriminations that ensued between members of the "old" and "new" organizations reflected poorly
on both sides and did much to convince historians of the Garrisonians'
"antipolitical" bias.

In attacking the Liberty party experiment, the Garrisonians proceeded from the well-founded assumption, validated by twentieth-century scholarship, that all of American society was uniformly hostile to
the cause of the slave.[4] The very structure of the American government,
the Constitution, reflected this verity in its many proslavery compromises.[5] So did the Garrisonians' own experiences. Congress, they argued, had simply responded to the dominant opinions of the nation by
legislating the censorship of abolitionist literature from the southern
mail, and by refusing to consider antislavery petitions in the House of
Representatives. "Non-resistants declare that, of all questions which
now agitate the land, none can compare in importance, *politically*, with
that of slavery," Garrison exclaimed in 1839. "Do the politicians agree
with them? No!"[6] How could the Liberty party expect "to make an
anti-slavery Congress out of pro-slavery materials?" queried Henry C.
Wright. "The nation must be abolitionized, before an abolition Congress can be created. . . . Why not then, lend all their energies to aboli-
tionize the nation [?] Then of necessity, the fruit will appear in an anti-slavery Congress and government."[7]

Implicit in Wright's statement are the assumptions of an effective
pressure group member, as well as the dreams of a perfectionist. He
affirmed his faith in the malleability of public opinion and stated that
elected officials react positively to public pressure. In short, Wright articulated his basic belief that the democratic process would respond at
all levels to the Garrisonians' special interest, emancipation of the slave.
Parker Pillsbury, the most zealous of non-resistants, once clarified nicely
the Garrisonian perception of American politics: "Men do not *go* to
Congress, they are carried there. They do not act—they are *acted upon*.
The active vote does not belong to Congress at all."[8]

Working from this analysis, the Garrisonians' decision to abstain
from voting and third party affairs proved tactically essential for their
political potency. Their immediate concerns were the opinions, not the
ballots, of the voters, and the actions of established representatives,

[4] See Winthrop Jordan, *White Over Black: American Attitudes Toward The Negro, 1550-1812* (Chapel Hill, 1968); Leon Litwack, *North of Slavery: The Free Negro in The North, 1790-1860* (Chicago, 1961).

[5] Staughton Lynd, "The Abolitionist Critique of The United States Constitution"
in Duberman (ed.), *Antislavery Vanguard*, pp. 209-239.

[6] *The Liberator*, Sept. 13, 1839.

[7] *Ibid.*, Aug. 30, 1839.

[8] *Ibid.*, Aug. 29, 1850.

not the creation of separate slates of candidates. Therefore, they correctly assumed that conventional political activities were restrictive and morally dangerous, "narrowing the broad dimension of the antislavery platform," as Garrison explained.[9] Liberty men were warned that they would inevitably pre-occupy themselves with party machinations, lose interest in emancipation, and moderate their antislavery platform to suit conventional tastes. Besides, as Garrison shrewdly observed, the act of forming a third party could amount to a sop to conscience, a surrogate for effective political action on behalf of the bondsman. "It has never been a difficult matter," he remarked, "to induce men to go to the ballot box; but the grand difficulty has ever been . . . to persuade them to carry a good conscience thither, and to act as free moral agents, not as tools of party." The Liberty party's faulty tactical presuppositions, and its willingness to work within the proslavery Constitution, would, said Garrison, cause it to fail as a permanent force for abolition.[10]

Of course, Garrison was right. By 1848 Henry B. Stanton and Joshua Leavitt, leaders of the "new organization," had abandoned emancipation for "free soil." The former began a new career as a political trimmer, and the latter henceforth worked to sell non-extension as a plausible cure for the slavery question. Others retired, disillusioned with politics.[11] Garrison was premature in his 1842 announcement that these individuals had all become "paralyzed" by "the sorcery of the new organization."[12] But by 1847, Wendell Phillips was already rejoicing privately at "how exactly" his and Garrison's predictions were being fulfilled.[13] Meanwhile, the Garrisonians had begun mobilizing themselves as a minority lobby around their theory of a responsive democracy, directing their efforts towards both the voters of the North, and elected representatives in Washington.

They found many opportunities to exert pressure between 1840 and 1860. These years were marked by mounting sectional tensions within the Whig and Democratic organizations which eventually produced the Free Soil and Republican parties. The extended Gag Rule controversies of the early 1840's soon merged with the issues of Texas annexation, the Mexican War, the Kansas-Nebraska Act, and the recurring debates over the extension of slavery into the territories. An even greater number of congressmen became indentified with antislavery opinions and began assuming sectional leadership in the political sphere.

[9] *Ibid.*, Sept. 13, 1839.

[10] *Ibid.*, June 28, 1839 (quotation); Mar. 11, 1842.

[11] Filler, *Crusade Against Slavery*, pp. 189, 247; Betty Fladeland, *James Gillespie Birney: Slaveholder to Abolitionist* (Ithaca, 1955), p. 265.

[12] *The Liberator*, Aug. 12, 1842.

[13] Wendell Phillips to Elizabeth Pease, Aug. 20, 1847, William Lloyd Garrison Papers, Boston Public Library.

Although none of these men qualified as an abolitionist,[14] their appearance nevertheless stimulated and heartened the Garrisonians. Radicals distinguished carefully between Liberty men, recreants from the exalted cause of moral suasion, and successful office holders elected from traditional constituencies, whose sectional activities marked not a retreat from, but an advance toward, abolitionism.[15] Free Soil Whigs and Democrats, and the Free Soil party itself, seemed to validate the Garrisonian formula of presenting moral arguments within the context of a responsive democracy, and Garrisonians quickly claimed the antislavery politician as their own creation. "It is not too much to claim these results as largely owing to the labors of the Abolitionists," declared Edmund Quincy in 1848, as he surveyed the havoc wrought within northern politics by proponents of free soil.[16] From the first, the American Anti-Slavery Society took this self-ascribed paternity seriously. Even while hurling invective at the Liberty party, they embarked on a program of supporting and challenging these new antislavery politicians and their constituents.

The Garrisonian criterion for supporting politicians was simple; only office-holders who dramatically publicized antislavery questions and disrupted their parties merited active aid. In November, 1841, for example, Garrison heard that a cabal of antislavery Whigs, directed by Joshua Leavitt, Joshua Giddings, William Slade, Seth Gates, and others, had been fashioned in Washington. Immediately, the *Liberator* reminded the antislavery Whigs that they were "pledged in good faith not to flinch, or to yield one iota," while calling on these congressmen's constituents to support their representatives with antislavery petitions. If the electors remained "faithful to themselves, their representatives will also be faithful," Garrison guaranteed.[17] Clearly, Garrison's "antipolitical" point of view did not blind him to the values of politics as an antislavery device. And soon after, Joshua Giddings resigned his seat after being censured by the House for his antislavery activities. Garrison was among the first to appeal to Giddings' constituents that he "be returned by an overwhelming (it ought to be unanimous) vote. . . ." Garrison would never vote himself, but he often saw the advantage of a properly cast ballot. Radical lecturers Parker Pillsbury and Stephen S. Foster rushed to Giddings' district to rouse the voters.[18]

While isolated incidents less dramatic than the above could be cited

[14] The term "abolitionist" is defined here as one who worked outspokenly for immediate, complete, uncompensated liberation for all American slaves. This definition is offered by James M. McPherson, *The Struggle for Equality: The Abolitionists and The Negro in The Civil War and Reconstruction* (Princeton, 1964), p. 3.

[15] *The Liberator*, Mar. 30, 1840; Sept. 22, 1843; Feb. 20, 1846; July 20, 1847; Feb. 8, 1850; Samuel J. May to Charles Sumner, July 12, 1848, Charles Sumner Papers, Houghton Library, Harvard University.

[16] *The Liberator*, Aug. 11, 1848.

[17] *Ibid.*, Nov. 26, 1841.

[18] James B. Stewart, *Joshua Giddings and The Tactics of Radical Politics, 1795-1864* (Cleveland, 1969), Ch. IV; *The Liberator*, Apr. 1, 1842.

to illustrate moment-to-moment Garrisonian support of congressional activity,[19] more instructive was their role prior to 1848 in fostering sectional splits within the Whig and Democratic parties. The first fissure of real consequence opened in 1845 when Democratic congressmen John P. Hale appealed from party policy to the people in opposing Texas annexation. As the powerful New Hampshire Democratic machine moved to terminate Hale's career, dissident Whigs, Democrats and Liberty men coalesced in his behalf.[20] The Garrisonians proved themselves equally ardent, if still non-voting, Hale men. Parker Pillsbury took over Nathaniel P. Rogers' financially shaky New Hampshire *Herald of Freedom* and began furiously attacking the old-line Democrats. Garrison, who had helped engineer the change of editorship, rejoiced that Pillsbury's columns were "never more needed than in this time of crisis, when New Hampshire is seeking to deepen her pro-slavery infamy by the sacrifice of the fearless and upright *Hale*." Stephen S. Foster stood up loyally for Hale at the state Democratic convention which purged him from the party, and the American Anti-Slavery Society sent agents into the Granite State to stimulate the voters in Hale's defense.[21]

Interesting, too, was the timing of Rogers' replacement by Pillsbury. Rogers, who had pushed perfectionism to the literal conclusion of anarchy, had bitterly assailed the Garrisonians as being "purblind with politics." He thought them sinful for their tending to "hover about the polls, to watch the balloting of others, and about the State House, where they can enjoy the turmoil of legislation." Garrison, clearly unwilling to let absolute perfectionism becloud political stratagems, ultimately purged Rogers from the movement.[22]

The Texas issue also produced party divisiveness in Massachusetts, this time among the Whigs. Here, a cadre of "Conscience Whigs," led by Charles Francis Adams, John G. Palfrey, S. C. Phillips, Charles Sumner, and Henry Wilson, began breaking with the party oligarchy over both annexation and the resulting war with Mexico. Garrison, deeply moved by these promising omens in his home state, willingly appeared with Henry Wilson at a "Conscience Whig" anti-Texas meeting, and began attacking the pro-southern "Cotton" wing of the Massachusetts Whig party in the *Liberator*.[23] Repeatedly, he urged the Conscience men to "snap the cords of party, and stand up untrammeled in the cause

[19] Issues of *The Liberator* during the 1840's and 1850's abound with radicals' endorsements of politicians' speeches, antislavery resolutions submitted in Congress, etc. It is impossible to cite them all, but even a casual perusal of *The Liberator* confirms this practice.

[20] Richard H. Sewell, *John P. Hale and The Politics of Abolition* (Cambridge, 1965), pp. 52-68.

[21] *The Liberator*, Feb. 7, 1845; Sewell, *Hale*, p. 57.

[22] *The Herald of Freedom*, May 2, 1845; John L. Thomas, *The Liberator: William Lloyd Garrison* (Boston and Toronto, 1963), pp. 294-295, 296, 300, 319-320, 343, 373.

[23] *The Liberator*, Sept. 26, 1845; Oct. 9, 1845; Feb. 20, 1846.

of liberty." Garrisonians, he explained, were "anxious" to give every Conscience Whig "a full measure of credit for what he has done, and to sustain him as far as he is disposed to go in his opposition to the Slave Power."[24] Throughout 1846 and 1847, Garrison, Wendell Phillips, and Edmund Quincy publicly fostered a bolter's spirit among the Conscience Whigs, enlisted prominent antislavery politicians from out of the state to speak to Massachusetts voters, and supported the divisive acts of "Conscience Whig" congressmen in Washington.[25] When John G. Palfrey defied his party by refusing to vote for "Cotton" Whig Robert C. Winthrop as Speaker of the House of Representatives, Wendell Phillips was among the first to endorse Palfrey's position. "Could I, conscienciously, throw a ballot," he wrote Palfrey, "I would spend one 1st of May at Middlesex & have . . . the pleasure of voting for a man who nails his colors to the mast."[26] Garrison defended Palfrey in the *Liberator* against charges from the enraged Whig orthodoxy, thus nursing the ensuing recriminations along.[27]

When 1848 brought with it a coalition of the Free Soil party, disaffected Whigs and Democrats with Liberty men, the radicals again claimed the movement as their own creation. Garrison, privately "hailing it as a cheering sign of the times," saw in the third party "unmistakable proof of the progress we have made, under God, in changing public sentiment."[28] Feeling definitely responsible for the appearance of the Free Soilers, many Garrisonians proceeded to encourage the movement. Samuel J. May, "deeply interested" in "the new party which seems to be forming," wrote to several of its leaders, trying to arrange rallies and public meetings, and he acted as chaplain when the Free Soil convention opened in Buffalo.[29] Edmund Quincy goaded a hesitant Horace Mann to abandon the "bloodhound candidate" of the Whigs, Zachary Taylor, and to "cast his lot with Palfrey and Giddings."[30] Wendell Phillips put aside his no-government principles long enough to ask Edmund Quincy's help in sponsoring the political aspirations of a young Massachusetts Free Soiler. "What he wants," Phillips explained, "is that you should show him an opening, if there be one, to make a few remarks & show himself. . . ." Any "courtesy you can do for him . . . " he told Quincy, "will not be thrown away."[31]

[24] *Ibid.*, Mar. 6, 1846.

[25] *Ibid.*, Oct. 2, 23, 30, 1846; Wendell Phillips to Joshua R. Giddings, Jan. 16, 1847, Joshua R. Giddings Papers, Ohio Historical Society, Columbus.

[26] Wendell Phillips to John Gorham Palfrey, Dec. 9, 1847, John Gorham Palfrey Papers, Houghton Library, Harvard University.

[27] *The Liberator*, Jan. 28, 1848.

[28] William Lloyd Garrison to Samuel May, Jr., Dec. 2, 1848, Garrison Papers.

[29] Samuel J. May to Charles Sumner, July 12, 1848, Sumner Papers; Samuel J. May to Joshua R. Giddings, July 11, 1848, Giddings Papers; Samuel J. May to Mary A. Estlin, July 16, 1848, May-Estlin Papers, Boston Public Library; *The Liberator*, Aug. 25, 1848.

[30] *The Liberator*, Aug. 4, 1848.

[31] Wendell Phillips to Edmund Quincy (confidential), June 30, 1848, Edmund Quincy Papers, Massachusetts Historical Society, Boston.

The most common Garrisonian opinion, however, held that the best way to promote these political malcontents was by continuing in the program of moral suasion. Edmund Quincy explained the strategy clearly in 1848, regarding the radicals' duty towards the Free Soil party. He called on Garrisonians to act as informal campaign workers, directing them to propagandize the electorate, to make "the conscience uncomfortable." "In nine out of ten cases," he observed, "the person thus acted upon, . . . desirous of relief . . . would seek it, in the first instance, in a Free Soil vote." Quincy vowed that there was no better way "to promote the antislavery movement in its every shape."[32]

Garrison's reasoning, when all but endorsing John C. Frémont in 1856, was little different. While warning his followers to eschew the ballot, Garrison observed that "if there were no moral barrier to our voting, and we had a million ballots to bestow, we should cast them all for the Republican candidate." He judged it inconceivable "that any voter, desirous of frustrating the Slave Power will bestow his suffrage upon either Buchanan or Fillmore." Republicanism had arisen as "the legitimate product of moral agitation" of northern voters by Garrisonians. Radicals could best promote antislavery feeling in all its manifestations by continuing to agitate in the traditional way.[33]

Here, then, was one important facet of the Garrisonian political strategy. By adhering to non-voting while acting on their belief in the responsiveness of American democracy, radicals remained unfettered by formal political ties, avoiding every possibility of proslavery compromise. Their position gave them the widest possible freedom to encourage sectional politicians of all parties as well as the voters who elected such men. Unlike the Liberty party, the Garrisonians' efforts in politics never caused them to abandon their demand for immediate emancipation. Wendell Phillips, while overstating his case, made the radicals' strategy quite clear when, in reference to the Free Soilers, he claimed that the Garrisonian movement "converted these men; it gave them a constituency; it gave them an opportunity to speak, and gave them a public to listen. . . . The antislavery cause gave them their votes."[34]

While the pragmatic promotion of candidates and the building of antislavery constituencies represented a major objective of many Garrisonians, they also pursued a second, more subtle strategy for polarizing American politics. Basically, they attacked northern political organizations by denying the Constitution and demanding the dissolution of the Union. They were most unkind in their attacks upon Free Soilers and Republicans. While, as we have seen, Garrisonians offered such politicians encouragement, they simultaneously scored all officeholders

[32] *The Liberator*, Aug. 11, 1848.
[33] *The National Anti-Slavery Standard*, Oct. 25, 1856; Wendell P. Garrison and Francis J. Garrison, *William Lloyd Garrison* . . . Boston, 1885-1889), III, 443-444.
[34] Wendell Phillips, *Speeches, Lectures and Letters, 1st Series* (Boston, 1863), p. 135.

as temporizers whose support of the Constitution actually made them tools of the slave power, accessories with hands drenched in the blood of the bondsman. Endlessly, the Garrisonians reiterated their claim that the only effective approach to abolition was for everyone to disavow the Constitution, that "covenant with death and agreement with Hell."[35]

To most historians, such assaults on the political system confirm only that Garrisonians were variously threatened by the rise of sectional parties, "ambivalent" towards them, or were simply ineffectual and psychotic individuals.[36] Many Garrisonians, however, had politically sophisticated aims in view when challenging the nation with the cry of "No Union with Slaveholders." Edmund Quincy was emphatic on this point: "The abolitionist who stands aside from the Government . . . does not renounce, but multiplies his political influence. The vote which a man casts is but an insignificant emblem of his political power."[37] Charles C. Burleigh, one of Garrison's most flamboyant radical associates, agreed wholeheartedly with Quincy that the disunion doctrine was framed for political ends. He vowed that "no more effective vote is ever cast, in its bearing upon the politics . . . of this nation, than that which is cast . . . from lips denouncing the Constitution. . . ."[38]

Exactly what Burleigh and Quincy meant by these statements comes clear only when one re-examines some of the Garrisonians' intentions in attacking antislavery politicians on disunionist grounds. Their essential objective was to establish a line of communication which would insure consideration for their radical ideas. In 1853, for example, Wendell Phillips engaged in a vicious press debate over disunion with Horace Mann, antislavery representative from Massachusetts.[39] While blistering Mann's replies with further rebuttals, Phillips assured Edmund Quincy: "I'll teach him [Mann] that the Garrisonians never go out . . . without their 'pockets full of rocks'. . . ." Phillips felt that winning this argument was especially important because Mann seemed to be showing disdain for the ideas of non-voting radicals. "Mann rode a high horse," Phillips told Quincy, "thought little of his foes and said, [']lo! I will ramble these vulgar Garrisonians into the mud.'" If radicals like Phillips hoped to cultivate lines of communication with Washington, they could not allow politicians to ignore their arguments, or simply dismiss them. Phillips, in this instance, had to

[35] Thomas, *Garrison*, pp. 305-337.

[36] David Donald, "Toward a Reconsideration of the Abolitionists" in *Lincoln Reconsidered* (New York, 1961), pp. 19-36; Walter M. Merrill, *Against Wind and Tide: A Biography of William Lloyd Garrison* (Cambridge, 1963) p. 322, and Avery Craven, *The Coming of The Civil War* (New York, 1942), pp. 117-150, reflect, respectively, these various conclusions.

[37] *The National Anti-Slavery Standard*, reprinted in *The Herald of Freedom*, Sept. 6, 1844.

[38] *The Liberator*, June 3, 1853.

[39] *Ibid.*, issues from Feb. 25 through May 6, 1853, contain the Phillips-Mann exchange.

assert and preserve the credibility of his doctrines. "If I floor him [Mann]," Phillips guaranteed, "no man will relish disputing my positions."[40] Referring to the Phillips-Mann encounter, Garrison summarized this dynamic neatly, observing that the quarrel was not seen by radicals as a personal one. Rather, he explained, "it relates to rights which are sacred, and to interests too momentous to be weighed in the scales of expediency." "The more faithful we are to each other," he concluded, "The more 'the enemies of the rights of man' will respect us."[41] Nothing pleased the editor of the Liberator more than antislavery politicians who listened carefully to Garrisonian attacks, and who treated their assailants' ideas with intellectual and political open-mindedness. Here were office holders who helped maintain the lines between Congress and the agitator. John P. Hale's "unfailing good temper" in holding himself "amenable to censure" evoked warm praise from Garrison. So did Joshua R. Giddings' "nobility of soul" in responding positively to criticism. Such men, instead of being "abusive and malignant," understood "the intentions and aims of ... PHILLIPS and QUINCY and PILLSBURY and FOSTER too well to fly into a passion...," and Garrison judged it "a pity" that more public men could not "set such an example or profit by it."[42]

In demanding this respectful attention, nearly all Garrisonians occasionally harbored the forlorn hope of totally converting northern politicians.[43] At other times many developed a more complex appreciation of how the politicians' acceptance of their criticisms could best serve the cause of emancipation. Charles C. Burleigh fell into the latter category, arguing that slavery would ultimately be eradicated through legislation enacted by anti-Garrisonian office holders. A sweeping northern commitment to disunion or even Free Soilism was unnecessary, so long as Garrisonians remained steadfast in communicating with the voter and the congressman. By agitating for disunion, Burleigh said, "The laws will be changed long before ... an entire majority is ready to come into the Free Soil organization. ... Men are not converted to the true faith at once. ... Some will come the whole way, some half way, some a quarter of the way."[44] Wendell Phillips was even more specific: "Our object is not to make every man a Christian or a philosopher, but to induce everyone to aid in the abolition of slavery." By publicizing radical doctrines, he continued, "We expect to accomplish our

[40] Wendell Phillips to Edmund Quincy, Mar. 22, 1853, Quincy Papers.

[41] The Liberator, Mar. 11, 1853.

[42] Ibid., May 27, 1853. Marius Robinson made similar observations about the "proper" responses which politicians should manifest toward abolitionist criticism. See The Anti-Slavery Bugle reprinted in The Liberator, Nov. 21, 1851.

[43] See, for example, Henry C. Wright to Richard Houghton in The Liberator, Oct. 16, 1948, and Marius Robinson to William Lloyd Garrison, Mar. 30, 1853, Garrison Papers.

[44] Burleigh's speech is here transcribed from the third to first person and from the past to the present tense. See The Liberator, June 3, 1853.

object long before the nation is converted into saints. . . ."[45] Two logical questions thus arise. What elements in the disunion arguments were consciously framed for political impact? How extensive and effective was the influence of Garrisonian communications with elected officials?

Garrison and most others in his circle spent a great deal of their ante-bellum careers explaining the meaning and intention of their disunion creed. Even so, many historians have overlooked its political purposes. First and foremost, the doctrine was framed to give northerners a reply of equal strength to southern threats of secession. Long before Garrison first announced northern disunion, a southern minority had invoked the right to dismember the national compact in order to protect slav-ery.[46] Until Garrison, the northern response to such threats had been entirely defensive and legalistic, merely affirming the Union's perpe-tuity while denying any anti-slavery motives. But Garrison, who judged Calhoun as "a man who means what he says, and who never blusters,"[47] keenly appreciated the deficiencies in northern retorts to fire-eaters. As early as 1837, he was deeply bothered by the polemical advantages held by southern radicals.

It is only for some few seditious hot-spurs at the South to brandish their . . . bowie-knives and shout 'We'll disolve the Union!', and straightway we turn pale, our knees smite together, and our tongues cleave to the roofs of our mouths![48]

The demand for "No Union with Slaveholders" was as much designed to correct this imbalance in the sectional debate as it was to satisfy the personal demands of perfectionism. "The lines are now definitely drawn," Edmund Quincy announced in 1847. "Calhoun in the South and Garrison at the North stand front to front. . . . Every man must needs be on one side or the other."[49] Wendell Phillips was, as usual, even more specific about the Garrisonians' intention to polarize national pol-itics: "If, as the South has so constantly contended, Secession is a con-stitutional right, well, we will commend the poisoned chalice to her lips."[50] Calhoun could sit in the Senate and appeal through the Consti-tution to secession in order to protect slavery. In opposing Calhoun's arguments while not even voting, Garrisonians aimed to make northern office holders aware of concepts and vocabulary with which to repulse threats of the "hot-spurs."

To be sure, no politician interested in re-election would openly en-dorse Garrisonian theories. Nevertheless, as the sectional crisis of the 1840's and 1850's ran its course, many free state congressmen indepen-

[45] Phillips, *Speeches . . . , 1st Series*, p. 120.

[46] William H. Freehling, *Prelude to Civil War: The Nullification Crisis in South Carolina* (New York, 1966).

[47] William Lloyd Garrison to Richard Webb, Mar. 1, 1847, Garrison Papers.

[48] Garrison speech reprinted in Truman Nelson (ed.), *Documents of Upheaval* (New York, 1966), p. 120.

[49] *The Liberator*, Nov. 26, 1847.

[50] *Ibid.*, Mar. 24, 1848.

dently came to appreciate, as had the radicals earlier, slavery's deep institutional power. Such officials usually harbored no desire to abolish slavery, but they did wish to express in the most effective terms possible, their opposition to the "slave power" in politics. Garrisonians had already spent years telling politicians that effective antislavery disputation must reach beyond Union and Constitution. Now these congressmen found themselves provided with words and ideas which increasingly fulfilled their needs. In short, politicians who had first been challenged by the Garrisonians on disunionist terms, ultimately found themselves perforce receptive to the radicals' "higher law" doctrine. Many Garrisonians had long been anxious to diffuse their concepts throughout the North in precisely this fashion. Herein lies a good deal of the motivation behind radical criticism of and communications with the likes of Giddings, Sumner, Hale and Mann.

Illustrative of this dynamic are Wendell Phillips' private remarks to Elizabeth Pease written in January, 1846, describing the heated political debates over free soil: "Men who would have whispered Disunion with white lips a year ago now love to talk about it. Many leading men will talk as we were once laughed at for talking a while ago."[51] Phillips, in fact, was understating the situation. As early as 1843, twelve northern congressmen, led by John Quincy Adams and Joshua Giddings, had issued a public appeal warning that the admission of Texas, with slaves, was tantamount to dissolving the Union.[52] In 1845, the Massachusetts and Ohio legislatures had both threatened to refuse recognition of the Federal laws enabling Texas to assume statehood.[53] By mid-1846, Giddings had released a nationally circulated "dissolution letter" which argued that any further increase in slave states would give northern voters perfect moral cause to sever all relations with the Federal government.[54]

Even on these occasions of the early and mid-1840's, northern congressmen had begun speaking against the South in Garrisonian terms, constructing rationales for non-compliance with enacted law. Obviously, such arguments by politicians in behalf of "free-soil" served far more conservative objectives than the Garrisonian demand for immediate emancipation. Nevertheless, as the sectional debate continued to develop, northern office holders increasingly applied this Garrisonian vocabulary when discussing their positions on issues short of abolition.

By April, 1846, Garrison found himself reflecting hopefully upon this heartening addition to the content of northern political rhetoric. Reminiscing, he remarked that in earlier days the radical cry for immediate emancipation had filled the North with loathing and disgust. But

---

[51] Wendell Phillips to Elizabeth Pease, Jan. 25, 1846, Garrison Papers.

[52] Ashtabula (Ohio) *Sentinel*, May 27, 1843; *The Philanthropist* (Cincinnati) June 14, 1843.

[53] Thomas, *Garrison*, p. 335.

[54] Stewart, *Giddings*, Ch. VI.

now, after years of arduous abolitionist labor, the slogan had insinuated itself into the vocabulary of most northerners. Even those who presently rejected complete and unhalting emancipation had accommodated themselves to the existence of the idea, "and the doctrine of *IMME-DIATISM* no longer occupies the time or demands the energies of the abolitionist." The same eventual acceptance awaited the dictum of "No Union with Slaveholders," Garrison asserted. He granted that the doctrine was still "as grossly misunderstood, as basely misrepresented, and as foolishly rejected" as immediatism once had been. But, he also predicted that hard agitation by the American Anti-Slavery Society one day would make disregard for Constitutionalism and law a common attitude in northern political minds.[55]

The utterances and actions of nothern politicians during the late 1840's and 1850's strikingly fulfilled Garrisonian's prediction. For instance, arguments posited by radicals to justify non-compliance with the Constitution were picked up and applied by northern congressmen opposing enforcement of the 1850 fugitive slave law. Garrison once stated, when defending disunion against the alternative of constitutional amendment, that "Dissolution may be [the] work of a minority. ... A man, or a State can refuse to recognize a law—it requires many to change one."[56] When it came to opposing the Fugitive Slave Act, politicians framed their arguments in terms strikingly similar to Garrison's. "We cannot be Christians and obey it," warned an Ohio Free Soil paper.[57] Before a Massachusetts court in 1851, John P. Hale argued in behalf of individuals charged with violating the Act. Using a Garrisonian mode of reasoning, Hale's most eloquent statements went beyond technical legality, defending the actions of the accused with the doctrine of "higher law". Ultimately, all of those indicted were exonerated.[58] Ben Wade, serving as a State Supreme Court Justice in Ohio, affirmed that while he would not recommend armed resistance to the law, he would still justify and dismiss from his court all acts of non-violent civil disobedience.[59] Joshua Giddings made comprehensive use of Garrisonian "higher law" arguments while speaking in 1859: "We say today 'down with the fugitive slave act; ... it is PIRATICAL, and we will not obey it!"[60] Horace Mann, Phillips' antagonist, was also intellectually indebted to the Garrisonians when opposing the law. "This doctrine—which is one of the off-shoots of slavery—that there is no higher law than the law of the state is palpable and practical atheism."[61]

Garrison doubtless understood exactly what Mann and these other

[55] *The Liberator*, Apr. 17, 1846.
[56] *Ibid.* Jan. 14, 1848.
[57] Ashtabula *Sentinel*, Sept. 14, 1850.
[58] Sewell, *Hale*, pp. 141-142.
[59] Ashtabula *Sentinel*, Nov. 14, 1850.
[60] *Ibid.*, May 26, June 2, 1859.
[61] Mann quoted in Filler, *Crusade Against Slavery*, p. 202.

political dissenters meant, for his American Anti-Slavery Society had begun circulating the same concept over a decade earlier, arguing that strict legal analysis could not meet the issues of slavery. Oliver Johnson was not indulging in self-justification when he observed, long after the Civil War, that "If Sumner and Wilson and Chase and Hale *did* breathe and do noble work . . . , it was only because they found a way to break through the web which the Constitution wove around them, and thus maintain their allegiance to the Higher Law." "That they were able to do this," Johnson continued modestly, "may have been owing largely to the influence of the Garrisonian movement in diminishing the popular reverence for the Constitution. . . ."[62] William Seward, the essence of conservative Unionism, presented ample documentation for Johnson's claim. The famous "Higher Law Speech" represented one benchmark of Garrisonian influence in northern politics. So did his "Irrepressible Conflict" speech and Sumner's "Crime Against Kansas" oration. Whenever confronted by sectional crisis, northern antislavery congressmen readily availed themselves of the theory which undergirded Garrison's demand for overthrowing the Constitution and applied it instead to the problem of the territories.

Seward, Sumner, Chase, and the others were hardly aware that they were employing antislavery language invented by the disunionists, so successful had the radicals been in making their vocabulary into "household words" appropriate to the perceptions and experiences of northern politicians. In turn, an increasing number of slaveholders came to believe that the American Anti-Slavery Society and the "Black Republicans" were one and the same thing and in 1861 reacted accordingly. Viewed in this fashion, the secession crisis represented the culmination of radical impact in the politics of antebellum America.

o   o   o

Wendell Phillips once remarked that "It may seem strange to some, this claim for Mr. Garrison of profound statesmanship."[63] Perhaps the suggestion advanced here for the political acuity of radical abolitionists seems equally foreign. Nevertheless, Phillips was correct when he observed that Garrison's own contemporaries had "heard him styled a mere fanatic so long" that they found it impossible "to judge him fairly."[64] Perhaps this comment has, until recently, also held true regarding students of the antislavery movement. Such historians possibly have overstressed the image of the "impractical" Garrisonian and have thus obscured these men's self-conscious attempts to influence American politics in the years after 1840. Many Garrisonians, unlike some of their chroniclers, realized that realistic political activity can mean more than just the building of party structures and collecting of votes.

[62] Oliver Johnson, *William Lloyd Garrison and His Times* . . . (Boston, 1880), p. 339.
[63] Phillips, *Speeches* . . . , *1st Series*, p. 152.
[64] *Ibid.*

INDEX